OUT OF THE AIR

# MARY MARGARET McBRIDE

OUT OF THE AIR
A LONG WAY FROM MISSOURI
HARVEST OF AMERICAN COOKING
TUNE IN FOR ELIZABETH
AMERICA FOR ME
HOW DEAR TO MY HEART
HERE'S MARTHA DEANE
STORY OF DWIGHT MORROW
BEER AND SKITTLES
NEW YORK IS EVERYBODY'S TOWN
LONDON IS A MAN'S TOWN
PARIS IS A WOMAN'S TOWN

# OUT OF THE AIR

## MARY MARGARET McBRIDE

1960   DOUBLEDAY & COMPANY, INC., GARDEN CITY, NEW YORK

*To* TEX *and* JINX MCCRARY
*whom I love*

# *CONTENTS*

I think about you very often these days as you are working on the radio book and recalling those wonderful and fabulous years. We listeners will feel that it's our book too because we lived it with you day by day.

The thought has come to me that this book should have a very special introduction done by someone who would have the feeling of the warmth and glow that came over those magic wires from one to two on weekdays. You brought us the war generals and correspondents throughout those heartbreaking times, the latest book reviews and authors, the Broadway hits and actors, and all the famous and great of our times. We even learned to like the commercials, the integrity of Bohack's, the fragrance of Sweetheart Soap, and the sweetness of Fanny Farmer's candy. With it all, you brought us humor, common sense, and your high standards of human behavior.

You added something very precious to my life, and I shall never cease to be grateful.

Margaret Oberfelder
May 1960

\* Requested and selected by the editor.

*"We don't know where Mary Margaret is, but we know she's bringing a most distinguished guest and that whatever may have caused the delay, they'll get here."*

That was Stella Karn, the first voice I heard when I picked a record at random to help me decide whether I wanted to write a book about the radio years.

"Why on earth do you want to waste all that money on recordings?" I used to ask Stella, my partner in the radio business for more than twenty years. "Who would ever listen to those old things?"

And she would smile and answer placidly: "Oh—when I'm old I'll sit by the fire and play them."

Now I was playing the records and she was not there—only her voice. The sample I had chosen featured Eleanor Roosevelt as guest. I'd gone to pick her up and heavy traffic delayed us so Stella started the program without me, and when Mrs. Roosevelt and I walked in, she and Vincent Connolly, our announcer, were doing the products.

Since the day more than a year ago when I played that recording, Hilda Deichler (my wonderful secretary for the part of my working life in which I could afford a secretary) and I have listened to hundreds of recordings for which Stella spent thousands of dollars. Hearing them, I have alternated between excitement and gloom. They cover twenty years of depression, recovery from depression, return to prosperity, preparation for war, war, and its aftermath. They record the voices and sometimes revealing thoughts of the leaders in many fields during that period.

There is a great book in them somewhere, and I've said often since I started this enterprise that I wish I had a genius ghost writer to bring it out. Unfortunately, geniuses don't ghostwrite—they're too oc-

cupied with their own deathless prose. So I undertook it myself with
the tireless and almost inconceivably devoted help of Mrs. D., as we
have called Hilda Deichler all these years; also noble assists which I
gratefully acknowledge from Janice Devine, the program's legwoman;
Cynthia Lowry, Associated Press television editor; Beverly Fleming,
advertising writer; and Lee Schryver, my always hopeful editor.

Whenever I see credits in the front of a book (and I'm a great
preface and introduction reader—I hope everybody is because this one
is important) I always long to know specifically what each helper did.
First we pooled our memories (all except Lee, whose acquaintance
with me began after the radio program was ended). Mrs. D. listened
to endless recordings and typed interminably (though Eva Dietze
made part of the final draft); Janice helped stitch together some of the
interviews that were taken word for word from the recordings; Beverly
typed industriously, ran errands, and listened eagerly to each chapter
as it was finished, commenting rapturously; Cynthia read, edited, and
argued about awkward phrases; Lee was a great help with the
structure.

Tallulah Bankhead told me that she never mentioned a person in
*Tallulah* (her autobiography) just because he was famous but only
when he belonged to her story, yet she was appalled when she saw
so many names in the index. I am worrying for a different reason. I
am so afraid I may have left out somebody who was kind to me or
somebody I love very much.

Although Stella had spent a fortune on recordings, there were gaps
in the collection, probably because when we cleared her office after
her death, some valuable items were lost. One missing set included the
broadcasts about the coronation and the Norwegian trip in 1953.
Luckily a devoted listener, Dorothy Becker, blessings on her, had
made tapes of almost the entire period, which she let us borrow. There
is one Helen Hayes interview after the death of her daughter—the best
talk we ever had—that I would give anything to find.

I wanted to include television critic of the New York *World-Tele-
gram*, Harriet Van Horne, because I have a fondness for her. Long
ago before I ever had seen her, I plucked up courage to ask her by
telephone what she thought a woman's program should be, since she
had been rather severe about the way we were. I anticipated icy scorn,
but to my amazement the soft-voiced person who answered the tele-

phone proved to be Harriet herself. Her unexpected kindness, even gentleness, won my heart that day, and though she has never been a particular booster of mine—as Ben Gross, radio and television editor of the New York *Daily News* has—I think of her as a friend. She was my guest on the air several times, but the recordings are missing.

Ben guested with me at every gathering of any importance, since I thought of him as a benevolent radio godfather, as his change of sentiment about my program helped to save my job in the early days. I searched for a wonderful interview he did about his childhood in the South, but it's gone. Gone also is one of the most moving conversations I ever had on the air. It was with General Carlos P. Romulo, during the war. I asked about his family. There was a silence that seemed to lengthen, and then he said huskily, "I know not whether they are alive or dead." He reached into his pocket and brought out a picture of a beautiful little woman—his wife. Both crying, we sat there then, talking about his wife and sons.

I have been fruitlessly trying also to find interviews with Marjorie (*Live Alone and Like It*) Hillis Roulston, to whom I am devoted, and some trace of fine talks I had through the years with Marjorie Mills of Boston and June Baker of Chicago, radio colleagues and dear friends. No luck, either, with interviews with old friends such as columnist Alice Hughes, Thyra Samter Winslow, Rex Stout, and Sophie Kerr—all of whom guested with me many times.

I searched frantically for a program done outdoors at the Haders', where John Kieran identified birds as they sang from the trees. Gone also is a hilarious interview with Margaret Kieran about taking up bird watching in order to be with her husband.

I find myself wondering, with the copy gone to the publisher, is Patricia Collinge, that writer and delightful monologuist in? Have I expressed somewhere my affection and indebtedness to writer Curtis Mitchell? Can it be possible that novelist Inez Haynes Irwin, my first real interview guest, and her husband, writer Will Irwin, are not here— two people who taught me so much about writing and true friendship? And a lovely nostalgic interview with author Rose Wilder Lane is among the sadly missing. No trace of Rae Elbrock, space buyer who believed in us more than anybody, or of Earl Wilson, Marie Torre, Nick Kenny, Hy Gardner, and Leonard Lyons, who were kind; Jack O'Brian named me "Queen of Radio" two successive years—no records to prove it, alas! Where, oh where, are those amusing interviews with Celeste Holm; Clifton Fadiman; Ed and Pegeen Fitzgerald, the first husband-and-wife radio team; with Dorothy Kilgallen and Dick Kollmar; the recording of that wonderful birthday party June and Wendell Fifield gave me at their wonderful old church in Brooklyn.

And I would like so much to hear again the interviews I did with Skulda Baner and Borghild Dahl, both of whom have coped with sight problems so bravely; Edna Kaehle who conquered cancer.

For weeks I hunted for the recording of the project Stella launched with the co-operation of the United Church Women, the National Council of Catholic Women, and the National Council of Jewish Women to find out what women in all parts of the country were doing for civic betterment. Myrta Ross of the United Church Women; Elsie Elfsenbein of the National Council of Jewish Women; Marietta Barkhorn of the National Council of Catholic Women; Fannie Hurst, celebrated novelist; Ruth Bryan Rohde, former United States minister to Denmark, and Dorothy Lewis, co-ordinator of radio for the United Nations, were the judges who presented awards on the program to these wonderful, dedicated women: Lulu Fairbanks of Seattle for her activities on behalf of civic betterment of Alaska; Kate Carter of Salt Lake City for the preservation of American history; Lillian Bishop of Topeka for her efforts on behalf of mental-health projects; Ruth Suddeth of Atlanta for her civic reform and prison work; Bertha Schwartz of the Bronx and Mother Alice of St. Clare's Hospital in New York City for their activities on behalf of the fight against narcotics and the building of hospitals, respectively.

Because I'll probably never have another chance, I wish to say that I think men and women in the publishing business are the most honest, the most friendly and generally delightful in the world! And I'd like to list the names of some without whose generous and capable help through the years I couldn't have done my program: Lynn Austel, Ethel Beck, Raymond Bond, Elizabeth Bragdon Easton, Ruth Brown, Dorothy Bryan, Lynn Caine, Virginia Carrick, Bill Cole, Susan Dempsey, Phyllis Egbert, Barbara Emerson, Hope English, Doris Flowers, Anne Ford, Barbara Frost, Seon Givens Manley, Janet Glennon, Elliott Graham, Mary Green, Irma Greenberg, Frances Grossman, Stuart Harris, Catherine Hayes, Ramona Herdman, Marion Hunt, Lucy Johnson, Eleanor Kask, Sonia Levinthal, Virginia Mathews, Maureen McManus, Patricia MacManus, Patricia Newell, Eleanor Nichols, Virginia Patterson, Mildred Salivar, Patricia Shartle, Ann Sylvester, Louise Thomas, Mary Thompson, Naomi Thompson, Betty Vaughan, Larry Vinick, Joan Washburn, Carolyn Wolf, Vivian Wolfert.

And finally, I want to send dearest love to the listeners who kept me on the air for twenty years, the happiest years of my life.

> Mary Margaret McBride
> West Shokan, New York
> May 5, 1960

# Part I  *THE PROGRAM*

# 1.  I MURDERED GRANDMA

MAY 26, 1934 *"Just then the door opened and in ran Penny and Jenny—they're my son Johnny's twins, his youngest. He has three girls besides—Judy, Josie, and Jessie."* [Pause—then a flat discouraged voice] *"Oh, what's the use? I can't do it! I'm mixed up again with all those grandchildren I've invented. I'm not a grandmother! I'm not a mother. I'm not even married. I made that up and it doesn't sound real because it isn't. The truth is I'm a reporter who would like to come here every day and tell you about places I go, people I meet. Write me if you'd like that. But I can't be a grandmother any more!" Martha Deane*

I had been on the air a little less than three weeks when I killed off Grandma with these words. After that I still wore a *nom d'air* but at least I was now myself—Mary Margaret McBride, reporter underneath Martha Deane, the name assumed for air purposes.

I believe that in every life there is one miracle and that radio, my third career in New York, was *my* miracle. I was middle-aged or nearing it (depending upon the charity of the estimator) when it happened to me, and I needed a miracle desperately. I had been jobless and broke for nearly four years. I was supporting two people besides myself, I was shabby, disillusioned, and rapidly approaching hopelessness.

I seldom turned on the small radio I had bought in my prosperous free-lance magazine period when an editor assigned me to do an article about the mysterious power that came out of the ether to hypnotize an old lady on a South Dakota farm into knitting a muffler for Jessica Dragonette and a young mother in Dubuque, Iowa, into naming her twins Amos and Andy. The article wasn't very good; I couldn't solve the mystery. As soon as it was done I stopped listening and went back to my old attitude of mild scorn for this interloper, a feeling shared by most people in the writing business. Some newspapers wouldn't run listings of radio programs and the more rabid tabooed even the name.

I had lines out for twenty-seven different jobs in the publicity, promotion, writing, and editing fields. I was holding down, temporarily and part-time, a sick friend's post as woman's-page editor of Newspaper Enterprise Association while I waited for her to get well and for something else to break. I loved Fred Ferguson, head of NEA, and Donn Sutton, managing editor, but the pay was only fifty dollars a week, and while I was thankful for it, it wouldn't pay my debts and manage my current obligations.

Then, surprise—a telephone call from my literary agent, Carol Hill. I hadn't heard from *her* for a *long* time.

"WOR wants you to audition for a woman's program," she told me calmly, after the amenities were over. I shrieked in quick disbelief, and she explained that Scott Lucas, a young man we'd both known as an editor on one of the national magazines, was now at the radio station and had asked that I come to see him. I was appalled.

"Carol, what is an audition?" I wailed. "I don't know," forthrightly admitted Carol, the usually infallible. "The best way to find out is to go see Scott."

I was used to taking Carol's advice, and no wonder. She had built me up during the late twenties into a well-paid feature writer with impressive sales to all the leading magazines. It wasn't her fault that the depression of the thirties caused editors to depend upon their staffs so that there was no place for a free lance, especially one with an agent who didn't much believe in compromise.

So—I telephoned Scott Lucas and he gave me an appointment for the very next day. At two that Tuesday I was taken into a little boxlike room with a small, strange-looking black contraption standing on a table. There was a big clock on one wall, and behind another wall, all glass, was an even tinier room in which two men were lounging.

Scott Lucas said: "Sit here and talk—talk about anything." Luckily I had recently been sent by the city editor of NEA to Baltimore to interview Scott Fitzgerald, and a strange evening I'd had, for the brilliant writer was in one of his emotional slumps and drinking whisky as if it were water. But the more he drank, the better he talked.

As I listened, fascinated, he spoke about his childhood, his marriage, his writing. He was in a bitter mocking mood that night, but most of his mockery was directed against himself. I was depressed for days afterward, and the whole experience was still fresh in my mind. I told about it just as it had happened. Scott Lucas listened but did not comment. I hadn't the courage to ask any questions as he shook hands and thanked me for coming. When I walked out of there I never expected to set eyes on him again.

I thought to myself, "I'm not what they want in radio. If they had wanted reporting of that kind, they'd have had it long ago." And I knew, too, that the only contribution I could ever make to anything would be as a reporter. That was what I'd been trained for—interviewing people, observing, setting down what I saw, heard, tasted, smelled. I didn't talk about the audition because I didn't expect anything to come of it. However, I began asking careful questions of people I knew who listened to radio. I didn't find out much that helped me except that nobody seemed to know of any women reporters on the air.

Then Carol called again. Scott Lucas wanted me to do another audition. This time I knew what an audition was and I planned ahead what I would talk about—life on the Missouri farm where I was born, myself as a little barefooted girl running down to the barn on a hot summer morning to have Papa fill my cup by milking straight from the cow into it; the one-room country school to which I traveled on an ancient bay farm horse behind my brother; Old Home Place on which my mother was born and where we lived when my little brother Buford was drowned in Salt River.

I thought I did better than before, but if I did there was no hint of it on Scott Lucas' poker face. As before, he thanked me for coming and said a courteous good-by. I was a little sad as I walked away, for I found to my surprise that I was getting attached to this odd medium. I did reflect, though, that if I ever talked, say, half an hour a day for a year, I'd have to develop more lives than a cat or I'd certainly run out of material.

Then something happened that put radio completely out of my mind. I got a magazine assignment, the first in more than two years.

*Good Housekeeping* sent me to Washington for a housing story. I had just finished collecting the material when Carol telephoned.

"Come home at once," she commanded. "Scott Lucas wants you to go on the air on Thursday!"

I was stunned and excited by turns, but fright was my principal emotion as I hurried back to New York. Scott Lucas was full of jubilant plans. He told me he had interviewed fifty women for the job and had chosen me because he believed I had the common touch. I wasn't sure exactly what he meant, but I was ready to do my best.

It was then that he unfolded his idea that I should be a very simple but wise and kindly old character, who had devoted her life to her large family. She would speak colloquially and dispense philosophy in great helpful chunks.

I was a little disconcerted by these instructions but not enough so to back out. I said I'd try, and in an effort to keep my word I gave myself a family of six sons and daughters, married them all off, and added an astronomical number of grandchildren upon whom I bestowed the favorite names I had been saving up since childhood for a real family.

Since I am a very forthright person, this experiment couldn't have lasted. When I blew up that day and committed mass murder, Scott Lucas was furious—fearful, too, about what might happen to the program. He really believed I'd committed radio suicide.

"You've done a terrible thing," he scolded. "The only hope is that nobody in authority heard you."

Probably nobody did, for no official attention was ever paid to the bizarre broadcast. There are women who sometimes tell me they remember the day I murdered Grandma but usually they are a little vague, so I'm not sure who was listening, if anybody. I only know that what caused the sudden demise of Grandma was that I got so mixed up I was giving Judy, Josie, and Jessie to the wrong parents.

I am sure now that if I had any listeners at all they would soon have found me out. So it was lucky that I beat them to it. Besides, though I've always been a g-dropper, often loathsomely folksy and not always grammatical, the Mrs. Dooley-type grandma was a little too folksy and ungrammatical even for me.

The reason I kept on being Martha Deane was partly that the station wanted me to have a name they could own, partly that I felt I might very well fail at this enterprise and it would be just as well to be anonymous.

William Rambeau, salesman in the Chicago area for WOR, had long pulled for a woman's program on the station, and so he took me to his heart and even helped to name me. He knew a successful radio Martha in Chicago. Scott Lucas had once been a minister and my Baptist-preacher grandfather had given me good grounding in the Bible, so the two of us thought of Martha, the sister who busied herself about many things while Mary worshiped at Jesus' feet. Bill Rambeau added, "Deane is a lucky name around this station."

I groaned, "I am certainly going to need luck!" We all said Martha Deane over a few times—it was easy on the tongue, would be easy to remember. So that's how Martha Deane was born.

The going was hard at first. Besides Scott, the only other person at the station who believed in me was Theodore Streibert, vice-president. Luckily, he was pretty powerful. I knew he was, because I wasn't fired. In time I discovered that one of the main reasons I got the job in the first place was that I had no exaggerated notions about what radio people were paid and never mentioned money. Scott, who got $200 a week for the program, paid me $25 and his little secretary, Lillian Cohen, $20.

Carol Hill, my agent, was against my tying up to such an unlucrative enterprise. She said I was an article writer, that already the magazine market was looking up and that all I had to do to step right back into my old niche was to get a lot of bright ideas. She predicted I would soon be swamped with orders. But I went ahead anyway.

One of my earliest handicaps was the discovery that Scott was a periodic drinker. The sieges lasted for as much as a week at a time, and, inexperienced as I was, it was hard to manage without him. Lillian and I covered for him as well as we could, but one day he staggered into the station and management found out.

That was the end of Scott Lucas and the point at which Stella Karn came into the picture. Vice-President Streibert told me they felt the program hadn't yet had a chance and that they would keep it on until there was more evidence of success or failure. He added that somebody to handle the business end would be needed—did I care to suggest such a person?

Stella was my first thought. She had been interested in radio even before crystal-set days, and back in my early free-lance period she had persuaded me to write a series with RCA's David Sarnoff about radio's beginnings. She knew more about the subject than anybody else I could think of, was also good at business, and besides we were close friends.

When she took hold I began to get more money right away. But I still wasn't telling anybody I was on the air. People would stop me on the street to marvel: "I heard a woman on the radio the other day whose voice was enough like yours to be you. Her name was Deane." I'd listen politely and promise to try to listen to this Deane woman. I suppose it was my usual dread of failure that kept me from admitting the truth. I really didn't think I would last, and I guess nobody else thought so, either.

I had been given what I finally discovered was conceded to be dead time on the air—from 2:30 to 3:00 P.M.—an hour when tired young mothers nap with the children, suburban matrons are on the way to the bridge club, and older women are gadding to matinees or shopping. I soon began to wonder if anybody would listen even if Clark Gable courted Greta Garbo at such an hour.

I went to Mr. Streibert and told him I wanted to be given a nice time in the morning when there were people at the other end to hear me. He said: "You've been given that time just because it is dead. If you can get listeners, we want you. If you can't, we don't."

Which settled that, but there was also the matter of technical knowledge. I had none. And nobody at a radio station in those pioneer days ever explained anything—not to me, anyway. They just shut me up in a little room and told me to go ahead. I was awful. I breathed wrong. I turned my head away from the microphone. I mumbled.

Once in the early days I did get one fragment of constructive criticism. In the control room, separated from me by thick glass, was usually Scott. I kept my eyes on him throughout those first broadcasts, hoping I could get some indication from his expression as to how I was doing. One day I was quite hoarse and cleared my throat twice. Looking through the glass, I saw his eyes bulging, his arms waving frantically. Later he told me that clearing the throat made a jarring, rasping noise over the air, something like a roaring lion caught under a rock. He warned me against sneezing and coughing, too.

After Stella Karn took over the business end she insisted that the station permit me to be myself, to say what seemed natural in my own way, to talk as I might to friends about anything I found interesting. But there was hardly a day that I didn't have trouble over some, to me, ridiculous convention.

For instance, there was the afternoon I arrived with a little story about clothes for pregnant women, including some fashion and beauty hints upon how a woman was to make herself look and feel better when she was having a baby. At the rehearsal—in those days we had a sort of rehearsal of the program—Jeff Sparks, my first announcer, was horrified. I mustn't say "pregnant" on the air, he informed me.

"Well, what shall I say?" I puzzled. "In an interesting condition? Expecting?" Both seemed worse. I finally decided on expectant mother. Was that all right? Jeff agreed, and the program began. But toward the end of my little fashion talk I inadvertently used the word pregnant and suddenly heard a piano playing. I thought they had taken me off; I continued—but with a heavy heart.

Only when the program was over did I discover that I had *not* been cut off—what I had heard was only somebody practicing in another studio. You can imagine how I had sounded, though, and it was my bad luck that an official listened that day for the first time. He said, "I thought you were supposed to be an ad libber, but it certainly sounded as if you were reading there at the end."

Times have certainly changed. Not long ago I heard a master of ceremonies on a panel show ask a young contestant in a matter-of-fact tone: "And when are you expecting your baby?" "Oh, in about ten days now," she answered, with a gay laugh.

"My goodness, I wouldn't have known it," commented the M.C. in surprise. "Oh, I never show," boasted the young woman, complacently smoothing herself down in front. "Just before my other baby was born people who hadn't seen me for a while would say on meeting me: 'Oh, you've had it! Was it a boy or a girl?' I didn't show up to the very last minute."

I remember Jeff said the only reason I wasn't taken off when I said "pregnant" was that the person whose duty it was to pull the switch wasn't listening to a mere woman's program. For a long time that was the attitude at the station, and I resented it. I didn't consider myself a woman's program—certainly not after I started doing interviews. I longed to be thought of as an intelligent person presenting guests who could talk excitingly about where they'd been and what they'd done. I thought that ought to interest men and women alike—and so it did. But I had to wait a long time for recognition of this fact.

When I finally told friends about my venture it was because I wanted help. "Write me lots of letters," I begged, and some of them really did send me a letter apiece every day for a good while. Most enthusiastic of all the writing friends was Sheelagh Kennedy, daughter of my dear friend Anne, who took my entreaties to write letters, lots of letters, seriously. Sheelagh certainly had the makings of a great fiction writer, and since then she's proved it by at least one successful novel. There was no end to her inventiveness in creating correspondents for Martha Deane.

One day she wrote as an old woman, the next as an old man. She changed her character, her sex, her nationality, her handwriting at will, and her efforts were so convincing, no matter what role she played —she carefully chose real addresses in case the station should turn detective—that even I was bewildered. Whatever letters I could not possibly identify as having been written by some other friend I credited to Sheelagh.

One of her efforts nearly caused a crisis at the studio. Scott got it in his mail by mistake. It purported to come from a girl whose address was a rather prosperous East Side apartment house. She had a beau named Joe, the girl wrote. One evening something had happened— she wasn't sure what, but she was afraid. Her father was severe. She couldn't go to him. Her mother was dead. She'd never been told the facts of life. The whole letter was a moving appeal to Martha Deane for advice and protection.

Scott wanted me to answer the letter over the air. Then he decided I must go to see the girl. But although the writing and language seemed authentic, I thought I recognized Sheelagh's style. She admitted at once that it was indeed the latest fine flowering of her talent. So I asked her please to lay off. It was time anyway, for, miracle of miracles, real letters from real listeners were coming in.

"I used to have a responsible executive job in a Manhattan department store," wrote one young woman. "I loved it. Then I met a young man, *the* young man. Now I'm living in the suburbs (New Jersey), trying to make a good home and waiting for my first baby. I get lonely and sometimes, though I love my life now, I miss the store and the

excitement of each day. You bring the world into my little kitchen—
the people, the sights, the sounds. I'm becoming an addict."

From then on I was part of her family. Her husband telephoned me
when the baby was born. I knew when Norman said his first word; in
nursery school he made a paper chain for me like the one he gave his
mother. I saw him through high school, and it was a great day for all
of us when he passed his college-entrance examinations.

By that time I was quite accustomed to the strange intimacies that
can grow up through air contact, but at first it was unbelievable to
me that a woman I'd never seen would take the trouble to write me a
warm, loving message.

I guess the first time I really said to myself "Maybe this is going to
last" was when a letter came that declared the two most wonderful
voices on the air were President Roosevelt's and Martha Deane's! That
amused Stella, who often said that my voice, Fred Allen's, and Jack
Benny's were the *worst* voices on the air but had the advantage of
coming over without any alteration by the ether waves.

I argued about my voice being awful, pointing to another note in
many letters which pleased me. "You're not like some of these women
on radio. You don't talk down to us," several women wrote. They
meant, I think now, that I didn't give them recipes and tell them
how to make pants for little Johnny out of the old curtains. There
was a good reason for this. I simply didn't know enough about anything to tell others how to do it. But I was close to getting the big
head over the compliment, the nearest I ever came to such a catastrophe.

One day Stella Karn asked me, "How'd you like to hear your voice
as it sounds on the air?" I cried delightedly, "Oh, *could* I?" "We're
going today to a place where they have a recording," answered Stella.

I shall never forget that afternoon. Several of the people from our
office came along. As we walked into a big room we were all talking
and suddenly I heard a woman's recorded voice. I remember to this
minute my reaction. I thought condescendingly, "Another of those
women—*I'm* not like *her!*" And then the voice said something quite
familiar and I stopped in my tracks, demanding, "Who *is that?*"
Everybody thought it was a great joke. "Don't you know your own
voice?" they asked. "Is *that my* voice?" I cried, horrified. Other people
may find this funny, but it was tragic for me. I sounded like all those

other women, and from that day to this, hearing my own voice has been torture.

That's why it has been a real chore to play the old recordings for this book. I farmed some out to my secretary, Hilda Deichler, who likes them, but I've had to hear myself all too often, using the same old mannerisms, saying foolish things, making ridiculous mistakes. Maybe if I had listened during the years I was on the air I could have improved, but probably the only result would have been that I'd have quit long before I did. It was better to go on making mistakes, maybe, than to have all the pleasure of broadcasting taken away. And broadcasting *was* a pleasure to me.

Almost as much of a bore to others as conceit is an attitude of perpetual self-depreciation. I know this very well, yet if I tell the truth about myself I can't avoid mention of this disagreeable habit which I've determinedly tried to break.

Sometimes I've attempted to analyze myself as I did other people, striven to understand myself as I used to try to understand those I interviewed. But while I think I can see myself as I am, I can't explain why I should have been miserable so much of the time in such a happy job. I suppose it's just that I was never satisfied. Oh, sometimes for a little while I might have a respite. I'd say to a really good guest, "This was wonderful. You were marvelous." And for an hour I would be quite complacent. But as the day went on I'd find myself muttering with a resigned sigh, a meaningless phrase like, "Well, that's the way it is in this world." Or sometimes, "How could I have been such a fool!" I wasn't able to keep myself from this kind of post-mortem.

"How did you go about interviewing?" a high school girl who wants to get into television asked me the other day. I tried to tell her, but I think she found my explanation too simple. I just sat with a guest and put questions now and then, interrupting when I felt one theme had lasted too long or was taking an uninteresting turn. But how wretched I often made myself over some point I hadn't brought out. The staff who had to bear with my groaning kept saying, "Nobody but you knows you had that material. It was a good show!" But I couldn't be comforted. I wanted perfection.

And always I was pursued by the fear that someday they would find me out. Radio was too good to be true—that I should have this job year after year, that sponsors should wait in line to get on the program, that I should actually be paid for a chance to perform for the public that ordinarily wouldn't have been drawn to a person with my lack of histrionic ability and training. It wasn't much comfort, but it interested me that more than one guest, especially actors and actresses, confided that they, too, dreaded they would be found out.

Arthur Frank Payne, a psychologist who had a program on WOR when I was there, told me that he thought I had, by going on the air under a name not my own, developed a second personality. This scared me at first, but when I thought it over I agreed with him.

For example, when I spoke of Martha Deane off the air, I never said *I*, always *she*. I felt quite apart from her. Dr. Payne said that was natural. He believed there are seven distinct personalities in the life of every normal person, clearly defined but not always noticed unless, I suppose, you do something like going on the air under an assumed name. He insisted that Martha Deane was the best thing that ever happened to me. Enjoy it, he urged. Get rid of the old personality and revel in the new.

I did have fun and I wanted my guests to be happy, too. This was partly self-interest, since if they weren't at ease they didn't talk well. Many of the broadcasts in the twenty years were done from my own home, and often we were alone, the guest and I, with the microphone between us and the engineer hidden behind a screen over in a corner. Quite often we would both forget that we were on the air, which was what I was working for.

I was talking about the prospect of this book to Faith Baldwin the novelist, one of my favorite guests, who said, "You know what you ought to do? Say what you really thought of all of these people. Don't repeat the flowery introductions you gave them and the things you put in to make them feel good. Come right out with your real opinion."

Probably I did sound flowery at times, but I rarely if ever was merely polite. Maybe I was often too enthusiastic, but I meant every word. I really *loved* a good guest. Even though I might have walked in three minutes before the broadcast and met the person for the first time, I sometimes felt that by the end of the hour we were best friends.

There was a time, though, when I was rather sorry for myself because I heeded those who kept saying, "You work too hard. You ought to go about more, play, see people, have fun!" It was true that if I went to a party or any other event it was to get a story. I was accustomed to leaving a first night after the first act (*South Pacific* was an example) because I had to dash home to get ready for the next day's broadcast.

All the same I went everywhere I was invited, provided there was a story in it. The hostess had to promise that. Carol in those early days invited me to what she said was going to be a very special dinner. Before I accepted I asked, "Who's coming?" "What do you want to know that for?" she demanded, startled. I sighed and reminded her, "I can't come unless I can get a story." She vowed that I was as bad as Queen Victoria, insisting on a list. But she sent me one and allowed me to choose where I would sit at table, too.

Later that month, my friend Helen Josephy, with whom I had collaborated on several travel books, asked me to dinner and told me a wonderful man was coming. "He works at the Bronx Zoo and has the most marvelous stories about animals," she assured me happily. She had invited me weeks ahead so she would have plenty of time to prepare, for Helen felt she must supply, in addition to the special guest, a delicious home-cooked dinner with at least one rare food that I could talk about on the air.

She had been my first legwoman on radio—that reporter who went about checking facts and getting tips for me. She decided on the zoo man, a former newspaper reporter, because she had learned that my listeners adored stories about animals and natural-history curiosities. She said the young man in question was full of such yarns. She had heard him holding forth at length at a party not long before.

Since I had been primed that William Bridges would make a story I actually came to the table notebook and pencil in hand. Immediately Helen told about my mission and tried to turn the conversation into zoological channels. But at that point our plans went awry. Mr. Bridges had never heard of the Martha Deane program or me, and he was immediately suspicious. A certain air of suspense hovered over the soup, congealed during the entree, and froze solid at dessert. It was obvious my hostess was on the spot.

To relieve her, I began a conversation with Mrs. Bridges. She was an amateur gardener, she told me, and for her birthday her husband had given her a load of manure. She was thrilled about it, and that was interesting, I thought. I led her on to talk about annuals and perennials until I realized that my host and the zoo man had gotten into a conversation about art—whether or not businessmen should take it up as an avocation. That was even more promising. Frantically I wrote away on the slips of paper in my lap, apologizing, but explaining that it was an absolute necessity for me to do this for my listeners' sakes.

After coffee the atmosphere grew less charged. Even the man from the zoo thawed somewhat. He admitted that it must be quite a responsibility to have a program on one's mind at a dinner party. He also grew a little curious. And finally contrite.

The upshot was that before the evening was over he was telling me delicious yarns about the home life of the bears and the llamas. In return I got a story from him about a book he had just finished, which I promised to talk about on the air. Before leaving he invited me to lunch with him at the zoo someday in order to be introduced to all his favorite wild creatures. Later, William Bridges became one of my best and favorite guests as well as a dependable friend.

## 2. RADIO FAMILY

*"Madame Queen, don't start to believe your own publicity!" Stella Karn, warning me by short wave four thousand miles away in Norway not to get above myself.*

Stella was my chief booster, frequent deflator, and head of my radio family. Before I began to have daily guests I depended a great deal on a group of friends and employees who appeared on holidays and special occasions or sometimes for no reason except that we felt like having a jam session, as our very informal unrehearsed gatherings around the microphone were called. Listeners grew quite partial to this feature.

The regulars included Stella; Hilda Deichler, my secretary through both the magazine free-lance and radio years; Janice Devine, whom Stella and I usually described as our legwoman because she chased around getting material about guests; Berta and Elmer Hader, children's book artists and our closest friends; Juliette Nicole (Nikki), who made my dresses and hats; Hattie Silverman, widow of the founder of *Variety*; Ben Gross, radio-television editor of the *News*; Patti Pickens, mother of the Pickens sisters; Enid Haupt, now the important editor of *Seventeen*, then a real Martha Deane listener with a greenhouse in which she grew the most magnificent orchids; Herman Smith, writer and food expert; Helen Josephy, with whom I collaborated on travel books; Olga Petrova, star of silent motion pictures; whoever was my housekeeper at the time—first Frances Gallacher, later Myra Washington. And of course there was always the current announcer: Vincent Connolly, and for a period, Dick Willard.

The radio family was rather like a permanent repertory company, though occasionally a new member joined. Marjorie Moffet wrote and recited special poems; monologuist Islay Benson often read from Dickens' *Christmas Carol* in season.

Nikki with her gaiety and her enchanting French accent was a great favorite ("We can't understand Nikki but we love her," the listeners wrote); Hattie, who made the perfect coconut cake, was unpredictable —we never knew what she was going to say any more than we knew what to expect from Patti, mother of the Pickens sisters, who once, to my shocked though pleased embarrassment, heaped so many compliments on me that, to hide my blushes, I crawled under the table the microphone stood on. Stayed there, too, until she finished.

Our cast contained a number of children who appeared chiefly at Christmas to sing "Silent Night" and "Hark! the Herald Angels Sing." These included my red-haired nephew Tommy, who was supposed to have been a girl and named for me; Mrs. D.'s Judy (who might never have been born, had radio happened to me just a little bit sooner, for Mrs. D. wouldn't have had time to have a baby); Janice's Michael (she did her best to have him arrive while she was getting stories at the World's Fair, for they were giving layettes to babies born on the grounds); Helen's Jay and Frances' Jimmy.

My various godchildren made occasional appearances, too—notably Tinka Streibert, daughter of Ted, my first radio boss, and Margaret, a wonderful friend; and the Lees—Calvin, Lily, and Bo-Lum—in colorful satin trousers and blouses, children of a Chinese-American restaurateur.

When Stella was going to be on, the salesmen gathered in the control room, for they found her stories of her circus experiences irresistible, especially the day she told about Pearl, a baby elephant that she used to take for walks on a boardwalk in California. "And from the back," remarked Stella solemnly, "you couldn't tell which was Pearl and which was Stella!"

People who knew Stella were divided into two camps, and they all used strong language to describe her. One group (and it was not small) called her unreasonable, hard-boiled, even cruel; the other hailed her as a great woman, a genius, the most generous, loyal friend anybody ever had. I and everybody who worked closely with her—Hilda Deichler and Janice Devine, too—knew she was all those things and more. It was impossible to move her, once her mind was made up. She was not introspective, and even when she was occasionally wrong she firmly believed she was right.

Life was never dull where Stella was because she was always interested and generally full of some brand-new venture. Long before we had anybody on the program telling about such subjects as spaceships or rockets Stella was interested in life on other planets and talking knowingly about interplanetary space. She had very clear ideas about it all and later insisted upon our interviewing every one of the authors who wrote about journeys to Mars and flying saucers, even when they seemed obvious fakes. Her favorites were a man who claimed he had talked to a Martian and another who had seen little green creatures get off a flying saucer in the Western Desert. She took these guests to dinner and questioned them exhaustively.

She was fascinated by China, Tibet, remote islands, and always planned to travel to them. Once she had an idea of equipping a ship and sailing with it all round the world to study the habits of people who lived on out-of-the-way islands. She enjoyed her class in international law at Columbia University because she met men from Siam, Africa, China, India, and even Outer Mongolia. She started to get a little of the money needed for the ship enterprise but in the end had to give it up just because nobody else could quite get her vision.

We were invited to visit Haiti and the Virgin Islands chiefly because Stella was so interested and persuaded me that recordings from such places would build program interest. In the Virgin Islands, Harry Harman, our engineer, then Commander Harman of the U. S. Navy, had to use a wire recorder, and the first batch of records we sent back to NBC, according to a frantic cable from Janice, couldn't be played because the wire had broken. Stella snorted and dictated a message: "Get Boy Scout Manual and learn to tie a square knot." Janice reported that it was quite a sight to see half a dozen grown men laboring over Boy Scout instructions but it worked. The scout knots repaired the wire in time for the program to go on the air.

In every place where Stella lived, or even stayed as much as three weeks, she had at least three telephones and handled all three at the same time. She would tuck one under her chin, hold one on her left shoulder, and the third was on the desk in front of her, leaving her right shoulder unhampered by an instrument so that she could juggle two receivers and hear three conversations with two ears. Somehow, too, she kept the conversations separate. She never relinquished any telephone book—even when the delivery man brought the new ones she kept all the old ones, not only from the five boroughs but all those of every year from other cities. She said that someday she might need an address that wasn't in the new books.

On one of her three telephones she might be bawling out a network executive (she had no regard for authority at all), on another she might be trying to find a job for some young person who had come to her in distress, and on the third she would be talking to the hapless woman who had sold her a dress in a Fifth Avenue department store. She bought dresses in the same reckless way she bought everything else—sometimes as many as a dozen at a time—and then when it came to fittings, though she didn't understand much about style, she and the saleswoman would have long, agitated conversations about every detail.

She was usually peremptory and demanding to sponsors who wanted to buy into the program, unless I was there. Then she was polite because she felt she had to defend them from me. She maintained that I was suspicious of anybody who wanted me to boost a product until some man mentioned that his wife or his mother wouldn't leave the house or even answer the telephone while I was on the air. At that point, she insisted, a light would break over my face and I'd suddenly turn friendly. Sometimes we lost sponsors because of my coldness. Whenever she wanted me to see anybody I reminded her of this, and she realized that if she exposed them to me she took a risk; but it was calculated because she thought we had to meet sometime and it was best to have it over with.

When I went to visit factories which I stipulated we must do so that I could tell the listeners exactly how everything was made, what went into it, what the employees were like, and how they felt about their employers, she went along with great enthusiasm. She was curious about everything, and long after I was bedraggled and unable to assimilate another idea she was still eager to see more. "Don't you want to look at this? Don't you want to have that explained?" she would urge.

One of the reasons I hated to be along when she was seeing sponsors was because she was an unashamed braggart where the honors and accomplishments of the program were concerned and equally unashamed when it came to ratings. She insisted that ratings didn't matter because our ratings never were as high as the soap operas which were opposite us. She used to say to inquirers: "I don't know what our ratings are. I don't care anything about them. Ratings don't matter. We don't sell ratings. We sell Mary Margaret McBride. Mary Margaret sells products. You want to sell your products, don't you?"

Any place where Stella lived, even a hotel room, became instantly outrageously different, and her office was uniquely hers. She never threw away any of the things she bought, and she was constantly buying. So wherever she was she needed plenty of storage space. At one point when I was writing a column for the Associated Press her suite at the Waldorf-Astoria contained hundreds of copies of the New York *Mirror*, which carried the column. She planned *sometime* to clip my pieces.

The office on West 45th Street had a main door which opened readily enough. But then you were in a tiny anteroom with a seven-foot-high partition that barred your way. The entrance through the partition was locked, but there was a small window that opened from the inside into a long general office with at least three times the number of desks and typewriters any office like ours needed. Finally there was Stella's own office with her three telephones, three or four clocks that were supposed to run by air, filing cabinets, numerous radios, bookcases, and an enormous desk piled high with papers, magazines, books, bronze elephants, and an interoffice communication box. She also kept some of the recordings in her office, but most of them were lined up in a storeroom which held not only tons of recordings but hundreds of magazines containing every article I'd done or been mentioned in, dozens of copies of every book I'd ever written, and every one in which I'd been mentioned.

She liked to have about six of even ordinary items just in case she might run out. It undoubtedly went back to the time when she was starting out, a poor little girl at sixteen, depending on her own efforts and never having enough of anything. She couldn't resist old silver and old glass, though sometimes the pieces she acquired were a little less ancient than she believed. She'd go into a shop, and if the proprietor happened to be a congenial spirit they'd begin to talk and pretty soon he would have saddled her with more than her weight in doubtful treasures.

She used to buy hundreds of dollars worth of Christmas cards every year but seldom sent out any because she put off addressing them. One time when I ran short of the Christmas message I was using for listeners she urged Mrs. D. to come to her office and help herself. Mrs. D. was appalled by the enormous piles of expensive cards that represented years of buying and begged Stella to let her help address and send some out. Stella produced a list and the two started off briskly, sitting at the big desk. Then Stella noticed that the tusk on one of the elephants lumbering across the far side of the bookcase was broken and that all her treasures looked pretty dusty. She dropped the Christmas-card project at once and began to dust elephants. Soon she left to keep an appointment. Mrs. D. stayed and finished the cards. Stella had failed to leave the key to her stamp supply, and although Mrs. Deichler put up a huge sign—IMPORTANT: These must be stamped and mailed immediately—and reminded Stella by telephone a dozen times, we found them just as Mrs. D. had left them when Stella was dead and we were closing the office.

I used to lecture Janice, who worked in the office, about restraining those buying impulses. Stella usually took her along on her expeditions out of the office. But as Janice confessed when she telephoned me after one: "It's impossible to stop her once she sees what she thinks is a bargain." She heard of a silver shop that had inexpensive sterling salts and peppers. She went in and bought six sets (she didn't need one), an ice bucket, and a bowl for fruit.

On our trip to Haiti and the Virgin Islands she spent every minute when we weren't in the middle of, or preparing for, a broadcast, shopping. She bought mahogany of every color in Haiti, she bought all kinds of handwork in the Virgin Islands, and when we went to Alaska she was the dealers' joy, for they sold her most of the silver fox, ivory, and totem poles they'd had lying around for years.

In New York she watched the papers for sales. Nothing delighted her more than an auction. She would bid on anything. The worst object she ever bought at an auction was a ten-foot-long jousting pole, purportedly used by medieval knights. It was the kind of object there was no room for in any home. Maybe a castle would have accommodated it, but a museum was the really appropriate place, if anybody wanted it preserved. Stella loved it. She stood it in the front hall up in the country and showed it proudly to everybody.

The reason Stella seldom opened the packages she accumulated was because she didn't need them. She just wanted them. The fact that she rarely unwrapped Christmas presents until she decided to give them to someone else also caused complications. Janice Devine declares that one day at the office she found several boxes so dusty that they must have been there for years. She bullied Stella into opening them and found among other now slightly ancient delicacies five pounds of five-year-old Christmas candy and six molding fruitcakes.

One day Stella was sitting in a restaurant with Cynthia Lowry. "Look at these nice steak knives," she commented enviously. "I must get some steak knives." Cynthia sat for one minute in angry unbelieving silence, then screamed: "Stella, I gave you a complete set of steak knives last Christmas. Where are they?" Stella had never opened the package, and when she did begin to inspect that year's Christmas haul she found three dozen steak knives in all.

She was fond of entertaining, though she never did as much of it as she really wanted to when three of us shared apartments in the Village. That was because I was so difficult about hospitality. In later years she liked to invite great crowds to her farm for weekends. If I was there she never told me beforehand, and the first indication to me that she was having a house party was finding a gentleman taking a shower in my bathroom, coming upon a sun bather of either sex, unbountifully attired, on the terrace, or from my room hearing the merry shouts of little children and realizing that this weekend Stella was entertaining at least one entire family. I am afraid I was often quite abrupt in such cases. I loved people out there at the receiving sets and I loved the people I interviewed, but I didn't have time or inclination to be gracious and hostesslike every weekend.

Stella did. The more people who came, the happier she felt. She would take infinite pains to give them a good time, to see that they were well taken care of, according to her rules.

A rigid one of these concerned the kitchen when she was fixing a meal. She refused to have any other person in there except maybe Berta Hader. Almost the only time she ever apologized to me for anything was once when I was in her big kitchen doing something harmless like dishing myself some cereal and she ordered me out. I ran upstairs with what she said later was the look of a wounded deer. And she pursued me to tell me she was sorry.

People said Stella bossed me, and I guess it was true. I did nearly everything she told me to, and the reason was that after I'd worked with her awhile I knew she was probably right. No matter how unlikely her ideas may have seemed to begin with, I usually had to admit in the end that by some miracle of intuition, she had called the turn. I never yielded without a struggle, and I'd argue for hours while she went straight ahead, hardly listening.

She could not be changed, and with a shock I suddenly realize that neither could I. It's difficult to understand how, exposed to so much assurance, I could remain the same timid, fearful, self-deprecatory person. Stella couldn't understand it either, but no matter how hard I tried I was never able to shake her faith in me. With every medium at her command she told the world that I was wonderful, and she really believed it.

Our battles were notorious. Berta and Elmer Hader, friends of long standing, tell about one time when we had such a stupendous row at their home on the Hudson that when we started back to town in Stella's car—Stella in the front seat and I in the back, where she kept me so she wouldn't hear my "back-seat driving"—they followed us because Berta said to Elmer: "No telling what they'll do to each other, they're so enraged." By the time they got to town (and very surprised Stella and I were to see them) we were calm and peaceful, chatting away as if we had never had an unfriendly word for each other.

Perhaps we needed the relief our wild quarrels brought us. I'm sure a psychiatrist would say that it was better than bottling up. I was never a bottle-upper, but Stella was. A month or six weeks would sometimes go by and she'd be rather cross with me the whole time, resenting something I had done or said, yet she'd never tell me what. I always have to do something right away when I'm angry—write a letter, make a telephone call, blow up one way or another. After that I feel no more anger, only remorse for my display of temper. Stella used to say, "Just because you say you're sorry doesn't mean that the other person isn't hurt."

Sometimes she was guilty of the same tactics. She and Janice were devoted to each other, but they, too, sometimes had stormy scenes. Afterward Stella might come out of her office and say to Janice, exactly as if nothing had happened, "Come on, Toots, let's go to lunch."

Janice says whenever she heard Stella calling her Toots, she knew she was going to let bygones be bygones.

Lunch sometimes was research for a cookbook which she had told me I was going to write almost before we had begun the radio program. She said there was a great book in the history of American food. I finally wrote the book but not the way she wanted it and the way it should have been written. If Stella had had her way we'd have traveled to the most remote towns and hamlets of every state and borrowed yellowed recipes out of treasured family books, listened to oldest inhabitants telling food stories from the earliest days. We did collect some of this material through the U. S. Department of Information and the state departments of agriculture and libraries all over the country, but nobody would ever have had enough money to finance a book such as Stella visualized, not that she cared about money. Sometimes to my horror she spent money that she didn't have. But in the end she got it.

She hardly ever talked about her benefactions, but I got a line on a few of the dead beats who victimized her. One told her his wife was out of her mind and he was having to pay $200 a week to keep her at an institution. He said he had lost his job because of worry and he must have $200 immediately or the institution would turn his wife out. Then he went off and bet the $200 on the horses. He got away with the same sad story twice before Stella grew suspicious and investigated.

She was touched by almost any kind of sob story and lent thousands of dollars they never paid back to men and women who came to her with improbable hard-luck sagas. This was not only generosity but the fact that she had gone hungry, had known what it was to scramble to get along in the world. Undoubtedly she sometimes believed the tales, but even if she wasn't sure, she helped just to avoid the possibility of suffering she understood so well—hunger, destitution. Mental suffering was more difficult for her to comprehend. She could be hard without ever realizing what she was doing to the other person. Perhaps subconsciously she felt it wasn't much use seeing the other person's side since the other person was wrong anyway.

When we were compiling recipes for the cookbook she put parsley and nutmeg into everything. I like nutmeg but I can't stand parsley, so I always took it out but she put it back. When she remembered a certain dish she'd had, she'd search the city until she found it and then have the chef tell how to make it. She spent a fortune buying test lunches and dinners. Just as she had known it would be, the cookbook was finished and published, though some time after her death. She had been right, as she nearly always was. That was the exasperating and wonderful thing about her.

The beautiful celebrity luncheon which Gene Leone planned and gave for the book was a sad day for me because I kept seeing Stella, full of zest and energy, welcoming her friends, tackling with gusto her favorite squab à la Leone, and making the occasion so much more exciting because she was there.

She went on a diet from time to time, and her idea of sensible eating was apple pie à la mode. "After all—what is it but a little bit of fruit?" she'd argue. "I don't touch the crust—and what's ice cream except milk? And I'm supposed to have milk." That's the way her mind worked. When she wanted to believe anything, she believed completely and irrevocably.

In the midst of one of our more violent quarrels I said suddenly: "Stella"—we were trying to figure a way for me to go to San Francisco for the opening of the United Nations—"why don't you go? You need a change and so do I." She agreed instantly (up to then we hadn't agreed on anything for days) and in three hours was on a plane. She had a wonderful time, interviewing mostly representatives of the little countries because she said they weren't getting any headlines. She was always more interested in small nations than big ones. I doubt if she slept at all for two or three weeks. Day and night she was rounding up men in burnooses, women in saris, Arabs, Egyptians, Yemenites, Lebanese. Daily her recorded interviews were vivid fascinating accounts of people and customs then unknown to the general public. For years when the men she met in San Francisco would come to New York they would head straight for Stella's office where, no matter how complicated her life might be at the moment, she would drop everything for long hours of fervid discussion.

One of her scoops was getting the first detailed description of secret factories in Luxembourg from which the Germans planned a terminal attack by a new and more deadly form of the V-2 bomb. That was when Stella decided she wanted the program to be broadcast from Luxembourg at the height of the rose season. She was planning that

trip up to a few months before her death, and Dora Miller, a Paris
friend of hers, was making the preliminary arrangements.

When she decided to come back from San Francisco by way of
Texas to visit her nephew Dick, in officers' training there, she ran into
what seemed insurmountable difficulties which she solved in a thoroughly Stella-esque fashion. Because of priorities ordinary people
hadn't much chance to get onto planes, and Stella, by going to Texas,
lost her chance to ride back to New York with other reporters in a
special chartered job. The situation was the kind of challenge she
enjoyed.

Investigation revealed that live freight could be sent by air if it was
crated to the airline's specifications. She telephoned the airline and
ordered a crate to measure five and a half feet by five and a half feet.
The request went from one official to another until the executive vice-
president finally asked what sort of live freight Stella planned to send.
"Me," Stella said. Everybody in that airline office hit the ceiling. They
kept arguing with her: "You can't go as freight." Stella would smile
that delighted guileless smile she had on such occasions and sweetly
read the printed regulations aloud. They said live freight and they did
not say that humans were excluded. Nobody knows who got bumped
when Stella finally took off—maybe a general, maybe a lesser person—
but anyway she boarded the plane with an airline vice-president there
to see that she did.

She visited her nephew, then chose a train which happened to be
carrying only sailors, slipped through the gate unnoticed, climbed
aboard, and had become such a favorite with the men that when the
train authorities wanted to put her off they made her an honorary
sailor so that it would be all right for her to ride on a troop train.
When I met her she came off the train surrounded by dozens of dear
friends—the sailors.

Stella Karn enjoyed life more than anybody I've ever known and
got more out of it. I'm positive that she even enjoyed her tantrums.
And because of her intense curiosity about everything, her business
sense and her intuition, she was the best manager a radio program ever
could have. If we had not met in our early twenties when we each had
a job in an interfaith organization, I am convinced I would have been
out of radio forever before my first six months were ended.

## 3. SEVEN-DAY WEEK

I soon got used to improvisation. I had to! One day I went to view an exhibit that I was counting on for my day's story. My reporter had already covered it, and details were already fixed in my mind. I only needed to verify them. But it turned out the reporter had made a mistake. The exhibit wouldn't be open for another week. The tough young director said they would sue me if I even mentioned it before then. I argued so long with the man that I just had time to hurry to the broadcast.

I was a little bit flustered because that day I had planned to do all the talking myself. Now I had no material. Luckily my taxi driver chatted most interestingly all the way to the studio, so I did my broadcast on taxi drivers and their ambitions. This one had written several popular songs, which he duly sang for me. He also had a method for combating old age. As I remember, he ate nothing but raw fruits and vegetables and drank vinegar.

Another time I went to dinner in the suburbs where I was to have duck cooked a special way. I had billboarded the duck on the air ahead of time. At the front door I was met by my hostess and her cook, both crying. The cook said, "I told the meatman that duck was no good." And the odor that wafted our way confirmed her worst suspicions. The cook finally ran around the corner and bought some pork chops. The story when I told it, as inevitably I did on the air next day, started an unexpected controversy among the listeners. That night's hostess had a job outside her home. Some of those wives who didn't have jobs said that if that woman had been attending to her chief business of homemaking, as she should have been, she wouldn't have had to be disappointed by a bad duck. Women wrote in about it for weeks.

Sometimes, listening to the recordings of those scrambling, stimulating years, I wonder how I did it all. Since the guests were the backbone of the program, preparation for them was my first consideration. Sometimes I read three books in a single night, making rapid notes until 3 A.M. or after and memorizing details until I was able, when I opened my eyes next morning, to recite to myself more questions and answers than could ever be used in a single broadcast—and this without reference to the notes.

It was like cramming for an examination, only more thorough and safer because there was no teacher to stump me. I was telling the truth when I said as I did to Orson Welles, "I've been thinking of you constantly for forty-eight hours." Incidentally, in spite of all that brooding, I was never able to decide whether Welles was shy or merely indifferent, conceited or covering up humility. Maybe he has, or had then, anyway, a kind of brusque bravado. A lot of people do.

"What does she do? Just sits before a microphone and talks! Who couldn't do that?" some people derided. My casual method of delivery, including the way I stammered and reached for a word, gave the impression that I was making everything up right on the spot. And it's true, after a fashion, for I never knew exactly how I was going to say what was packed in my head.

When I had only one broadcast I got up at seven o'clock in the morning, but when after the second year I did two broadcasts my work would start at five-thirty. This was the best part of the day, for the staff didn't come until nine-thirty and all to myself I would plan the commercials and collect my thoughts. Immediately after the broadcast was the most frantic time. Stella Karn would usually try to spare me as much as possible, but sometimes there were business matters that I had to know about and any day there might be half a dozen persons waiting to see me—writers, future guests, sponsors, artists' representatives, salesmen, network publicity men, insurance agents, press agents.

Some evenings after the dinners and the parties where I got stories I went on to big charity balls where there were lots of colorful people. In odd moments I answered much of my mail in my own hand.

To get stories I scurried about like the proverbial eager-beaver reporter on a newspaper. I spent the whole of one terrible night in Long Island Sound on a tiny boat seining for fish with a professional fisherman. Each smelly, squirmy catch was thrown on deck, and though I can get seasick in a rowboat tied to a dock, by some miracle of will I restrained myself the entire twelve hours from throwing up.

I covered the night courts of the city and heard firsthand the sordid, sorrowful stories of those who get in trouble with the law. Down on the water front I got life histories from families who spent their entire lives in cargo barges on rivers and canals. One spring I hurried out to Maspeth, Long Island, to visit with a gypsy queen and her subjects before they started traveling. I spent a night in a listener's trailer in order to tell what it was like (in one word—crowded!).

Stella tracked down and I spent some time with a bunch of hobos and was written up in their magazine by Georgina, one of Tommy Manville's wives. I floated over New York in a blimp, went up in a helicopter with Igor Sikorsky, who invented it.

It exhausts me now even to think about all the places we went and the things we did. Some weeks I must have shaken as many as five thousand hands. No wonder I seemed about then to be getting chronic bursitis in my right arm! . . . And eat! Nobody was ever satisfied when I took just one helping of anything, for I was reputedly a mighty trencherman.

In the South they fed me spoonbread, corndodger, beaten biscuits, country ham, black-eyed peas, and fried chicken. In Pennsylvania my hosts put on the table the traditional seven sweets and seven sours (seven sweet dishes and seven sour ones), besides special sausages, shoofly pies, and a dozen other viands.

In Connecticut, Mrs. Israel Putnam introduced me to that pumpkin bread (made with a female pumpkin) that I've talked and written about ever since. And for dessert we had the scorched custard that I said Mrs. Putnam ironed. That gracious lady of the old school never contradicted me publicly, but she gently insisted in private that touching a flatiron lightly to the brown sugar on top of a pudding wasn't really ironing. However, I'd used too many flatirons in my youth not to recognize ironing when I saw it!

As if five days a week weren't enough Stella Karn one day decreed that weekends must be devoted to expeditions that might turn out to be adventure stories to be told on Monday. So many Fridays when the broadcast was over we—Stella, Janice, and I—set off by automobile or airplane for some spot, usually historical, that would provide material. These broadcasts quickly became highlights in our week, and invitations poured in.

The Middle West—my part of it, anyway—is not strong on history, and I never cared for it in school. But I was entranced by the old salt-box houses in Connecticut that had been lived in by the same families for six, seven, even eight generations.

At Guilford, for instance, we saw an old salt box on Crooked Lane with floor boards worn completely through. The owner of the house, Comfort Starr, was a tailor. He stood all day, this hard-working Connecticut Yankee, in front of his cutting board until he made a dent. In Guilford, too, lived a hatmaker who was town clerk, magistrate, and representative at the General Assembly. His name was Sam Hill, and to this day people round there say, of some paragon of industry, "Why, he works like Sam Hill." Guilford also was put in our broadcast for that Monday because of Acadian House, where a man named Samuel Chittenden gave shelter to a whole family of French refugees driven from their homes in Canada, as in Longfellow's poem.

At Beekman Arms in Rhinebeck, New York, I found a window seat in the original dining room worn into a hollow by being sat on for more than two hundred years. Among those who helped wear it down were Benedict Arnold, Alexander Hamilton, Aaron Burr, Lafayette, DeWitt Clinton, Martin Van Buren, Theodore Roosevelt, and dozens of others (not all at the same time of course).

Upstairs in the Beekman Arms stands a little hooded cradle made of rough pine with a patchwork quilt folded at the botton. The touching legend about it is that it came through the terrible Cherry Valley Massacre with the baby tucked safe inside.

A listener invited me for a weekend in Bordentown, New Jersey, to inspect the escape tunnel in the house that had been lived in by Joseph Bonaparte, Napoleon's brother and ex-king of Naples and Spain. I looked at the tunnel but came across another story in Bordentown that I liked better.

The heroine of this was Patience Lovell Wright, Quaker, who had lived in a little stone house. She began carving funny faces from loaves of bread to amuse her children. Then her husband died and she had to make money. Everybody marveled at her bread faces. She thought maybe she could do the same in wax and sell them. She couldn't sell any around there so she packed up and took the children and the miniatures to England. There her wax images of important people soon made her the rage. She got to be friends with the king and queen; called them George and Charlotte, Quaker style, and they called her Patience. When the revolution broke out she told her royal friend George her sympathies were with the colonies, moved on to Paris and there she did even better with her wax portraits of local notables.

In Cooperstown, home of James Fenimore Cooper, I saw the baseball museum—overrated, I said on Monday—and picked up the story of Mrs. William Cooper, mother of James Fenimore, a reluctant pioneer and proud of it. She sat down in her rocking chair in her home at Burlington, New Jersey, and when her husband wanted to move to New York State announced she would not stir. Nonsense, she called it, going off into the wilderness just because her husband liked the looks of a valley he'd seen when he climbed a tree on a hunting trip! But if she was made of stern stuff, her William was made of even sterner. He ordered the household goods piled on a wagon, all except the rocker she sat in and the carpet under her feet. Still she refused to budge. So William picked up chair and wife and put them aboard the wagon. She didn't stir during the trip, and when they arrived at what is now Cooperstown, New York, she was still determinedly seated in that chair.

In Richmond, Virginia, they told me tales of what war was like in privation and suffering for southern women. My favorite resident of the Confederate White House is Nina, the smuggler doll. Nina is faded and battered now, but she's so illustrious that the United States Government twice had her portrait painted. She was carried aboard an English ship by a little girl whose father, a doctor, wanted desperately to bring morphine and quinine to the suffering Confederate soldiers. He knew he couldn't hide the drugs on his own person or in his luggage, so he borrowed his little girl's doll, and inside Nina's china head, with its cherubic blue eyes and painted hair, he stuffed stores of the two medicines.

I went to Cape Cod just at the time the roses were climbing over the Cape Cod cottages with the funny little square porches set on the roof. Widows' walks, they call those, because sea captains' wives kept hopeless vigils there, looking far out to sea for the ships that never came back.

The Pilgrims' monument up in Provincetown, Massachusetts, furnished me with an all-American theme one Monday. They told me in the town that the design is Italian, the architect was of French and Swiss descent, the men who built it were mostly Irish, and the Portuguese take care of it. So I preached a little sermon about how we are all one and none of us has the right to look down on any other.

With sand everywhere, you'd think Cape gardens would be pretty bleak; instead they're a mass of color and bloom all summer long. The reason, I was told, is that they're rooted in earth from every corner of the world. Brought in as ballast on the old sailing ships, the dirt was unloaded in Provincetown and used for lawns and gardens. So the rambler roses on a cottage roof and the orange poppies blowing in the wind may be planted in soil from England, France, or China—or other faraway places visited by the clipper captains.

My weekend in New Castle, Delaware, was the one that finally sold me completely on history. I walked through the cobbled streets lined with tall elms and maples, some of them two centuries old, shading houses of mellowed brick with immaculate white gates and great fan-lighted doorways. There is a small room in the courthouse that they believe was the original town hall, built before 1682. William Penn stood in that old building and received bits of turf, some twigs, and water as a sign of his ownership after he had taken the key and locked himself inside alone for a few minutes of prayerful reflection.

The Village Green is shaded by immense elms and crisscrossed with paths worn by people like old Peter Stuyvesant, who used to stump across in the days of Dutch rule; William Penn; George Read, signer of the Declaration of Independence; George Washington; and Lafayette. Packet Alley is the cobbled street used by travelers who arrived by packet and took the stagecoach route out of town. Just past it is Amstel House, standing solid and sedate in its two-hundred-year-old garden with clipped box borders, brick paths, and a sun dial announcing, "I only mark the hours that shine."

Every house in New Castle has treasures from the past. One that I especially loved was a queer-looking silver gadget kept under a glass globe. It's an old tongue scraper, and the reason for the glass is that nobody can resist trying it. In another house is a cumbersome old umbrella, four times as big as our modern umbrellas, with real whalebone holding the tattered blue silk. It once had William Read's name in cross-stitch and a coat of arms on its tip.

Sometime around 1790, William Read was walking down the Strand with his grand silk umbrella sheltering him from the rain. A gust of wind from the river whisked the umbrella out of his hand and blew it far out into the water. He gave it up for lost, but exactly a year later there was a knock at his door and an old sea captain handed him the umbrella. It had blown straight onto the rigging of a sailing vessel bound for China and had journeyed over all seven seas before it finally got back to New Castle.

One weekend in June we arrived in Chocolate Town, Hershey, Pennsylvania, to see the rose garden famous all over the world. Stella and Janice were in a silly mood and registered themselves as secretary and maid, respectively, with the result that one night for the three of us cost me about $75. And we couldn't even get hot chocolate when we tried to order it at one in the morning. The roses were lovely, though.

I flew alone to Charleston, South Carolina, to see the unforgettable thousands of flame and scarlet azalea and camellia blossoms mirrored in the lakes and just as clearly and colorfully in the black-surfaced paths of famous Middleton Gardens.

In Nantucket, I explored old houses and visited with four people I love—Marjorie Mills of radio and television, actress and writer Patricia Collinge, who was one of our favorite guests, and the naturalist Kierans—John ("Information Please") and Margaret. I even threatened to go on a bird walk with John, but I suspected he was not hospitable to the idea. Margaret, however, has become almost as good at spotting birds as her famous husband.

One of our most delightful broadcasts was with John, high on a hill on the front terrace at the Haders' home on the Hudson. The birds were singing fit to burst their throats, and John identified each in turn. We broadcast from Hader House for a whole month that summer and were so enchanted with the rosy dawns, golden sunsets, and companionship of animals and birds that we decided to accept Marjorie Evans' invitation to move our equipment to Larchmont the next summer for an even longer period. Marjorie was a listener who one day got sick of hearing me complain on the air about the heat, noise, and dirt of New York.

Her opening gambit on the telephone (I'd never even heard of her until that moment) was, "Haven't you any sense at all? Why don't you get a few electric fans and a ventilator for your bedroom that will shut out noise and dirt? A great big radio person can certainly afford a few comforts . . . Never mind, I'll be there within the hour with some fans."

She was, too, and next day sent a man to install a ventilator in the bedroom. She has never been what I'd call a flattering friend but she certainly is stimulating, and the summers in her house overlooking Long Island Sound with the sailboats lazily floating in the sun were very happy.

Mildred Helms found a terrace at the Towers Hotel in Brooklyn where I could watch the ships and the incomparable skyline of New York. That was after I had undergone an operation for anal fistula and had to sit on a rubber ring for several weeks. Listeners loved the mournful whooing of the ships, and Stella said any change in routine helped the program.

Before I had healed enough to give up the rubber ring I had to appear at a convention in the Waldorf to receive an award. I decided it was better to be frank, so I took the rubber ring along, waved it at the crowd, and told about my operation in painful detail.

Some of my happiest broadcasts away from the studio were done on the stone terrace of Stella's farm in the Catskills with a view of mountains and water that reminded almost every guest of his favorite scenery, wherever located—Scotland, Switzerland, Italy.

I got into a good many books during the twenty radio years, sometimes as myself, often thinly disguised. I was murdered twice, and three times—that I know about—I was the murderer in mystery stories. Authors who want to picture you as murdered or a murderer but don't want to be sued for libel have a little trick that I got wise to after the first time it was worked on me. They mention you by your real name in a complimentary or at least innocuous fashion. Then they feel free to go ahead with you under another name that they are using for their nefarious purposes.

I was cartooned by "Believe It or Not" Ripley, profiled by *The New Yorker, Look,* and *Life,* proposed to in his sports column by Red Smith of the *Herald Tribune* and got into the annual Christmas greetings of Frank Sullivan (in a poem) and Burris Jenkins' enormous Christmas card in the New York *Journal-American.*

*Reader's Digest* got and printed this little yarn from one of my listeners: "When I brought our new baby home from the hospital, I brought a nurse, too. For the six weeks she was with me, everything went fine; Andy was a model child. After she left, things were different. Every afternoon, at one o'clock, the baby started to whimper. Nothing I tried to do would quiet him. One afternoon, the cleaning woman remarked, 'Maybe he misses Mary Margaret McBride. Miss Lynch always had it on.' I tuned in at 660 and, sure enough, Andy stopped crying at once!"

This is fame? Well, it's a reasonable facsimile and rather fun.

For my second vacation (the first one I spent having the fistula out), I went to Europe with a friend, George Schmidt, on the lighter-than-air ship *Hindenburg*. This created a real panic among my listeners. Hundreds wrote to wish me a safe voyage. Some scolded me for frightening them by taking what they thought was a most perilous trip. They sent gifts that ranged from rabbits' feet to hazelnut cake and included the caul of a seventh daughter of a seventh daughter. One listener wrote me later that she persuaded her husband to drive her to New York from Trenton, New Jersey, in order to go past both the station and my apartment so she could say the Mizpah at both places.

Any number of my rooters declared they sat up all night and tuned in their radios to find out how my journey progressed. They were afraid that there might be an accident over the sea, and if I was being plummeted down they wanted to know about it.

As a matter of fact, there *was* a storm that night, but I didn't hear it and I never felt safer in my life. When after its return trip the *Hindenburg* caught fire and burned up, I was stunned. Captain Lehmann, who had been the commanding officer on my crossing, was fatally injured. I was sad for I'd liked him. He had let me sit beside him on the bridge and listen to him reciting his own poetry. I walked with him over every inch of that ship on narrow catwalks with the ocean in plain sight below. I can't imagine how I could have been so venturesome.

Captain Lehmann took me to lunch in Frankfort with his wife, and she and I talked chiefly of war. She said, "Women don't want war, and somehow they've got to see that it is stopped." Then she and I looked at each other and there was complete agreement in our eyes—a question too. We women didn't want war. Why did men bring it on us?

It was when I came back by boat from the *Hindenburg* trip that I brought a goat, Pierrot by name, and the two of us became front-page news for a few days. *L'affaire de Pierrot* started as a joke planned by Nikki. She was in Paris when I left and presented me with this goat, which she had dressed in a cute little bonnet and neck frill. During the voyage on the *Ile de France,* Pierrot lived in the dog kennel.

When we got to New York he had to be checked through customs, and as he came down the gangplank he ate his declaration. However, he got past immigration all right, and Hattie Silverman, who met me, fell in love with him so I gave him to her for her little grandson up in Westchester. I saw Pierrot ride off in great style in Hattie's limousine and thought it was the last of him. Little did I know! It was August and there wasn't much news, so the ship news photographers had made a lot of Pierrot and me. Next morning we were all over the front page, and silly we looked, too. I felt deflated and miserable—but helpless.

Then the telephone rang and a stern masculine voice said that he was representing the Department of Agriculture. Where was the goat I had brought from France, that I had taken from one of the worst regions of hoof-and-mouth disease in the country? "It will have to be sent back at once or it might infect thousands of animals in this country," he declared. I, who am afraid of authority in any form, stammered when I told him I didn't know where Hattie's son lived in Westchester but I'd find out. I telephoned frantically to Stella, who was absolutely delighted.

"We'll get the goat back," she promised, "but meantime the papers will keep writing about it. It's a dull season." How right she was. I stopped answering letters, telephones, or doorbell, for if it wasn't the Department of Agriculture it was a reporter.

Finally Hattie brought Pierrot back and the Department of Agriculture made me come down to the pier and put him on the return sailing of the *Ile de France.* Much later a friend of mine was sitting at the captain's table on a voyage of the *Ile* and my name came up somehow. The captain exploded: "Don't talk to me about that woman! I hope I'll never hear of her again. The immigration officers in France refused to admit that goat of hers and put him back on our ship, so he traveled back and forth—a goat without a country—until we finally ate him up."

Now when television is so flooded with celebrities that people claim they get tired of looking at overadvertised faces, I wonder what Stella would suggest if I had a program. Maybe I'd have to go back to talking and getting stories, because even the biggest programs have a hard time producing exciting guests and are driven to trading turns with one another. One thing I'm sure of—Stella would think of something.

It was well that dauntless woman was around when I made my first big public appearance at Grand Central Palace. It was my second broadcasting anniversary and twenty-five thousand women came. It was a complete surprise to everybody, since we had expected at most a few hundred. The women couldn't hear and they couldn't see and there were no chairs for them to sit on. Stella said there weren't that many chairs in New York City, short of Madison Square Garden (a prophetic utterance that turned out to be). As to the defeat of the loud-speaker, she explained that the equipment had been checked the night before, but the engineers had failed to take into consideration that when the hall was filled much of the sound would be absorbed by the crowd and its clothing.

"Anyway," she added, "the only important thing was that people came." Later when stories began to be written about me, she was equally practical and, I thought, hard-boiled. She would find me crying over something that had been said about me. She was always honestly astonished. "Just look," she would urge. "Look at all the space you got!"

Now I know that I was overly and stupidly thin-skinned. I know it because I reread the other day a profile in *The New Yorker* that a nice girl named Barbara Heggie wrote. She haunted me for a good many days and since she was an excellent interviewer used various devices to get me to reveal my innermost thoughts. As I nearly always did when being interviewed I talked too much, but when I reread the story, to my surprise I found I liked it very much. I couldn't even remember what I had been so upset about at the time.

I might even decide someday to take a look at the *Life* profile. A photographer from that magazine accompanied me all the way to my home town in Missouri, climbing to the top of the Paris National Bank in order to get a bird's-eye view of the water tower and antagonizing the citizens because he was more interested in pictures than people. There were no developments from that first siege with *Life* except thousands of pictures, but a while later Jeanne Perkins revived the idea of profiling me, and this time *Life* really did me to a crisp—or so I felt. I cried for three days after the magazine came out. I can't defend myself. I just admit it to prove what I've already hinted—that I'm a spineless slob—and of course a suffering slob.

## 4. NEAR CATASTROPHE

I don't think Mary Margaret McBride really enjoyed Martha Deane much at first, even though Dr. Payne recommended it. The truth was this strange poised woman frightened me. I didn't frighten her, though. She wasn't afraid of anything. At that microphone she was monarch of all she surveyed. I must have ended by assimilating at least that much of Martha Deane, because for twenty-odd years, even after I dropped the name, I still was queen of the world—my world, anyway—when I sat before my own microphone. That's why I had such a fine time being on the radio.

Ordinarily worried about what people would say of me, when I dropped down in front of that leering little instrument I didn't think of myself at all, not until I got up and changed back into my ordinary self. Or maybe I should say except at times of near catastrophe—as when my old-time boss came, Henry L. Stoddard, who'd been editor of the *Evening Mail* when I was a cub. I'd never heard him swear in all our years of association, but he at once began to tell about my coming in to ask for a job and saying I was from Paris, Missouri. Mr. Stoddard then quoted himself as ejaculating, "My God, where is Paris, Missouri?"

Then there was the man who started out calm and agreeable but suddenly began to rave. He was an explorer, and I never did find out what the person he was bitter about had done to him, but midway in the broadcast he started calling his enemy a cheat and a liar. It was a spontaneous broadcast all right, and about all I could do was utter little soothing sounds and try to switch him to a safer theme such as jungle animals, which he was supposed to know a lot about.

The most nervous guest I ever had in all those years was, of all people, a newspaperwoman. I'm shy, but I've never thought of my

fellow workers as being in that category. This one, however, certainly
was. She was so scared that people on the receiving end could hear
her teeth chatter. I tried to gentle her down before the broadcast began and after it started, but she never did feel at home and to this
day probably thinks of that as the worst hour of her life.

In time I got used to near catastrophe and learned how to avert it.
I succeeded pretty well the time a redheaded Irishman, unexpectedly
come to town, insisted upon defining the position of his country in
relation to England, while a blond English general fumed and tried to
put in a few words of rebuttal. I had my work cut out, but I finally
brought my two guests together on the beauty of American girls and
the excellence of corn on the cob.

Once I had asked two authors on the same day. Neither had known
the other was coming and both were late, arriving just before the
broadcast. My production man took one horrified look at them bris-
tling at each other and whispered that they were deadly enemies, that
almost the whole writing world knew how they detested each other.
How had I ever missed this feud? With fear and trembling I edged
carefully into the interview. When you're determined to avoid any one
subject it stays perversely in the forefront of your mind and usually
you end by saying the very thing you'd determined not to. In this case,
horrified, I heard myself praising one of the authors to the other.

"He's about as loyal a friend as anybody could want. Why, he even
said that if I advertised arsenic sandwiches he'd go right out and buy
one."

"And if he'd eat it himself," the other author instantly countered,
"I'd make it for him."

Eric Herud and Henry Gabrielson, my engineers, had been in radio
since the days of crystal sets and earphones. They were not easily upset. Newsroom bulletins rushed into the middle of a program bothered
them not at all. They juggled voices expertly. Their panel of dials and
knobs were like test tubes to a chemist; they knew how to mix and stir
sounds until they got them properly balanced. But as Gabe sometimes
pointed out, he couldn't change words. He could only change the way
they sounded.

And even though I was sitting near enough to a guest to choke him,
I couldn't alter the phrases pouring from him unless I really did
commit violence! I could only try to keep control of the interview and

pace it by the odd sense of timing that develops in your head after you've been doing radio for a while, a sort of tickless clock that lets you know when a story is getting too long, when the moment has come to start commercials, when a guest is talking too much. Right now I can tell time almost to the second without looking at a clock.

But the tickless apparatus in your brain doesn't always suffice. It didn't when I had a bubbling middle-aged southerner on the air, who not only didn't stop talking but didn't stop for breath. I plunged head-long into the stream of honeys and you-alls and reckons. The only question I could think of that called for a brief answer, giving me a chance to marshal a few similar questions was, "Where were you born?" This is absolutely safe ninety-nine times out of a hundred, because most people will say, "Harrisburg, Pennsylvania," "Louisville, Kentucky," "a farm near Davenport, Iowa." This guest, however, flashed her coyest honeysuckle-and-roses smile and went into another monologue.

Fifteen minutes later she was still going. She had described her home down to the last portico; she had traced her family tree back to the Crusades; she had told how many beaux pursued her before "that big old handsome Vuginnyah gentleman" came along. It was the first, last, and only time that I was really outtalked, left helpless and silent, with the minutes marching by toward sign-off time. Risking the charge of discourtesy, I had to cut into the middle of a sentence, telling my guest that the chamber of commerce of her city ought to put her on the payroll but that my payroll was going to be nonexistent unless I got a few sponsors mentioned.

At the opposite end of the dilemma is the guest who won't talk at all. I sat with perspiration beading my forehead the day I tried to interview a pretty blond singer who'd got back that day from overseas. She had been everywhere. Starting with South America she'd sailed and flown to islands all over the Caribbean, toured the Gold Coast of Africa, made a forced landing in Russia and stayed overnight in a barracks for Russian women soldiers. But when I asked her to tell about it she hesitated, took a deep breath, and said with finality, "Well, it was interesting." South America was interesting, she admitted. So was Africa, and Russia was not only interesting but cold.

Then there was a young man who has written books I wish I'd written—which is my highest compliment to man or woman. But the

memory of our one broadcast together is mutually bitter. He had a
novel coming out and ordinarily I wouldn't have invited him, since
most novelists (I hate generalizations, but this one is fairly safe) write
much better than they talk. I agreed to have Mr. R. because the publisher's publicity girl, of whom I was especially fond, made a fervent
plea. Then I dispatched Janice with stern instructions to get something interesting for me to go on.

She found the author more opposed than I to the interview. He said
flatly that he did not want to go on the air. They discussed this at
length in his office at *The New Yorker* magazine, and then he suggested they repair to a nearby restaurant and talk further. Over a tall
drink (or two) they arrived at some stories of his having lived in Tahiti, a description of how a profile is put together for *The New Yorker*,
plus a few anecdotes about people he'd personally profiled. It wasn't
world-shaking and it took Janice a whole afternoon, but I agreed we
could make something of it.

However, the morning before our broadcast I tuned in another network and heard Mr. R. being interviewed! Hadn't he been told, I
stormed, about my rule that I must have guests first? And here he was
—same day, same stories. I telephoned Janice and told her to cancel
him at once. She tried, but our friend at the publishing house explained that the big boss had made a special point of his author ap-
pearing on *my* program. The poor writer had been recorded by the
other network, and it was a schedule slip-up that had put him on at
the wrong time. Please—wouldn't I have him? Finally Janice went
scurrying over to the magazine to try to dredge up some new stories.
Tahiti was the only thing he'd missed on the other program. She found
the novelist very unhappy.

"Look," he said, "my editor has telephoned, my agent has called,
Mary Margaret has bawled me out, and now here you are. All I did
was write a book. Why does this have to happen to me?"

He added that he didn't have any more material, he didn't know any
anecdotes, and furthermore he intended to have a drink. Janice, pro-
testing, followed him to a downstairs bar and then, knowing me and
my allergy to alcohol, founded in my temperance upbringing in Missouri, bought him some breath sweeteners and dragged him to the
studio.

I can smell even a hint of alcohol on a person a room's length away, and the breath sweeteners just emphasized the aroma. It was all I needed. Grimly, I started the program and gaily the guest announced to the world that he had been on the air that very morning.

"That's tactful of you," I remarked—and did two commercials. Mr. R. seemed to be dozing when I again got round to talking with him. I told the name of his book, gave a brief summary of it, and began: "You lived in Tahiti, didn't you?"

"Umm," he said, "ummm?"

"Tahiti," I said. "Didn't you live in Tahiti?"

"Oh, Tahiti. Yes."

"Well"—with increasing grimness—"tell about it. What was it like?"

"Tahiti—— Oh, Tahiti. Nice place, Tahiti—liked it there."

"Well, where in Tahiti did you live?"

"In a house—yes, lived in a little house."

I hope this gives some idea of what that broadcast was like. I don't believe I spoke to the man after it was over, but I learned later that he returned, shattered, to the magazine and for years thereafter warned all fellow scribes never, never to go on the radio. As for him, I'm told he's not been on the air since, though he keeps on turning out excellent books.

There is nothing you can do in cases like this, unless you're lucky enough to be able to answer your own questions. After a few such crises you see to it that you *do* know a few details before you tackle any subject on the air. In time I learned not to ask a guest for a story I couldn't tell myself. One of the horrible occasions that drove me to this starred a man who I thought had written (or at least compiled) a popular history of medicine, filled with odd lore, exciting stories, and technical, unpronounceable names. I introduced the guest and tried to launch him on the history of the first operation performed under ether, only to have him look at me coldly and explain that he had merely taken the pictures for the book—he didn't know a single word contained in it and didn't want to, either.

I blessed then the hours I had spent over that difficult material. So I was able to laugh and murmur, "Isn't that just like a photographer —interested only in how the pictures came out!" Then I launched into the stories, announcing that I would try to sell him on his own book. He turned out to be a good sort, listened quite interestedly, laughed, and the program ended smoothly.

Most of the time the audience out on the air is happily unconscious of tense situations in the studio. My interview with foreign correspondent Jim Linder, for instance, brought floods of enthusiastic mail. Listeners never knew that he chain-smoked nervously throughout the broadcast (against all rules, this was then) and as he finished each cigarette, sent it arching into the air with a flick of thumb and forefinger, so that I had to fight the urge to turn from the microphone each time a cigarette took off, to see whether the studio was on fire!

To balance him was another foreign correspondent—a handsome, bronzed six-footer back in the United States after five years of South Pacific wandering. Until I got him on the air I had no hint of what home-coming was like for those men. He told me afterward that he hadn't known it himself, but when I asked him, "What did it feel like to get back?" he hesitated so long I was worried. Then he burst out with, "I was scared—just plain scared!"

He'd covered seven invasions, had broadcast from PT boats, planes over Japanese lines, and foxholes on beaches. Yet—"I was so scared that first day back that I locked myself in my hotel room for twenty-four hours. I couldn't face New York. It was too complicated. For years everything had been figured out for me—where I was to go, what I was to eat, if anything, where I'd sleep, even what I'd wear. I no longer knew how to handle responsibilities that used to be everyday routine."

Taking it from there, he did a better job than any social worker could have done in telling of the big adjustment families would have to make to help their boys when they jumped into peacetime lives from discipline, security, and war's strange combination of adventure and duty.

I can remember only one time when I really almost signed off and ran from the studio. That was when the zoo came to call. Neither I nor the station will ever forget that program. Animals were all over the place. It had been my own idea to have them in the background for atmosphere, more or less free from restraint. The interview with a zoo official was rolling along hilariously when the kinkajou, a three-foot-long weasel-like creature with a definite leer behind its whiskers, escaped from its keeper, scrambled up my leg, ripped my stocking to shreds, and landed belligerently in my lap. I managed to say with outer calm, "Well, I have just lured the kinkajou to the microphone—

does he make any sound?" The zoo man answered, "No, but he bites—and he's got a prehensile tail." While he and I explained that a prehensile tail meant he could wrap it around me and hang on, the keeper managed to remove the kinkajou.

By this time the baby dromedary had been given a nursing bottle of milk to calm him down, and as if propelled he marched up to the microphone and burbled milk audible into the ether. As the program signed off on a note of restrained frenzy two tiny owls flew to the top of the three-story studio and perched with dignity on a sort of shelf up there. Frenzied studio attendants sent for a ladder. They climbed it nervously, one holding a box for the owls. As the first man reached out his hand both little birds unfolded their wings and sailed slowly to the other side of the room.

By now the orchestra scheduled for rehearsal in the studio was trundling in drums, trombones, and bass viols. The conductor arrived and declared furiously that he could not rehearse with birds in the room.

The studio men retorted, "All right, catch them then." I left, stuffing bills into the attendants' hands and explaining to an unbelieving reporter from the newsroom that yes, it was true—I had interviewed a baby dromedary, and yes, a kinkajou had broadcast, but no, it was not a fact that a lion cub was loose in the halls of the radio station.

It's a surprise and not a catastrophe of course to find a guest nicer and more co-operative than you anticipate. You'd expect a fan dancer on a radio program to be, to say the least, a breezy guest. But I started Sally Rand off on her farm childhood, and she talked as tenderly and lyrically as any poet about the sudden pink of apple blossoms in the Missouri spring, summer nights in the country when you can hear a rhythmical insect chorus through the murmurous dark, the suppertime fragrance of hickory-smoked ham and browning potatoes.

The Good Friday on which photographer Margaret Bourke-White quoted one of the bombardiers on a bomber over Japan as saying "gee-sus!" when her flash bulb exploded unexpectedly (unexpectedly to the bombardier, anyway) was a very difficult day. It much upset Mel Ferrer, now a very important actor, who was our director at the time. A director was appointed by the station to keep tab on whether we did our commercials and report to the front office on anything untoward. I thought then and I think now that Mel considered a woman's program pretty small potatoes, and I imagine his report that day was anything but flattering. I felt much worse than he did, for I was always sick at heart when something was said that might hurt or offend listeners.

I went through agony the day Laurette Taylor, talking about her southern accent acquired for *The Glass Menagerie*, thoughtlessly referred to "a nigger accent." As always on the air, once it's said, it's too late. I knew instinctively that making an issue of it then would be a mistake, because with something I felt so deeply about I needed time to think, to plan carefully what I wanted to say. The broadcast ended with the guest not even realizing what she had done. I couldn't work that afternoon and wandered aimlessly into a motion-picture theater where I sat without seeing anything on the screen, so deep was my unhappiness.

But sometime between boy meeting girl and the final clinch I decided what to do. I remembered Walter White's story of his life, in which he told with painful honesty about his childhood. He was the one to undo the harm if it could be undone. Walter said of course he would come, and I got to the point at once, explaining to him about the guest and what she'd said, adding—"I'd do anything to keep such a thing from happening on my program. When it does, it breaks my heart. It was not said deliberately nor with malice, but thoughtlessly; yet I can't help believing that if people understood—well, they wouldn't allow themselves ever to be so careless."

Gently and with no bitterness Walter White began to talk. He put it very simply but unforgettably. There were many groups of people in the world, he said, who had a hard fight to reach even the ordinary goals—the life, liberty, and pursuit of happiness they were taught about in school. These people—some call them submerged, some minorities, some underprivileged—these people have hurt and struggle enough. Sometimes those names, those condescending labels that set them apart, prove the final hurdle and they feel that they can't make the grade after all. He said he was sure that not many people would deliberately wound a fellow man in that way. His voice had a softness, an almost biblical quality. He never said them, but you could almost hear the words, "Forgive them . . . they know not what they do."

It wasn't a catastrophe in the serious sense, but the day Stella and I had one of our more unrestrained arguments (thinking we were, so to speak, alone) on a ship-to-shore telephone conversation and were picked up by, it seemed to me, most of our listening audience, lingers in my memory as a day less than happy. For months we were hearing from women—and men—who quoted verbatim everything we had said, mostly Stella complaining about the goat I was bringing back not being a lamb. "Mary and her lamb would be a wonderful story," she kept repeating sorrowfully.

Sometimes when I had guests who were obviously thwarted or at war with their own lives I was unhappy about them afterward. Often I was afraid they'd said more than they really meant to say, and I felt responsible. Leicester Hemingway, younger brother of Ernest, had written a novel about two brothers with a tragic relationship. I put to him, of course, the obvious question—"Is it autobiographical?" He said I reminded him of a story about Arnold Bennett, who when asked that about one of his books answered, "Young man, you remind me of a coroner who did an autopsy on a suspected murder victim and when he found arsenic in the body, was so surprised!"

Leicester assured me, however, that Ernesto (as he called his brother) had urged: "Write it. Write anything you please and say any resemblance to real people is accidental." But I was sorry I'd brought the matter up.

Howard Fast, as a thrilling young writer, was one of my great favorites for a while—in fact, until he became an avowed communist. Rumors had preceded the avowal, and one day right on the air I asked him if he was a communist. He looked me straight in the eye and said, "No, I am not a communist." Afterward, when I found out that he really was one, I remembered a time when he was discussing a book about George Washington and we got into a terrible argument because Howard Fast said that generals had to lie, that they always did, and that they also had to tell very good lies. So perhaps that was the beginning of his belief that a lie is necessary sometimes and that very important people tell them. I wonder what he thinks now. I've never talked to him since he denounced communism, though I've read some of the things he's written.

Ben Gross, in his book *I Looked and I Listened*, describing a near-catastrophic encounter of his on my program, failed to record my emotions on that occasion. We were celebrating Ben's twenty-fifth anniversary as a radio critic, and I had planned to have Eddie Cantor and Ben reminisce. But when we were all three seated before the microphone I suddenly realized that there seemed to be no glad-handing between the two. Laughing at the foolishness of the question, I attempted to break the ice by the arch observation, "Certainly you two know each other!"

There was a slight pause, and then Eddie extended his hand to Ben and said, "Ben and I had a little misunderstanding some years ago. But I must tell you, nobody ever could have guessed it by his comments on my show. I may not always agree with him, but he has been a fair-minded and honest reporter."

And Ben said, "No one could give a newspaperman a more welcome compliment." After that it was all right, but I had to wait until we were off the air to find out the whole story and I was still shuddering at what might have been.

It seems that Eddie sometimes engaged in feuds with critics who panned his shows. In one instance it led to a suit for libel against Eddie by Ben and his assistant on the *News* radio column—Abe Greenberg—now a Hollywood publicity man. Cantor, explains Ben in his book, riled by the comments of some metropolitan newspaper pundits, struck back and in an interview in a fan magazine said that every New York radio critic "except one" was either a chiseler or a logroller. All the critics wondered about the identity of this journalistic pillar of virtue until Nick Kenny took a bow by writing, "Thanks, Eddie, for the compliment."

"Well," said Colonel Frank Hause, managing editor of the *News*, "I see Nick admits he is the honest one. Cantor's certainly not going to dispute that; if he does, it'll give Nick a good case. And if Cantor keeps quiet, he is merely adding to the insult to all you fellows. You and Greenberg gotta sue him."

"We did," wrote Ben, "for $100,000 each—and without coming to trial the case was fought on legal points up to the Court of Appeals in New York State. The precedent-setting decision was published on the front page of the *New York Law Journal*. It held that because at that time there were only a limited number of radio critics in New York City, each could suffer injury through the comedian's blanket accusation. In other words, a group if small enough could be libeled, and all that remained was for a jury to determine the amount of damages.

"Eddie settled for a nominal sum, paid the court costs and the legal expenses for both sides. He has the satisfaction, however, of knowing that this decision, with due publicity to him, is still being cited in almost every action for group libel brought in the U.S."

Almost equally a facer for me was Ole Olsen's calm comment when humorist S. J. Perelman had finished telling a story about a plot he narrated to three dogs, the poker-faced Marx Brothers, and about twenty-five members of their families without getting a single laugh. Then after a lengthy pause Groucho said, "It stinks."

"Oh yes," said Ole interestedly referring to the Marx Brothers' picture, *Monkey Business*. "That was our title—*Monkey Business*—and Chic [his partner, Chic Johnson] and I thought we'd sue the Marxes." My heart sank, but Ole continued calmly, "We dropped the suit, though, because we had to put up a $2,000,000 bond." I don't know who looked more relieved, S. J. Perelman or I.

I considered it a catastrophe when an English author who talked composedly through the broadcast and went off quite calmly after it was over was written about next day in my morning paper as having been knocked down and robbed on her way to the studio. What a story I had missed because of the restraint of the English.

I suppose the major catastrophe for me would have been a long illness. But it was odd about that. Naturally in more than twenty years I had my share of ailments, but I always got them on the weekend. In the entire twenty-odd years I was absent from only three broadcasts because I was sick and that was when I had my appendicitis operation.

The second day I wanted to go on the air, but the doctor made me wait until the third. Broadcasting from Doctors Hospital, surrounded by so many flowers my room looked like a funeral parlor, with nurses running in and out, I managed quite a dramatic effect.

Sometimes through the years I would get neuritis or bursitis—the doctors never seemed sure which—in my arms and legs so that I couldn't even dress myself, but I always managed the broadcast and even forgot for one full hour all my aches and pains. Ten minutes after it was over I'd be just as sick again.

I was only once late to a broadcast for physical reasons. That was the time I had an encounter with a zipper that got nationwide coverage in a picture magazine as well as on a radio hookup. A long-distance

call had delayed me one day when I was dressing to broadcast at
the Waldorf before a group of several hundred women. At twenty
minutes to air time I was struggling into my corset and reflecting hopefully that I'd be able to leave the apartment in five minutes. Trying
to hurry, I gave the zipper an extra yank and it plowed into me.

I attempted frantically to dislodge it. It held on. I howled for help.
Everybody in the place came running. They took turns trying to extricate me. Blood flowed freely. My helpers winced. It hurt me more
than them, but I couldn't stop to suffer. My eyes were on the clock.
I kept screaming that I had to get to the broadcast. Then I fainted
and was brought to with spirits of ammonia.

Myra, wringing her hands, scurried to the house telephone to call
the handyman from the basement. He came racing up with his tool
kit and started working on me with pincers, wire cutters, and saw.
The apartment superintendent and the elevator man stood by to as-
sist. The zipper resisted all.

It was now ten minutes to one, nine minutes, eight minutes, six
minutes. Mrs. D. suddenly remembered there was a doctor in the
house and tore down to bring him up. He was just setting out on a
round of calls but recognized an emergency and came quickly. The
hands of the clock moved on. I began to cry. "It's one o'clock," I
sobbed desperately. "The broadcast has begun." Just then the handyman applied a bigger wrench and the zipper gave up, taking a large
chunk of me with it.

The doctor plastered me with a big bandage, I threw on the rest of
my clothes, jumped into a taxicab, and got to the broadcast ten minutes late. I had to explain my tardiness somehow and so told the truth,
in all its gory detail. After an astonished gasp the audience roared with
laughter and I realized with pained surprise that here was a funny
story—to other people!

Later *Life* came to take my picture—because I'd been caught in my
zipper—and months afterward I met a United States senator who said,
"I know you! My picture was going to be in *Life* about an important
Senate measure I was sponsoring, but *you* got caught in your zipper
so they took me out and put you in!"

In a way I sympathize with the senator. He probably felt a little as
I did about my three chances to act. They began with an M-G-M
scout watching our broadcast and deciding I might be able to take up

where Marie Dressler left off in Hollywood. He hired a dramatic teacher for me, and for weeks I worked out acting problems in my spare time: denouncing and being denounced; jilting and being jilted; killing and being killed.

Then I had a test. Nothing came of it.

Another time Joan Blondell, then married to Mike Todd, suggested that I might do a small bit as myself in a Broadway play he was about to produce. I made a test in full make-up. Result—nil!

You'd think I might have learned my lesson by this time. But no, in Paris my old friend Dora Miller introduced me to a friend of hers who was producing a motion picture starring Grock, Europe's most famous clown for half a century. The idea was that I should be shown doing a radio interview with Monsieur Grock. Cynthia Lowry, who was with me in Paris, served as the announcer and said: "It's six o'clock in Paris, one o'clock in New York, and here's Mary Margaret McBride."

ME  Monsieur Grock, is it true you are married?

GROCK  For thirty years. (Only Grock has a little trouble with English so it came out, "For certy yearrss.")

ME  Really?

GROCK  Eet's no joke!

That was all, but never have I worked so hard. At the studio at dawn where the make-up crew took over. Onto the set to wait around for the shooting. Doing the bit over about twenty times the first day.

Then, next morning at six, Bluette, one of the producers, called to say apologetically that the electric current had been weak the day before and the film was ruined. Would I mind coming back for another day of shooting? So back I traveled to Joinville and went through the whole thing another twenty times. The third day was just to make sure, and for the weary fourth and fifth nobody was making any explanations at all.

Finally, though, it was really over and I could scrub the final make-up from my tortured skin and go about other concerns. The picture was supposed to come to America to be shown, but I doubt if it did. Except for one small comment from Dora Miller, who saw it in Paris, I never heard of it again.

"You were not in it at all," she reported forthrightly.

So apparently in spite of earnest effort I ended up as a face on the cutting-room floor.

## 5. LETTERS, WE GOT LETTERS

*"I can't stand a woman's voice on the air. Why don't you stay at home and take care of your family?" Slightly poison-pen letter quoted by me on the air.*

When the mail count became astronomical I got in the habit of carrying it around with me in big grocery sacks. Then if at a party, a fitting, or shopping I had a few seconds to spare I dug into the sack and read letters. This innocent enjoyment was halted by my agent, who, coming upon me one day heavy-laden, said I looked undignified. From then on she sent her office boy to deliver the mail to my apartment. I loved every piece and grieved when patriotism (and Stella) caused me to contribute three and a half million of my treasures to the war effort, when the government called for paper.

People don't write letters like those any more. One man sent me a daily tome for more than a year, detailing his often quite sensible and practical views about the state of the world, and carbons of communications to senators, representatives, and foreign ministers. Sometimes he included a letter stamped for mailing with instructions to read and, if I approved, to send it on to the dignitary he wished to reach.

Pretty soon the handwriting on some of the envelopes was almost as familiar to me as my mother's. And I felt I knew my correspondents better than many members of my own family. I loved them, too. After all, they were making possible for me a life I loved, and I wanted to embrace them all, I was so grateful. Why did they write? Partly because they felt sympathy in me, I suppose, but mostly because I was not bound up in their families, communities, friendships, and feuds, so they were unself-conscious about telling me ideas and emotions they felt they couldn't confide to anybody closer to them.

I came to have great respect for what I had previously thought of vaguely as the public. Their letters divided them into separate human beings—sad, funny, bright, frustrated, lonely, ambitious, conservative, forward-thinking—and I began to realize that I couldn't accept figures about them. Statistics told me their average intelligence was that of a twelve-year-old child, but I got out the latest batch of mail and proved to my own satisfaction that this just wasn't so. If I had talked down, planning my programs on the basis of such an estimate, not one of these thousands of people would have written to me again. They wouldn't have listened either.

Somewhere I hit a balance, decided there was almost nothing I couldn't tackle on the air, get away with, and have people understand, if I found the book, person, play, or picture dramatic enough to illustrate the point. Were city people interested in soil conservation and the future of farming? They certainly were when writer Louis Bromfield talked about it to them. After we had him the first time, there was a letter from a woman who had known Bromfield's mother. It was a story in itself.

"I go back six generations in Ohio on both sides, and my grandfathers were farmers. Louis's mother was of pioneer stock, strongminded and determined. She made up her mind when Louis was on the way that the child would be a great author. She read good books every minute she had. When he was a little boy he had a sister and she was to be a great musician. While she practiced, Louis had to spend the same amount of time reading the best literature. His sister was a fine musician too."

After another broadcast a woman sat down to write: "I was so excited when Eddie Dowling spoke of Barney Turner making the sets for their play—well, Barney was our carpenter with the Way Down East company years ago. We were great friends, all young together. He had a wife and I a husband. My husband died this past Christmas and I had lost track of Barney—but because of your program I know where he is and can write to him now. I was married forty years, and now I am left alone in our little house with just our dog and two cats . . ."

I wonder how that story turned out.

After I had reviewed a new collection of O. Henry stories a woman wrote me of knowing him well during her childhood. She remembered

". . . seeing my younger sister riding around the floor on his back and looking through his pockets for treats. He never quite overcame his unhappy prison memories, and often he would lapse into a sad thoughtfulness—which was a signal for us children to re-start our games and get him to romp with us."

The first day Eleanor Wilson McAdoo came on a letter arrived from somebody who had known the Woodrow Wilson family and told of making the bridal wreaths for both Jessie and Eleanor, and of secretly twining her own hair among the wax orange blossoms because it was considered good luck. She'd painted the sashes Margaret and Eleanor wore as bridesmaids, too, because no ribbon could be found to match the flowers in their bouquets. She described a moleskin hat with an embroidered band that she made for the second Mrs. Wilson to wear for her marriage, and other hats she'd helped put together for the wives of the Theodore Roosevelts, senior and junior, the Tafts and Hardings.

Lots of men wrote—about everything from blondes to toothaches. I tried a one-minute toothache cure sent by a dentist who guaranteed at least temporary relief!

"By examining the side of the upper back part of the neck, just below the skull, you will find a tender place. Apply the tip of the first finger or first two fingers to that place and with firm, deep pressure, massage the part by moving the finger tips in a small circle. If your fingers are too weak, get some man to do it for you. In many cases the tooth pain does not return—but if it does, massage again."

A newspaperman wrote about "quite my oldest girl friend—a sweet old lady, 93, although totally blind, knits all kinds of things to be sent to the world's forlorn children, from Kentucky to Greece."

A woman told of collecting spider webs. The spider-web collector added "passers-by consider me not quite sane, seeing me atop a stepladder armed with scissors, can of talcum powder and cloth-covered cardboard, cutting and dusting, as far as they can see, the air. But I've had some beautiful webs. One, very small, adhered so closely to the silk that I could touch it with my finger without disturbing it. My other collection is intangible. It doesn't have to be dusted or rearranged. It is pictures—of some rare loveliness I have seen, like the golden light of a sunset in the tall rocks across the river from us, beautiful cloud formations, or, like last night, the moon riding high and wearing a rainbow."

A typed page with the first three words in red began, "They do not," and went on in ordinary black type to state firmly that Scots do not wear anything under their kilts! The question had come up when the author and producers of a play involving a Scottish leading man told on the air that they didn't know and wouldn't tell, even if they did. The letter was from a man who'd been in a Scottish regiment, and, as he pointed out, he ought to know. He added that they were very uncomfortable in the trenches, but in the ordinary world—fine. They kept him warmer, with their nine yards of box pleats, than any clothes he'd worn before or since.

Should chicken be fried with or without batter; did O. Henry really use perfume; which is the real clam chowder (with New Englanders denouncing any touch of tomatoes and New Yorkers demanding them); how did doughnuts begin and where and how did they first get holes in them; and were crullers and doughnuts the same?

And there was a woman who tuned in and found me talking about her own grandfather! She wrote: "He was the leader of that group of strong young men who went up into British Columbia and Alaska to survey for the projected telegraph to Russia. It was to go all the way to London, and the project was undertaken because the first Atlantic cable had failed. Grandfather picked up a nugget of pure gold in the Yukon Valley and it became my grandmother's wedding ring and her prized gold thimble."

A touching letter, evoked by a day of reminiscing about my own farm childhood, told of a sentimental journey home, only to find that "what I had remembered as a virtual mansion was only a rambling, run-down old farmhouse, that the mahogany stair rail and the magnificent hall were strangely shrunken, and my children who had heard me brag were politely silent the whole time."

The writer swapped memories with me.

"Did your farmhouse have a washup sink for the hired men, and a looking glass, very wavy, with a comb attached, and a Boston rocker with turkey-red cushions? Did you sit down all together, the hired men at one end of the table, and stuff yourself with green corn and watermelon and 1-2-3 cake, and after dinner did you darken the room and take small tree branches to drive the flies toward the door? And was

there a buttery—with a big green bin always full of gingersnaps? Did
you have a black pony, as we had—and 32 cats! And down by the
creek, the yellow jackets to dodge? Did you believe that if you took
a hair from a horse's tail and let it lie in the water three days, it would
become a snake?"

Advising me not to try retiring from radio to farming, another listener wrote, "How can city people make good in a business—and farming is a business—when they don't know a shoat from a bantam? Miracles do happen, but I'd hate to pin my hopes on one. My husband
and I did that very thing when we bought a view, and woods, and
sunsets, and the marching glory of the nightly firmament as seen from
a hillside. But we couldn't eat any of it, and none of it paid taxes.
I was amused at first, then irritated, when visitors said, 'What lovely
milk, and to think it costs you nothing.' No—nothing except the cows,
their feed, housing and care—there's nothing free on a farm. You pay
for it all, in money and labor."

Stella Karn used to tell everybody about the letter and gift of one
listener which touched her very much. At a studio party this woman
stood in line to shake hands with me—a little bent creature carrying a
package wrapped in tissue paper. When she reached me, I saw that she
had been crying and I pressed her hand and murmured sympathetically. She didn't say anything—just held my hand for a minute, kissed
it, and went off leaving me with the tissue-wrapped package.

Inside was an old-fashioned cut-glass bowl and a tear-stained note
which read: "Tomorrow they are coming to take me away to the poor-
house. This is the only thing in the world I have left that I value. It's
been handed down in my family for generations. I won't let the
sheriff get it when he comes for my bed and chair. You mean more to
me now than anybody so I'm giving it to you as a keepsake."

There was no name and no address, and though Stella tried and
tried to trace the woman, we never were able to do it.

I never allowed any message to go unanswered if I could help it.
On the *Hindenburg* trip I sat up until three in the morning writing
with my red pencil to everybody who had remembered me. (Those
cards are collectors' items now because of the *Hindenburg* stamp.)

Later I got a letter from a woman who had sent me one of the
packages that made the *Hindenburg's* freight cargo heavier that trip.
She said that she had reason to believe her nieces and nephews

were conniving to get her money. Something particularly bitter had happened before she sent me the present, and afterward she thought of herself as a fool and wished she hadn't done it. My post card from the *Hindenburg* with its red pencil scrawl had somehow restored her faith in human beings. But she scared me because she threatened to leave me her money! I could just imagine what the conniving nieces and nephews would have done to me, but she evidently had sober second thoughts (or else she never died) for I heard no more about the money.

A sort of proof of Dr. Payne's theory that I was at least two people was my experience with a professor from a western university. When I met him, he told me that he began listening to Martha Deane against his will when he was stuck in a Pennsylvania hotel room on a rainy afternoon. He was on a lecture trip, and WOR was the only station he could get clearly. Though he didn't like women's programs he listened and got interested in spite of himself.

He wrote me regularly and finally we met, but it was evident that far from being charmed by me in the flesh, I rather bored him. At the same time it was equally clear that I didn't in any way disturb his affection and concern for Martha Deane. In fact, he sat there telling me what a wonderful woman *she* was—exactly as if I were somebody who didn't know her. And he kept on writing to her.

On the same order was the encounter with a young American woman who had come back from Europe after having lived there for many years. She was lonely and confused while trying to adjust to the change, and listening to me became important. She wanted to meet me, but when we did I discovered immediately that I wasn't really the person Helen was interested in. She didn't dislike me, but it was Martha Deane she had longed to know, not Mary Margaret McBride.

One day when she came to take me to tea I was grumpy and complaining because of some fancied injustice. I said I was going to give up radio. Helen sat listening like a person in a daze, and soon excused herself. Next morning I had a frantic note from her saying she couldn't bear to have Martha Deane leave the air. After she left me, she walked to her apartment with tears streaming down her cheeks, concocting a scathing letter to the president of the station demanding that they keep Martha Deane on the air. She was wild at me because I had even dreamed of letting them fire me—which was what she thought they had done. When she found I had just been grumbling about some fancied injury she never liked me so much again.

Our announcer Vincent Connolly, the Princeton-graduate announcer Stella Karn picked after she came into the picture, was much beloved by the listeners as was later Dick Willard, who was with me for four years. Both were such nice young men that listeners felt it over the air. People would write that they had named all kinds of objects for them and for me. One woman knitted Martha Deane sweaters, another made a quilt. Babies, newborn calves, and even goldfish were called for us. I knew (by letter at least) talking dogs, piano-playing cats, and fortune-telling parrots. At least one of the talking dogs came to see me and did say "Martha," or so I thought. My listeners instructed me by mail about everything. If ever we mentioned a symptom of any kind we got hundreds of remedies, with follow-ups to ask why we were still coughing. Hadn't we tried that asafetida or the honey and vinegar?

One listener wrote amusingly about how she got rid of mice. She first cleaned up the mess they'd made in her cellar, then left a letter standing up against the coalbin. The letter said politely: "Please go away," and she claimed the mice did. I told about that letter one day, and right in the middle of the program a listener telephoned to say, "It's not true. There's a mouse looking at me right this minute from the front of the desk I'm sitting on. Though I've written him the nicest note I'm capable of, he won't go away."

The telephoner was furious when Vincent and I shrieked with laughter, thinking she was joking. She banged up the receiver. Later she wrote to say that she was telling the absolute truth—that she had to telephone for a neighbor's help to get rid of the mouse.

The letters weren't all charming by any means. Everybody who deals with the public as an entertainer gets his share of poison pens. They come from cranks or just ill-tempered men and women letting off steam. The first I ever got was ten pages long and went into detail about every program that I'd had for weeks and weeks, carefully tabulating just what the writer didn't like about each one. I couldn't understand why she didn't just turn the dial. But I suppose I had some strange fascination for her. She was certainly a listener—nobody else could have known so much.

Some of those who wrote adverse criticism later became my friends.

I always tried to win them over by presenting my side and sympathizing with theirs. And often they had a great deal on their side, too.

Men listeners often expressed pity for Vincent and Dick, sometimes facetiously, sometimes in earnest. One of these was the radio editor of the New York *Sun*, a man named Bragdon, who wrote in his paper that there was one man on the radio who should have a vote of condolence from all men—Vincent Connolly, forced during an hour of announcing a woman's program, to listen to some pretty silly talk. Mr. Bragdon reported later in his column that as a result he got seven letters, a post card, and a chocolate cake, the latter an effort to soften his heart. Hundreds of my listeners assured me that they had expressed their displeasure vociferously, not only to Mr. Bragdon but to the owner of the paper. Mr. Bragdon finally admitted that he hadn't really listened very often to us.

One of my masculine regulars wrote to Mr. Bragdon and claimed he was quoted by the recipient out of context. "Maybe you can forgive him," declared my defender. "I never can."

A boy long in the India-China-Burma theater—his mother had listened to us while he was growing up—visioned coming home and asked me to tell his relatives that he would do very odd things for a while. Like examining a slice of bread at dinner "because it's many moons since we've had a bug-free piece," picking up the sofa pillow before he sat down—a hangover from days when pillows usually hid scorpions; shying away from the cane-bottom chairs on the porch, because over there they were ideal breeding places for bugs and lice; staying in the bath longer than any human being has a right to because for so long "a tub was a myth." And finally—"We shall make all sorts of blunders when we come visiting you those first few days and weeks, and we shall be unable to find the right words for thanking you. The warmth of our handclasp will have to tell you how we appreciate your patience with us—and how mighty, mighty glad we are to be back home again."

People often ask if I got many proposals. I did—but I'm pretty sure if I had ever accepted any of them the proposers would have taken to the woods. However, one of these, a westerner, telephoned from Washington, D.C., that he was on his way to New York to claim his bride. Mrs. D. sent a hurried telegram warning that I had been called away suddenly, and Stella hired a private detective as my bodyguard for the next two weeks!

For years a blind man wrote enchantingly of his adventures in the city streets where he made his living by begging. He described himself as a cynic who knew the world from its seamier side but was in love with a dream and I was the dream. He saw himself as a knight in shining armor ready to rescue me from unimaginable dangers and terrors. He was not blindly adoring, though, for he kept close watch of the program and if I violated by so much as a word his conception of me, he rebuked me gently and begged me not to behave like that ever again. I do not subscribe to the theory that a good letter writer could necessarily turn out salable articles or novels, but Hal's case seemed so different that I begged him to try it. He never did, and one day his letters stopped coming.

My most touching male listener lives on Staten Island. Ever since my mother died he has sent me yellow roses (her favorite flower) on her birthday and the anniversary of her death. At Christmas, I get a box of fruit and nuts he has gathered and my favorite milk chocolates. Since I have been writing this book he has mailed me a carefully kept log of my broadcasts of the thirties and forties, together with dozens of clippings about me that he had carefully preserved.

Most of my male admirers apparently worry about my getting enough to eat. Gus in Moberly, Missouri, painstakingly cracks and picks out black walnuts and hickory nut meats for me each fall. Walter sends wonderful cheese from Wisconsin, and John from upstate New York, sausage like my father used to make back in Missouri—all these with letters admonishing me to take good care of myself.

There have been a few bad moments with packages. Like the day in wartime that a carefully wrapped parcel marked "Fragile" and in very small unobtrusive letters "Danger" produced a rattle when slightly shaken. "A bomb!" cried office assistant Florence Wagner, who was opening mail that day. Everybody quickly backed away, and Stella had the object taken to the basement for gingerly opening. It proved to be nothing more alarming than a china teapot, and the word danger evidently was an attempt to discourage rough handling.

Mrs. D.'s assistant, Jean Grenier, a fastidious French girl who knew and liked good food, often was made unhappy by some of the edibles that came through the mails. "Please, Mrs. D.," she would plead, "you can't let Miss McBride eat those cookies. They're indigestible, I can tell!" One time she hurried into the office earlier than usual because she dreamed I'd eaten a chocolate cake that came the day before and it had been poisoned. She found to her relief that the cake was intact, and that was one pastry that disappeared before I even saw it. For the most part, though, listeners sent me delicacies they knew I liked, and I enjoyed eating them. I still get wonderful salt-rising bread from Sallye in Evanston, Illinois, nut cake from Bertha in Pennsylvania, panocha and cookies from Florence in Binghamton.

Whenever I read a poem or a guest made some noteworthy remark the procedure was reversed. Then the listeners asked me to send copies. We had a flood of requests for the Thanksgiving story done on the program by my red-haired nephew Tommy, then seven. Luckily we had recorded it, for he did it ad lib.

My young guest arrived Thanksgiving Day a few minutes before we went on the air. His mother, who was with him, said a little anxiously that he hadn't slept much but he wouldn't tell anybody what he was going to say, nor would he accept help.

Here is what Tommy did to history that day:

"These people were in this England—and there these people were Pilgrims and they wanted to go to their own church but the government said you shall go to our church. So they went to that church for one Sunday and then these Pilgrims said, 'We shall get across this big ocean.'

"And finally the English people gave them lots of money and they bought a big boat called the *Mayflower* and they went sailing down the river with a thousand more than three thousand people on the deck— and they went very far across the Atlantic and finally they came to the shore and a rock—and the rock was called Plymouth Rock. And they all got off on that rock.

"And then they thought they'd make houses, but when they found out there were Indians and that they were friendly, they helped each other and these Indians gave them a lot of corn to plant in the ground. And when it came up very high and they had nice corn they thanked God for all these things and they thanked Him that they could have a holiday and they called it Thanksgiving. And they had all these turkeys and things and that's how we got Thanksgiving started."

"It was beautiful," wrote a moved but amused listener, "and at least it allows a few more ancestors for all these people who claim their forefathers came over on the *Mayflower*."

It was wonderful hearing from these blessed men and women from everywhere who tuned me in (or out, as I deserved) and who guarded me from the awful conceit and self-satisfaction that might swiftly have wrecked both my job and me.

## 6.  THEY PAID THE BILLS

DECEMBER 13, 1940  *"Broiled grapefruit! It's the most horrible thing I've ever heard of! Hot grapefruit—gives me the willies just to think about it!"*

Actress Florence Reed has a carrying voice and her diction is perfect, so there was no chance, when she said "most horrible" right in the middle of a Florida grapefruit commercial, for a desperate broadcaster to translate it into "most edible" or anything else complimentary. I did venture hopefully that perhaps she just preferred her grapefruit fresh and uncooked. But *no!* Miss Reed would have none of that. "I don't like grapefruit," she announced flatly. What could I do? I laughed—a little hysterically—but I went on talking about the virtues of grapefruit, accompanied by quite audible rumblings of disapproval from my guest.

You'd think the experience might have taught me something, but no. Whenever I could see what looked like interest in a guest's face I was sure to drag her—or him—into the fray. Or I would even interrupt as I did one time when Queena Mario, opera singer, was talking about the rigors of training the voice and got onto diet.

"Of course for my diet I rely chiefly on fruits and vegetables," she declared, and I interposed brightly (because I was advertising Andy Boy broccoli at the time), "I suppose you eat lots of broccoli?" Miss Mario's response was swift. "I loathe broccoli," she asserted firmly.

For some reason I never understood, humorist James Thurber, on what must have been a perverse day for him, insisted on talking about a rival radio program, and when he left the studio he was blithely whistling a musical commercial of a competing soap.

As far as I know I never lost a sponsor because of a guest's negative attitude, which is probably an indication that the sponsor never listened to the broadcast or, if he did, felt people would remember his product better because of a little diversion. I'm inclined to agree with the latter point of view. Though they happened in the comparatively early days of my broadcasting, when I meet old listeners even today, many of them bring up two instances when I was the culprit in a sponsor difficulty.

I was advertising Cushman Bakeries, and a big batch of chocolate, caramel, jelly, and coconut masterpieces had that day been delivered to my apartment. I was rhapsodically describing them when I realized that announcer Vincent Connolly was upset. His face was beet-red, and he was moving his hands as if he would like to restrain me. "What on earth's the matter with you, Vincent?" I broke off to ask tartly. "Oh nothing, nothing," he answered in tones that indicated there was on the contrary a great deal the matter. "You are talking about those wonderful Cushman cakes, aren't you? Just go on talking about *Cushman!*" "Of course I'm talking about Cushman cakes," I answered irritatedly. Then suddenly with misgiving: "Wasn't I?"

But even as I said it I felt, almost *knew,* that I had been saying not *Cushman* but *Schrafft!* I didn't try to rectify it then, just went on piling up adjectives for Cushman cakes.

Another time, long after the cake company had left me (but not for that fiasco), I had taken on a flour sponsor and had been talking about a one-egg cake, very inexpensive but delicious, that could be made with this flour (Swansdown). I had been promising Vincent that he might come and watch me bake the cake so that he could join me in testimonials to its perfection. Finally we set a day, Vincent appeared according to schedule, and I went to work. This is the way Vincent reviewed the spectacle next day on the air (we had promised our listeners a blow-by-blow description).

"First Mary Margaret—fortunately, as it turned out, wearing a gingham apron that covered her from neck to ankles—got out a yellow crock. It seems her mother always used a yellow crock for making cakes and so Mary Margaret can't manage without one. She put into the crock some sugar and butter and began to mix them together with her hands. Her mother did it that way and it's called creaming. Then she sifted flour and baking powder together and beat an egg and got some milk and added all these, a little at a time, to the butter and sugar, beating and stirring industriously. Finally she poured the mixture into a pan and put it in the oven.

"Then she began to make the icing. She used butter, cream, sugar, and chocolate and it smelled wonderful when she was cooking it. Afterward she beat for a while, and at length it was time for the cake to come out of the oven. It had risen way up and looked beautiful.

"She cooled it for a little while, but soon she got impatient. Besides, as she pointed out, she had to put the fudge frosting on before it got cold—and so she began to pour icing on the cake. At first it was all right, but the icing was so rich and thick—and heavy—that suddenly the still too-warm cake collapsed exactly as if it had been struck by an earthquake, and as we watched, appalled, it became just a mass of delicious crumbs surrounded by fudge."

I didn't lose my Swansdown account either. In fact, the sponsor (General Foods) almost immediately offered me my first network show, fifteen minutes across-country for several of their products. Except that the items I touted all belonged to one company, the participating sponsorship idea was the same as my Martha Deane program.

The advantage to Martha Deane customers was that a company could buy, for a relatively small sum, participation in a show with an established audience. I always figured that I had a solid base of listeners who would try at least once anything I recommended and, better still, would attempt to get it the very day I spoke about it, or at least the next day. This created an instant demand and gave me a chance to bring up my reserve forces—the women who took a few days to make up their minds. The reason the listeners did what I asked them was because they knew I never recommended a product unless I had not only tested it but proved to myself that I really liked it. That was my invariable rule, though it took considerable doing to persuade advertising agencies that I meant what I said.

Stella hooked up with a laboratory, and we paid to have all possible checkups. Sometimes even then I didn't like the product, and so we turned down a great many more than we ever accepted. One radio personality owed her successful program to our turning down a cold cream. The agency was so provoked with me (the product was perfectly good—I just didn't like it) that it started the other woman off.

I recently listened to myself talking about one of my sponsors on her eighty-fourth birthday. Mrs. Knox almost didn't become a sponsor because she was so outraged when we said we'd have to test her product. She felt that Knox Gelatin was so well known that we were being impertinent. But we tested anyway. I said about Mrs. Knox: "On her birthday I expect that Mrs. Charles B. Knox will go to her office as usual. Up to the time her husband died in 1908, she was a home woman but when she had to she stepped in as head of the Knox Gelatin Company and built it up to be the biggest business of its kind in the world. When anybody asked her how she did it, she said: 'Well, you just use the same methods in the factory as at home. Apply the same principles of common or horse sense. Don't try to be masculine. Be a woman. Men don't like masculine women. Dress like a woman, keep your feminine charm but for goodness' sake, don't trade on it. Don't go around asking men to do things for you because you are a woman and don't accept favors that you don't deserve and that are given to you because of your sex.'"

Then I added about Mrs. Knox: "What I like best about her is that she's supposed not ever to have said an unkind thing about anybody. Reason (according to her) is that it always comes back at you! Long ago she put in the five-day week, gave her employees two weeks' vacation with pay, time off for doctors, dentists, and sickness. Eighty-five per cent of those now working for her have been with her for twenty-five years or more. She raises orchids, and every girl who gets married is allowed to pick a big bouquet of orchids for her wedding."

This was rather more time than I usually gave a sponsor, but since no one client owned me, Stella and I made our own rules. If I decided the program was too important to be associated with products (though goodness knows they were pretty vital to me) I would just list the clients and add that I depended upon every listener to buy twice as much of everything as usual. I believe they did it, too, for many of them felt it was their program as much as mine.

When I had three quarters of an hour I advertised twelve products. When I became hour-long, I added four more. So they took up a good deal of time unless, having stayed too long with a guest, I wadded them all together at the end.

But when I did this I usually had a plot to hang them on, hoping thus to hold the listeners' interest. Mrs. D.'s daughter Judy and Janice's son Michael were practically brought up on the program. Their mothers in long, newsy, and often amusing letters told what they were fed, how they were clothed, what was used to clean them and their high chairs and play pens. And always the letters recounted not only stories of the children but of the products. Best of all, the tales were true, for my employees knew that I didn't want false testimonials, no matter how attractive.

I had one brilliant inspiration that poor Vincent suffered under for months. I made up little plays about our sponsors for Vincent and me to act out. Sometimes I was little Susie and he was little Willie. Other times I became Mama, who sent little Willie on errands to the grocery store. Many listeners entered into the spirit of this foolery and contributed sketches which I adapted to my purposes. Others, to Vincent's not too secret relief, said—but kindly, not nastily—that our plays were silly and eventually we gave them up.

However, I thought of other devices—riddles, including musical ones, for Vincent to answer with the names of the products, testimonials from my mail. One day my comments were all from men, another all from women I envied for one reason or another—(one lived on a farm and could have thick yellow cream to whip for the top of gingerbread made from my mix!).

Once I had a letter which asked, a little irritatedly, "Don't you ever get tired of superlatives? Why don't you now and then try understatement?" So next day I did, and a good many ardent supporters wrote that they stocked up double because I was so restrained.

It was hard for agency people or even clients to believe that the women felt as they did unless they saw firsthand evidences. Fortunately for me, many of them did.

One of the earliest of my listeners was a charming southerner—Myrtle Campbell—who lived with her sons and daughter-in-law in Bronxville. She rarely allowed anything to keep her from hearing the broadcast—telephone and doorbell rang unheeded, appointments were put off until we had left the air. Her son, Lawton, was a very important executive at General Foods. He trusted his mother's judgment ("Martha Deane products popped up at every meal and all over the house," he told me) and decided to let me try a dry-run with the flour. He must have been satisfied, for he signed me for the network show and it lasted for several years.

I had another product for a long time because an advertising man-

ager's crippled father, confined to a wheel chair, waited for the program
every day. "That woman can sell anything," he told his son.

The most important victory, though, was a much earlier one. Ambra
Diefenthaler, the wife of the head of a coffee, tea, and spice company,
a soft-voiced but determined lady, heard the program from its very
beginning and after weighing it for a while advised her husband that
she had found exactly the right advertising medium for him—me!

Mr. Diefenthaler immediately called William Rogow, salesman at
WOR, who had been begging him to try the station. Bill went gallop-
ing to Mr. Diefenthaler's office in a downtown section redolent of
browning coffee and pungent spices. Mr. Diefenthaler soon shattered
the salesman's elation. When he heard what the client wanted he
shook his head. He was an honest man.

"I'm sorry, Mr. Diefenthaler," he declared dolefully. "I can't sell
you that program. I don't believe in it. I think it's going nowhere but
off the air!" However Mr. Diefenthaler thought Mother knew better,
and so he bought the program and stayed with it for years.

Bill Rogow apologized to me later, but he didn't need to. I like
honest men, and he was not alone in his skepticism. It took a good
while for any of the old hands to get accustomed to the Martha Deane
approach. After we were going strong, sales manager Neff liked to tell
the story about a day he took a difficult agency man into the sponsors'
room to listen to me. I had only been on for a few months and sponsors
were few. This agency man was really interested in buying, and the
sales manager hoped that I might give recipes that day and tell the
women how to do something useful around the house.

Instead I embarked delightedly on a description of a flea circus
which I had visited the day before. The sales manager sat frozen while
I went on talking about how fleas were trained and how they ate their
suppers off the trainer's arm. That was the ultimate blow, for the product was a food and never in this world, thought Walter Neff, would a
food advertiser want his wares extolled on a program that went into
graphic details about the disgusting care and feeding of fleas. But the
advertising man had a sense of humor and signed a long-term contract
that very day.

By this time I had learned to treat a sponsor respectfully. I knew he
was to be handled carefully and made to feel important. Before that,
sponsor was a dirty word to me. To the end I retained my suspicions of

anybody who wanted to become a client, but I at least behaved more hospitably to most of the later ones than I did to the very first. This first one was a cleaning powder, and the sales department, after many futile efforts, were overjoyed at making the sale. They thought I would be, too. Instead—"Have I got to have a sponsor?" I wailed. They assured me that I had to, indeed, if I wanted to stay on the air, and when I could find nothing to object to in the product it was scheduled to start in a week.

I was miserable during those seven days of waiting, though I was rather interested to discover that Oakite, the new client, was used to clean the George Washington Bridge, the Holland Tunnel, the New York Public Library, and the laboratories of Johns Hopkins Hospital. These would all make fine stories, but at the same time I was tormented by a dread that the sponsor might try to boss the program. Sure enough, on the morning Oakite was to start the advertising manager telephoned. After cheery inquiries as to my health (which I answered gloomily) he said briskly: "I suppose you are all ready for the broadcast! I'll be in the control room!"

Then I blew up. "Don't you dare come to the broadcast!" I screamed at him. "I know what you want to do—you want to tell me how to run my program! Well, you can't. Let's just tear up the contract right now!" The poor man gulped and tried to calm me by assuring me that if I didn't want him to come, certainly he wouldn't. And he didn't. In fact, he never came near as long as I had the account, and after the contract was ended he stopped using my program for good, though he spent a lot of money other places.

Professional radio entertainers know, of course, that a program pays only when it induces sponsors to buy time—in other words, when it becomes commercial. I suppose the reason I didn't understand at first was because I had worked always on newspapers and magazines where editorial was editorial and advertising was advertising and never the twain could meet. In fact, on some magazines I'd written for, it was considered almost a crime for the editorial staff to mix in any way with the advertising staff, and on newspapers several floors usually divided the two departments.

But in the end I came to enjoy the products. They were a challenge to my ingenuity. I had lots of help, for while some guests made it harder for me commercially—or so it seemed at the time—many others, charmed by the novelty, took over and "did" the sponsors in unforgettable ways.

I think some of them came back again and again to my program just to relax. They often tried to tell on the air what it was they liked about our daily jam session, and perhaps famous band leader Fred Waring expressed it as well as anybody when he said: "You can be as silly as you like here and nobody stops you." It would have taken a more determined woman than me to stop Fred when he got going, especially if *Hellzapoppin* Ole Olsen was teamed up with him, as he often was.

I met Fred first in the elevator of the apartment building opposite Central Park South into which I had just moved. He lived there then too. His first words to me were: "When are you going to have me on your program?" I looked at him, startled, and the elevator man interposed nervously. "This is Mr. Fred Waring." So I invited him to come the next day. He arrived with a wonderful poem set to music in which all my products were mentioned. He sang it to me with gestures and from then on, whenever he appeared, insisted on doing the products in rhyme beginning with his favorite "Bulldog Blues," continuing that melody even after the bluing it extolled had departed from me.

On my ninth anniversary on the air Ole Olsen and Fred moved in and took over the entire program, concentrating so much on the commercials that there was hardly anything else. They threw the ball back and forth, ignoring me completely, and even the control room abetted them, for on the recording my attempts at protest were drowned out completely. The audience packed into our biggest studio at NBC didn't mind the commercial aspect and laughed and applauded their way through the gay hour.

It might be interesting to give a blow-by-blow description of one ordeal by fire with comedian Frank Fay and producer Fred Finkle-hoffe. Fred and his then wife, Ella Logan, had been my guests not long before, and, as I told Fred rather grimly, "I'm lucky that I still have any sponsors after what you and Ella did to me." "Oh, I'm so sorry," crooned Freddy, overflowing with false sympathy. "We'll never do that again."

But immediately the slaughter started. "Did you ever hear of a split pea?" Fred asked Frank Fay. "No-o-o! Why would they split a pea? Does she do it?"

m.m.m.   Frank, please tell about winter and summer French. [This was a reference to a routine in the play Freddie was producing and Frank was acting in.]

f.f.   Oh, get her. *Please.* You take care of your split peas and I'll take care of my material. We only have two or three good jokes in this show and if we tell them to everyone, where shall we be? You wouldn't want us to tell how you split the peas, now, would you?

m.m.m.   Yes. I wish you'd do it at your next performance.

f.f., *plaintively.*   Have you got any wake-up products? Did you see me tottering as I sat down? No, don't answer. All right—this is Fay taking over. When I came in here there was nothing but two men standing watching and another man nodding in the control room and all of a sudden the door opened and now the place is covered with Massachusetts women and she asks where they're all from. "Hello," she says. "How are you—it's nice to have you here—you're from Brooklyn—well, how do you do, Mrs. Fefferell." That's what I'm going to do from now on. Meet the people and then you can't flop. She's fixed it so everybody says she's *sweet*. So now I'm going to do that at the theater. "Oh, I'm so glad to see you—it's so *nice* to see you!" So then when you come on the stage, you can't fail.

*Nervously* vincent *seizes the moment to start doing a Bohack commercial.*

f.f. *interrupts.*   I know what sponsors are. I had one once. [vincent *mentions the price of pears.*] Are they split? . . . No? Then pardon me for being so plebeian. But what is this Bohack?

m.m.m.   They're a chain of stores that sell wonderful steaks.

f.f. *interrupts again.*   Can they hear my name good from where I am? I have had to put up with split peas so if they have an old steak lying around, they could send it to me at the Shubert Theatre.

m.m.m.   You can make ice cream out of Van Camp's——

f.f.   Really. I shall whip up some chocolate myself this afternoon.

m.m.m.   I'll make you some ice cream if you'll be quiet. I'll bring it to you.

f.f.   Where will you bring it?

m.m.m.   Backstage.

f.f.   Backstage where?

m.m.m.   Shubert Theatre.

f.f.   Thank you. And what is the name of the show?

M.M.M., *obediently, if sulkily.* "Laugh Time." [*Then with a surge of hopefulness*] Ruby Lane Stores have a blouse special.

F.F. I'm just loaded up with blouses. I'm sorry.

M.M.M. Well, then, Bulldog Blue.

F.F. This will slay you, Fred. This was my big surprise for you, Fred. You think split peas are something. Well, get a load of this. A chubby little bottle [*picking it off the table and holding it up triumphantly*]—imagine punching a hole in that cute chubby bottle.

M.M.M. And this tall brown bottle—it's for taking fruit stains off.

F.F. Well, that solves my problem.

M.M.M. Then comes my bread.

F.F. I never in my life was at a place where they talk about more things to eat and never give you a mouthful—not even a coffee bean.

M.M.M. Thousands of women buy these products.

F.F. In a little chubby bottle?

M.M.M. No, that's the bluing. . . . Now for the apple juice.

F.F. Does that come in the tall brown bottle?

M.M.M. No, this is in a green bottle and it's the whole good of an apple squeezed out.

F.F., *indignantly.* I think it's unfair to an apple to mash it all over the place and put it in a bottle! That poor little apple when it was born thought it was going to hang on a tree in the sunshine and enjoy itself with all the other little apples and what happens—it ends up being mashed and put into a bottle. Is that any end for an apple?

VINCENT Shall we pass on to something else—maybe paper napkins?

F.F., *gloomily.* We won't need them for anything we've had here.

FRED FINKLEHOFFE Why don't we talk about Sweetheart Soap, my favorite?

M.M.M. They went off the air after the last time you were here.

FRED FINKLEHOFFE, *with mock humility.* Oh, did I drive them away? I want to apologize to them.

F.F., *sadly.* Even sweethearts go off without two weeks' notice. No warning or anything. Leave you flat.

M.M.M. By this time you both know what you do with split peas— you make soup of them.

F.F. *Really!* What *we* have are split *weeks*.

M.M.M. What are split weeks?

F.F.   That is when you play three days here and three days there—
that was in vaudeville when I was a child—but if you aren't so good in
the theater where you played the first three days, you might not get
to play the other three days.

FRED FINKLEHOFFE, *in a high falsetto imitating* M.M.M. *as* VINCENT
*makes a despairing gesture indicating that we must get off the air.*
That's it—good-by, you all.

I was glad he had signed off for me. I was so choked with laughter
I couldn't have been heard. I suppose many of these things were much
funnier to us and the listeners then than they are when I tell about
them. But in the dark days preceding and during World War II laughter was one of the commodities I was peddling.

I even turned the dignified Admiral Richard Byrd into a commercial,
though before I went on the air with him I had definitely promised
myself I wouldn't. I was advertising a starch, and I had a story about
the admiral that was a perfect lead-in—only the way I'd obtained it
was questionable. But when the moment came I blurted it all out—
how one summer on Mt. Desert Island in Maine, I was on a party-
line telephone with the admiral, who had a summer place there, and,
tempted beyond my strength, used to listen in when I heard his ring.
But the only real information I ever got, I assured the admiral, was
how he liked his shirts starched.

I didn't have to maneuver Olga Petrova, star of the silent motion
pictures and always an electric personality. She sat down in front of
my microphone and calmly announced without ever having mentioned
it to me beforehand that until she heard my soap commercial she
hadn't washed her face for thirty-two years! *Life* magazine picked that
one up, and correspondents were so skeptical that Olga finally wrote
them confirming the story.

One day I started a program by saying, "If I told you this guest sang
at the Metropolitan at seventeen, you'd guess who she is so I'll just
hint by saying that she whistled before she sang and I'll keep you
guessing while I do some products." I started with a chocolate pudding, and a voice piped up: "Gosh, that sounds wonderful."

M.M.M., *accusingly.*   Now they've heard your voice!

GUEST, *defiantly.*   I can't help it. You make me want to rush right
out and get some.

M.M.M.  Well, I'll bet a nickel you can't sew!

GUEST  Oh yes, I make my own clothes. Is that a good entrance to a commercial?

M.M.M.  That's a wonderful entrance because I advertise a sewing machine.

I finished my plug and the guest gave an even better one from her own experience. By this time the audience knew that she was Patrice Munsel.

The first author I ever had who mentioned one of my products in print was Betty Smith in *A Tree Grows in Brooklyn*. Her heroine washed a horse with Sweetheart. And so that the other sponsors needn't feel left out, I got lead-ins from the book for every one of them. Betty ended by signing my copy of *A Tree Grows in Brooklyn* "With love from one of your products, Betty Smith."

In Henry Misrock's *God Had Seven Days*, the story of four badly wounded veterans who are cured by a miracle, the author told how they visited my program and talked about their Bible experience. As a result the country was sold out of Bibles before the week was out and readers were clamoring for more copies. This would have made a wonderful story for a sales prospectus if only it hadn't been fiction.

For a long time we advertised a gingerbread mix, and it was our custom to serve cookies made from the product. Since our usual hour was one o'clock in New York, guests had often not lunched when they arrived. Recurrent ones had grown to depend on the prospect of cookies and were reproachful if none was forthcoming. Emil Ludwig, distinguished biographer, was one of these and journalist-author Louis Fischer another. "No cookies?" complained Louis when he visited us for the first time after spending six days with Gandhi in India. "You're starving me the way Gandhi did. He gave me a great deal of intellectual food but not enough for the stomach."

Perhaps the most surprising lieutenant I ever had was the wise, wonderful historian, biographer, and scholar, Carl Van Doren. I met Carl at a Writers' Board Meeting soon after our entrance into World War II. He told me then that he was a listener, also that he lived near me, and after that he came often to sit in my kitchen where we drank quantities of strong hot tea and talked about everything under the sun and some things that aren't, for even then he was speculating about space and other worlds. When I invited him to be a guest on the program, to my amazement he turned up with plugs for several of the products and even a nonsense question and answer about the cleaning tissue I was selling then. The question: May I tiss oo? The answer: Yes. *Yes* was the name of the tissue!

That was my favorite Van Dorenism, but here are two other specimens of Carl's commercial aid. "Memorandum to Mary Margaret McBride:

> *Calcium is a metal*
> *Found with limestone, chalk, gypsum.*
> *When you drink Starlac*
> *You are bound to sip some.   Love, Carl.*"

"Dearest Mary Margaret: Just in case you and your Sutra sponsor do not know it, you may like to be reminded that *sutra* is a Sanskrit word meaning thread or rule, and specifically is applied to a brief moral maxim or teaching in Hindu or Buddhist literature. What other program besides yours puts Sanskrit thoughts into a listener's head?"

The loyalty of my listeners still fills me with awe. They had Martha Deane or Mary Margaret weekends and dinners. It became a sort of personal game among them to find new uses for products and then write me about the way the family reacted. Oddly enough, some who were worried at first about the commercial aspect became the most devoted addicts of many of the new products. One letter now before me says, "I was disappointed when you first began to interrupt your program with commercials. But when I happened to notice a box of your cleaner at a store where I traded, it seemed the most natural thing in the world to buy it. I like it so much that I feel differently about the whole commercial idea."

I think I must hold one or two records. For instance during the war years I was paid to persuade people to buy less of their favorite candy, to be satisfied with only a half or even a quarter of a pound. This was because the makers couldn't get enough quality ingredients to manufacture in quantity. I remember I came back from Rockville Centre where I had been speaking for the Red Cross to tell Vincent triumphantly that the mayor had presented me with a half pound and I'd eaten it right on the spot.

A possible second record: it is reported and certainly it's down on several of the recordings that I threatened to eat a whole hand of bananas if the sponsor would send me that many. Some say I did it. I don't remember—I've always been a big banana consumer, but maybe I didn't, since listeners wrote and telephoned to beg me not to.

A campaign of Stella's was responsible for still another record. One day she came out of the control room to command the listeners to go right to their grocery stores, inspect the soup shelves, and if our soups weren't in front, to see the manager and get them put there.

"And if you have to make a fuss to get to the manager," counseled Miss Karn, "do it." They did, too, and so belligerently that the sponsor had to suggest that the ladies go a little easier with the grocers, who felt badgered. Whoever heard of sponsors begging a broadcaster to be less persuasive?

Some products naturally brought in better stories than others. Cat or dog foods were best of all, because people liked to write about their pets. Everyone had a wonderful yarn about his own Fido or Fluffy. My favorite was the dog who loved to answer the telephone and also enjoyed eating leather. He ate every handbag and answered every telephone he could get his paws on. His owner therefore kept him away from telephones and handbags, but one day after she left the house she remembered that her brand-new handbag was on the couch within easy reach of the dog, so she went straight to the telephone and called him. Then she started home in a hurry but stopped at pay telephone stations so that the dog would be kept busy and wouldn't have time to finish the handbag. Sure enough, when she got home the handbag was barely tasted. (No, I don't know *how* the dog returned the receiver after each call!)

Now and then, as in the case of Mrs. Knox, the sponsor was unusual enough in some way to furnish me with copy. One wrote the most enchanting letters about his farm and his fancies, and he used to get triple time because I was so charmed by his masterpieces that I read them aloud. Pretty Jane Redfield, now one of my closest friends, came into my life as the sister-in-law of a gingerbread-mix sponsor. Poor modest Jane, who is not very fond of publicity, found herself being linked to so many gingerbread commercials that she finally begged me please to lay off.

I got into the habit of including the good looks of the manufacturer every time I spoke of one product. I think my references to this handsome man really did sell extra amounts of the product, but I quit that

in a hurry after an encounter with his wife. She greeted me in quite
a friendly fashion and then suddenly sprang like a cobra: "I want you
to stop talking about my husband and his neckties and about how
good-looking he is," she commanded. "I don't like it and he doesn't
like it either."

If all other devices failed there was always long-suffering Vincent.
One Friday I remarked brightly: "We've got a new sponsor coming on
next week."

VINCENT   Going to tell now?

M.M.M.   No, but I'll see if you all can guess. Know what? I'll send
a lock of Vincent's hair to anybody who can guess the new sponsor.

VINCENT   H-m-m. Out of your millions of listeners at least a thousand might guess right and I'd be completely bald!

M.M.M.   I can't help it, Vincent—I've got to have something nice
to send them and I think a lock of your hair, right there where it is
curliest, would be perfect!

VINCENT   I bet they'd much rather have yours.

M.M.M.   No, no—it's settled!

And it was. The new sponsor was butter. A number of listeners
guessed it, and for a good while Vincent went round with a shorn
head.

# 7. PRIDE GOETH BEFORE A FALL

*"Congratulations, Mary Margaret. Four more sponsors went on our waiting list today." Stella Karn, just as we went on the air one day in 1935.*

Those early years of Martha Deane, after the settling in was over, were wonderful. My prosperity went up with that of the country. Business was booming under the New Deal, everybody was advertising, and no sponsor wanted to leave the Martha Deane program. But if one did drop out now and then, dozens (Stella said hundreds) were waiting to take the departed one's spot. In addition, I was doing a network show under my own name and enjoying making new friends and getting letters from all over the country.

Some of the local letter writers discovered me on the network and wrote to Martha Deane, "There's a woman imitating you but she's not as good as you are, darling." There were plenty of real imitators, though, and Stella welcomed them. It made something else to brag about. Letters came from many station managers and from ambitious girls who wanted "to have a program like Martha Deane's." Stella invited them all to come and see how we did it and spent hours proudly explaining the details.

During the years that I earned most the newspapers used to quote my income as one of the highest paid to a woman in any field. The trouble was that they calculated every cent the program took in as my income. In a small way it was like attributing to the head of U. S. Steel all of steel's earnings in a year. I hated that—I couldn't bear listeners to think I was rich when I wasn't. They realized that because of my job I went to exciting places they couldn't go to, but otherwise they knew I was one of them. And they were fond of me.

Popularity was a heady business, and while I was always apprehensive that the powers were about ready to send me packing, I got accustomed to taking for granted the perquisites of being in the public eye. I never asked for them and I don't approve of special privileges, but I did accept extra attention in restaurants, shops, or airports; gifts, compliments, recognition. Everybody, it seemed, wanted to do something for me. People who knew me *when* sprang up from nowhere— a man I couldn't remember who said he took me to my first dance; classmates from schools I'd never gone to; even roommates enough to fill a small dormitory. And, of course, chiselers.

An unemployed carpenter whose family came from Paris, Missouri, he said, needed $59.60 to get his tools out of hock. He gave an address in Brooklyn, and when Stella, failing to convince me any other way that he was a phony, went there, it was a cemetery.

Sick mothers were my worst hazard, and next came women who needed fifty or a hundred dollars to start a little home cookie-baking or pickle-making business. I kept giving sums for several months to one woman under the delusion that I was keeping her from committing suicide. Mrs. D. unmasked her. It was a game, the woman finally admitted. It amused her to see just how gullible I was. She didn't even need the money—her husband was a prosperous traveling salesman, but she had no children and his long absences left her with too much time on her hands.

I learned to say at once to suppliants like her that since I had no way of checking the good faith of any request, I must confine my efforts at helping others to established organizations. I can remember only one instance where I gave money to a stranger who was not later proved to be a phony. And of all the people who borrowed from me through the years, only two ever paid any of the money back. Those two gave me such a glow of renewed faith in humanity that I wanted to tear up their checks. Money never has been very important to me, though I am miserly at times about small items, I think because of having been poor and worried about mortgages when young.

One of the plusses of those earlier years was having a rose named for me. To this day it is the honor I most cherish, but in a way it's terrifying. Because for the rest of my life I must live up to my rose. Roses are never renamed. There have been instances where the namee has gone down to deserved oblivion, but the rose namesake blooms on.

If the namee becomes too notorious, the rose may just fade away like the old soldier but never will its nomenclature change. So the Mary Margaret McBride—even if I should, heaven forbid, commit murder— will still be the Mary Margaret McBride.

I wish I could say that Charles Perkins of Jackson & Perkins, who became a well-loved friend, admired my program and me so much that he begged me to let a rose be called for me. But I'm afraid it was, like many such grand-sounding honors, essentially a publicity deal. Amy Vanderbilt, etiquette queen, had not then begun her march to fame and fortune as the arbiter of manners, and she was doing publicity for the Jackson & Perkins rose garden at Newark, New York. She and Stella evolved the plan as of possible mutual advantage. And so one lovely June day I journeyed to Newark to broadcast from the biggest rose garden in the world.

The program that day started on a tragic note with a bulletin about an allied submarine that had gone down. We all looked grave for a few moments, remembering that even though we were not, much of the world was at war. But soon we cheered up; the sun was shining and three thousand acres of flame and gold roses surrounded us.

My beautiful rose was there, too—number 34-14168, now Mary Margaret McBride. I argued about the color. They called it salmon pink, but I made them open a can of salmon to prove that it wasn't. I said it was the color of summer sunrise shot with gold. Charley Perkins, hybridizer Gene Boerner, and I got up at dawn to make sure. We wandered about the garden, exquisite in the morning light, with dew on the roses. Finally all agreed with me about the color of Mary Margaret McBride. I also learned that it had taken eight years to develop me, for I had to be sent to eighty-seven experimental stations to find out whether I had stamina.

All kinds of other honors (many, I'm sure, also negotiated by Stella) came my way, and I was as happy as I was ever likely to be. Then the blow. My network sponsors wanted to change my time. No, it was more than that. They wanted to put another program in the time I had come to consider mine (I'd had it several years) and give me a later hour. They offered a raise in pay, but in spite of that I was hurt and, against Stella's advice, insisted on giving up the sponsor. This was one of the happenings that I magnified into a tragedy. Not long afterward I found out what tragedy really meant.

My mother had been ill, and I was planning to fly to Florida to see her that weekend. At four in the morning on Tuesday the telephone rang and I knew it for what it was—the worst news I could ever have. My mother was dead. Always I had dreaded that ring and now that it had come, nothing seemed very important.

All my friends, especially the ones I had made on the air, tried to help me. They poured letters, telegrams, and flowers into my mother's home in Winter Park, Florida, but I was numb with pain. Even my beloved program seemed remote and of little consequence. I came back to work the day after my mother's burial and went on the air at once. Among the records is the one in which I talk about my mother in a tight, strained voice that is like that of a very little girl. I have heard it only twice, and I doubt if I'll ever play it again.

She was a pioneer, my mother, with a kind of courage and self-sacrifice that seems to be passing. At the time of her death a beloved friend of mine, Nina Oliver Dean, a Florida writer who used to show me the state and help with my broadcasts when I was there, wrote about my mother in the Orlando paper.

"Mrs. McBride's life story is a true tale of the American Way," Nina said. "She represents a type that is fast vanishing from the American scene, a woman we read about with quickening pulse and stare at in the movies with a touch of awe, a woman who, in spite of calico dresses and cotton stockings, possessed a radiance that cannot be found in a beauty parlor and a resourceful intelligence that cannot be won in a college—the pioneer American mother.

"Elizabeth Craig McBride was the daughter of a Baptist minister. She fell in love with Thomas Walker McBride at a county fair where he drove a pair of high-stepping horses and paid pretty compliments to all the ladies. She raised her family of four children on a Missouri farm. She had her babies in the old farmhouse with the aid of a country doctor if he happened to be in the vicinity, without him if he didn't. She made butter in an ancient wooden churn with a dasher, lard from hog meat over a fire of hickory chips, soap in a great granite kettle, and put up enough pear preserves and green-tomato pickle in the summer to stock the pantry shelves for winter.

"She awoke at four o'clock every morning, winter and summer, at the summons of an old dominecker rooster who acted as her alarm clock, went to the well for water, made a fire in the kitchen stove, and cooked a breakfast of ham and eggs and biscuits for her family and the hired man. If it happened to be haying time, there were seven hired men to be fed instead of one.

"Her daughter said, 'I can't remember that I ever saw Mama sitting down unless somebody had come to visit.' And this mother still wasn't too busy when Father McBride brought in some snow to make snow cream for the children with cream, sugar, and a drop of vanilla. Nor was she too busy to plant sweet peas and a pansy bed for the Mc-Brides always had flowers even in the worst years when the mortgages pressed and the crops failed."

From the day I came back from my mother's funeral I was listless, uninterested, and tired. One day Stella told me that the Florida Citrus Commission was proposing to buy us for the network. That meant another fifteen-minute show across the boards. The thought of doing it in addition to the Martha Deane three quarters of an hour seemed just too much.

I said, "I think I'll do only one show a day from now on." I threw this out mainly to see what Stella would say. She said nothing and so I asked, "Do you think the Florida Citrus people are in earnest?" (After a few years of sure things that didn't come off I had grown cautious.) She assured me that these men really wanted to buy the program. So I proposed that she make an appointment for us to see them. She did and I met LaMonte Marvin, business manager of the Citrus Commission (father of Lee Marvin, television star), and Charles Gannon, representing the advertising agency for the Commission.

In spite of glares from Stella, I confided that I had decided to do just one program from now on and if they could meet our price, theirs would be it. The two men left for Florida that night, and in a few days they were back with an agreement at our terms for an exclusive program.

Stella and I had been arguing in a desultory manner ever since their departure about the exclusive clause. She never for a moment believed I'd meant it about giving up the Martha Deane program, which she knew to be something very like the breath of life to me. But now I said that I *had* meant it, that I had pledged my word and that I must go through with it. This was pretty silly because the Citrus Commission didn't really care how many other programs I had as long as theirs didn't suffer. They produced the contract ready to sign, but I said I must tell Ted Streibert first. This was really hard; I loved Ted and he had stood by me loyally. At first he simply didn't believe me. When I convinced him that I was in earnest he literally threw up his hands and uttered one explosive word that his emphasis made into an epithet: "Women!"

I told him I knew a fine person who would do as well or better for him—Bessie Beatty. He said he'd never heard of her. I explained that she'd appeared several times on my program—that she was a writer and editor of great ability. I promised I would enlist all the listeners in her behalf and turn the program over with a flourish. He shook his head gloomily but promised to see Bessie Beatty.

I did not tell him that Bessie Beatty was a close friend—she wasn't. More precisely, she was an intimate of friends of mine. The reason I chose her was that one day she confided to me not only that she was worried about finances but also about the welfare of somebody she loved. I knew too well what she was going through; I had experienced both anxieties and that desperation which makes you feel you have nowhere to turn. I told her in confidence about the possibility that I might leave WOR and promised I would try to get the job for her.

So when I went to Ted Streibert my mind was made up. Some of our closer friends were hurt and bitter afterward that Stella and I had not given them the chance, but once I've promised, no matter what the circumstances, I go through with it. The results often show that I've been pigheaded and stupid.

I told Ted Streibert, in succeeding discussions when he brought up other candidates for the job, that I would not turn the program over to anybody but Bessie Beatty and stipulated that she was not to be called Martha Deane. So it was finally agreed. And I signed the citrus contract.

For the first time since Martha Deane began Stella closed down for six weeks and we went to Alaska for a so-called vacation. I was already beginning to regret, and have only the vaguest remembrance of snow-capped mountains, golden sunsets, and flame-colored sunrises. I told about it later on the air, though, and made it sound wonderful—how the sun colored the snow on the mountain peaks, and to my surprise I heard myself saying on the recording that there was a full moon all the way there and back. Rather a feat since the trip took a month. I was sort of dazed, I guess. One piece of scenery was nice—I had never seen a glacier before and was fascinated when sirens' blowing made pieces fall off. Stella had a field day with her motion-picture camera, and I was her favorite foreground for glaciers, mountains, forests, churches, even totem poles. Luckily, I came out just a blur.

Back on the air, we broke the news that I was giving up the program. A week later I turned it over to Bessie Beatty in a great gathering at Town Hall with all my regulars on hand, handkerchiefs out, ready to reminisce and weep. "Beautiful Lady," my theme song, was being played for the last time on the organ and "Here's Martha Deane," said Dick Willard. I mournfully intoned, "The last time Dick will say those words."

Then we set about a real jam session, reviewed all the family jokes, not funny at all to others but hilariously so to us—like the time I was broadcasting from Bamberger's and called it Wana-berger's; the recipe for rice pudding from Jack Dempsey's Restaurant when frantic listeners telephoned, "It's a cup of rice to three cups of water, instead of the other way round. Yours would be cement"; the awful day I lost my temper when the newsroom kept sending in the same bulletin over and over and the loyal listeners wrote to say, "We understand but suppose somebody strange was listening. We just can't bear to have anybody think you're like that so please, please, Martha Deane, try to control yourself."

Hattie Silverman said, "The show that stands out in my memory is the one after you came back from your mother's funeral. 'The show must go on' applies to radio as well as to the theater, and the show did go on. I was in the goldfish bowl and the tears were streaming down my face." Then Hattie told how she found me. "I tuned in on a voice one day. I listened and it spoke of WOR, Newark, New Jersey. I thought, here's this poor little schoolgirl way over in Newark so I listened next day and I tried to put a face to that voice. I got the face all right—a pretty, roly-poly face with pigtails, for it was a child's voice.

"For a year I listened and then came a letter. Mrs. Sime Silverman was invited on the Martha Deane program—it was the Women's Exposition of Arts and Industries, and to my astonishment a pigtail-less Martha Deane came over to shake hands. She said, 'Would you like to see some of the exhibits with me?' But I never got to—she was so mobbed with people shaking hands and getting autographs. When she finally came back to me, I said, 'Sorry, but now I've got to go home,' so she threw her arms around me and kissed me—which was unusual. People don't like me, at least till they get to know me, and from that time on Hattie Silverman and Martha Deane have been the very best friends and now it will be Mary Margaret McBride and Hattie Silverman—and I'll have to practice saying Mary Margaret, Mary Margaret!"

Herman Smith declared: "You always made the Martha Deane program a living thing, but I best remember the broadcast about my Christmas pageant in the little village of South Salem when you described it so it sounded like an old-fashioned Christmas card. You got the spirit of the reverence of those simple people. Then I'll never forget the time at Hearn's when I went with you and you were twenty minutes late—the crowds were so thick, you couldn't get through. It was your first public appearance, and you didn't think anybody would be there!"

Stella Karn reminisced about the day I was sailing over New York in a blimp, having luncheon and expecting to be five or ten minutes late for the show. "Well, I was to get the program started," she related. "I did and you suddenly appeared, swept me off the chair in the middle of a sentence, and finished it with me flat on the floor."

Mrs. D., who was taking notes, said, "This book in which I keep a log of the programs is really *my album*, and every broadcast you've ever done is here. Yesterday I looked through 1934, '35, '36, '37, '38, '39—and then 1940, and on nearly every page there was a broadcast that I had found interesting and exciting."

Janice Devine struck a less tender note. "The first time I heard you, you didn't appeal to me at all. I was writing about the Ephrata, Pennsylvania, Cloisters for a magazine, and suddenly there was this voice telling about the Cloisters and about features that weren't in my story —and I had lived in that vicinity! You even knew how many windows were there—I didn't—and about a footprint I'd never heard of; so you can imagine how I felt about you that first time."

Mildred Helms recalled the time my mother told on the air about when I almost missed the train going back to boarding school and lost my skirt right before the whole town, standing revealed in long purple bloomers. Commented Mildred: "I am here now to say that you haven't changed. Every day we leave the house, go down the elevator, get into the car—and you suddenly have that look—you're sure you've forgotten this or that. And you always have!"

The Whites, Maud and Mitchell, my good angels from Mexico, Missouri, were there also, and Dick's father and his mother, who is the best cook alive. They and the Haders had refused to talk, but I made them stand up and be applauded.

Then I finished by saying: "Now I've got to do a delicate and difficult thing because some of you have been upset—you thought WOR was firing me, that I was being badly treated, that some woman was going to step in and take the name Martha Deane, and you were ready to fight. Frankly, it tickled me to have you take on like that. In fact, it's going to be hard for me to be as nice as I want to be because I'm desperately jealous of this woman who is to be my successor.

"But this whole change was my idea. You know when I used to have two daily programs how difficult it was and how I worked twenty-four hours a day. So I decided to do just one broadcast that would go all over the country. I wanted to tell you the truth—that I'm to blame—so you wouldn't hold my going away against this station and the nice people—Alfred McCosker, Theodore Streibert, George Schmidt, Frank Brower, Gene Thomas, Jeanette Land, Bill Rambeau, and the many others who have been wonderful to me. WOR let me choose my successor, and the person I've chosen is Bessie Beatty."

Then I said some complimentary things about her, introduced Bessie Beatty—and I was no longer Martha Deane.

The next thing I knew I was doing only one show a day and that a measly fifteen minutes. Perhaps I should add that time on the network is so expensive that fifteen minutes seemed a fine big chunk to everybody but me, accustomed to three times as much. The truth is I can do a program in fifteen minutes if I have somewhere else to tell all the little funny personal things that are so important to a loyal audience. I was accustomed to live my life before the microphone, almost like a continued story. I started the story one day and the next I told how it came out. If a woman had to be away from the broadcast she either called a friend or our office. Our telephone operator had a blow-by-blow description every day of what went on so that she could answer questions.

"You've sold your birthright for a mess of pottage, and I for one won't listen any more," one old listener wrote.

I agreed with her that the broadcasts had lost their old-time flavor. I worked harder than I ever had getting enormous amounts of information about each guest and boiling it down into what I hoped would be the absolutely right questions for a neat twelve-minute interview (the sponsor had to have at least two minutes of the fifteen—and the station another half minute.) But it is impossible to hold a guest to a plan unless he's reading. That I wouldn't have, for part of the charm had always been the ad-lib digressions that often turned up delightful surprises for me as well as the audience.

The Florida Citrus Commission was not much better pleased than I was. First, I had too many bosses (there were hundreds of members of the Commission); and second, they didn't know much about radio regulations. They couldn't understand why I didn't spend the entire fifteen minutes talking about oranges and grapefruit. At a time when I most needed an approving sponsor, I had my first doubtful one, with only dear Monty Marvin for comfort.

In the meantime, Bessie Beatty was doing fine in my old spot. One day I met an acquaintance (rather a spiteful one, I decided later) who had just come from a party where she claimed Bessie was saying that a comparison of my listening audience on WOR during the week I came back from vacation and her present one (after some months of running the program) showed that hers was much larger. Of course I was wild. To compare a check made when the broadcaster is just back after the program has been closed down for six weeks is unfair anyway, but for *her* to speak about it was too much. Yet if I hadn't been miserable in my job I'm sure I could have laughed it off. But with the situation as it was, I felt as if the world had ended for me. And it was no comfort to remind myself that the whole idea had been mine.

That first Christmas Bessie was on the air I went to Berta Hader's as I had done for fifteen Christmases. Bessie was there. I climbed the stairs with my bag and came right down again.

"I'm sick, Berta," I told my hostess miserably. "I have the most terrible indigestion. I guess I tasted too many of the Christmas cakes and candies people sent me when I unwrapped my packages yesterday. I'm going home."

I did have indigestion, too, and I had it for two years. In that time, also, I never again went to Berta's for the holidays. I gave Elmer and her new names in my broadcasts—Allen and Amelia, I called them—

and when listeners asked, "Why do you never mention Berta and Elmer any more?" I ignored the question.

At one time, when I was going through the worst of my bitterness, I
wrote to Berta that I was going to stop seeing her or trying to be
friends. Berta (and this shows the kind of person she is) hurried to
New York and with tears streaming down her face (I was crying, too,
of course) said, "I am not going to let you cut yourself off from us.
You need your friends now more than ever."

She was right and she made me see it. She loved Bessie, too, and
she managed to keep on being friends with both of us without dis-
loyalty to either. Only such a staunch, wonderful woman could have
done it.

I have tried sometimes to analyze my emotions in that bad time. I
had sincerely wanted Bessie Beatty to make good. After all, she was
my choice and I had fought for her, but I hadn't dreamed she could
really take my place. And on top of that, I was, for the first time
since I had begun radio, wretched in my work. I knew then and I
know now that she could have mended the situation by offering to
turn back the program. I wouldn't have taken it and even if I had
wanted to; WOR wouldn't have let me. They were still angry at me
but growing less so in their pleasant surprise at her great success.

I truly believe if the situation had been reversed I would have offered to give the program back, praying hard that she wouldn't take
it. I wasn't faced with such a decision, and I might have behaved
quite differently than I think. Anyway, for that year of the Citrus Commission broadcasts I was inwardly bleeding. I was learning, too, that
bitterness, suspicion, and jealousy are a terrible sickness.

A year later my old friend Marion Young was brought in by WOR
to be Martha Deane. I was hurt because she hadn't told me about it
in advance, but for some reason I was never jealous of her—I suppose
because I really love her, and when once I love somebody, nothing
changes my feeling. I must admit that I tried to grab off guests before she got them and made a fuss if I failed, but that was business!

For a while, at least, I was the only one who recognized that my
move in going completely network was the beginning of disaster. On
the surface I seemed to be having a whale of a time. I appeared on
many CBS nighttime programs, notably Fred Allen's. I christened a
cargo-attack vessel and got invidious notice in the newspapers when

some group, maybe the Senate, questioned the money spent on gifts to christeners. (I got a jeweled pin, very pretty, which someone immediately stole.)

One national group named me the most listened-to woman on the air, the hairdressers' association picked me (and this really was to laugh) as the best-tressed woman of the year. Lingerie makers dubbed me all-American collar-and-cuff "girl"! I got the radio oscar, Governor Stark of Missouri set aside November 22 as Mary Margaret McBride Day, and Stella made me buy my first fur coat to wear to Mexico, Missouri, for the celebration. She already had one, and she declared emphatically that she wasn't going to have my fellow Missourians think she, as manager, was cheating me.

In Mexico I rode down Main Street sitting like a real dignitary on top of the back seat of an open car. Later I was told by my old friend Curtis Mitchell, who also had lived and worked in Mexico, that Stella, learning no parade had been set up, quickly organized this one. For an impromptu effort, it certainly had style and energy. In front of me was a motorcycle policeman with a screeching siren. In back was a military escort—knee-high-to-grasshopper cadets from Missouri Military Academy. The high school brass band in scarlet uniforms led the procession. (Almost the only solemn face I saw all day belonged to a boy in the band who told me he had walked fifteen miles from his family's farm with a heavy trumpet and case.) Placards on every lamp-post we passed said "Welcome, Mary Margaret." The climax came when the procession passed under an arch with my name in electric lights, while photographers snapped pictures from the roofs of nearby tall buildings.

At my old desk in Mitchell White's *Ledger* office I pounded out the story of my arrival. Then they gave me a dinner with five-year-old Missouri ham and red gravy, fried catfish, sorghum molasses on corn bread, damson, peach, and cherry preserves, salt-rising bread, hot biscuits, new peas in cream, mustard greens cooked with side meat, mashed turnips, mashed white potatoes, sweet potatoes with marshmallows, caramel cake, apple pie. I ate it all! And while the bulbs flashed Governor Stark and I toasted each other in country buttermilk, the very same kind I used to pour from the cedar churn in the old summer kitchen.

Before the day was over I'd been guest of honor at six other parties.

When I staggered into the final one I flopped down in a comfortable chair and slipped off my pumps. Just as I was beatifically wiggling my happy-to-be-released toes the governor arrived at the party. Frantically I struggled to get my shoes on again. No use—my feet had swollen. There was nothing to do but greet the governor as I was. His eyes twinkled.

"I wish I could do that," he said, and sounded wistful. I knew he was remembering back just as I was, to a Missouri orchard and a barefooted child munching a green apple and enjoying the soft grass caressing feet covered with stone bruises and chigger bites. Those are memories you never forget. I hated to leave Missouri to go back to my problems. But it had to be done.

Monty Marvin decided that it might help strained relations with the sponsors if we went to Florida to broadcast. Stella and Janice left ahead of me to start research. Once in Florida, Stella realized the political chaos into which our program was being plunged. All the disagreements among members centered on me. By the end of the trip I was heartbroken—and convinced that my career in radio was finished. (It almost was.) Every day there was a new hurt. Once I walked across the lobby of a hotel and a man said to his wife, loud enough for me to hear, "There goes two million dollars of our money." I really think he and others believed I was pocketing all the cash they were spending for time, agency, and everything else.

Marjorie Kinnan Rawlings, author of *The Yearling,* was the nicest thing that happened on that bleak trip. I went to her farm, Cross Creek, in a primitive, palm-fringed section of swamps, live oaks, and ghostly gray Spanish moss. Jungle crept to the edge of the little orange grove, and panthers, deer, and bear crossed the land quite casually. Here women, leather-brown from sun and wind, heated water for their washing in iron kettles over smoky pine fires and their men scratched a living from hunting, fishing, and tending their groves.

Marjorie talked on the air about her own struggles to make a living by her typewriter. One day nothing at all was left in the cupboard except a box of crackers and a can of soup. Hanging up her washing that morning and looking affectionately at the jungle, she said aloud, "It will have to get tougher than this to take me away from here." And at that very moment, in approved slick-magazine fiction style, the mailman arrived with a $500 check!

It was during the tough days that Marjorie began making blackbird pies. On my program she described these pies, which are all right in nursery rhymes but strictly against the law in Florida. The station reported in alarm that Marjorie had broken the game laws and might be arrested. To my relief the authorities decided to let the offender go with a warning.

The rest of the Florida trip is too painful to tell in detail. Nobody would talk openly about the political rivalries into the middle of which we had plunged, but the atmosphere was supercharged. Every night I would go to sleep worn out from another day of strain and after two or three hours jerk awake to face bleak reality.

It was hot too, and I was making five or six appearances a day between broadcasts. Once in a while I hysterically rebelled and declared I wouldn't go on the air, but when the time came I always did. In fact, my listeners wrote enviously. They thought I was having a lovely mid-winter vacation. Only Stella knew the whole bitter truth—that the agency was going to lose the account and we, our network program. Because I always believe *I'm* to blame, no matter what the circumstances, Stella couldn't bear to tell me. But I found out and was sure that final ruin and failure were inevitable.

As usual I couldn't see a single gleam of light. I didn't want another fifteen-minute show—we could get that easily, Stella said. I didn't want anything except my lovely forty-five minutes back—and time to turn around in to tell my listeners everything that I saw or heard. What did I care about a national audience? I just longed to feel warm and snug around me again the approval of the listeners who had been with me from the beginning. I'd never have believed it then if some miracle in time had let me see a line from a magazine article of 1947 by Barbara Heggie which asserted, "Mary Margaret McBride no longer has to seek for fame and fortune. She has them."

For once the optimistic Stella also was affected. She succeeded in having our program cancellation announced as gently as possible in the press. Then she went to work. Friends close to her and worrying about her overdoing told me later that she lived on her battery of telephones and talked her way past insurmountable opposition into the offices of network VIPs and advertising bigwigs.

They told her time was at such a premium it couldn't be had. Stella refused to believe that. She had made up her mind I was going to have forty-five minutes on the air again and on a major station. All summer she worked. She gave up her vacation, developed a baffling skin ailment which kept her, delirious half the time, in her bed for weeks. She got out of it to fly with her nurse to Chicago, where she saw a famous doctor—and landed a sponsor! So when the fall broadcasting season reopened there we were—in the choice 1 P.M. spot on NBC. And Stella, sitting at the welcoming luncheon with executives, eyes bright, a spot of color on each cheek, had a fever of 104. She went to bed again when the luncheon was over and this time stayed there.

We had a great send-off the first day at WEAF. The Vanderbilt Theatre was packed with welcoming listeners to whom I confessed that I had made a mistake by giving up my long program and had paid with a year of heartache. All the regulars were on hand, and the air was full of the perfume of flowers and hope. Not so many sponsors though. I had thought the fifty to eighty who had been standing in line to get on Martha Deane would want to come to Mary Margaret McBride, but I got a rude shock.

One year away from a participation program had changed the picture, and with Stella too sick to fight for me, I did mighty poorly for most of that first year. I spent hours on the telephone learning the hard way what Stella must have endured for years, experiencing everything from formal politeness to rude rebuffs. Yet in that time I exasperated NBC salesmen by turning down some of the prospects they brought in. They couldn't understand how I could need sponsors so desperately and not take whatever was offered.

Heaven knows I was sorely tempted, but much as I wanted that program, I could not accept sponsors I didn't believe in. It wouldn't have done any good anyway. I can't sell unless I believe. I never knew how near NBC came to letting me go before we finally picked up our full quota of clients. But Stella, getting better at her Catskill farm, heard rumors and came flying back to New York to throw herself into a determined fight to save the situation. Her rest had done her good, and she was soon her old irrepressible self.

By our first anniversary at WEAF, we had sponsors waiting in line again. If only there hadn't been war!

## 8.  WAR *IS* HELL

I was weekending with my friends Hal and Jean May in Long Island, and on Sunday, December 7, 1941, we'd eaten one of Jean's marvelous fried-chicken and hot-biscuit dinners with chocolate icebox cake for dessert. Afterward, like millions of other well-fed Americans, we were idly listening to the radio. At first nobody believed the news flash that told about the Japanese attack on Pearl Harbor. A few minutes later we were all excitedly walking the floor and exclaiming, one of the men swearing softly under his breath.

Next day I came to the broadcast direct from the NBC news room where we had listened to President Roosevelt designating December 7 as that date which shall live in infamy.

Still a little dazed, as everybody was, I looked out a window in Rockefeller Center and saw men replacing burnt-out bulbs on the giant Christmas tree. Life was going on, even preparations for a merry Christmas or whatever kind we were going to have.

Nothing *really* was as usual though. Everybody was being caught up in a great wave of activity. Men were enlisting in the services without waiting to be called; women were signing up for Red Cross first-aid courses and enrolling in civilian defense.

That Christmas Day, I ate turkey with the recruits, many of whom looked as though they ought to be trying out for the high school football team, at the United States Navy Receiving Station in Brooklyn. Some of the boys came to the microphone and talked about Christmas back home. They ate a great deal of turkey and stuffing and had two desserts; then they bellowed out the wartime lyrics of "Beer Barrel Polka." After that we sang "Home, Sweet Home," I off key, the listeners and Vincent insisted. Then I went to my apartment and cried for an hour. I couldn't stop remembering that many of those rosy-cheeked lads would never see another Christmas.

Every day we were on the air there were heart-stopping bulletins. Sometimes we were pre-empted by Roosevelt, Churchill, the Pope. Later Italy surrendered on our time, and I said wistfully: "I hope Germany and Japan will choose our program too."

I guess I was too solemn at first; even mothers with enlisted sons asked me please to be as gay as possible. That is one reason we went ahead with the celebration of our eighth anniversary on the air—that and the fact that the program was dedicated to the American Theatre Wing War Service and Stage Door Canteen. Our friends Helen Mencken and Florence Reed were spokeswomen for the two causes.

A line of listeners formed in Rockefeller Plaza by eight that morning and stretched all the way to Fifth Avenue. Some clutched pictures of their boys in uniform to show me; others had letters for me to read.

I said as we opened: "I know we're entering a very serious year—we can't foresee what will happen, but since the weekend I am an optimist. I can't believe the world is going to end. Friday I went to Stella's farm on the side of a mountain with other mountains rising all around, their heads reaching into the clouds. I looked off into the valley at the little white church and even as I looked, the bell began to call the children to Sunday school. There was a kind of peace over it all. In the orchards apple trees were blossoming, pale pink and white. Two old lilac bushes in bloom were spreading their perfume and not far off, as I sat on Stella's porch, was a cherry tree with the blossoms beginning to fall so that every time a gentle breeze blew, I was covered with a snow storm of cherry whiteness.

"I had that ache in my throat that comes always when I see almost unbearable beauty, and the ache grew worse as I thought of all the things wrong with the world, including me."

My extracurricular war effort consisted of bond selling and making speeches in nearby towns for the Red Cross, the Blood Bank, and other causes. I went out four or five times a week, told about celebrity guests, the nightgown story (how I got locked out of my Hollywood hotel room in a very thin nightgown) and anything else I thought might make my audience laugh, then ended with a serious plea for whatever war effort needed most promotion in that area.

I was so emotional all the time that it was no trouble to be as eloquent as I am capable of being about the need for sacrifice and devotion. Sometimes after reading the letters from my listeners which told of their sons and husbands, missing or lost, I would come to the broadcast actually trembling with my desire to help.

When the war started I had hoped to do much more than just make speeches. Even before Pearl Harbor I had my heart set on being a nurse's aide. I went to see Mrs. Walter Lippmann, head of the Nurses' Aid Committee. She was charming but firm. She didn't *say* I weighed too much, only that she was sure I could do more good by making speeches. It was a great disappointment to me.

I helped sell thousands of dollars worth of bonds in nearby towns like Tarrytown, Westport, Connecticut, and Rockville Centre, Long Island; and even in Buffalo and Philadelphia. In Westport, I was auctioned off and eventually belonged to several hundred bond-buying Westport citizens. Usually we went at the bond selling in teams. Comedian Eddie Mayehoff, carried away by zeal, offered to work free as houseboy for a day for anybody who would buy $25,000 worth of bonds. When I saw him later, I asked him how he came out.

"Oh, the houseboy part was easy, but I had a little more trouble with the pigs."

In those days I often got impassioned and angry. So did Fannie Hurst. One day in 1943 she came to my microphone and denounced the "women of leisure who are simply not using to the limit their spare time in this effort. Mrs. Roosevelt said it best: 'There is no way to superimpose the psychology of the blitz upon an unblitzed people.'"

Fannie Hurst continued, "We are such an unpunished people; it's hard for a woman in Kansas to look up into the clear sky and say, 'Now I have to do something about this.' There is no threat that she can see, no sudden thrum of bombers coming to destroy her farm.

"And now I feel we are beginning to relax from that first white flame we felt on Pearl Harbor Day. We're beginning to relax to a point that is dangerous."

At this point I told Fannie a story Bob Considine told me. That industrious reporter, columnist, and feature writer had been touring war theaters. A young American army nurse was ministering to a desperately wounded man.

"I wouldn't have your job for a million dollars," a bystander said.

"Neither would I," she answered quietly.

One day when we were making a special plea for the Red Cross, Geraldine Farrar, that great lady, drove down from Ridgefield, Connecticut, to help us. What she said that day gave such a wonderful picture of what the small community with a dedicated leader can do (could do in peace, too, for a real cause) that I reproduce it here.

Miss Farrar, who had been retired for some time, came right out of retirement when the need arose.

"If you're persuaded of a mission you get the strength to go on almost beyond human endeavor but not really beyond because you are loaned something that comes definitely from another realm," she said.

"Our little village has 3800 people—340 lads in the service—a lot for a small village to give up. You miss that boy who is gone because you see his mother. She isn't just somebody you read about in the newspaper or somebody you hear a friend talk about; she sits beside you in the workroom, sharing what you do. We're just learning a little brotherly love because of this tremendous catastrophe that has thrown us all together. We shall make something out of it, but the sacrifice is tremendous for mothers, fathers, and sweethearts as well as the boys who go.

"Human nature won't take hints. It has to have an avalanche and the avalanche descends upon the innocent as well as on the guilty.

"A little village is a symbol of the best part of our United States just for the reason that we do know our neighbors. I have night classes of some Italian ladies, and I call it the Opera Table. We speak Italian, and they are beautiful workers. They come to the classes after their children are put to bed and their husbands sent off to their defense-plant jobs. They make most beautiful surgical dressings, but they are shy so I thought of the opera table and it has helped. We sing a little bit too.

"Somebody is taking on my duties at air-raid control today so that I can be here; somebody else is substituting for me on the ration board, which is a headache and I'm glad to give it over to them. We have home canteen and home nursing, first aid, and—by the way—we have a quota of 390 but a trained personnel of 448. Doesn't that speak well for us?

"No boy who goes from our town but gets his letter, his kit bag— some evidence from the home people who do not forget, no matter where he may be.

"My day? My only free time is Saturday afternoon when I listen to opera on the radio. I'm an early riser—you have to be because we have unheated houses so you get up with the sun and go to bed with it too. You keep warm and you keep well that way. Our people do not complain. When there's a blizzard we come in to work just the same, bundled up like Eskimos. Some pioneer ancestor lunges to the fore and gives an added push. I was born in New England, and if at the first fall of snow I have to wrap myself in cotton wool and run to Florida or California, then I'd better give up.

"To go on with my own day: I have my coffee and then I take the electric heater into the bathroom in order not to congeal entirely before I get dressed. Then I dash to the garage with my flashlight and unroll the garage door and push the car out—sometimes it needs a lot of pushing because it freezes. I go downtown and my working day begins at nine o'clock either in the workroom or at some spotting post, and at five-thirty I call it a day. I come home and have something hot —sometimes just hot water, since coffee and other pleasant things now are somewhat scarce. I go to bed at eight o'clock because that's the only place where I can keep warm!

"We gave two Christmas parties for all the workers. Our clergyman said a benediction and we sang songs, ate cookies, and had a charming time, quite like the quilting parties they used to have in my grandmother's day."

When I was in Ridgefield to sell bonds we went way over our quota, and I ended that triumphant evening standing between Geraldine Farrar and Marion Anderson, all of us singing "The Star-Spangled Banner."

That was a lift and I was grateful for it. Some days the war pressed down pretty hard. Robert Sherrod, correspondent returned from the South Pacific, said wearily to me: "I feel as if I've never written about anything but war."

Sometimes I felt as if we never talked about anything else either. Whoever the guest and however we started, we always came to war before we finished. Refugees and soldiers, reporters, diplomats, and entertainers—all talked about some face of war.

Actress Judith Evelyn, on the program because she had opened in a play on Broadway, soon began to tell about a memory that she said would forever haunt her. The ship on which she sailed back from England was torpedoed. She was packed with seventy-nine others into a lifeboat.

"The horrible unforgettable memory is of sitting on the edge of the boat with my feet slipping down the side and onto a baby lying in the bottom. I did everything I could in the cramped space to keep my feet away from the baby and was thinking, 'If I could only get it up and hold it on my knee!' But the mother didn't understand English and she was very seasick. Though I didn't know what she was saying, I could tell that she felt she must keep the baby close to protect it. So there seemed nothing for me to do except try desperately to keep my feet out of the way.

"When a rescue ship came up to us, our lifeboat got caught in the swirl of water from its propeller and went down. We had no life belts and there was little hope of anybody getting clear. Only eight of us did—seven, really, because one man died. The baby I tried to keep from crushing never had a chance."

Another actress, Lilli Palmer, had her baby during the worst of the London blitz. She said she was frightened but not as much as she would have been if they hadn't kept the cribs with the newborn babies under the beds of their mothers.

"That way we could look after them when the air raids came," Lilli pointed out.

"What could you do?" I asked.

"Why, we were there with them," she answered surprisedly.

"It's because I was so afraid of cellars when I was little," explained Luise Rainer, great star of an era before World War II, when I asked how she came to be so dedicated in her work for the United States Committee for the Care of European Children.

"My first memories are of rushing into a cellar whenever there were air-raid alarms in World War I. It was years before I found the strength and peace that a child needs so desperately. When this war began, my thoughts went to children and I resolved to try to help them escape some of my mental agony."

Setting for the scene violinist Albert Spalding described was a ward for shell-shocked soldiers. The great artist was playing for them. Suddenly a boy shuffled forward. "He reached for my two-hundred-year-old Stradivarius," the musician said, voice still muted by the memory. "I handed it over, my heart in my mouth. He stood there with it for what seemed an eternity. Finally he muttered, 'Break—break,' smiled, and gave the violin back. The doctor said those were the first words that boy had spoken in six weeks."

Spalding was not really surprised, since he had learned from experience that music has power to soothe the troubled breast. In addition to this therapeutic work for mentally disturbed servicemen, Spalding, who spoke Italian, broadcast short wave for the Office of War Information to Allied partisans and guerrillas in northern Italy.

"I explained what they were to do when the Mussolini government fell and how they could help when Allied forces landed in Italy."

Albert Spalding told one story that was at least a relief from the gloom of war. He sat next to the king of Italy at a dinner.

"There was a marvelous pastry for dessert and, not thinking, I took a second helping," he remembered ruefully. "Suddenly I realized that the chief chamberlain was fixing me with a chilly glare. I was the only one with a second helping of dessert. I wished I could slide the delectable trifle down my trouser leg, anything to be rid of it. But the king saw my dilemma, summoned the waiter, and asked for another pastry. Then the two of us solemnly ate our second helpings!"

On Thanksgiving Day, 1942, my guests were three with prices on their heads, each with a history of courageous opposition to a common enemy.

"Frankly I don't think bombings are very interesting. They bored me at last because they stopped me from working," said Kari Berggrav of Norway.

If anybody should have known about bombings it would have been pretty Kari, who had been through twenty-six of them at the time she faced me across the microphone. The other two guests were Boris Furlan, then under official sentence of death in Yugoslavia, and Bella Fromm, who had got out of Berlin just ahead of the Gestapo.

Within days after that program two physicists at the University of Chicago produced the first nuclear chain reaction, thus making 1942 an even more ominous year than it seemed to us then.

Kari, who had been a photographer with the Norwegian high command, counted as only one the bombing that lasted two days, and as for the shot that whistled through her fingers, she was reluctant even to mention it. I persisted.

"Well, I was in a little shack listening to the radio news and mimeo-

graphing it," she finally told me. "Three big English trucks were outside, and the Germans spotted them and began to shoot. The flimsy
shack was no protection so I started to run across the road to a shelter.
Too late—the bomber plane was upon me, so close I could see the
pilot's face. I lay flat in the road and they shot at me. One bullet
whizzed between my fingers on the left hand and another grazed my
hip."

One of Kari's jobs was cook on a fishing boat that brought part of
Norway's gold supply out of the country. It was a trip full of danger,
but Kari remembered best the stairway of gold bullion the boys built
to make it easier for her to get into the galley.

"The resistance in Norway came from all ages," the girl said proudly.
"A German truck loaded with captured Norwegian guns stopped at an
inn and sixty small boys from the neighborhood stole all the guns and
got them back to our side."

She couldn't give all the details then, but Kari's fantastic escape
brought her to Russia a month before war started there, then to Iran
and through the Persian Gulf to Bombay, around South Africa to
Capetown, and finally to Montreal, where she stayed at a Norwegian
pilots' camp.

She knew the young pilot who'd sat across from me a few days before to tell of his own escape, aided by courageous Norwegian friends.
I'd suggested that he omit names for fear of reprisals. His reply chilled
my blood.

"All those concerned have already been dealt with," he answered,
and there was no emotion in face or voice.

Kari listened without any change of expression and said only:
"That's how it is in war."

Boris Furlan, professor of political philosophy and jurisprudence,
declared that when he heard from a friend that he was under sentence
of death he had his first good sleep in months.

"There is satisfaction when the enemy recognizes you," he explained, "and I suppose I was a little gratified that I was important
enough to get a death sentence."

I remarked how wonderful it would be if someday the whole world
could celebrate Thanksgiving in unison. "Am I an optimist?" I asked.

Dr. Furlan assured me: "You *must* be an optimist, otherwise you
achieve nothing. But the whole world must collaborate to have the

good turkey on the table for everybody on the same day. When there is no starvation there will be a new world."

Bella Fromm, my third guest, wrote to a friend in 1923: "There is a new party in Germany that's causing plenty of trouble. It is led by a man called Adolf Hitler, and he seems to have a sort of hypnotic power."

Bella, a columnist then, had the unpleasant distinction of having her hand kissed by Hitler.

"It was in 1933, and he had been in power for three months," she told me. "Hitler always said he could smell a non-Aryan, but mine is not an Aryan hand—and he kissed it twice. I felt spoiled and poisoned. Though I hated him, I recognized his power over women."

The worst, she said, was what Nazism did to families. She told of happily married friends with three little sons. The boys became involved in the youth movement, and one day the eldest came home in his uniform and drew his knife on his mother when she asked him to perform some small chore. "His mother asked me, 'What shall I do?' but I told her it was too late."

Soon the Gestapo came to the house to ask of the father why he spoke against Hitler. They said: "We know everything. Your boy told us." When the father asked his son why he had done such a thing, the boy said: "First comes Germany, then comes Hitler, and then my family."

Another friend of Bella's, a well-known intellectual, gave a party to which he invited both Aryans and non-Aryans. The Gestapo arrested him and warned that if he again entertained Jews he would be sent to a concentration camp. He found that the informer was his own small grandson, who said it was his duty to report to the Gestapo that there had been Jews in the house.

"On my first Thanksgiving here," Bella recalled, "I worked as a waitress, and I had to carry in a turkey platter that must have weighed more than twenty pounds. But I was so happy in that job. It doesn't need a special day for me to give thanks I am in this country. Every morning I am grateful that I live in a land that is free."

I had already decided not to mention any products that day, and to my own surprise as we reached the end of the emotion-charged program I found myself talking to God about as I did to listeners.

"Dear God, please, please keep America the land of the free. Please keep it so that when we read our Declaration of Independence we do not put in any parenthetical exceptions where it says 'created free and equal.' Let it be the kind of country it was intended to be, please, dear God—a country for all races, all creeds, all heartbroken people; all people who haven't found a refuge anywhere else."

Stella arranged that the celebration of my tenth anniversary planned by NBC at Madison Square Garden should be an occasion for recruiting women for the war services and invited many of the celebrities who had been on the program to be guests of honor. Fred Waring agreed to be master of ceremonies and bring his famous band and choir. Billie Burke and Eddie Dowling promised to star in a play.

I went through my usual misgivings. We sent tickets and there were thousands more requests than there were tickets, but I somehow was sure that a catastrophe would keep everybody from coming.

The morning of the party was filled with telephone calls, telegrams, great masses of orchids, lilies of the valley, and roses. Perhaps I should have been reassured but I wasn't. As I put on my new navy blue dress with its white collar and cuffs that Nikki had so painstakingly fashioned for me, I got more and more jittery. By this time I absolutely knew there wouldn't be anybody there.

I was crying when I got downstairs and into the cab driven by a young man I called Red, who usually was waiting to take me to the studio. My driver's fiery hair was especially brushed, and he was all dressed up because he knew this was a great day. When he saw my tears he began anxiously trying to comfort me. I soon convinced him that the party was going to be a flop and nobody would be there.

"My wife will be there with my little girl," he consoled me. By that time he, too, was crying. So we drove sadly to Madison Square Garden and to a side door.

As I went in I saw a man I knew and said hopelessly, "There's nobody here." He agreed solemnly: "There's nobody here," then led me to the stage of Madison Square Garden. As I walked on I heard a roar of voices and the next thing I knew, 25,000 women (and a few men) were on their feet applauding and cheering. They *had* come after all.

One section was reserved for my own special Red Cross chapter (Queens County, New York), who in their uniforms formed a Victory V. Fred Waring introduced John Golden, who in turn introduced Mrs. Franklin Delano Roosevelt. She made a moving plea for women volunteers. (She also said two sentences that I cherish to this day: "I always rejoice when a woman succeeds. And when one succeeds superlatively, as you have done, Mary Margaret, it helps us all.")

Billie Burke, Eddie Dowling, Margaret Culkin Banning, César Saerchinger, Julia Shawell, Fannie Hurst, Robert St. John, John Roy Carlson, Adela Rogers St. John, and Margaret Bourke-White put in pleas for our cause.

All this time Fred Waring was doing a masterly job of keeping the show at high pitch, and when Niles Trammell, president of NBC, came on to say some pleasant words and give me a silver Lazy Susan from the network, Fred, with total lack of respect for rank, admonished him not to turn away from the microphone.

Mrs. Michael Schultz gave me a Red Cross identification bracelet from my chapter; Florence Smith a diamond microphone from New Jersey press women, and Joseph Auslander read a congratulatory poem he had written especially for me. I introduced my radio family: Stella, Mrs. D., Janice, Mildred, my redheaded nephew, Nikki, Hattie, Herman Smith, Patti Pickens. Fred Waring's chorus sang the "Battle Hymn of the Republic" and "The Time Is Now," and the hour was over.

The party went on, however, all afternoon, with Nikki's fashion show, Jane Pickens and Wilbur Evans singing, and introductions for Ralph Dumke, actor; novelist Homer Croy; actress Jessie Royce Landis; Bill Corum (sports columnist of the New York *Journal-American* and a schoolmate of mine from the University of Missouri); Russel Crouse (we had worked together on the *Evening Mail*); Harry Hershfield; John Sousa, grandson of John Philip; Edwin C. Hill; author R. V. C. Bodley, whose seven-year sojourn in the Sahara had fascinated me. I never knew exactly how many young women we recruited. I think the release of such statistics wasn't allowed, but the services told us the publicity was a help. And probably the fact that most war news was good now helped most of all. I went on speaking, selling bonds, until the war in Europe ended.

On June 6, 1945, a flustered page located Stella Karn.

"There's somebody in that line waiting to get in to the broadcast who looks a lot like General Bradley," he told her excitedly. He said he had tried to give this distinguished-looking man in uniform a seat but the woman standing beside him had said, "No, no—we'll just wait for Mary Margaret. We tried to send word that we'd like to hear her program today, but we couldn't reach her. We'll just wait."

Stella hurried out and it was Omar Bradley and his wife, Mary, with whom I'd gone to school in Missouri.

Here, standing in line for a broadcast, was the most headlined general after Eisenhower. War in Europe was ended, war with Japan still was on. Only a month before, on the morning of May 7, the news of Germany's surrender had reached the world.

When I got Omar Bradley before a microphone I asked what he had thought when he knew of the surrender.

"I don't remember all the things I was thinking, but I walked into headquarters and saw my cap with the four stars on it, lying on a map. Five years before I had been a lieutenant colonel in civilian clothes. Now I looked at the map with forty-three United States divisions stretching over a 640-mile front. I wrote the date on it—D Plus 335— and then I pulled down the blackout curtains and looked out the window at the spring morning."

It was on D Plus Two that General Bradley received a report from me in Normandy. His only daughter, Elizabeth, was married at West Point, and since her father was occupied elsewhere I went as the general's private reporter. I hadn't worked as hard on a piece of copy since my first story for a New York newspaper.

I did my report on the air, and NBC picked up the copy and sent it by one of our war correspondents to France.

"I was in my trailer about a mile in from the Normandy beach when the NBC man found me," General Bradley told me. "I sat under an apple tree to read it."

"I hope I got over to you how perfectly beautiful Elizabeth looked —blond and young and shining."

"You did—and I was mad all over again at missing my only daughter's wedding."

"I wondered what would happen when you became a four-star general, but you've stayed simple and natural," I said to Omar Bradley.

"I hope so," he said fervently. "I, too, thought that it might change a man to be a general—and I worried."

I'd heard that Bradley, known as the GI's general, was often so near the front that headquarters worried. He didn't deny it. "You have to get into the field with the men now and then," he explained. "Unless you know your men, unless you value their lives and unless you're tormented by what they're going through, you are not fit to command."

I asked whether a general's decisions were always based on such a high moral plane.

"Well, I believe you must try always to make a decision that will cost the least number of lives. Out in the field you see war for what it is —a wretched debasement of all the thin pretensions of civilization. It's not an adventure. Most of the time it is exactly what General Sherman in the Civil War said it was."

I asked about his meetings with the Russians, and he told how Marshal Koneff, receiving him at his headquarters, had a whole Red Army chorus singing our national anthem, and a corps of beautiful ballerinas to dance.

When Bradley commented admiringly, the marshal said: "Oh, just a few girls."

"So when Koneff came to return my visit and admired the marvelous technique of a thin man in khaki playing the violin, I tossed off: 'Oh, just one of our American soldiers.' I didn't add that we had borrowed this particular soldier for the occasion—and that his name was Jascha Heifetz."

I got Mary Bradley to the microphone then to ask what she planned to feed her husband during his brief home visit.

"Swiss steak with cream gravy," she answered promptly, "and apple pie with ice cream."

When we went to Toots Shor's nearby restaurant after the broadcast —walked because we couldn't find a taxicab—a parade gathered behind the tall, blue-eyed general.

At the restaurant, over his double order of ice cream, Omar Bradley told about a day when he and General Eisenhower were sitting by a roadside and a bunch of GIs came up with short snorters—those pasted-together dollar bills on which they collected autographs. "Would the generals sign?"

"So of course we did," said Omar. "I signed Brad and he signed Ike."

Though he didn't really say so, we could feel that General Bradley believed the war with Japan would end very soon.

It did. On September 2, 1945, Japan surrendered aboard the battleship *Missouri*. A few days later artist Clayton Knight, who was there as official artist, came to tell us about it.

"I had to be in a position to do my drawings," he explained, "so finally I climbed to the range control just under the radar equipment, pushed my sketching outfit on the range finder, and slid out after it, my legs tucked under.

"I was just in time because the Japanese were coming toward the *Missouri.* They looked shabby in the third-rate tugboat they'd been given, undressed, their shoes not shined. It took a long time for the old prince to get up the companionway—he's a cousin of the emperor's, old and quite lame. As General Sutherland started forward to meet them, I saw one of the Chinese generals grab his nose and hold it hard as the Japanese walked by.

"I couldn't tell how the Japanese were taking it. I studied their faces through my binoculars, and their expressions never changed. It was quite simply and quietly done. General MacArthur looked very impressive and did the job with great dignity."

Clayton Knight had promised Tex McCrary, then public-relations officer for our Air Force, that he'd try to include in his drawing some of our planes as they flew across.

"I was at the top of the ship, looking down, and I thought I hadn't a chance to see the airplanes above me. Then, just as the surrender was being signed, a B-29 swept across the top of the mast and cast its dramatic shadow over the ceremony."

I asked Clayton and all those connected with the war whom we interviewed after the bomb was dropped on Hiroshima whether we should have dropped it. To my surprise, since I felt so strongly that we shouldn't have done it, opinion was about evenly divided.

Serene-faced Father Hubert Shiffer gave us a firsthand report of what Hiroshima was like when the bomb fell.

"I had gone through so many bombing raids in Tokyo that I'd been sent off to Hiroshima for a rest," he said. "It was eight-fifteen in the morning, and I was reading the newspaper. There was no noise, no warning—just suddenly the room was filled with fire, there was a terrific flash and finally a crash as the room exploded. I was blown into the air and then I blacked out.

"After a while I began to realize that I was still alive, but I could not see and the silence was so complete that I thought I'd gone deaf as well as blind. It was like the end of the world concentrated in one city.

"At last I began to talk to myself and realized I was hearing my own voice plainly. That frightened me even more because then I couldn't understand the dreadful silence that had overtaken a whole city.

"Somehow I managed to crawl out of the debris. Our earthquake-proof building was so shattered that I could see straight through it. Then I heard the voice of our Father Superior asking: 'Are you still living?' And three voices replied: 'Yes.'

"When he saw me all black and bloody, with my clothes ripped off, he said I must get to a doctor, but the doctor's house was no longer there. We tried to locate the hospital, but everything was flattened. We couldn't even see streets. I was so close to bleeding to death that the Father Superior said I must leave and find aid for myself, while the others stayed to help the people around us.

"He said to me: 'If you get to heaven first, will you tell the Blessed Mother that we intend to rebuild this church?'

"I answered: 'You don't look too well yourself, so if you get to heaven first, will you deliver the message in person?'

"After that I just wandered about helplessly until a cart picked me up and took me to a first-aid station outside the city. The trip was so painful that once I asked to be laid beside the road to die in peace. But they refused. They had to cut more than eighty splinters of wood and glass from my body."

I suggested that since he had miraculously survived, it was fine that he could live in quiet and comfort here in New York.

"No," he answered quickly. "I am a missionary. I shall go back to Japan in the summer."

As soon as the war in the East ended we began getting firsthand reports of what prison camps in both Germany and Japan had been like. Agnes Newton Keith, who with her husband and two-year-old son George had been held by the Japanese for more than three years in Borneo, gave the most vivid account.

"That first night after we were brought to the island we had no food or water, for we were afraid to drink from the tank outside. There were no fires, beds, baths, or lights. Our children were weary, frightened, crying, clinging to us tightly.

"A few days later we were addressed by Japanese commanding officers: 'You are a fourth-class nation now and you will be treated as such. In the past you have had proudery and arrogance. You will get over that now.'

"There was no furniture; we slept and ate on the floor. Centipedes lived under us and rats lived over us. The rats ate soap and buttons as well as food and bit our bare feet in the dark.

"To eat we had mainly broken rice with powdered lime in it to keep the weevils out (it didn't), and a green vegetable that had to be swallowed in ropes because it could not be chewed. The children got dysentery, malaria, worms, skin diseases; and sanitary conditions were unspeakable."

Mrs. Keith herself contracted beriberi from undernourishment and her body swelled. Then she got boils. The years were a dreary monotony of dreadful food, hard physical labor, disease, and often pain inflicted by the captors.

This was Mrs. Keith's credo voiced after the war was over and she and her family had survived.

"I believe that: While we have more than we need on this continent, and others die for want of it, there can be no lasting peace. When we work as hard in peacetime to make this world decent to live in, as in wartime we work to kill, the world will be decent and the causes for which men fight will be gone."

I had asked Omar Bradley then about my going to Europe as soon as the war in Japan was over, and he thought it would be a good idea. I had wanted to go to the war zone long before the end, only it was obvious I would have been more of a hindrance than a help. But now Stella, too, liked the idea and made arrangements. Nikki, who hadn't seen her family during the war years, came along.

I talked to everybody—taxi drivers, chambermaids, hotel clerks, shopgirls. I would interview a woman in the afternoon, speak about her over the air from London, Paris, or Berlin in the evening. I tried to give a picture of human beings who had been hurt by a terrible war— men, women, and children who might have been us.

It wasn't easy. The shocks kept hammering at my mind and heart. In two weeks I lost fifteen pounds—which certainly never happened to me before. After I saw the people and listened to them and stood for hours in their food lines I felt as if I would have no right to anything I called mine until I had made some effort to help. I didn't know all the political issues involved, but I couldn't see why those issues shouldn't be made simpler. Here in the United States we seemed safe and secure, but I decided we were like a little oasis in the desert and I believed the desert would swallow us up unless we did something to stop it spreading. I felt that even if we had been unwilling to help those people (which God forbid), we *had* to do it to save ourselves.

In London I found so much wreckage—a little church that I had loved gone, a gaping hole where there'd been a hotel I'd stayed in, the little flower shop of my old friend, Constance Spry, with windows boarded and the roof a sieve for rain and weather after being bombed four times.

Constance wore a dress she had bought on her last visit to the United States nine years before, and it was her best. Her underwear was ribbons, her household linen rags. I had brought her a box of chocolates. She and her friends were excited about them, but after they had eaten only a few candies they tried not to let me know that they were ill. The confection was too sweet and too rich. Their stomachs hadn't known anything like it for years.

But desperate as conditions were in London, they were worse in Paris. At least in England everybody had a part of what there was to have. In France there was inequality, probably because of the black markets.

I saw a blanket burned full of holes and with the binding torn away offered for sale at $75. A man's threadbare suit of clothes was $90. A friend paid $18 for a chicken to serve at a dinner for guests.

And Monette Michou, Nikki's sister, who had been living in Paris throughout the six years of German occupation and what came before and after, had absolutely nothing in her pantry. She got together the best dinner she could to welcome her sister and me. It consisted of brown bread and an infinitesimal pat of butter with tea Nikki had brought from New York. Then Monette brought out a tiny apple tart she had made—by what sacrifice I can't imagine—and watched with anxious eyes as we ate to see if we liked it. It was contrived somehow without sugar and shortening. It was the most awful and most beautiful little apple tart that ever was and forever will symbolize for me six years of sacrifice, courage, and hope. Monette's hands, once soft and well cared for, looked as if they would never be white again. Her nails were blackened and broken. It's a many-times-told tale now, but then it hurt almost unbearably.

In German-occupied Paris the Gestapo used to take Jewish children away, Monette told me. No one knew where, no one ever saw them again. They came for the three little girls of Monette's neighbor. Screaming and tearing out her hair, the mother dragged the children to an upstairs window, threw them into the street, one by one. Then she flung herself from the window and died with her children. Monette told everything in a flat, almost unconcerned way that made the horrors seem more horrible. It was as if she had stopped feeling.

I thought nothing could be worse than France, but when the B-17 assigned to fly me to Germany landed me there, I decided this was the most upsetting part of the tour. I went about with a feeling of dread. I couldn't overcome fear of what I kept hearing about the German character. Reporter though I was, I had no heart to get into conversation even with the woman who ran the house in which I was quartered in Berlin. It was her house and she stayed in the attic.

The plane had a crew of five, full of high good humor now that the war was over. Veterans of dozens of bombing missions, they would look down as we passed over a city leveled and all but wiped from the earth. "We did that one," they would comment casually. I couldn't see that their experiences had made them much different from American youngsters who hadn't been to war.

Once we struck a stretch of rough going, and I discovered to my horror that both pilot and co-pilot were asleep. I was out of my seat in the quickest move I've ever made, to shake them awake. They were already shaking—with laughter! They were teasing me. They thought it was so funny that I had to pretend to agree. But I didn't get over it for hours. I wonder where they are now, bless them—darling boys every one. Lt. Richard Warren, S/Sgt. John Coch, Lt. Lyle Wade, S/Sgt. Thomas Vincent, and Lt. Byron Smith . . . hail, wherever you are.

Roy Porter, NBC foreign correspondent, who had me in charge and arranged every detail expertly, must have groaned when he got the assignment, but though he ruled me with a will of iron he never let me feel that I was a tough job. He interested General James Gavin of the 82nd Airborne Division in our project, and the general who became and has remained my hero gave me a scarf (it was my dearest possession), made from a parachute, that I wore around my head for the weeks I was in Europe. Boarding our B-17 was no easy task for a woman, especially one my size. It was a combat ship with bucket seats and no gangway. At first it took the whole crew to push and prod me aboard, but as I lost weight and got more agile I was able to manage by myself.

I wore a navy blue suit throughout the trip, and one night in Berlin, at the Press Club, although only one other woman was there, I came up against the stiffest competition of my life—Marlene Dietrich, in a bronze dinner gown that looked as if it had come straight from Paris and she looked poured into it. She'd been overseas for some time, entertaining our troops, traveling in trucks, jeeps, and combat planes. She had nearly died of pneumonia and almost lost her hands from frostbite, but she was chic, beautiful, and unruffled.

Getting back to America was a relief but also a painful reminder of the contrast between them and us. A Montclair, New Jersey, church asked me to talk from the pulpit one Sunday morning about what I had seen, and afterward several other churches invited me. I tried my best, but it wasn't possible to get over to relatively well-fed, well-housed Americans the suffering I had felt firsthand. How could I make a woman fretful about meat coupons understand Yvonne of France, who said, very simply: "Of course my baby died. I couldn't keep him warm, I couldn't keep him fed, I couldn't even keep him dry. I just had to watch him die."

To realize what had happened to the Dutchwoman in the displaced persons' camp, one had to look into her eyes as I had done when she told me in a dead-level voice: "I had a husband and two sons. My husband was taken away, and my older son went into the army. I do not know whether they live now. One day my little boy went out in the yard to play and when I called him, he did not come. They took him away, and I shall never see him again. I shall never see any of them again." I wonder if she ever has.

Back in America, at my microphone I said on that broadcast recorded fifteen years ago: "It's wonderful to be back—to be in my apartment on Central Park South; to brush my teeth with water I can use with safety; to have orange juice for breakfast; wash with a cake of soap that doesn't feel like sandpaper.

"My friend Juliette Nicole went with me, and I saw her when it burst upon her what had happened in her city of Paris, her country of France. She cried and kept saying: 'I knew but I never realized.' So when all of you keep hearing people say, 'Oh, France and her hard-luck stories—and now they've got their hands out saying gimme, gimme . . .' well, what do you know of it unless you've had six years of semistarvation, heatless homes, fear, and shame? One woman I talked to, Goldie Antignac, said she couldn't have borne it if she had known beforehand what it would be like. Her six years seemed endless walking, standing in queues for a bit of fish and then when they got to her, the fish was gone and she walked somewhere else and stood in another queue, and at the end of the day she was lucky if she could buy a turnip and some bread.

"It hurts to remember the look in the eyes of the people who had been in concentration camps. A woman told me what she minded most was not the physical torture but what the whole degrading experience did to them as human beings. She said, 'I knew a prisoner who killed one of his cellmates for bread. That's what can happen to human beings.'

"In Germany the best houses had been taken over by the victorious Americans, French, English, and Russians. I was billeted in the home of a German woman. It is a strange, disturbing experience. She is paid by her own burgomaster and was supposed to look after my comforts. You bring your own towels. I didn't, so I used my petticoat.

"Many of the Germans are living in ruins. They have no coal, and you see them in the woods and parks hunting for wood. Many will die this winter. I had the impression that my landlady hadn't wanted the war. But maybe I was wrong. I remember one correspondent staying in a house like mine. His landlady came on a book in his room, on methods of dealing with war criminals, and she was furious.

"You find law and order on the surface, but you hear stories of looting and black markets. You see men selling matches and chocolate. I heard that a carton of cigarettes might bring as much as $15."

I agreed with John Hersey that the role of an occupying nation is an uneasy one. Hersey's hero in A Bell for Adano—Major Joppolo—was sent to the little Italian town of Adano as chief officer of our Allied Military Government. With him were Americans, some stupid and selfish, none really very bad.

Said John: "What this man was able to do in one town represented, in miniature, what America can and cannot do in Europe. Major Joppolo was a good man. That's why I wrote about him—because we all have need of him. He is our future, more important than treaties and theories on paper and even stirring speeches—because these can't guarantee us anything. Only men can guarantee, only the behavior of men under pressure."

I was constantly crying out against war those days and trying to find somebody with a remedy. That wise man and great photographer, Edward Steichen, did not believe rehearsing the attendant horrors would ever stop men fighting.

"The smell of rotting human flesh won't do it—it simply revolts us and makes us want to forget. I think only a universal consciousness of how wrong and stupid it is, can do away with war."

He believed pictures could help and had been dreaming for years of an exhibition to show ordinary, everyday life all over the world—not automobiles, chromium iceboxes, and fancy trickery, but life . . . the sweetness of home and family, children and schools.

"Even in places where life is primitive these things have an inner beauty," he declared. "Such pictures will make us conscious of how wonderful is what we have. I'm not sure about the value of our high standard of living. Sometimes I wonder whether it isn't destructive— whether it doesn't keep us from being sensitive to the really sweet things of life."

In October of 1945, former Secretary of the Treasury Henry Morgenthau, Jr., had a plan, too—quite different from Mr. Steichen's. His concerned the future of Germany. He told of being with Franklin D. Roosevelt at Warm Springs the night before the President died and talking about the Morgenthau plan for postwar Germany.

"The President said, 'Bring it out'—but I am afraid it will never be brought out now. Yet Germany must be deindustrialized. The important industrial centers are in the British zone and they must be taken apart. We must not make the same mistake we made in World War I when we left Germany intact with her factories. We know now that at the end of the First World War, Germany was already planning the next one. And it's the same now. Laboratories and factories have been left intact so that jets and bombs can be produced."

Mr. Morgenthau's idea was that we ought to make Germany a strictly agricultural community.

"I'll be asked what to do with the men who understand technology so well. I'd simply put them where they can't make the weapons they know so much about. Most of them were Nazis anyhow. So let's replace them with American chemists; let's transport the factories to Holland and to other countries."

It was interesting to hear again on the recording what Mr. Morgenthau said in 1945.

"If we carry out the Potsdam agreement, Germany will not be made to suffer as it has made other countries suffer. Franklin Roosevelt thought that Russia had demonstrated her desire to be a member of the family of nations. But many people in the United States say and write opinions which must give the Russians cause for suspicion of us. If the Russians felt that their neighbors did not want to wage war against them, then I think they'd be glad to stay within their own borders."

One night during the forming of the United Nations at the San Francisco Conference in 1945, Stella called me on the telephone. "I want Eleanor to tell you something she's just told me." She put Eleanor Wilson McAdoo on:

"My sister Margaret was sitting with Father the day before he died," she began. "He had been very sick. She thought he was asleep. His eyes were closed. Suddenly he seemed to rouse and she heard him say: 'You know, daughter, it was right that this country did not join the League of Nations—no, I haven't gone mad. Listen, Margaret, you must remember this. If this country *had* joined the League of Nations when I asked the people to it would have been a personal victory for me—but I know now, it wouldn't have worked. They weren't really convinced. They didn't really believe. I think God knew better than I did. The next plan will be better than my plan and the American people will join it, believing with all their hearts in it and trying hard to make it work.'"

Then Eleanor Wilson McAdoo added: "I think my father was right, Mary Margaret, but how we have to believe and how we have to work! It will be hard."

Then to me: "You have a great obligation. You sit before a microphone and out there people listen to you. We all have to work, but the people in radio and television and on newspapers, they have to work harder than anybody else. I want you to think of that always, Mary Margaret, of the obligation laid upon you."

I said, through tears, "Eleanor Wilson, I accept that. I'll care for nothing except a good peace, a right peace, a working peace for this world. I'll take this as a sacred charge from your father, Woodrow Wilson."

In the strangest way I did feel a sense of dedication. I wish I might have done more.

I was haunted by the endless stream of homeless people all over the world, moving from place to place, going nowhere because they had no place to go. I learned much during the war years about the human spirit and its incredible powers of survival, perhaps never more vividly described than by Leo W. Schwarz, soldier, social worker, writer.

"The lesson we get from these people who must flee from place to place is not from their suffering but from their extraordinary vitality and resiliency," he pointed out. "To those of us who are anxious about the world and the atomic age, there is inspiration and hope in their stories. The people who have suffered so much prove that you can live through anything and even live through it with grace.

"I met a man in Munich who told me how he and three friends lived in underground bunkers in Poland from 1933 to 1944. They couldn't have survived without help, but some of the fine, simple farm people took their lives in their hands by bringing these men the news from the outside world, throwing slips of paper down into the bunkers, telling them of the fall of Stalingrad, the Allied occupation of Rome. They set up a little communication system between bunkers and worked out a code so they could invite each other to dinner and exchange ideas and opinions. In those eleven years they never gave up.

"When I met this man he had collected every scrap of paper, every tiny poster they'd made, the notes they'd written, the stories they told —and last year he shipped it all to Israel where he has set up a little printing press and is full of high hope, looking to a sunny future in his own land."

Leo Schwarz told of a mother who had managed to keep her baby alive somehow in the dreadful death camp at Belsen. Then, just forty-eight hours before the liberation, the child's face turned blue, the pulse seemed to vanish. But the mother would not give up. She held the child in her arms, and when the liberators came doctors were able to save the little one's life. Today both are healthy and happy in Israel.

He quoted from the fourteenth chapter of Job: "There is hope of a tree, if it be cut down, that it will sprout again and that the tender branch thereof will not cease. Though the root thereof wax old in the earth, and the stock thereof die in the ground; yet through the scent of water it will bud, and bring forth boughs like a plant."

## 9. EVERYTHING HAPPENED TO ME

*"She was new at radio and so was I. We at WOR had some free time
and wanted a woman's program to fill the hour . . . The experts said
her technique was deadly and her voice impossible, but we had a
hunch she was something new and different in radio. . . ." Theodore C. Streibert at Yankee Stadium*

For a long time her friend Poppy Cannon, writer and food expert,
had been urging Stella to take the program to the Virgin Islands
where, she said, people tired of tension, noise, and crowds were relaxing in an atmosphere of peace and beauty. So on a March day we
flew away from bleak, cold rain in New York to land twelve hours
later in a world of soothing sunshine, emerald hills, green-blue water
that was sometimes almost opaque, like a semiprecious stone that combined jade, aquamarine, and sapphire. This was the little town of
Charlotte Amalie in St. Thomas and I'll never forget our relief when
Poppy, down to meet us, relieved us of our heavy fur coats that had
felt good at La Guardia but now were an embarrassment. Marjorie
Evans and Marion Thayer came, too—for the ride, they said.

We stayed in a house with great white pillars and a porch overlooking white sailboats on the Caribbean. At night the stars were silver
candles and there seemed always to be a full moon, like a stage setting.
The town in the valley had red-roofed houses in peacock blue and
cobalt, with jalousies and wrought-iron balconies. I fell in love with
the country people, coming to town or going home on winding mountain roads, baskets balanced on their heads. That first day one woman
even carried a letter on her head. The wind came up and she put a
stone on the letter to hold it down. All along the roads were wonderful
trees: the flamboyant with black pods, Brazilian rose tree with yellow

flowers, Mexican tulip, mahogany, cork, kapok (for stuffing mattresses), cannon (with a pod that explodes), calabash (called "woman's tongue" because the leaves rattle when there's a strong wind, candle cactus with a sort of candelabra effect, and at night the fragrance of jasmine everywhere.

Governor Hastie, a fine man, welcomed us and confirmed the report that there are only about ten degrees' difference between winter and summer temperature—and no mosquitoes. Later he also made clear something more important—that the matter of race was not important in the Virgin Islands. People got along as human beings and nobody paid attention to color of skin. It was a real demonstration of democratic living without tension, without race consciousness.

I'd like to go back and watch again the people coming in at 3 A.M. riding on their jack and jenny asses for the outdoor market with strange foods—plantain, papayas, mangoes, sugar apples, custard apples, soursops, geneps (small berries, very sweet and good), tanya, pigeon peas ("eat them and you come back to the Virgin Islands"), gooseberries that grow in bunches on trees.

I ate all the unusual fruits and goathead soup, stewed cashews, soursop sherbet, herring gundy (served on Good Friday without vinegar because Christ was given vinegar on the cross), man soup that men take when they go to work in the fields and heat over a fire they build.

A gentle, lovely place, the Virgin Islands, when I saw it. I was told that many tourists came afterward as a result of our broadcasts. I hope they haven't ruined the rare charm that I felt strongly and tried to describe.

Hardly, it seemed to me, were we unpacked from the Virgin Islands safari, when Stella arranged with Gladys Petch of the Norwegian Information Service for me to open the new Norwegian broadcasting short-wave system (very high-powered to reach Norwegian sailors on distant seas) with a series of live hour programs over the four thousand miles of ocean that separate Norway and America. I had been decorated by King Haakon some time before, and Stella said it would be nice for me to thank the king in person. So off I went again—this time with Gladys Petch (very amiable and Norwegian-speaking) for a traveling companion.

Stella regretfully stayed in New York to attend to business, taking comfort in the thought that the program was going places even if she wasn't. She was an indefatigable slave driver, even four thousand miles away. She knew me for a lazy sight-seer and was determined I shouldn't miss anything. Every day she checked rigidly on my schedule.

I got to Oslo just in time for Norway's Day of Independence celebrated May 17 with the booming of cannon at dawn from the fourteenth-century fort and fifty thousand children in the bright colored costumes of their districts, marching in a great parade accompanied by sixty bands. I watched from the palace plaza, and on a balcony above stood the king in a high hat which he continually doffed to the children who shouted "Long Live the King!" as they passed. One little girl was in a wheel chair and another limped, but though there were no fat little boys and girls they all looked well cared for and healthy. I knew how much they had suffered during the occupation, and what the Norwegians had been able to do in the way of recovery seemed unbelievable to one who had recently seen the gaunt, pitiful children in displaced persons' camps.

All nature helped with the show that day. The sky was bright blue, the sun was golden, and everywhere were blooming lilacs, tulips, chestnut and apple trees. The kind Norwegians showed me fjords and waterfalls, mountains and celebrities, including explorer Bernt Balchen, their great national hero.

The king was as hospitable as everybody else. The car that was sent for me arrived fifteen minutes late, and I fumed because Mrs. J. Borden Harriman, once our minister to Norway, had told me what a flutter of protocol and etiquette she was in at her first audience with the king. She even had to change the dress she'd bought especially for the occasion. It wasn't dark enough or long enough, and she stressed that you must be on time for royalty.

The crown prince, whom I saw first, looked pointedly at his watch, but King Haakon didn't appear to have time on his mind at all. Except for tardiness and forgetting my white gloves, I was dressed according to regulations in a navy blue dress, dark enough and long enough.

The king seemed to know about my work and said graciously that he had heard my voice and that it was familiar to his people. He added, "We are all glad you have come."

We talked about farming, as I had already done with the crown prince, and about the war. King Haakon made several comments about world leaders that I wrote down but didn't talk about because I considered them said off the record. I was saving them for this book, but I put them away so carefully that now I can't find them.

I told the king that some of his subjects had bragged to me about what a fine man he was and how much they loved him. It may not have been protocol, but I'm sure kings enjoy compliments, just like anybody else. He smiled and recalled an incident that happened during the occupation, when he and his government were in England. In the Norwegian schools the children were not allowed to speak or write about the royal family, but one little boy, assigned to produce a composition, selected King Haakon as his subject. The teacher told him to write instead about cats. The child obeyed but finished off his essay with, "Cats don't have such a good time now in Norway as when the king was here, for then they got good meat to eat."

Before my week of broadcasting was finished I had adopted Norway as my second country. I liked the intelligence and the straightforward attitude of the people. They seemed to like me, too, but they are more formal than we are, and I think the casualness of my method was a little shocking at first.

"Of course you and that lady in New York [meaning Stella] weren't on the air when you had that—that—conversation about the music," ventured one spectator hopefully, after Stella and I had exchanged heated words over the four thousand miles. When I assured him that we were indeed on the air and added, "Our program is like that," he went away shaking his head.

After Norway, Stella's next enthusiasm was television. She had me sold to five sponsors and had a time spot before she even consulted me. I had been on many of the early experimental television shows in heavy sun-tan make-up that dripped off me as the lights beat down, but my own nighttime program following Milton Berle was something else. Before I began I wanted to do it and then I didn't want to, and after I got going I knew I really didn't want to—but I had to finish out the thirteen weeks.

"If you plan to stand up and walk from here to there, we must know the exact time," the director would inform me. "Do you think it will be all right to set it at nine-fourteen and three quarters?"

I would wail despairingly that my program was ad lib. How could

I know what would be happening at nine-fourteen and three quarters? They drew chalk lines to establish positions, they poked cameras at me, they set up prompting boards which I couldn't see without my glasses; and in the end, after the rehearsal, we ad-libbed while the control room went mad and Stella kept calling the camera shots and explaining: "Mary Margaret never followed a script in her life—just take it easy, and shoot her the way you would a baseball game!"

The program which shook the TV staff most profoundly involved a mud turtle which had its own room at the Waldorf, a praying mantis which almost got eaten on the air by a marmoset, and a lovebird that said "good-by" at the start of the program and "hello" at the end. And a toucan that bit me.

Even for that program the director insisted upon a rehearsal. One of my favorite naturalists, Edwin Way Teale, had brought his prize praying mantis. This creature with his eerie ability to turn his head and stare with popeyes looked quite improbable in a close-up. The cameramen were so enchanted when he stood on a microphone and pounded out a drumlike rhythm that they kept him doing it. Finally Edwin warned: "I do have a stand-in mantis in this box and if you tire this one I'll have to use him, but I warn you, he has no personality. His close-ups will be terrible."

At this point the marmoset, a tiny, bad-tempered monkey, was brought on by Ivan Sanderson, another of my favorite nature men. Ivan moved into the camera, marmoset on his shoulder. Just then the little monkey caught sight of the tap-dancing mantis. Here was an unexpected banquet, and he leaped through the air toward the juicy morsel. Just in time Edwin snatched his prize from the hungry jaws. The marmoset, seething with frustration, got himself into such a state that a quiet studio had to be found where he could rest in complete silence until show time. By then I was as upset as any of my creeping, crawling cast and I went home to a quiet room.

Meantime, Stella had decided to present for the first time a mud turtle which had earned some local fame by living in a glass jar under scientific observation. The turtle was an unremarkable-looking creature but valuable to science because it was the only one of whose habits a complete record had been kept from birth. So when Stella telephoned to ask the owner to bring over his pet she was told that this could be done only if the turtle need not make the round trip in a single day. That was when Stella, with her eye for news and her unfailing showmanship, put the turtle up at the Waldorf-Astoria Hotel!

The show went pretty well, people said, although I was at such a pitch of anxiety that I couldn't tell. The toucan, with his outrageous coloring and pirate's profile, was a sensation with the public—especially when he leaned down and took a swipe at me . . . funny on camera but personally upsetting since it missed my left eye by inches. The lovebird, looking angelic, said "good-by, good-by, good-by" every time anyone gave it a chance, and at the end of the program when I told it, "*Now, now* you can say good-by," the perverse thing cocked its head and squalled, "Hello, hello, hello."

I think we did a good deal of innovating on our television series. We had a program on humor which starred Bennett Cerf, Ilka Chase, and Ogden Nash (Ogden read his own wonderful poetry)—their first time before any cameras, years before "What's My Line" and the like were even gleams in producers' eyes. We did a foreign-correspondent show with famous newspapermen who talked prophetically about Russia.

We staged a dinner party at which the distinguished guests cooked. Actor-singer Burl Ives, in an overwhelming chef's cap, presided over a mulligan stew at a shiny new electric stove. He said he had to have sherry for the concoction, and since Stella was masterminding the show it was, of course, not cheap cooking sherry but Bristol Cream. The first bottle vanished mysteriously during rehearsal, and Stella promptly locked up the stand-in bottle until show time.

Crosby Gaige, the famous gourmet and expert on herbs and spices, did the hors d'oeuvres, and Lucile Watson brought a roast chicken which she refused to cook on camera. I suspect she had it done at her local delicatessen, but anyhow it looked properly brown and tender.

Dessert was being created by James Montgomery Flagg, the noted artist and illustrator whose shaggy white eyebrows were a sure-fire camera stopper. The party got under way with me nervously trying to guide table talk and at the same time keep an eye on the kitchen to my right. During a conversational lull I said brightly to Lucile Watson, "I know you acted with John Barrymore—you loved him, didn't you?"

"Oh no, my dear," she contradicted in her throaty voice. "I couldn't bear him. He was a dreadful man. He got drunk—he didn't give cues. I *loathed* him."

At this point James Montgomery Flagg, eyebrows awag with indignation, leaned across the table and roared, "Who's talking about my friend Jack? There's no actor—and no *actress*—could hold a candle to him." Lucile came back with, "Well, I could tell you things . . ."

A free-for-all seemed to be threatening so I pushed back my chair, signaled for the camera to follow me, and rushed into the kitchen to talk to a surprised Burl Ives, who was caught with the soup ladle in his mouth, testing his stew. By now the control room was in hysterics and the viewing audience was having a lovely time. I glanced at the clock and thanked heaven we had only a few minutes to go. Burl and I were trading theories about the origin of mulligan stew when across the kitchen stage loomed the figure of James Montgomery Flagg.

"My dessert," he moaned. "You've spoiled it. You turned off the oven and it's nothing but soup—and that's how you'll have to eat it too." Grimly he took hold of the too-hot baking dish and bore his creation to table. Last seen, my TV dinner guests were valiantly coping with a soupy sort of custard—which they were eating with forks!

In retrospect our thirteen weeks in the impossible position of following Milton Berle, then at the height of his popularity, were not so bad. I remember Pearl Primus, the talented Negro dancer and folklore specialist, singing a Calypso she'd invented for me—this long years before Harry Belafonte. And the beautiful dancing of the then young, unknown Destine from the West Indies. And the language of drums explained by two talented artists recently arrived in Harlem. There was a Far East program, too, with Nobel prize winner Pearl Buck sitting beside me in a theater box built on our set, talking about the philosophies of the Orient while a gilt and brocaded dancer performed on stage.

I had insisted that my eleven-year-old nephew Tommy help with the commercials. One night when the time came for a plate of cookies to be brought up, I discovered that Tommy had quietly eaten them all off stage. Luckily, that made an even better commercial than the script called for.

I suppose the show that most delighted everybody but me was the one in which we were presenting such weird underseas characters as the piranha—tiny, murderous fish of South America known to reduce a man to bones within minutes of his immersion in their waters—and an ugly-looking electric eel. Whatever made me, I don't know (yes, I do know—the urge to have the best possible show); anyway, at the end of the program I walked over to the tank and touched the eel. We left the air with me leaping a foot off the floor and uttering most undignified squeals.

My reviews were mixed—some very good, but Jack Gould, the critic of the important New York *Times*, gave me a bad notice and I was rebuked by an NBC vice-president for answering him back on the air. All the same, while I wrote Jack Gould that I thought he was partly right, I think some of our programs were better than many that are on right now.

Almost ten years later when I substituted for Jinx Falkenburg on the Tex and Jinx show, while Jinx covered the Grace Kelly wedding in Monaco, I applied some of the knowledge I'd learned the hard way. I wouldn't rehearse. I insisted that my guests not talk to me or anybody else before we went on the air. I wouldn't let the show be gimmicked up with things to look at unless they added to the program content. I thought, and still do, that people—what they think, how they've lived, what they've done—are infinitely more interesting than conversation-wrecking items the producer thinks will look well on camera. And apparently producers have finally come to the same conclusion.

We had offers, and Stella would have tackled television again if she had been well. She was always restless when we weren't doing something new and challenging. She would have liked us to broadcast from different places every day, and when Poppy Cannon arranged for the government of Haiti to invite us there, of course we went. President Estimé welcomed us in his great white palace, bigger even than our White House, with its mahogany floors, exquisitely carved chandeliers, paintings and sculptures by Haitians. President Estimé had asked his people to do everything they could for us, and Madame Maria Franco, I thought, reached the apex of hospitality. She moved out of her little house, redecorated it, and gave it to Stella and me, with two pretty girls to look after us, for the whole of our stay.

Poets made poems for us, song writers created songs especially in our honor, and all day long musicians drummed and chanted them

to us. It was carnival time, the first since the war. Parades were everywhere, and whenever I woke in the night I could hear the beat of the
cowhide drums and sometimes my name being chanted. Our wire recorder, manned by faithful Harry Harman, broke down now and then
and once, we suspected, put out of commission the entire electrical
system of Port-au-Prince, but Harry with unfailing good humor saw
that everything was fixed up and we went on. Anne Kennedy, an old
friend then living in Haiti, Edith Efron, a Brooklyn girl married to a
Haitian, and Jean Brierre, Secretary of State, were particularly helpful
in those crowded days during which Stella Karn still found time to
pull off a romance between our beloved Harry Harman and Jeanne
Perkins, who had researched me for a *Life* magazine profile and become my friend in spite of it.

Stella had invited Jeanne, who was on vacation, to spend the Mardi
Gras period with us in Port-au-Prince. She had confided to me that
Jeanne and Harry were just right for each other and she always claimed
that they fell in love the minute they looked at each other. Jeanne
says no, it was propinquity. After everybody else went to bed they
sat up until dawn—under my window, so I know—talking about life
and love. Jeanne claims the rest of it was the fact that Harry, six feet
two and known as athletic, wrote poetry and painted in secret—"and
longed for somebody to ignore his muscles and appreciate his mind."
While she, on the other hand, with a Phi Beta Kappa key and a reputation for a fine mind, had been waiting for someone who would just
say she was pretty instead of smart. So she was enchanted when Harry
told her he found her more attractive with her mouth shut. Best of
all, she thought his rather impractical dream of living on a houseboat
and starting a business in the Virgin Islands with only the savings
from his navy pay as capital was a fine idea. So they flew to the Virgin
Islands and astounded both sets of parents with cablegrams which
said that they had just married each other. Up to then, Jeanne's
parents had never heard of Harry Harman and Harry's mother and
father had been equally unaware of Jeanne's existence.

The Harmans started a glass-bottomed boat business and now have
a prosperous sight-seeing business and a daughter to whom Stella Karn
became godmother.

A few days after we came back from Haiti, Stella telephoned. "It's
about time we started talking about your fifteenth-anniversary party

at Yankee Stadium," she said casually. I shrieked, "Yankee Stadium!" "Of course," soothed my manager.

There was no "of course" about it to me, and for days I kept putting obstacles in the way which Stella demolished unhurriedly as they came along. Soon she was putting on extra girls to take care of the ticket requests.

It's history now—extra policemen, special subway trains with banners on the sides reading "To Mary Margaret McBride's Yankee Stadium," the official police count that showed fifty-four thousand persons checked in. It was a hot sunny day, the loud-speaker often failed, there were dead spots where nobody could hear anything, half the hundreds of celebrities who came (invited, too, by Stella and me— well, Stella anyway) didn't get on the air. Some of them resent it to this day, and I don't blame them. I was more miserable than anybody. Fannie Hurst says that when she came I was being serenaded by Scotch highlanders who were waiting to pipe in Mrs. Roosevelt.

"Isn't it wonderful, Mary Margaret?" Fannie enthusiastically greeted me. "Just look over there at those vacant seats," I commanded furiously. "I don't believe there're more than forty-five thousand people in this place!"

Whether I was happy or not, the program began. Fred Waring was master of ceremonies, his band and chorus were on hand for the music.

Fred Waring—to a thunder of applause ("Mary Margaret calls him her favorite man in all the world," buzzed the listeners)—"This is the biggest anniversary party I have ever attended! I'd like to give you a picture of Yankee Stadium where we are now. We're on a huge platform on the Yankee diamond. Mary Margaret McBride has just been piped aboard by Scotch bagpipers. Here on the platform are hundreds of distinguished guests come to wish Mary Margaret a happy fifteenth anniversary. The dean of photographers, the dean of radio commentators, the greats of sports, radio, screen, stage, Pulitzer prize winners, cartoonists, musicians, composers, a visitor from the Solomon Islands, an eighty-four-year-old lady wearing a forty-five-year-old dress, poets, the most famous partygiver, psychologists, psychiatrists (I'll be needing one myself), a man who breaks dimes in half!

"Some were here at 6 A.M. this morning with lunches under their arms—now the lunches are under their belts and they are ready for what is to come. Paul and Grace Hartman were here for the party yesterday. (That was true, they got the date wrong.) Five years ago Mary Margaret McBride celebrated her tenth birthday in Madison Square Garden and the streets were jammed. So that is why we are at Yankee Stadium. Somebody said that the next celebration will probably be in the Grand Canyon."

He introduced President Niles Trammell, who said NBC was "proud to be connected with this great program . . ." and then he presented *me*.

I said: "I feel a little more dead than alive with excitement, but I am glad so many of you came. I'll try harder to be better after this."

Fred brought on Ted Streibert of WOR, my first radio boss. Ted said: "She was new at radio and so was I. We at WOR had some free time and wanted a woman's program to fill the hour. Mary Margaret McBride had newspaper and magazine experience and although the experts said her technique was deadly and her voice impossible, we had a hunch that she was something new and different in radio. The rest you know."

Frank Connolly, my first sponsor, said: "Back in 1934, we down at Oakite attempted to tell her that we were going to sit in the control room while she broadcast. Mary Margaret said, 'Mr. Connolly, you can tear that contract up—I never want to see you again if you are going to interfere.' I never laid eyes on the queen of radio for six years!"

Ben Gross confessed: "The first time I heard Mary Margaret McBride I panned her because I didn't like her way of speaking. But I tuned in a month later and I was captivated. I wrote about that in the *News*, and the piece appeared on the very day her station was considering whether to renew her. She was renewed. . . . Anybody who can call this crowd to Yankee Stadium doesn't need the support of radio critics."

Morton Downey called out: "This is for you, Mary Margaret," and sang "Let Me Call You Sweetheart."

H. V. Kaltenborn, dean of radio commentators, took the microphone: "Why is Mary Margaret McBride the miracle woman of radio? Where could you find one who pretends to be so ignorant when she is so wise? Who is smart enough to be willing to appear foolish? Who asks a thousand questions to which she knows the answers?"

Tex McCrary admitted: "The first time I was asked to be on Mary Margaret McBride's program I said, 'No, it's only a woman's program.' A few nights ago Mary Margaret and I played the balcony scene from *Romeo and Juliet* together. And if Jinx is listening, I'm not kidding."

Fred introduced other friends who spoke with affection and humor that wasn't entirely stingless of the program and then he announced that I was getting three awards—from the President of Haiti, the governor of the Virgin Islands, and the mayor of Vienna.

Now we were coming to the serious part of the program. I asked Margaret Bourke-White to tell about the message from Mahatma Gandhi which she got a while before his death. "On the morning of his death Gandhi's last message to the world was nonviolence," she told us. "I asked him: 'What do you think about the atom bomb? Do you think Americans should stop manufacturing it?' Gandhi answered: 'Of course they should stop.'

"I asked him how he would meet the bomb. He said: 'I would meet it with prayerful force. I would not go into hiding. I would face the pilot of the bomber so that he could see I did not have a face of evil against him.'

"I asked: 'How would the pilot see your face?' Gandhi answered: 'I know the pilot could not see our faces, but I would send out a prayerful yearning that he should not harm and his eyes would be opened. If the people of Hiroshima had prayed, the war would not have ended so disastrously. Who are the victors? The victors or the victims?' It was time for me to leave. I looked back at him and said, 'Good-by and good luck.' A few hours later he was struck down by bullets."

"I envy you, Margaret Bourke-White, having known the great man of our time," I said fervently. "What makes me heartsick is that there are people who because they were born another color or religion consider themselves superior to that magnificent leader. Because I feel as I do, this program today is dedicated to the cause of justice and human rights."

Then the program went on with Lawrence Tibbett singing the national anthem of Israel and the presentation of a dramatic sketch—"Unfinished Business U.S.A."—written by Morton Wishengrad with Melvyn Douglas narrating. Mr. Douglas listed as our unfinished busi-

ness: anti-Semitism, discrimination, poll tax, unequal education, legis-
lation against civil rights.

After the stirring sketch I asked Eleanor Roosevelt whether, as chairman of the Commission for Human Rights of the United Nations,
she thought things were going better for human rights. "Sometimes
I think they are better and sometimes I think we're going backward,"
she replied thoughtfully, and then she urged me to go on trying to
help good causes.

And so the program ended with me going down to shake hands
with all the fifty-four thousand. Rather absurd, except for the human-
rights effort, it seems in retrospect—the whole proceeding a little on
the childish side. But no more absurd than a football game, when
you come right down to it; and perhaps, considering our avowed
aim, which was to fight intolerance by a spectacular use of all the arts
combined with some of the biggest names of the time, this occasion
may even be said to have had its uses.

All I know is that I wouldn't want to go through with it again, and
it's a wonder those important people came. True, many were my
friends, nearly all were enlisted in the cause of justice, and a few, I
suppose, were there out of sheer curiosity.

On the whole, reaction was good, though we were criticized for
having Lawrence Tibbett sing the national anthem of Israel and not
"The Star-Spangled Banner." The truth was time ran out and "The
Star-Spangled Banner" was played after we got off the air. I was also
rebuked for kissing Walter White in public.

## 10.  A WITCH HUNT AND A CORONATION

*"Counterattack says I advertise Polish hams. Where do you suppose they got that piece of misinformation?"*

That was how I started a rather angry broadcast toward the end of what I always think of as the radio witch hunt. The fifteenth-anniversary celebration was probably the real cause of my involvement in this. *Counterattack* was a sheet which appeared regularly with items about people in public life whom the editors linked either outright or by implication with communism. The only time I was ever mentioned was the item that had me along with a radio colleague advertising Polish hams. *Counterattack* did not say so, but the inference was that if we were willing to talk about Polish hams, we probably were fellow travelers, if not worse.

But I not only was not advertising Polish hams, I never had even been asked to advertise them. I telephoned the editor of *Counterattack* to say so, and he was rather taken aback. At first he was inclined to argue.

"How could our information have been wrong?" he asked plaintively. I said I didn't know but I was positive about me and Polish hams. While I had the gentleman on the telephone I went on to utter a few more words that had been welling up in me. For while *Counterattack* had found nothing except the nonexistent Polish-ham account to badger me on, some of its friends had been busy with my guest lists and my sponsors. The first I knew of this was when the advertising manager of one of the companies I advertised telephoned Stella, very upset because of a call he had that morning received from a delegation of women. They had brought with them a list of two dozen names, people they claimed were suspect who had been guests on my

program. And lo, Eleanor Roosevelt led all the rest! Then came Pearl
Buck, Carl Van Doren, Fannie Hurst, and many more of my best
friends—people whose political opinions I absolutely knew were above
reproach.

There were others mentioned of whom I knew little—but I resolved
I was not going to condemn them unheard just because a small group
of women said they were guilty of having served, perhaps innocently
enough, on some committee that later was said to have leanings toward the Reds. That was my contention throughout this time—that
nobody has the right to be accuser and judge all in one operation.

Yet, I confess it shamefacedly, except in cases where I was sure from
long knowledge what a person's convictions were, I finally yielded
to pressure and turned down several who were on the committee's
lists. If radio as an organization had backed me and others who believed in fair play, there would have been fewer acts of injustice, heartache, and even illness and death as a result of hasty accusation treated
as proof.

It is the blackest memory of my radio life that I did not stand up
determinedly for what I believed—that a man should be considered
innocent until proved guilty. Among friendly performers I admire very
much that we rejected as guests in this period were a famous folk
singer and a distinguished actor. Our lawyer, whose wife had been
smeared and blacklisted, advised Stella in this course. He said it was
that or go off the air. We lost only one sponsor that I know of as a
result of the witch hunt, and that place was filled at once.

Florence Eldridge and Fredric March, two of our favorite guests,
who were on the *Counterattack* lists, carried the matter to court and
got retractions. Pearl Buck threatened to do the same, and she, I know,
retained a lawyer. So did Stella ("as staunch a Republican anti-com-
munist as I could find," she comforted me). Anyway, after a while
we were apparently dropped by the volunteer guardians of our safety.
Maybe it was coincidence but the turning point seemed to be reached
after I pointed out that I had not advertised Polish hams!

I want to make clear here that I'm sure many, if not most, of those
involved in drawing up black lists (or red lists) really believed they
were doing useful work to guard the country. It was their methods
which were wrong. They made charges and sat in judgment all in one.
And they used pressure before proof as in the case of the Marches,

who told me that they lost thousands of dollars in their profession and spent thousands more before they got the retraction. Except for the one sponsor (and lots of spiritual agony) I never knew of any other personal loss until the other day when an editor told me that I was being seriously considered by a magazine for a series of articles at the time and was eliminated because of having been in *Counterattack* for selling Polish hams! I was too busy to have done the articles, but the injustice infuriates me.

It is rather sad to have to relate that after our expensive Yankee Stadium birthday party Stella came to blows the very next year with the network over a proposed time change. She felt that "One o'clock and here's Mary Margaret McBride" was by that time a valuable trademark, and after a good deal of palaver and offers from WEAF of bonuses and fringe benefits in a new contract we accepted a very good bid from American Broadcasting and, trailing all seventeen sponsors, Henry Gabrielson, our engineer, and considerable notice in the public prints, we journeyed to ABC.

It wasn't really much of a distance to travel, since we still used my same old studio in Rockefeller Center for that first broadcast and for the weeks of 1950 that followed. In 1951 we moved to my apartment on Central Park South, and a very pleasant arrangement that was. The first ABC program was, as might have been expected, full of pretty speeches from my new bosses, old friends, and a great armful of flowers (Mary Margaret McBride roses) from Robert E. Kintner, president of ABC and then and always one of my favorite people. Also there was a new recording of my theme song made by Paul Whiteman. Jane Froman, the brave singer and an alumna of my university, talked about courage, and Ole Olsen brought his eighty-year-old mother and Denise Darcel, who had just come from getting a marriage license at City Hall.

The ABC people were wonderful to us. Our contract must have stipulated that we were to have anything we wanted, for I had only to express a desire to have it gratified. Soon our show was being taped for ABC's network, and so I was back with my national audience again. And when I decided I'd like to cover the coronation of Queen Elizabeth II, Mr. Kintner agreed at once and the news department included me in plans for ABC's coverage.

I may be the only person in the world who had a ticket for West-

minster Abbey on the great day and didn't use it. Knowing that my
assignment for ABC was not in the Abbey but across the street in
Middlesex Guildhall, I decided it would be helpful if I could see the
dress rehearsal. A friend, Lord Donegall, succeeded in getting me a
ticket for that, and next day I was being paged all over town by the
ticket service at Buckingham Palace. When I finally got the message
and called back, a very British voice informed me that he was holding
a ticket for me in the Abbey for the day of the coronation. I knew
I couldn't use the precious piece of cardboard that millions in London
would have given anything for, and I wondered what the British would
do to me. I left poor Lord Donegall to square me and he must have
done it, for that's the last I heard of it.

Cynthia Lowry, then top Associated Press reporter and feature
writer, at Stella Karn's urgings gave up her vacation to go along as
my badly needed aide. I couldn't possibly have managed without her,
since we had to schedule strange guests in a strange land, get advance
information about them, and attend to the mechanical details of
broadcasting during an exciting occasion that turned everything topsy-
turvy.

ABC had engaged a flat for us in Dolphin Square. The owners,
like so many other Londoners, charged an enormous rent (about 500
per cent profit, we heard) and went off to the country for the duration. Thrown in with the place were two helpers and some goldfish.
Mrs. Moon, the regular accommodator, delighted us by addressing us
as "Ducks"—"Ducks, shall I do the bawth now?"

We'd read about such charwomen in English books; now we were
experiencing one. She was worried at first by our bad habit of dropping
papers wherever we went, but in time she took us to her bosom. Nellie,
the extra, was not so tolerant. She said, "I never saw this place looking
like this before!" But finally even she conceded, "It's only surface lit-
ter. You're not really dirty people!"

Cynthia had an idea that to live up to what the English expected
of her, she must be extra-American, so she was soon sprinkling everything with "gee whizzes" and "oh boys." She claimed that I, on the
other hand, got so English she could scarcely understand me. And she
swore that for one whole week, even on the air, the only "h's" I used
were in the wrong places—influence of Mrs. Moon and Nellie.

Among those who came to talk with us over the thousands of miles were author G. B. Stern; historian Sir Harold Nicholson (he got there late and left early so I've never spoken to him off the air); editor Fleur Cowles; General Omar Bradley, the president's ambassador to the coronation; his wife Mary, my old schoolmate (her dress was reported to have cost $1000 but she said it didn't); the Marquess of Bath (who told of his plans to drive to the coronation in a carriage drawn by beer-truck horses, the only kind he could find for hire in all of London); writers H. V. Morton, Virginia Cowles (she'd done a book about Winston Churchill), Frank Swinnerton, and Hesketh Pearson; novelist Angela Thirkell; Lady Cynthia Asquith; Ian Hamilton, who stole the Stone of Scone from under the coronation throne and took it to Scotland; Lawrence Tanner, authority on coronations; Poet Alfred Noyes, then seventy-two, who read some of his poems, including one written especially for the coronation and "Kew in Lilac-Time"; Sir Alexander Maxwell, head of British Travel Information, who in a sense was host to all us reporters; Selma Holland, the future queen's beauty expert, then married to Oscar Wilde's son.

We also kidnaped Lady Nancy Astor, who was waiting in the lobby at BBC to broadcast, but didn't know with whom. Somebody telephoned us; Cynthia went down and brought her up. With her usual spirit she inveighed against what she called the whole world being Hollywoodized. "I feel bitter always having to hear about Hollywood representing America. I have nothing against those people out there —God help them and God bless them with all those divorces, remarriages, suicides, and what not."

I don't know how we got on the subject, but I must have told her that I took the Temperance Pledge at six. She is rabid on the subject and said, in a gratified tone, "I might have known you were a Temperance girl—you've got such nice skin."

Mixed in with the other guests at frequent intervals were Constance Spry and Lord Kilbracken, otherwise John Godley, an Irishman whom I called my private peer. John filled us in on all the coronation gossip, Constance on solid facts. She was in charge of the special floral decorations for the city and could get us places we never could have gone without her. Later she was decorated by the queen with the Order of the British Empire, which we felt she richly deserved. We'd have starved if she hadn't sent baskets almost every day of wonderful things to eat, for rationing was still on and it was difficult for us to buy much food. "Ham, ham, ham," mourned Cynthia's notes because we ate that every day except when Constance's banquets of fresh salmon, gulls' eggs, caviar, and other delicacies arrived.

As often happened in short-wave broadcasting at the time, one broadcast didn't get through at all and reception was sometimes spotty other days. Alec Templeton made an amusing report of how one of these sessions sounded to the American listener.

"M.M.M.  'Now we have the distinguished Sir Bang-bang-bang whoo——'

"VINCENT  'We're not hearing you, Mary Margaret.'

"A VERY BRITISH VOICE  'Ahfter that they killed bang bang whish ——' And then silence from the London end.

"STELLA, *disgusted*.  'Reception is not very good today.' "

As the whole world knew, it rained in London on Coronation Day. Cynthia and I got up at dawn and drove in a car, engaged months ahead for that day, to Middlesex Guildhall, where a scaffolding and platform had been built outside the third floor to accommodate broadcasters. To get to my position I had to crawl on my knees through a small opening that had been a mullioned window. I went in sideways like a crab, and even then Cynthia had to push to get me through. Though it was June, it was bleakly cold and raw. I wore every scarf and sweater I had brought, but even so, we had sometimes to creep inside to get warm.

Since I was the only woman covering for American Broadcasting, I had the task of describing what I could see of the women's clothes, including the grass and bark robe of the tall, handsome Salote, queen of the Tonga Islands in the Pacific. Just as Queen Elizabeth passed in front of us in her golden coach the sun came out for a brief moment. It shone on her again when she stepped out in front of the Abbey.

From eight o'clock on, Cynthia and I made a game of spotting earls, dukes, marquesses, viscounts, and barons as we watched the peers and peeresses go into the Abbey. They wear scarlet capes with ermine collars and little black ermine tails on the collars. The rows of tails give you the score: a duke has four rows: a marquess three and a half; an earl three; a viscount two and a half; a mere baron only two. They lined up at the entrance, and it amused us to see that the nobility queues up too.

At six that evening (one o'clock New York time) I did my regular broadcast from a makeshift studio in the Guildhall with one microphone on a pillow in the center of a big table. We all sat on telephone books and when it was time to speak, stood up, leaning toward the microphone and practically yelling into it. My guests were all peers and peeresses who had been in the Abbey—Stella, Dowager Marchioness of Reading; the Marquess and Marchioness of Donegall; and Baron Kilbracken.

They were still in their red and ermine coronation robes with coronets and swords. My private peer acknowledged that his grand habiliments were rented, and Lady Reading said comfortingly, "In the last coronation I had on jewelry of an American guest and everybody was wearing borrowed things. I don't think there's a tiara in town that didn't go to the Abbey today—and some were borrowed and some rented!"

Lady Donegall contributed: "One friend of mine had a terrible burglary about a year ago and borrowed from a kind friend some stuff for today, but last night they had another burglary and *that went!* You know I kept hoping with all my heart that my coronet wouldn't fall off. It didn't but it could have very easily, because while there are two little pins, they don't meet in the middle. I tried a hatpin and I tried a knitting needle before I started, but the knitting needle came out so far at the other end that I decided I'd stick to my two little pins."

I asked about her dress. "White satin brocaded with silver, very plain—and no train." Lady Reading commented: "It is lovely. I wore this gold sari because my husband had been viceroy in India, and I have his jabot he used to wear when he was Lord Chief Justice—sentimentality, you know."

Lady Donegall smilingly put in: "You were not the only one with that feeling for the past. I think my husband didn't know, but I put the same steel buttons on his suit today that he wore when he was six and a half. He was the youngest peer in the Abbey for that coronation!"

John Godley thought the most moving moment was right after the crowning—". . . when we all had to put on our coronets and the sort of togetherness with which the peeresses lifted up their long-gloved white arms and fiddled for about three seconds with their safety pins —during those three seconds five hundred pairs of white arms were poised in the air like a thousand swans sailing down a river of diamonds."

Then, manlike, my private peer, fearing he was getting mushy, told about the last coronation and the trouble they had getting everybody out of the Abbey afterward. The peers leave according to rank, and it's a slow process. Some were getting a little impatient when suddenly a refined English voice was heard coming over the loud-speaker system in the old Abbey, saying, "The viscounts have hoofed it, but the barons are getting restless!"

Lady Reading sighed. "I wish everybody could have seen it—the dignity, the color, the wonderfulness—and then the queen, finally invested in her crown—a very moving moment. Her face looked almost worried in its seriousness as she followed the meaning of the ceremony. I'm supposed to be hard-boiled, but I had something in my throat and a terrible twitching in my eyes. I was so lucky that I could see everything that happened because I was in the third row facing the throne and the queen mother. The queen mother may have been nervous but never would anyone have known it—and alongside her was her small grandson, who played his part as gracefully as his grandmother hers—the concentration of that child and the way he behaved with every single eye on him, and knowing he was being televised."

Lady Donegall: "I think our hearts went out to the queen mother, too, when the queen went by and the mother made a little curtsy to her daughter."

Lady Reading went on: "After the ceremony was over the peers and peeresses went to the House of Lords for a meal. It was raining hard, so we put our trains over our shoulders to keep from getting pneumonia, and when we came there we watched the procession go past —and there came Cinderella's coach with not a fairy princess inside that golden carriage but a lovely girl we've all seen grow up—a woman we respect—and a queen we all admire and will loyally follow."

That coronation *was* moving. Even Cynthia, who likes to feel she is unsentimental, cried a little. We were both dead tired, but there was no time to rest. Though we were summoned, we couldn't go to Perle Mesta's great party, since we had to pack right away for Norway. Before I left America, I had accepted an invitation from the Norwegian government to be its guest in a flight to the northernmost tip of their country to see the northern lights.

Gladys Petch had promised me this trip on my first visit to Norway when there was no time to go north. She had intended to be my companion but wasn't well, and so patient Jon Embretsen, director of the Norwegian Information Service in New York, and his pretty wife, Florence, with their tape recorder, became Cynthia's and my escorts. I dedicated the broadcasts to Gladys, and my grateful thoughts often went out to her because this, too, was a memorable experience.

It was marred just a little because two days before I flew to London, I had been attacked by sciatica, which I believe is the most painful ailment of all the many pesky plagues that afflict humanity. The agonizing part of it was over, but the pain persisted throughout the London sojourn and became more acute as I began to clamber in and out of airplanes in Norway. I mention this, I suppose, to prove that I'm not such a bad sport as I've occasionally been accused of being. To balance my sciatica, Cynthia has a deadly dread of airplanes, especially when they take off or land, so Florence and Jon had a lot to put up with. However, we scrambled out of seaplanes, army carriers, and old-fashioned commercial jobs that sometimes bucked like bronchos over the rugged black mountains.

What we always refer to as the trip with the blond viking is the one I still shudder about. This blue-eyed six-footer looked about sixteen but undoubtedly was a little older. We boarded his army plane for a flight over mountains so rugged and isolated that it was obvious no human had ever invaded their swift-running mountain streams. Cynthia and I sat on rudely contrived seats in back of the pilot and co-pilot. The latter spent most of his time with a screw driver, apparently trying to undo the plane.

The viking flew with careless grace, occasionally glancing at what looked like a pamphlet in his lap. We came within inches, it seemed to me, of some of those jagged black peaks, and my sciatica was raising Cain because I was cold. I would tell the viking to put on more heat. Cynthia on the other hand said she was so hot she was feeling faint and would order the poor boys to shut the heat off.

"You'll be sorry if I can't even get out of the plane," I warned her gloomily.

"You'll be sorry if I faint," she riposted. And both of us were hoping above everything that we would just live to reach our destination.

Finally the viking set us down in a fjord. Then he turned round to me and grinned.

"I'm just as glad to get here," he admitted. "I've never flown that route before." And then and only then did I realize that the pamphlet in which he had seemed so interested was an automobile road map!

There was one maddening day when we were trying to take off from a fjord in a small seaplane and attempted time after time with no success to rise from the water. Most Norwegians speak English (I did a program with a housewife, a journalist, a schoolgirl, a grocer, and a farmer, all of whose English was better than mine). But this pilot understood not a word of Cynthia's entreaties please, please to go back. Finally, however, even he conceded it was hopeless, and we waited while a bigger ship was telephoned for.

Our broadcasts were in the form of a travel diary, part Baedeker, part rapture, and mostly done on airplanes with the conversation of other passengers and the sound of the motors for background. My voice, rather louder than usual to combat the din, sounded excited:

"We're on the most magnificent air route in the world. We'll pass the Polar Circle at 66 degrees 33 minutes latitude north, which is about 23 degrees from the North Pole, and yet because of the gulf stream the climate remains temperate. We're further north than Iceland and the northernmost part of Greenland—skerries are rather like the little island in the middle of the lake on your place in the Catskills, Stella —maybe a little bigger. Anyway, people live on them and the sea washes right over them. The mountains look like fantastic animals in a child's picture book. We're seeing in rapid succession waterfalls that roar, rivers that sweep with great rapidity and the last of the glaciers, barren plateaus, vast expanses of the murmuring pine and the hemlock, cultivated farmland and busy towns. . . .

"Oh, now we are passing the Black Glacier—on our right here. How absolutely thrilling! It's one of the largest—312 square miles and from a height of five thousand feet it reaches into the shadows of the fjords —the sharp ridge and peaks of the Lofoten Islands are below us." And then as if the listeners could see them—"Look, all snow-covered, and just see those pearl gray mountains with the sun on them and the snow. Even Cynthia is speechless."

We broadcast from restaurants too. "We're in Bodo having smorgasbord—open-face sandwiches with the tiny shrimp of Norway, curls of mayonnaise and cucumbers, paper-thin, cheese and ham and tomato on crusty bread, and perfectly delicious cake." I pick up again when we are flying. "After that we walked a few muddy steps and got into a little motorboat which chugged us out to a tub of a seaplane.

"It started up, and now we're flying rather clumsily and lazily out of the fjord, with the most rugged coast line we've seen yet. Gulls are crying farewell to us—— Oh, now we are passing low over little villages with houses clustered on the hills, mountains on both sides sprinkled with snow and so magnificent I keep wishing for my mother. She had a way of shaking her head, looking with all her eyes, and saying, 'It's grand, just grand.'

"Now the scenery is getting wilder and fiercer—it's beyond description. One mountain is like a charging elephant, another like a castle, one is like a prison that might be full of criminals. . . .

"Oh—we're so close! Jon, did anyone ever run into one of these mountains? Mountains on the mainland and mountains on the islands —black, black with snow dotted on them as if some great artist had arranged it. And now we are emerging from clouds draped like scarves —soft white and gray clouds—and the water sullen-looking and dark, then suddenly emerald-green and blue.

"Soon we'll cross the Arctic Circle and get into that part of Norway which is the Land of the Midnight Sun, and at that moment the pretty little stewardess will come and announce it in English so you'll hear it—it's like crossing the line of the equator or the North Pole. Sure enough—here she is: 'We are now passing the Arctic Circle'— and each of us gets a certificate to mark the occasion."

When we were registering at the hotel in Tromso, the town that is the gateway to the Arctic and therefore as nearly out of the world as one can get, the clerk looked at my signature and said, "Oh, New York is calling you, Miss McBride." And sure enough Stella had located me there, cutting yards of red tape and finally getting the Norwegian consul in New York to persuade the telephone company to put through a transatlantic call at a forbidden hour. The call mainly consisted of "What'd you say?" and "I can't hear you—speak louder," but, as Cynthia said, it was a comfort to think that somebody knew where we were.

Finally the great moment. "We're in a seaplane now on the way to the midnight sun. It's eleven-thirty and we are traveling in an army

Catalina. I'm sitting in the blister which in wartime carried the guns but it has been refitted with cushions. Beside me is Major Aberso, officer commanding the air force station, who came along to see that we're well taken care of. Captain Johanson is our pilot and beside me also is Captain Olaf Norvick, the stationmaster at Tromso." A pause and then: "Here we are—it's the midnight sun. I hope you're hearing me—we're circling now over the northernmost city in the world— they've put on extra power and I can hardly hear myself talk—it's eleven-forty by our watches and the major says this is the darkest part of the night."

At 4 A.M. of this strange day we were still sitting in the hotel lobby sipping tea, eating sandwiches, and talking it over on the tape recorder. We'd been at it from 10 A.M. the day before—working every minute. Jon was so tired he was putting the mike instead of the earpiece to his ear.

Cynthia's final words were: "I've spent this entire trip hunting Mary Margaret's glasses and looking for hairpins. She's dropped hairpins from the North Cape to Oslo and left her glasses in at least two hundred restaurants along the way."

Lord Kilbracken wrote in *Punch* as good a postscript as any to the whole adventure. After describing our exploits in London he ended with: "Mary Margaret then went to Norway whence, just as easily as from London, cat's meat and gingerbread can be admirably advertised."

# Part II   *THE PEOPLE*

# 11. SMOKE-FILLED ROOMS

*"I have a spiritual headache today. I've seen just too much in the past twenty-four hours of deals, spoiled children, broken promises. This week it's Republicans, but week after next the Democrats will start out fresh and new with carnival buffoonery, charges, empty oratory. They will utter words carelessly, recklessly, make promises they don't intend to keep. Oh, why can't we elect a president in a quieter, more thoughtful, more prayerful way?"*

I said this in Chicago on a July day in 1952. I'm sure I had voiced almost the same sentiments in 1944 and 1948 when I covered the political conventions of those years. I know that on a blistering day in June 1944 in Chicago, I glared at Stella, the leering microphone, and the insolent empty chair where a Republican senator should have been sitting and shouted, "I'll never again as long as I live and have my senses report a political convention!"

Stella shrugged, the empty chair and microphone continued to mock me, and I resignedly set about putting on a program without the missing senator. In July, I was back in Chicago for the Democrats. In 1948 there was I in Philadelphia for the duration. In 1952 I went to Chicago again for both incredible gatherings.

I missed meals. I spent sleepless nights. I agonized over guests lost in caucuses and committees and traffic snarls. I inveighed against political practices.

But I enjoyed every absurd minute of it, even struggling to get through the crowd and into the Bellevue-Stratford Hotel in Philadelphia, and hearing the familiar sirens trying to clear the way for one of the VIPs who rushed back and forth across the city. Hoping it might be our guest of the day, we stopped and stared, as did hundreds around us. A black limousine swept up, motorcycles fore and aft. The chauffeur leaped out, whipped open the door—and nobody got out. The escort had arrived but had left the VIP behind.

That's how it was at political conventions in the forties and fifties. I sympathized with an important state leader who was being courted day and night by other leaders who wanted him to swing his delegation their way. He posted a large sign on his hotel door: "Go Away. I Gotta Sleep Sometime."

Maybe he got some sleep. I couldn't. Too many things were happening too fast. Everybody tried to get on the air—except the ones you wanted most! One radio man, Graham McNamee with a single microphone, covered the Coolidge convention in 1924. The politicians made few concessions then to the new and still awkward medium. Twenty years later radio was a major consideration of most speakers.

In 1944 a dampening item was the shadow of war. Also preconvention excitement over the Republican nomination had sputtered out when it became evident that the forces of Governor Thomas E. Dewey of New York were too well organized for opposition to hammer them down.

We all knew that back on his farm at Pawling, New York, Dewey was awaiting the call to fly to Chicago. As reporters, we were frustrated at not being able to get interviews. I had close friends of the Dewey family trying to snag Frances Dewey as soon as she arrived in Chicago. The network was alerted in case we managed it. But I had to wait four more years for Frances. In 1944 she simply said, sweetly but firmly, "I am not the speaker of the house."

The press was reserved in its attitude toward Dewey. Some said it was because of his formality, his unemotional attitude, and his air of efficiency. I think it was because he looked so infuriatingly cool. The night he was whisked from the Chicago airport to convention hall the temperature had dropped outside to the high 80s. But in the hall it still sizzled at 98. My cotton dress looked as though I'd been swimming in it. Delegates in their shirt sleeves, dripping with sweat, swigged lukewarm soda from bottles. Officials on the platform mopped at themselves with soggy handkerchiefs. Even the poised and beautiful Clare Booth Luce wilted under the bright lights.

Then with a blare of music and a glare of spotlights, Mr. Dewey came on stage, immaculate in a crisp white shirt, a perfectly pressed dark suit, not a hair of head or mustache out of place. He wasn't even perspiring. You could almost hear an envious murmur.

By the time the Democrats arrived for their 1944 convention it was cooler. Not much, but enough to support a facetious rumor that Chicago's Mayor Kelly had installed electric fans over the lake for the Democrats. We had a hard time finding news at first, since it was known that Franklin D. Roosevelt would be renominated and that he was going quietly west by train to a Pacific coast naval base from which he would broadcast his acceptance.

What excitement there was centered on the vice-presidential nomination. At first I concentrated on Henry A. Wallace, who seemed the most likely choice. We heard from his supporters about his dawn walks, his devotion to Old Testament prophets, his eccentric diets featuring soybeans. When Stella learned of Wallace's eleventh-hour arrival in Chicago to fight for his political life she spent a whole day trying to get him for the program. I haunted pretty Mrs. Wallace and described every move she made, every dress she changed to. But neither would be interviewed.

About this time Stella and Janice discovered an air-conditioned underground, a closely guarded room beneath the speakers' platform where political strategists plotted. If we corralled a good subject there we informed convention news headquarters and sometimes were put right through on the network with what I can only describe as catch-as-catch-can interviews.

One was with Mrs. Emma Guffey Miller, veteran Pennsylvania political leader fighting to keep delegates in the Wallace corner. She had just learned that a letter was coming from President Roosevelt constituting anything but a real endorsement of Wallace and subtly informing the convention that Senator Harry S. Truman would also be acceptable as a running mate. Mrs. Miller was furious and tartly loquacious about the tactics of the Kelly-Hague group. Meantime, the convention was giving Wallace a thunderous ovation and Mr. Truman was sitting quietly among the Missouri delegation munching a hot dog. But Mrs. Miller said the decision was made for Truman.

Our news chiefs decided that since I was a fellow Missourian, I must be on hand to try to extract a few words from Bess Truman. My Washington reporter friend, Bess Furman, warned me that Mrs. Truman shunned publicity and that it was believed she had made a tearful plea to her husband not to accept the nomination. It was likely, too, Bess said, that Truman preferred his powerful position in the Senate and that both were tormented by the fact that six times in our national history the death of a president had catapulted a vice-president into the White House. Photographs of a haggard, careworn Roosevelt were causing alarm everywhere.

Thinking of this, I stood by the Truman box from ten in the morning until seven or eight at night when Mr. Truman walked in front of the battery of platform microphones. Mrs. Truman was kind. She knew me all right, but she said she didn't have anything to say. Finally I got her to promise that I might put her on the air for a few minutes if her husband was nominated. She knew he would be. We all did. She was ready to keep her word, too, but at the last second I realized that I'd have to hang from a shaky wooden railing to get the microphone near her. Six-foot-two Bob Trout was at my side, so I handed him the microphone. I think Bob generously gave me credit, but it was a disappointment to me all the same.

Four years later at a party in Washington that Bess Furman gave for Mrs. Edith Helm, secretary to many first ladies, President Truman and I reminisced about that day and about Missouri hog killings, fried chicken, and county fairs. That was the day Stella insisted I have my picture taken with three first ladies, Mrs. Truman, Mrs. Wilson, and Mrs. Roosevelt. They made no demur, but I was so embarrassed I tried to get away. No use—Stella had made up her mind, and I decided it would cause less confusion to go ahead than to balk. In retrospect it seems to me the most pushing thing I ever did.

In Kansas City, after the Trumans were out of the White House and back in Independence, I was speaking to Theta Sigma Phi honorary journalistic organization, and to my surprise found both Mr. and Mrs. Truman on the dais. Mrs. Truman sent me a welcoming orchid, and Mr. Truman served as my willing stooge for the entire speech. They are nice people, those two.

Even in 1948, when we were all (men, too) scurrying to Philadelphia drugstores for make-up, there were only 350,000 television sets for people to see us on. Nobody knew how you should look or what you should wear, though everybody had an opinion. One of my women guests got slapped into a ludicrous brown lipstick and mauve face-do. Luckily she never saw herself, for she looked more like a clown than a rather pretty and very dignified minor stateswoman.

There were some bad mistakes that year, television-wise. Now and then a special event telecast by one network would even be carried by another. I used sometimes to doubt whether I'd been on the air at all, and when letters and telegrams came commenting on some special program I was relieved to know we'd been heard or seen by somebody.

It was almost as hot in Philadelphia as it had been in Chicago, but there was a carnival air to this first postwar convention. Besides, Republicans were sniffing victory in the summer air. Nobody would have turned down the G.O.P. nomination in 1948.

We were located just across the street from headquarters, the Bellevue-Stratford Hotel, which creaked in every Victorian timber with the weight of delegates, press rooms, candidates' headquarters, radio and TV news rooms. Getting across the street was a major undertaking, and I used to start a full half hour before I was due to go on the air.

Stella and I wanted two very special interviews from the Philadelphia G.O.P. convention. Ohio's Senator Robert Taft was again in the running, and so was New York's Governor Dewey. We wanted each candidate with his wife, and we were able to promise full network coverage—even a pool of all networks if the time could be cleared.

Getting an exclusive newspaper interview with a potential candidate was hard enough. But pinning him down, with his wife, to a specific time and place for the air was next to impossible, especially since we wanted the interviews at the deadline hours, when the battle to hold delegates kept convention leaders up all night.

We buttonholed family friends, we cajoled politicians, we hung around candidates' headquarters. Finally we got word that both the Taft and Dewey interviews were set. One room of a Bellevue-Stratford suite served as our television studio, a small table with white flowers the principal prop, and there, on the day of the scheduled Taft interview, I waited.

Six blocks away at the hotel where Taft had his suite Janice Devine found Mrs. Taft—but no senator. He had been called to a vital last-minute meeting with a key group. Whether he was nominated might be decided then and there. Janice got as far as the closed bedroom door, Mrs. Taft at her side, and they held whispered consultations with the senator's chief aide. It was ten minutes before air time when they decided to leave for the broadcast and trust that the senator's session would end in time for him to come along later. The Tafts' official limousine waited, and they started driving toward the Bellevue-Stratford. Amid the mass of people in the street was a band merrily shrilling, "I'm looking over a four leaf clover," the Taft campaign song. But there was no getting them out of the way for Mrs. Taft.

Martha Taft proved that day why she was so important to her husband's political career. A woman of quick and sensible decisions, she told the chauffeur to pull to the sidewalk. "We'll have to walk," she said. And running, not walking (Martha Taft was neither very slim nor very young, either), she and Janice battered their way through the crowds, squeezed into an elevator over the operator's loud protests, and arrived at our makeshift studio with less than a minute to go. Somebody flicked make-up in Mrs. Taft's direction, and we started the interview. *Time* magazine later reported that I kept peering anxiously at my watch, but I don't wear a watch and, besides, Mrs. Taft did such a beautiful job that I was fascinated. Maybe I did look toward the door now and then, but Mr. Taft never came.

Toward the end of our half hour his wife said: "It shouldn't have happened to you, Mary Margaret. But I must tell you, it's happened to me my whole married life!"

Not once during the interview did she show the deep anxiety and concern she was feeling over the outcome of that meeting back at their hotel. We knew later that an effort had been made to join the Taft and Stassen forces against Dewey which, of course, didn't materialize and I suppose wouldn't have worked anyway.

By the time my television date with the Deweys arrived it was fairly certain that the nomination was his. But another last-minute caucus was called at noon, and again poor Janice was sent to try to pry the guest loose. I was particularly anxious to bring off this one, since the Deweys had never appeared together for a TV interview. But again I had to sit clenching my fists and watching the clock. Mrs. Dewey came first—alone. Janice was still ten floors above, handing desperate notes through the door to the governor's secretary, later President Eisenhower's press chief, James Hagerty, whom she suspected of being highly unsympathetic to anything but the business of the hour—clinching the nomination. This time it was only fifty seconds before one o'clock when the door swung open and out came Dewey.

"Come on," he called to Janice—and they started on the run toward the elevators, which were passing their floor packed with people. Finally Janice yelled up the shaft, "Please stop—it's Governor Dewey," whereupon an elevator screeched to a halt and the operator asked two very annoyed delegates to step out and make room for Mr. Dewey. We were on the air (both radio and television) when he walked in. I practically kissed him (in fact I think I did). He said gravely that, after all, he'd given his promise to appear—and here he was. That's why he has my eternal affection, admiration, and gratitude. He was delightful with his wife, and because he knew she had been nervous he protected her gallantly.

We didn't try to make political news that day. There were political analysts behind every microphone, in front of every TV camera, so this interview tried to be what my old city editor used to call human interest.

"Is it true—all the reporters are saying so—that you've changed?" I asked Thomas Dewey. (I meant changed in that he was easier, more informal with the press, and gayer.)

Before I could explain, Governor Dewey said, "It's only the people I don't know who are saying I've changed. Though I suppose everyone changes a little as he gets older. If I haven't learned anything out of being in public life for eighteen years and governor of New York for six years, I ought to quit."

He added: "When you're in public life, people invent stories about you, your childhood, your hobbies—and many are sheer fiction."

Was it fiction that Thomas E. Dewey had been a model boy?

He snorted. "I certainly wasn't! Once for misbehaving my tricycle was shut up for a whole year. That was a tough year. I was unlucky as a boy—even caught the measles during the summer holidays!"

Frances Dewey, pretty and poised, for all her timidity, told of meeting young Tom Dewey when they were both studying music in New York, he fresh out of Owosso, Michigan, she from Sapulpa, Oklahoma —an American boy-meets-girl story if ever there was one. She gave up her promising singing career after one minor part on the Broadway stage and turned her talents to such wifely tasks as condensing the books she thought her busy husband ought to read, cutting out clippings for him, seeing that he frequently got his favorite Berkshire soup, made with tomatoes, corn, cream, and egg yolks.

Mr. Dewey talked of his two sons and his farm, and admitted, his dark eyes sparkling, that he'd just had some wonderful news. But alas it was a secret! The Deweys left in a glare of camera flash bulbs for a session in the Bellevue-Stratford ballroom, the floor of which had been scrubbed at seven o'clock that morning by the very chic, good-looking Marjorie Hogan, long-time friend of the Deweys.

When she noticed and mentioned out loud that the floor was pretty dirty she was told by a porter, "You can't scrub a hardwood floor."

"I've been keeping house for too many years for you to tell me that," Majorie said crisply. And on hands and knees she proved her point!

Popular response to the Taft and Dewey television interviews indicated the political importance to candidates of making a good impression via this tricky and often too candid medium. Radio had made the political voice important, television was to analyze the political smile.

In contrast to the confidence marking the finale of the G.O.P. convention, the Democrats came to Philadelphia muttering discontentedly. Their defeatist theme was "Truman can't win." In fact, of the twelve hundred delegates it was estimated at the start that less than a hundred were firmly for Harry S. Truman.

The President stayed quietly in Washington until the squabbling ended in a none too glorious victory for him.

Meanwhile, in Philadelphia, two women were certain Harry Truman would win not only the nomination but the election—his daughter, Margaret, and India Edwards, head of the Women's National Democratic Committee. Both were saying that Harry Truman would positively win the election. Both went right on saying it when in the next months every poll in the country proved the opposite.

Margaret of course was a prejudiced witness, but she was convincing even at one o'clock in the morning just after Mr. Truman had made his extraordinary acceptance speech—off the cuff and fighting mad. She came to a tiny studio high up in Convention Hall, where a nice girl from *Look* magazine and I had been waiting for hours to do a pool interview—that is, for all radio and TV networks.

We asked her the usual arch questions about men in her life and suggested that she really ought to be a White House bride. The impression we left was that if she didn't hurry she might lose her chance to be married in that historic pile. Margaret smiled serenely and came back again and again to her contention that her father would win the next election.

India Edwards, probably the most influential woman in the Democratic party then, would, I'm convinced, have had the vice-presidential nomination in 1948 if the convention had gotten up courage enough to chance running a woman for that office.

India herself said, "If I were a delegate maybe I'd try to start some excitement by nominating a woman."

I suggested that her fellow guest on the program that day, the famous partygiver, Perle Mesta, *could* put a woman in nomination since she was a delegate at large from Rhode Island. The matter never got further than on my radio program. But India Edwards did say she believed women to be achieving some political independence.

"I don't think they're all doing as Dr. Gallup said recently—voting exactly the way their husbands tell them. When a woman is smart and has an opinion of her own she's more likely to influence her husband's vote than the other way round."

Just as I was starting an interview with Frances Perkins a while later, a bulletin was handed me announcing that Mr. Truman had okayed Alben Barkley as the vice-presidential candidate. I said to Frances Perkins, then the only woman who had ever been a member of a president's cabinet:

"If I were Mr. Barkley I'd rather be senator. After all, we haven't had a vice-president for some time, and who's missed him?"

Miss Perkins agreed. "You're quite right. The vice-presidential office in normal times is not very powerful or important."

Frances, whose concern for social justice, to borrow a Quaker phrase, led her to crusade against child labor and to fight for a fifty-four-hour week for women (the words sound almost archaic), had the toughest battle of all when she served as Secretary of Labor under Franklin D. Roosevelt. He was her hero, and she felt that Democrats were missing the lift and stir he gave them.

"But we have to face the facts of life—we get a genius only about once in a thousand times, and I believe there are plenty of less gifted leaders who can carry out FDR's ideas and aims and plenty of people in the party who are dedicated to those ideals. They just can't express them as attractively, that's all."

Frances Perkins told touchingly about the time she really wanted to resign. The brickbats had been flying at her thick and fast. Roosevelt had just been elected for the fourth time, and before he set off for Warm Springs, Frances went to see him. "He looked sick and exhausted," she remembered sadly. "He knew I was tired, too, and wanted to be free of it all. But he said, 'No, I don't want you to go now. I don't want to think of changes—not now.'"

The former Secretary's voice broke. "He never flattered, and complimentary words didn't very often pass between us. But that day he put his hand on mine and said in a weak voice, 'You know you've done awfully well.'

"Tears came to both our eyes, and I had that sense of precious communion and closeness that you get only occasionally with another human being—that instant of real contact between two old friends. I never saw him again."

During both 1952 conventions in Chicago we occupied a suite high up in the Hilton Hotel. Equipped with an engineer and a production man, I did interviews day or night, moving down a few flights for network television. I never left the hotel at all, not even for the convention hall. I had discovered in common with other correspondents quartered downtown that I could cover the proceedings beautifully by means of the big television set installed in my living room. One columnist who turned out brilliant analyses confessed that he lived mostly in the air-conditioned railroad lounge deep under the convention hall floor. Handy were free food, drinks, an upholstered chair, and a giant television set to make his assignment quite different from the days of shoving through crowded aisles to seek out candidates and delegates.

I believe John Foster Dulles was the first public figure I asked the question that became a sort of theme for me in 1952: "Do you ever compromise?"

The reaction of many political leaders was a startled silence, then a certain amount of hemming and hawing. George Halvonic, our engineer, and Dick Languirand, our production man, were so fascinated by the answers to this particular question that if I hadn't yet brought it up they'd pass me a note toward the end of any interview: "Aren't you going to ask him if he compromises?"

Mr. Dulles, who was to be our Secretary of State within a year, was perhaps prophetic in his answer. "In my work, as foreign-policy adviser, I don't feel I ever have to compromise with my principles. So far, in the foreign-policy plank we've drawn up at this convention, there is nothing I do not believe in. But perhaps in government—well, maybe one must sometimes compromise."

Mr. Dulles said much that day in 1952 that I found interesting eight years afterward: "There is anti-American sentiment in all parts of the world. Even though we've given away or loaned forty billion dollars since the end of the war, we're less popular, more disliked than ever before in our history. Powerful countries are always suspect. Some feel we're pressuring too hard. Others fear we are trigger-happy and may start an atomic war. There are countries that fear our military policy more than they do that of the Russians."

Mr. Dulles described Korea as mishandled. "You remember our Secretary of State announced that we had no interest in Korea—and we pulled our troops out. That was an invitation to Russia to push her satellites in." (Satellites meant follower-nations in pre-space 1952.)

Mr. Dulles also emphasized our neglect of South America and of Asia; said Asians felt we'd written them off, because in nineteen trips abroad since the end of the war our Secretaries of State had not once visited Asia.

Listening all those years later, I felt sure John Foster Dulles was one man who would have chosen exactly as he did even if he could have foreseen the jet-propelled existence, the millions of miles, the crises and anxieties, even death, awaiting him.

That day he insisted we must get back the good will of the world. "It's the most valuable asset a country can have and in a crisis is apt to be a decisive factor. Nations unpopular and unliked in the end will lose out. We came into this role of being the most powerful nation without much historic preparation for it and we bungled in the beginning, but I think this can be corrected. I think we'll settle down to a better pace—especially if the Republicans get in!"

I had planned my question "Do you ever compromise?" especially for two controversial senators at the 1952 convention—Joseph McCarthy and Wayne Morse.

Senator McCarthy failed to show up for his appointment, though he had not canceled ahead of time. I was told that he was located, fast asleep in his suite in the hotel, a few floors below me. He had been up late, an embarrassed aide explained, and besides, he had decided he'd rather not make any public statement prior to his scheduled speech before the convention that night.

Senator Wayne Morse of Oregon appeared on time. He is, I guess, the only one to whom I put the question about compromising who answered without hedging: "No, I do not and will not compromise."

He did say, though, that he would never bolt the Republican party!

I teased: "I read day before yesterday you might become a Democrat."

Senator Morse, emphatically: "No danger of my becoming a Democrat. I see no more hope for the Democrats getting rid of their reactionaries than the reactionaries getting out of the Republican party, but I'm going to keep on struggling in the Republican party to come forward with both a candidate and a platform to give the independent voters what they're looking for—an excuse to vote Republican."

Unexpected drama was added to the broadcast I taped on July 21 at 2 P.M., edited at 3 A.M. July 22, and finally put on the air July 22 with Vice-President Alben Barkley and his wife as guests.

I had to explain the circumstances to the listeners. "Early this morning the country heard the news that Vice-President Barkley had withdrawn from the contest for the Democratic nomination for President," I said. "When the Veep and his pretty wife were here with me yesterday, surrounded by secret service men, he seemed serene and confident. But at one point I thought Mrs. Barkley looked wistfully at him as he answered a question of mine about the close relationship between him and President Truman.

"Was it because even then the Barkleys had begun to hear rumors that the White House was getting ready to support Adlai Stevenson? Did they find waiting, when they left me, a message that confirmed the apprehension that was in Mrs. Barkley's voice?"

I still don't know the answers to my own after-the-event questions, but here is part of what we talked about the day before it all happened. I told the Vice-President that a man on his staff had said rather mournfully, "That guy never gets tired."

Since Mr. Barkley was seventy-four at the time, I was impressed.

"I've never had a feeling of fatigue or exhaustion in my life," declared the debonair Veep. "Maybe that's bad because if I did get tired, I might rest now and then."

Mrs. Barkley agreed. "It's true. I can't keep up with him. One time when he was campaigning in Kentucky, making five or six speeches a day for weeks, he went from place to place in a small private plane. The pilot was so worn out after this terrific campaign that one day he suddenly realized to his horror that he had dozed at the controls and the Vice-President was running the plane. I must add that Alben knew nothing about flying, which added to the pilot's alarm. Luckily the machine was uncomplicated to fly, as airplanes go, but the poor pilot stammered, 'Oh my, Mr. Vice-President, for goodness' sake!' Whereupon Alben said, 'That's all right, Charlie. You looked as though you were tired and needed a little nap.'"

Later in the interview Mr. Barkley said he did not like written speeches. I said I didn't either and that I thought it would be fine to have a president who didn't read—at least not obviously.

Mr. Barkley commented: "I'm just made for the presidency if that counts—and if physical endurance does—because the presidency demands many vital decisions."

"I think you are the most popular vice-president the country has ever had," I told him, and then asked how he got the pat headline title, "Veep."

"I'd been a senator for twenty-two years before I became Vice-President, so everybody was used to calling me senator. At my daughter's house one night, after I'd become Vice-President, we were talking about this. I'd keep answering telephone calls by saying Senator Barkley, and at the other end the caller would say, 'Oh, the Vice-President?' One of my grandsons said idly, 'Why don't you put a couple of "e's" in there and make it Veep?' A few days later I mentioned the suggestion to a reporter—and I've been Veep ever since."

And Veep was the way the headlines read when Alben Barkley died.

I hadn't caught up with Thomas E. Dewey in Chicago, but in New York, exhausted from putting on twenty-two radio and television programs at the G.O.P. convention, I talked to him again. He was tired, too, after the dramatic convention-floor show he had staged, polling the New York delegates and swinging the nomination to Dwight D. Eisenhower.

All his talk was about retiring to private life. "I tried awfully hard two years ago—even had an apartment picked out and a school in Riverdale for Tommy. But I was afraid the Korean War might turn into total war and I was convinced I had a duty to do."

I wondered how he could survive the bitter attacks I'd heard during the convention.

"You can't achieve anything without being criticized," he answered. "Of course if you're going to be a door mat and let the wrong things happen, then you can avoid abuse." He added wistfully, "But if I don't get back to private life at the end of this term, I'll be the unhappiest man you know, Mary Margaret."

Back in Chicago for the Democrats, I had India Edwards and Perle Mesta again on the air.

"I'm still getting into the news about a party you gave in 1948," I told Mrs. Mesta. "Seems Dorothy Thompson was quoted as saying that your party had everything—Rebecca West, Mary Margaret Mc-Bride, a guest who fell flat on the floor. I'm still trying to explain that I did *not* fall flat on the floor—that the comma should have been a semicolon."

I reminded India of our conversation of four years back about the possibility of having a woman vice-president and informed her that news commentator Elmer Davis was right then running around hotel lobbies wearing a sign: "India Edwards for Vice-President."

"Suppose you did get the nomination?" I asked India. "Do you think it would help or hurt your party?"

"I couldn't modestly answer that," she parried, "but I will say that I think the Republicans would have done far better to have nominated Margaret Chase Smith for vice-president on their ticket."

What if they had—and she had won. Would she have been the Republican choice for president in 1960, I wonder?

Adlai Stevenson, reluctant candidate for the presidency, was still trying to say *no* the day Stella Karn kidnaped his sister and aunt, who were on their way to the convention hall but found themselves instead in our hotel studio.

Mr. Stevenson's bubbly little Aunt Letitia turned out to be one of my listeners. That's how Stella got them. Aunt Letitia took Elizabeth

Stevenson Ives firmly by the arm and said, "Come, dear, if Mary Margaret wants us, we must go."

Aunt Letitia was the daughter of the Adlai Stevenson who was Vice-President of the United States in the Cleveland administration. She told of watching a television program in which President Truman did a guided tour of the White House.

"I kept wondering whether they still had that lovely old red sofa in the diplomats' waiting room and sure enough, they did—the sofa I used to sit on in the Cleveland era. Mr. Truman told how they dragged it out of the cellar and had it recovered. Official dinners in Cleveland's time were far more lavish than now. An eighteen-course state banquet was commonplace. My father went to some and survived, but they probably killed off a lot of poor old senators."

It was obvious that Aunt Letitia would be enchanted if her nephew were to go to the White House. His sister, Elizabeth Stevenson Ives, was doubtful that her brother wanted to be president but certain he'd be good at it. She told a wartime incident that to her proved his reliability. Admiral Nimitz chose him to be the bearer of an important message to the President, so confidential that it could not be put in writing, and Mr. Stevenson had to memorize it. When he reached Washington his first meeting with Mr. Roosevelt was at lunch. The President asked whether there was any special news from Admiral Nimitz. Stevenson said yes, but it was a message he must give to Mr. Roosevelt alone.

"Oh, I think you can tell me right here," said FDR.

"So," concluded Elizabeth Ives, "since no matter what the President said, he felt he couldn't *tell* it before others, Adlai sat there and wrote the message which informed the President of a rumor that the Russians and Germans were ready to sign a separate peace."

"Yes," put in her husband, Ernest Ives, who'd arrived in search of his family, "Adlai wrote it on the back of a White House menu."

He then helped us out with the portrait we were trying to draw of the absent Adlai. "He hates waste and unnecessary extravagance."

"And he doesn't like to buy his own clothes," Elizabeth contributed. "Once his house burned down and he said, 'It's awful—now I have no old clothes to wear!'"

In spite of his reluctance, Adlai Stevenson accepted the nomination and made, I thought, the finest speech I'd ever heard. I listened to it from the comfort of an easy chair in my hotel suite where a few hours before Dorothy Thompson had talked for an entire hour on the telephone to Adlai Stevenson. I think Dorothy and I set some kind of record for women and reporters that day. She never told me or anybody else what he said. I never asked, nor did I try to eavesdrop!

# 12. UNFORGETTABLE CHARACTERS

*"Mary, that house they've given me to live in—it* stinks!" *Mayor La Guardia about Gracie Mansion.*

By a character, I mean an unpredictable person who says what he thinks and does what he pleases without regard for the conventions and restraints that we ordinary people live under. My "characters" all have a streak of nobility interlaced like the fat and lean of bacon with a streak of arrogance that can become relentlessness. They are the stuff of which martyrs, patriarchs, and tyrants are made.

Only one man in my years of radio and television had the habit of telephoning (or having his secretary telephone) at 10 A.M. to announce that he was coming to my program that day! He was Fiorello La Guardia, rambunctious little mayor of New York City, and because he always had something to say I invariably managed to make room for him.

The something he wanted to say was usually directed to women and often concerned a city crisis he feared they might not hear about. Fifteen or twenty minutes after we had gone rather uncertainly on the air (since we never knew at what moment he would descend on us and everything else had to stop when he did), La Guardia would arrive with his entourage. Just before he entered the studio an anxious aide would whisper to him: "Her name is Mary *Margaret,* sir—everybody knows her as Mary *Margaret.*"

And Mr. La Guardia would bounce in, beaming, and greet me with, "Hello, Mary."

I was Mary to him and Mary I remained until the end. One morning I got up at dawn and spent the day with him. We drove in his car, equipped with a telephone, shaving gear, a dictating apparatus and a little table for writing, all over the city inspecting bridges, markets, and slums.

The Little Flower told me what he hoped to accomplish. Chiefly he intended to do away with want, and he firmly believed he could. At his office in City Hall we had orange juice and sandwiches (ham and cheese for him) and then he showed off a little, since, of course, he knew I was going straight to the microphone and describe our day.

One by one he called in the heads of city departments—his cabinet —and to each he laid down the law. Some of them almost winked conspiratorily at me as they left, though they all looked properly contrite when His Honor, rising to his full height, pounded the desk and shrilled reprimands at them for something left undone.

On my program he used to stand up, too, when he wanted to emphasize a point about housing or discrimination. "I think the people ought to know about this," he would cry.

On his first visit after moving into Gracie Mansion he announced that he didn't think much of the place. "Mary, that house they've given me to live in—it *stinks!* The rugs haven't been cleaned—there's grease all over them." (The rugs had been loaned by the Metropolitan Museum and they were rare as well as old, but that didn't appease the Little Flower.)

"The dining room is full of portraits," he continued relentlessly. "They came from the Metropolitan Museum—and there they are on the walls staring at me—but not a single one is related to me. How would you like to eat with a lot of strangers staring at you? And, Mary, you women know about wash day. Well, I want to tell you that in this Gracie Mansion there isn't a single place to hang up washing. My wife can't cook a meal, the kitchen's so filthy . . ." [He drew out that word.]

"Now, Mary, I don't think the people of New York want their mayor living in a place like that!"

The women at least agreed, and as a result of the broadcast a civic committee was formed to see to the renovation of Gracie Mansion.

An encounter with Fiorello La Guardia was like an ice-cold shower, numbing at first but wonderfully invigorating in the end. I miss him, and I think I shall not see his like again.

Sam Goldwyn, though he gave me more notice than the Little Flower, was another man who used to let me know on occasion that he would like to borrow my pulpit. He came one day from making a speech at the Harvard Club, where he had accepted one of the many awards he was constantly given for making pioneering motion pictures.

In his speech, which I had covered, he insisted that he didn't pay any attention to critics. "I just make pictures and let the dice fall where they may," he said. Then he added that he didn't need critics for he depended for success upon "word-to-mouth advertising."

That same day with me Mr. Goldwyn declared solemnly that the legendary Goldwynisms "are usually invented by press agents and newspaper reporters."

I think perhaps he believed it too. Two minutes later he was explaining that he had refused to use GI Joe as the name of the hero of his Academy Award picture,—*The Best Years of Our Lives*. "Every Tom, Dick, and Harry is called Joe," he snapped. I never let on, for I knew Sam with his foibles and vanities and I was genuinely fond of him.

Over the years I learned to let him say, as he always did, that while the picture he'd just finished was perhaps the greatest picture ever made, the one he was going to do next would be even greater. After he got this off his mind, Sam would talk about his childhood on the Lower East Side and Hollywood and his son, of whom he was proud, and Frances, his wife. Frances often came to New York on some scouting errand for Sam, and sometimes she and I talked about him.

Also among the people who recurred in my radio and television life was James Montgomery Flagg. That unpredictable man, with eyebrows only a shade less formidable than those of John L. Lewis, had a wicked gift of caricature, as he himself admitted. "I sharpened my most malicious pencil," he said about his sketch of Mickey Rooney.

Before I could ask him a question at our first interview, he asked me, "Aren't you sick of celebrities?"

"Only when they won't do what I want them to do," I warned.

"I wish I'd been alive to paint Abraham Lincoln," he went on, as if I'd brought it up. "I'd just as leave be dead now if I'd had a chance to do that. We're a pretty young country though. Imagine—I can sit here and tell you that my grandmother Flagg was held up by her nurse to watch Lafayette go by! And even my own lifetime has covered quite a span of our history—it seems almost impossible to me that I painted

Mark Twain in his shirt sleeves. He'd lectured around the world to
make $200,000 so he could pay off debts his publishers actually owed.
That's the kind of man he was. He didn't like sitting for portraits either. He said, 'I'd rather have smallpox.' But he sat for me when the
Lotos Club commissioned me, a youngster in my twenties, to paint
him."

The youthful artist went to Mark Twain's home in Connecticut for
the sittings. He described what happened when the mail came. "Mark
Twain would throw all the letters on the floor in a line, march up
and down, picking the ones he wanted to read. Then he'd hurl them
all down again and cuss. And could he cuss! His poor wife couldn't
cure him of it. She sat in a front room, knitting, and ever so often
we'd hear her say, 'Oh, sugar,' in a furious tone. Mark Twain would
mutter to me, 'The recording angel is going to hold that just as black
against her as my swearing against me. She means exactly what I
mean.' "

Years later in Hollywood, James Montgomery Flagg, who thought
so little of celebrities, was horrified when he was besieged by auto-
graph hunters.

"They had old bottle tops, toilet paper, everything—and after I
signed and signed, I got tired and sneaked off to lean against a wall
and rest. An old lady followed me and whispered, 'Mr. Flagg, isn't it
true that you are the author of the Gibson Girls?' 'Nope,' I whispered back, 'it's a secret, so don't tell, the Gibson Girls are by Howard
Chandler Christy.' She went off thinking she'd got something hot off
the griddle. They don't even know or care who you are as long as they
think you are a celebrity."

I thought maybe we'd better identify Gibson and Christy for the
listeners. The artist sighed. "I guess so. Isn't it awful that there are
people who don't know who Charles Dana Gibson was—and Howard
Chandler Christy? They think of Gibson as a martini or am I not
supposed to mention martinis on the air—seems everybody's bucking
taboos. Arthur Godfrey even asked forgiveness the other day for saying *heli*copter."

I asked, as I always did when anybody'd met the woman I've always
been frustratedly curious about, what had he thought of Greta Garbo.

"It's my one regret that I didn't let Garbo come on to New York
and be my model," he answered sadly. "She kind of took a shine to me

and *wanted* to come East. But I was trying to be a good married man and I didn't want complications. . . . Yes—she is beautiful and she has character in her face, although character and souls have nothing to do with beauty. Beauty from an artist's point of view is physical. It's simply skull and bones surrounded by flesh."

I believe James Montgomery Flagg would say anything that came into his head, anytime anywhere. So I think would Lucile Watson. At seventy-three this *grande dame* of the theater was pretty mad at audiences of the 1950s.

"There is something wrong with them, but I have noticed this of audiences over the past fifty years. After World War I people had become so used to horror that they weren't affected by it any more. And they laughed raucously at what they called sentiment."

Miss Watson was convinced that the reason audiences had changed was because "people who once sat in the gallery got money and moved into the expensive seats. Their attitude toward the drama was different."

Disagreeing with Lucile Watson was like disagreeing with Einstein, so I didn't. I merely said she sounded snobbish.

"No, no, no," she insisted. "I mean there was a time when the theater suited a certain kind of select group, but now it's for the masses."

I muttered something about not believing in class distinction, but she went right on. "Yes, audiences have changed for the worse. Adrianne Allen, the English actress, went with me to Laurence Olivier's *Hamlet*, and we were both sick when the audience laughed at Ophelia's madness. Imagine roaring with laughter at that tragic figure. Audiences laugh at vice now too. Vice should make you cringe, not laugh. They've lost reverence for reverence, awe for awe, and their sense of delicacy to boot. This makes me sad in my old age."

We talked a bit then about growing old, and Lucile Watson said she wished she had been born earlier so that she could join the ladies of a rapidly vanishing era.

"I mean the ones you find in books chronicling the doings of the Four Hundred. They never knew what the workers knew, so it could not corrode their minds. Their intentions were good, their minds were touchingly pure—and they had a graciousness. Altogether they were delightful creatures."

Madame Watson then predicted (wrongly, as it turned out, and I'm so glad) that she had six years to live. She based this prognostication on the Bible.

"When I was sixty-five," she explained, "I picked up the Bible and it opened at a page where King Hezekiah was dying, and he prayed to the Lord who granted him fifteen more years. Since I was sixty-five then and I am now close to seventy-four that gives me six more years!"

I was not sure I saw the connection and I said so.

Lucile Watson smiled sweetly and became more explicit. "I always guide myself by the Bible. Once I was trying to decide whether or not to buy a house on Sixty-third Street. I went to the Bible, opened it at random, and it said, 'I will lay thy foundation of sapphire, I shall make all thy windows of agate, and all thy borders shall be of precious stones.'"

Yes, she bought the house.

Ethel Waters also reads the Bible for guidance. I introduced Ethel on the air on publication day of her autobiography—*His Eye Is on the Sparrow*—by reading a sentence that I said tore my heart out.

This was it: "There I was, born too big, always too big to sit in anybody's lap. Nobody's protective instinct seems to be aroused by a huge girl."

Ethel Waters smiled at me and said, "Right."

"But isn't it wonderful what has happened to you since?" I exulted.

"Mary Margaret, you're the first person who expressed it that way." Ethel was pleased. "It *is* wonderful what has happened to me. So many people think of my life in terms of tragedy, but it has been rich and full of meaning. In my later years I've watched people who had been sheltered and protected all their lives, and then when they went out in the world they were so unprepared—and five years later you'd hardly recognize them. Life had struck them such blows, and they don't know how to combat blows.

"Mine isn't a color story," she went on. "It's a human story. It applies to everybody and to all nationalities. I don't say everybody could have stood up to it, but I was blessed to the extent that we were all together on the other side of the tracks. We shared and shared alike, and there was loyalty and integrity—in a crude form, maybe—but to me a liar is still a liar, a thief a thief. I'm not going to question what makes them that. But you know, if a person in what you call the plebeian class steals something they say, 'Put him in jail—he stole that,' but if a banker does the same thing they call it misappropriation of funds.

"Usually I call a spade a spade, but I'm grateful to God that I *can* conform and use a word that sounds better in the correct spot—such as prostitute when I'm speaking over the air, but when I'm not I'm more likely to use a less respectable synonym that's been drilled into me from childhood. When I learn better, I try to benefit, but I hate hypocrisy."

Ethel is known to be deeply religious, and I asked whether she had ever had doubts. She thought about that.

"Well, if there is no hereafter, let that take care of itself. Maybe my faith is blind but it works, and until I get something more reliable I'll cling to it. When I was a little girl I was comforted by the picture 'Rock of Ages' in my home that often seemed to have a light shining on it. But I guess it was going to that school in Philadelphia that really gave me something to hang on to.

"Everywhere else they'd turned me down. The sisters took me in, and it was their gentleness and understanding that gave me to realize just how much I wanted love and affection. At first I fought it because I was suspicious. Those sisters were white, and it had been drummed into me that light people are no good. Then I realized that to those sisters I wasn't separated from the neatly dressed other child, even though I was black and dirty with knotty hair and a runny nose. That's where I got religion.

"Maybe I'm not a real Christian, but I have Christianlike thoughts and I believe in heaven. Only I hope God will give me a little more time to clean myself up before the summons comes."

Who but Ethel Waters could or would have said that?

I guess what I have been longing for through the writing of this book and especially this section of it is a James Thurber to do it for me. Thurber is at once my love and my despair. I love him because practically every piece he ever wrote I wish I'd written. I told him when he came on the air with me that most humorists bore me but that his writing has for me the special quality of quiet laughter, so rare in our world.

I was glad that he didn't make a flip answer. Most humorists, embarrassed by the compliment, would have. Thurber then was midway in his battle against blindness. Instead of making a tragedy of it he explained without bathos: "All I can see are public libraries and dirigibles—and so I have to write in my mind. I've been doing that since 1940."

I said how extraordinary to be able to read from the tablets of your mind.

"It's just a faculty I happen to have. My psychology teacher was the first to discover it, out in Columbus, Ohio. One day he read three hundred words to our class, then asked us to write down as many as we remembered. I got down 90 per cent. Three weeks later he said to the class, 'Remember that passage? I wish you would write down as much as you can remember now.' I got 60 per cent. Later, when I was a newspaper reporter, I'd take down a lot of things in my mind. It was a dirty trick because usually the other reporters, seeing that I wasn't taking notes, didn't take any either."

Having been a note-taking reporter myself, working against a non-note-taker and absolute rememberer, Marguerite Mooers Marshall, I sympathized with the colleagues of James Thurber. Did he draw in his mind, too, I asked, referring of course to the famous Thurber dogs and to the awful stringy-haired women and lunging males in his Battle between the Sexes series.

Thurber objected to my describing his women as awful. "Anyway, your sisters apparently don't agree. Most of my mail comes from women, 90 per cent, I'd say. The 10 per cent of men who write usually ask whether I 'really get paid for that stuff.' But, Mary Margaret, I'm a feminist. I'm only mistaken for a misogynist because I can't draw pretty or attractive women."

I, hesitatingly: "Still, the men and dogs do come off better in your drawings."

"The truth is I draw like a child," he explained. "When I was forty-eight my wife said, 'Well, you've become twelve for the fourth time!' When I was thirty I wrote a farewell to youth. Nobody would publish it. They said I was too young. At forty I was scared because at forty your legs begin to go and the faces of girls you loved in your youth are as misty as dreams. Now at fifty-nine I can see them again, quite clearly."

I asked him about the absurd, hilarious stories he'd written about growing up in Columbus, Ohio, and James Thurber said thoughtfully:

"One incident I never did get written—the best Christmas I ever had. It was when my brothers and I threw all our gifts at one another before they were opened. Then we had to take presents to our grandparents, and we continued the fight while walking over. Candy canes were flying all over the place. A footstool for Grandfather made a wonderful object to hurl—you got hold of a leg and whirled it around your head and let go. I don't remember any serene Christmases in the Thurber family, but that was the most unserene and the best of them all."

I went back to the business of Thurber being able to write and keep the continuity of a story in his head.

"It's good," he said, "because I can write wherever I am, and then go over and over it. I can have several plots working in my head at once. Right now I could repeat three thousand words of the one for next year.

"But it can be a bother," he noted wistfully. "I've got a hundred and sixty-eight telephone numbers in my head that I'd like to get rid of— addresses, too—they keep bobbing up. I even remember the telephone number my family had in 1913. I have no further use for it because the house burned down, telephone and all."

I suggested that he list the numbers for me—maybe then they'd go away. Instead, he wrote a wonderful piece about old telephone numbers that linger in your head. Imagine a wonderful piece about old telephone numbers. What a talented lot they are, my unforgettable characters!

Looking across Central Park at the Guggenheim Museum, I remembered back years ago when Frank Lloyd Wright gave the first preview on our program of that controversial structure. He said it would be a museum designed for looking at pictures, and he added that Samuel Guggenheim, who left $8,000,000 to further the art of the future, "was the only millionaire philanthropist who stayed with his convictions right to the end. Most of them, when it comes time to die, cuddle up to the past and leave their money for what they are sure is respectable. But Samuel Guggenheim believed in my design, and kept on believing even when everybody he knew laughed at him."

Frank Lloyd Wright came many times to be my guest. I introduced him once as that merry, bitter, lively, ambitious, and beguiling man, a quotation from an article about him.

Mr. Wright liked it all except the "bitter." I insisted, "You *are* bitter some days when you lash out at authority and at almost anything else that has disturbed you that morning."

"Bittersweet, perhaps," he finally yielded.

That day certainly he was sweeter than he was bitter, because we got to talking about his childhood in Richland Centre, Wisconsin, and this blazing iconoclast turned out to be almost as sentimental about his mother as I was about mine. His was a rebel family; his Unitarian-preacher grandfather came from Wales in search of freedom, and the middle western neighbors wanted to try him for heresy.

"One should select one's grandparents with even more care than one's parents," Mr. Wright decided, lifting his fine head with its white hair. "My grandfather believed in the druidic shibboleth of truth against the world. He was eighty when I first knew him. I remember him presiding with such vigor in chapel—we had a family chapel with rocking chairs for the uncles and aunts. I was with him when he bandaged an injured pine tree, talking all the time to me about saving precious life. That tree survived and grew to be eighty-three feet tall."

Before he was born Frank Lloyd Wright was destined by his mother to be an architect.

"She hung pictures of cathedrals in my room so I should see them mornings when I woke up and nights before I went to sleep. I never questioned her belief that architecture was the finest profession in the world. She was a woman of real character." There was a glow in his blue eyes when he said that.

He was not sentimental about the house he was born in, though—far from it. "It was imitation Cape Cod; it has disappeared, thank God," he declared grimly.

He said about war that "the men who had so little sense as to make it deserved to be wiped off the face of the earth." He seriously advised women to "strike and refuse to have children until war was outlawed!"

But sometimes I thought that his hatred of war was not animated so much by his worry about the people who would be destroyed as an advance protectiveness for the buildings, his kind of buildings, that he was fiercely determined to give to the world.

"What is art?" I asked.

"I find that when people talk about art they usually mean painting," he said annoyedly. "I don't understand painting. Children do it best, and I consider it the most primitive form of art. Architecture is the highest form."

"Writing?" I suggested.

"Yes, it's fascinating, but for me—it gets away from me. I can say things best with bricks and mortar."

We were doing the program that day in my studio apartment, and Frank Lloyd Wright observed that I was "an example of decentralization," because I was broadcasting away from the studio.

He was convinced and never failed to voice the conviction that cities are obsolete—that decentralization is the only solution. "Every city is bankrupt," he kept repeating. "It can live on its birthright no more than three years. The trouble with us in this country is that we've wasted most of our time on manufacturing, merchandising, making money, going right on with the colonial ideas we brought here instead of creating our own."

When he talked his face lighted up like the face of a very young man with all the world still to search out. "I *am* young," he insisted. "Youth is a quality, not a circumstance."

I think of all the men I ever met Frank Lloyd Wright was the luckiest. He never compromised with his principles. He nearly always said and did exactly what he felt like saying and doing with no regard for consequences. And at an eager-eyed eighty-four he had produced that controversial Guggenheim Museum at Eighty-eighth Street and Fifth Avenue.

The monument funny-men Olsen and Johnson leave behind them is less tangible, but real just the same, built of the hours of laughter they have given to all kinds of people. John Olsen once shoved a large brown bear into the control room of the studio from which I was broadcasting. Stella rushed at the bear, yelling, "Get out," and when he stood immovable she punched him. The bear rather halfheartedly punched back, ripping her dress. The bear didn't mean to do it, Ole, now entering to claim the bear, explained. "He has a cold and is scared of Stella."

I didn't know about any of this until later. The first intimation I had of the bear was a gasp in unison from a hundred women watching my broadcast. I lost the thread of what I was saying and looked over my shoulder. There was the bear, bowing politely to the audience from the control room.

Ole was supposed to be a guest that day, but not the bear. Except that of course I never knew who or what Ole Olsen and Chic Johnson might bring along when they came. They created havoc in my life often, but I love them both dearly. And not entirely because they gave me my chance on Broadway.

It was when their zany production *Laffing Room Only* was playing at the huge Winter Garden Theatre that Ole and Stella decided I should have my name in lights for one night at least.

Afterward Ole said on my program: "Mary Margaret McBride's histrionic contribution to the theater had us rehearsing for six weeks for the two lines she spoke." I protested that it was six lines, at least—and seemed like sixty. "Well, all I know," Ole went on, "is that Mary Margaret starred in the Winter Garden one night and practically the next the theater was sold. But I'll tell you this—she got more flowers than any star—in fact, she looked like a well-made grave."

The electricians took down Olsen and Johnson to put me up in lights, and I felt numb opening night, the way stars had told me they did. I opened and closed the same night, but in that short period I suffered all the agonies of stage fright, fluffed my lines, and burst into tears backstage. Those are the things I remember best. Also an enormous bearskin coat that I wore for one scene that was so long and heavy that I stumbled going on stage and stumbled going off. Luckily I didn't fall—I had very little on underneath that coat.

I think the bravado of putting me on the stage even for one night shows the kind of character Ole Olsen was. His object in life was to think of and execute zany stunts. His darling little mother was one of his favorite victims. In from Indiana for a visit, she came on the air with me and told indulgent stories about her son.

"One day he telephoned to say that a friend was driving through and would stop and visit with me. So I sent my daughter out to get a few things like bacon and eggs in case he stayed awhile and was hungry. That evening a bus drove up and thirty-nine people got out. John is a wonderful son, but he is the kind of person who will say one man is coming to dinner and then thirty-nine will show up. You have to get used to it."

It was obvious that she was proud of her son's lunatic imagination. She liked to act put-upon, but she loved being a part of *Hellzapoppin*, even out there in the middle of Indiana. Another time when she'd complained of not getting enough letters from him, Ole gave her address to more than a hundred inmates of a nearby penitentiary. They all wrote, putting their cell numbers on the outside of the envelopes. Mama Olsen wrote back happily, and years afterward still kept up a correspondence with a chosen twenty or so. Ole frequently was confronted by a beaming ex-con backstage at the Winter Garden, sent there by Mama, who just knew John would get him in to see the show, and John always did.

Four ex-convicts were waiting for the comedian the first time I went backstage at the Winter Garden, a harassed secretary was handing out Olsen and Johnson ties with "Stolen from Olson and Johnson" printed on them to a dozen soldiers and sailors, the mayors of two middle western cities, and half a dozen out-of-town police chiefs. Ole dashed in and greeted them all by their first names.

Yet anywhere but in his own dressing room if he goes up to a person, he'll say at once, "I'm Ole Olsen." John Kieran at the height of his "Information Please" fame always identified himself too. Mary Martin does it and, of all people, Mrs. Roosevelt. But Ole Olsen has, more than anybody I know, the ability to make people feel known and important.

Occasionally his practical jokes bounced back. Oscar Levy of Seattle, a leading jeweler and a much put-upon friend of Olsen and Johnson, took to boarding up his store and posting a sign—"Closed until Olsen and Johnson leave town."

One time when the company reached Seattle, Ole told me, "Levy brought a group called the Athletic Roundtable to the show. Chic had a thing he did—he'd come out wearing a hat and I'd say, 'Who are you?' and Chic would say, 'The lone eagle' and take off his hat and out would fly this pigeon. It was a homing pigeon and would go right to its place backstage. Well, these Athletic Roundtable guys all had their hats on with pigeons underneath, and at that line they let the pigeons fly. It was almost a panic; the rest of the audience didn't know what had happened.

"I got the Roundtable together afterward and they had to collect those birds. It took almost three days. I haven't had trouble in Seattle since then.

"Another time the company was met at the station by eight ice trucks loaded with two hundred and fifty cakes of ice, and the company had to sit on the ice while the trucks took us to this place for lunch. And there was the mayor, carrying a shoulder of lamb. It cost him a lot of time and money, but he gave us the cold shoulder all right."

Very few ever gave Olsen and Johnson a real cold shoulder, for their contribution was to make gay, joyous children of us all.

Though of course there are children and children. Some are older than most adults. Quiz kids, for instance. It seems a long, sad time ago since these prodigies delighted us on radio. There weren't any isolation booths then. Nobody was winning half a million dollars. Children though they were, I approached a program involving two Quiz Kids as guests with some trepidation. Especially after my reporter returned in a state of mild confusion from talking to that young demon, Joel Kupperman (married and with children now, I suppose).

"Joel," she said doubtfully, "may be difficult. He's small, looks about six, and his father sits in a corner while Joel hangs upside down from the chandelier in their hotel room, answering questions the while. He's certainly smart but—— Well, I wish you luck!"

The broadcast began with Joel imitating the Quiz Kids' roll call: "I'm Joel Kupperman, I'm nine years old and in 5-B in school in Chicago."

Harvey, the second and older of the Kids, had not yet come. The two were in New York to act as bat boys for a benefit game between two teams of youngsters, labeled East and West. Two of the star players were also in the studio and they answered politely. One, seventeen, was to play first base, the other sixteen, an outfielder. Since it was a roll call in the tradition of the Quiz Kids' program, Vincent Connolly rose to the occasion. "I'm Vincent Connolly, announcer for this program, and I'm thirty-five years old."

Whereupon Joel endeared himself to Vincent by whispering quite audibly, "He seems like fifty."

I gave up the roll call and asked Joel about being a mathematical wizard.

"I'm mathematical," the little wonder said, "but I ain't a wizard, and I don't even read the stories about myself. I haven't hardly seen any of them."

"That's just as well," I admonished, feeling rather like a stern maiden aunt. "But is it true that before you were five you wrote to the author of a mathematical textbook to tell him one of his answers was wrong?"

Joel said yes, it was true—but he didn't remember what he said.

"That's just as well," I rather confusedly repeated myself. "You're going to be a bat boy, Joel. Does a bat boy play an important part in baseball?"

"No," replied the disconcerting little boy, "not really—only he has to be careful. If the bat boy handles the bat a certain way, ignorant superstitious people think it's bad luck."

At this point the young genius was playing with his microphone and hopping about like a flea. I said, "Aren't you the one on the Quiz Kid program who always messes up the microphone?"

"No," retorted Joel.

Somebody came through from the control room. "That sounds like Harvey," commented Joel in a slightly apprehensive tone. It *was* Harvey. He sat down composedly beside Joel and remarked accusingly, "I heard that—and of course you do mess up the mike, Joel. He sits next to me on the program, and it is my duty to make sure he sticks his nose in the microphone. He used to sag back and forth and I'd have to grab him by the scruff of the neck."

I admitted that the only other Quiz Kid I'd met was Ruthie Duskin, and she at a tender age had found a mistake in the Bible. I asked, "How do you acquire so much knowledge?" Harvey answered thoughtfully: "The best thing to do is learn how to read. The biggest advantage of the Quiz Kids is they have good memories and they're kind of quick when the question is asked. When I first got on I thought I had to read every textbook I could get my hands on, and when the broadcast came I was so mixed up with all I'd read I made a bad score that night. Now I read about an hour a day, but I don't cram. I listen to the radio a lot, though."

Joel couldn't stay still any longer. He said he listened to the radio, too, but only when a ball game was on. He turned to Vincent: "Vincent—in the eighth inning with the bases loaded, a batter hits a home run. No man touches the base, yet all four of them score. How can that be?"

Vincent, a bit stiffly, confessed Joel had him.

"The players are women," Joel shrieked triumphantly.

I believe that the Dionne quintuplets (unique but except for that not characters in the sense that Joel Kupperman was) were interviewed as a group only once on the radio. That was on my program in 1950, and it was not what I'd call a very good interview. The five dark-eyed little Canadian girls were sixteen years old. Listeners that day heard one sentence repeated five times: "We are having a wonderful time."

I'd had to promise Papa Dionne not to ask them anything except a routine question or two. And indeed they were so shy and so unsure of their English that I'd probably have got little more out of them if I'd had permission to go ahead full steam. But they were such a world legend that their mere appearance in the studio brought reporters, cameramen, and so many people that we had to move to one of NBC's big theater studios, and even then the crowds were waiting in the streets.

The girls had come at Cardinal Spellman's invitation to attend an Al Smith dinner, a benefit for a new memorial wing being built at St. Vincent's Hospital. They were housed in the convent of St. Patrick's Cathedral, guarded, chaperoned, with, as far as I could determine, not a single moment to themselves.

Poor lambs, I thought, as they filed into the studio, attended by family, clergy, and civilian advisers. They've lived in a goldfish bowl all their lives, and today I'm certainly not helping much.

They looked at me bright-eyed when I opened the program by telling them that they were born just three weeks after I went on the air, and that the newspaper syndicate I worked for sent me to Canada the following May to report on their first birthday.

"You were so cute lying in your five little beds, smiling and contented. Then, as if on cue, one of you—I think it was Yvonne—started to cry and in two seconds all the rest of you joined in."

They burst into laughter. Glancing at Papa Dionne I ventured one question: "What time do you get up in the morning?"

"Six-thirty." (I think it was Emilie.)

"Do you say your prayers?"

"Yes!" (That was in concert.)

Lillian Barker, the reporter who'd done forty-one stories and a book about the Dionnes, told then how they'd hated being cooped up, and when they were four and five years old had begged to play in the road with their brothers and sisters.

"Emilie told me one time that the animals on her papa's farm were better off—*they* didn't live behind bars. They called themselves 'the poor little quints.'"

Lillian watched the children grow up into five poised individuals with five separate personalities.

At this point Yvonne said, in French, that they would be very pleased to sing for us because the night before at dinner they'd learned a new song in English. Whereupon five high, sweet voices sang out in memory of Al Smith:

"East Side, West Side, all around the town . . ."

Al Smith would have loved it. He was an unforgettable character himself. He came one day to talk about hospitals and spoke of himself as a radio talker.

"Didn't you used to say 'radio' differently?" I asked him. "You said 'raddio,' didn't you?"

"Yes, but I got out of the habit because I was afraid I might not be right about it. I was backed up by the professor of English at Yale, though."

I said disappointedly: "I thought you were the kind of person who, once you made up your mind, went straight ahead."

"Well, it caused too many laughs so I thought I'd drop it."

"But we need laughs, don't we?"

"That's all right when they ain't laughin' at you!"

"What hat did you wear here today?" I asked.

"I wore a brown soft hat on account of the rain. I'm very careful about my derby."

"I always wondered if you wore it every day."

"Only on fine days."

"How'd you ever start with that brown-derby business?"

"Well, when I was a young fellow everybody had a brown derby for the off season. There were no soft hats at that time and you had to wear the black one all year if you didn't change for Easter and the fall to the brown derby. They were very fashionable."

"And when you got into politics they described you as Al Smith with the brown derby."

"Well, that came about in a funny way. They used to have a stunt dinner for legislative correspondents, and in a little play an office employee said to a character supposed to be one of my opponents: "Do you know you've got to start out campaigning Monday? You'd better get a brown derby like Al Smith."

"Were you really sorry at first that you went to the Assembly?"

"Well, I didn't understand it. They didn't even know me the first year I was there. The speaker asked one of the clerks if I was a page boy or a member."

"But you kept going back, didn't you?"

"Oh yes, I went back twelve times. When I commenced to understand it, it was interesting."

I was curious about one other item—Al Smith's degree of F.F.M.

He explained: "Oh, that came about one day when there was a hot debate going on and an old man from Buffalo, in order to calm the debaters down, asked to be recognized. When he was he said: 'I just wanted to let the Assembly know that Yale won the boat race.'

"One debater said: 'That doesn't interest me. I'm a Harvard man.' Another snorted: 'It doesn't interest me. I'm a Syracuse man.' All the others called out their schools. So that left me all alone. Some fellow hollered out: 'What about you, Al?'

"'Well,' I said, 'I'm an F.F.M. man.' And Jimmy Houghy, who was sitting behind me, said: 'What does that mean, Al?' I said: 'It means Fulton Fish Market!'"

Al needed no degree to be important and remembered.

It's strange how sometimes one meeting with a person makes for an unforgettable memory. Tiny Amy Otis Earhart, mother of Amelia Earhart, came one day to present me with a bronze citizenship medal that had a bust of her daughter on it. She was past eighty but said she was still hoping to learn to fly.

"I had a letter from a man past ninety who just learned," she told me.

She had chosen to go to California to live all by herself, and she commented: "It's taught me a great many things. I always wanted an understanding heart. I've had such experiences in my life—and now I'm beginning to think maybe I have learned to have an understanding heart.

"My father wanted all his children to have seeing eyes. He was an interesting man. When Lincoln called for men to join and bring Kansas in as a free state he went with a group of New Englanders and helped with an underground for escaping slaves.

## FETED, CITED, HONORED:

"She was the only radio personality who held an anniversary (her tenth) in Madison Square Garden. 'Which I thought was bad enough,' she said, 'until the fifteenth was held in Yankee Stadium and fifty-five thousand people came. That's almost as much as a World Series, isn't it?' "—*Sidney Fields*

"Seventy-five thousand people jammed New York's Yankee Stadium . . . the celebration of her fifteenth year on radio."—*Celebrity Register*

(*Cosmo-Sileo*)

Tenth anniversary, Madison Square Garden.    Fifteenth anniversary, Yankee Stadium.

(*Abstract*)    (*N.B.C.*)    (*Jackson & Perkins C*)

McBride on Times Square.    Eddie Cantor presents the One World Award to her.    Jackson and Perk names a rose after h It wins the grand pr the first time exhibit

At United Nations, named the most important women in America, with Mrs. Roosevelt, Sister Kenny, Dorothy Thompson, and Emily Post.

State of Missouri dinner in celebration of the Missouri day named for Mary Margaret McBride

(*N.B.C.*)

## SOME OF THE PLACES SHE WENT:

Boarding the *Hindenburg* zeppelin. The next trip was its last.

(*Jimmy Sileo*)

(*Cosmo-Sileo*)

(*Cosmo-Sileo*)

*Middle left:* To a sugaring-off in New Hampshire, at Bette Davis' farm.

*Middle right:* The crew that took her far north of the Arctic Circle to the land of the aurora borealis.

*Bottom:* On Christmas Day, she took her listeners to the Cloisters, the medieval museum in New York City.

"You brought us the latest books, reviews and authors, the Broadway hits and actors and all the famous and great of our times. We even learned to like the commercials. . . ."—*A Listener*

(*Nickolas Muray*)

"She and her personal friends would privately test the claims made for the product by its manufacturer. When a product survives . . . the news is relayed to the radio audience in a white heat of Evangelism. 'Will you just try a box of it?' Miss McBride cries into the microphone, arms outspread. 'Will you try it?' "—Profile, *The New Yorker*

"The products she boosts range from shoe polish to noodle soups, and dog biscuits to grated cocoanut. The net effect of any broadcast would be sheer pandemonium without the soothing touch of a master mind to make it jell." —*Bennett Cerf*

e most outstanding example of reli-
· upon the word of a human being
e commercial field."—*Printer's Ink*

"I ate so many oranges I ought never to catch cold."—*A Listener*

## ACTORS AND CELEBRITIES

"The list of McBride guests includes authors, actors, politicians, Swiss bell ringers, screwball inventors, trapeze artists, hog callers, and flagpole sitters."—*Tradewinds*

(*Cosmo-Sileo*)

Bob Hope and Jinx Falkenburg        Fred Waring

(*Cosmo-Sileo*)           (*Impact Photos Inc.*)                      (*Cosmo-Sileo*

Russel Crouse        David Sarnoff and Tex McCrary.        Dinah Shore, Missy, George Montgomery

(*Wide World Photos*)

Olsen and Johnson                            The Zoo

# AUTHORS

"Authors are so at ease they frequently forget they are broadcasting . . . an all-out McBride recommendation is reflected immediately in the sale of a novel or autobiography"—*Bennett Cerf*

(*Gary Wagner*)

hor Heyerdahl, author of
on-Tiki.

(*Cosmo-Sileo*)

Carl Van Doren

Fannie Hurst

(*N.B.C.*)

uentin Reynolds

Mary Garden

(*KLM Royal Dutch Airlines*)

Poppy Cannon

(*U. S. Coast Guard*)

ok and Author Victory
an Rally, Buffalo, N.Y.

Sinbad, author of *Sinbad of the Coast Guard*.

(*Cosmo-Sileo*)

Jean Thomas

(*Cosmo-Sileo*)

General Omar Bradley chose her program in preference to a score of others for his first interview after his triumphal return from Europe. "Maybe my wife will appreciate me at last," he said happily. Mary Margaret with General and Mrs. Omar Bradley.

(*Wide World Photos*)

(*Ellingsen Photos*)

*Middle:* Mary Margaret with the first ladies—Mrs. Truman, Mrs. Roosevelt, and Mrs. Wilson.

*Bottom:* Mary Margaret being made up to broadcast from the G.O.P. Convention, 1952.

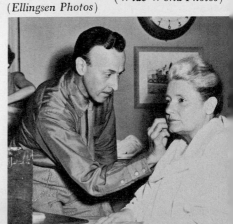

(*Cosmo-Sileo*)

Vincent Connolly, Mary Margaret, Janice Devine, Mrs. "D" (Deichler), Stella Karn, Henry Gabrielson.

Mrs. George Lee, and Mary Margaret's god-children Calvin, Lilly, and Bo-Lum.

Nephew Tommy's first birthday, on the air.

"As a young child I can see us sitting around the fire on hassocks listening to his stories, wide-eyed. Later I realized how important they all were."

I said she ought to write some of them.

"No," she demurred. "I never felt I had a gift for that, though I write lots of letters. I almost write letters in my sleep. Once I wrote to a hundred school children interested in Amelia's around-the-world flight. You know, teachers and children followed her flight on their globes.

"One darling little girl in Connecticut wrote me afterward: 'Dear Mrs. Earhart: Every day I take my National Geographic map down and look over those South Sea Islands, hoping I can find the one where Miss Earhart is and can tell you so you can go and bring her home.'

"Amelia was reserved," said her mother, "shy and shut-up like a clam. Her sister Muriel made the speeches. Amelia cared most about investigating things. She took to flying and flew like a bird. She didn't have to learn it. She was interested in the scientific side of flying; she didn't go at it haphazardly. Her plane was a laboratory."

Broadway was John Golden's laboratory.

My first real indication of what producer John Golden was like was when the reporter I had sent to see him said, "John Golden is determined to bring notes."

"Did you tell him that I don't allow anybody to bring notes to my broadcast?"

"Yes, but you don't know John Golden. He's going to bring notes!"

From that first appearance in 1942 until his death, more than thirteen years later, I loved John dearly, despaired of him, and indulged him as everybody did. He had his own barber chair in his office, and usually when I dropped in to see him, he was in it, being shaved and meanwhile dictating messages to his secretary, Clarence, and shouting for Alice, his receptionist-secretary. A boy was shining his shoes and at intervals he talked through the soap lather into an extension telephone.

For that first broadcast he had made Clarence print large cards which he planned to keep in front of him. These were to remind him to talk about the John Golden Theatrical Loan Fund; his producer's prize; his Equity Library Theatre; drama critics; USO entertainment for our armed forces ("I invented it in the First World War," he informed me parenthetically); and about presidents he'd known. He collected quotations from Wilson's speeches, wrote a tune for them, and sang the song at the White House. He was told by the President: "I don't know about your tune, but my words are damn good!"

Luckily I got to the studio rather early that day, two minutes instead of my usual thirty seconds before time to go on the air, and scornfully brushed John's array of cards off the table onto the floor. We began with John belligerently announcing to all the world that "Mary Margaret just threw all my notes on the floor so we can't do this program at all"—but we did it and while I got exactly what I wanted from him, he got in all his projects too.

A broadcast people talked about for a long time was on New Year's Day from my apartment. John wanted some special money for the Actor's Fund. I agreed to help but said I would do it in my own way. So I put him in the kitchen and locked the door. "I'll let you out when I'm ready for you," I assured him.

We started the show and had talked for about two minutes when the listeners heard John breaking open the door and talking at the top of his lungs about my gingerbread.

In lily-of-the-valley season he used to get up early and pick great bunches to leave at my door, and one morning he came up with the flowers to tell me he was having a first ladies' luncheon at Sardi's. He had a special table there and on this occasion had invited Mrs. Roosevelt, the wife of the mayor of New York, Helen Hayes, and Dorothy Shaver, president of a department store, for a wonderful lunch, including—because of me, he said—a confection made of cake, whipped cream, ice cream, nuts, and chocolate sauce. He scolded about my overweight, but he couldn't help indulging me just as I couldn't help indulging him.

Mrs. Roosevelt brought John along once when she came to do a show, and he caused such confusion that the first lady told him to sit down.

John said: "Ladies and gentlemen: I came here accidentally. I want to save my real appearance for sometime when Mary Margaret and I can be alone and make confessions, but I happen to be lucky enough to be Mrs. Roosevelt's attendant. I was told to sit down, but I saw something so shocking I'm not over it yet. Mary Margaret has a screen some six feet high with the names of the great, the near-great, and the hope-to-be-great of the theater world and the other world on it. It is so packed with signatures there's no room for more except at the extreme floor level. So I just saw the First Lady of the World lying on her stomach on Mary Margaret's floor writing something on the screen."

Mrs. Roosevelt commented dryly: "You'd better add that you did the same!"

# 13.  THEY'RE ALWAYS ON

NOVEMBER 18, 1952  *"Mary Margaret McBride is a liar."* Danny
Kaye

The above direct quotation from a broadcast with Danny Kaye
hints at, if it does not entirely explain, the reason that I usually got
very little sleep the night before a comedian was to guest on the program. Comedians are unpredictable, or rather I could always predict
with certainty that whatever they did or said, it would be unlike anything I had hoped for or planned. Sometimes it's true they pleasantly
surprised me. Thus Danny Kaye, after I had spent at least half an
hour cajoling and fencing, came through with some serious talk that
I thought was from the heart. But that half hour!

"Well, good afternoon, ladies and gentlemen," he began lecturishly.
"Here it is one o'clock and we're sitting here with Mary Margaret Mc-
Bride in this very nice studio—can I tell them it's your home?—sur-
rounded by a great many books which Mary Margaret never reads."

M.M.M.   I do so read them.

D.K.   I don't even think you have time to collect them.

M.M.M.   I read nearly every one of them—and I'm eager for you to
write your life, Danny Kaye, because then I can have a wonderful
time interviewing you. As it is I have to depend on such sketchy
sources.

D.K.   I take umbrage at that remark. This is no sketchy source. I
will give you information about myself [*sotto voce*] which has never
ever been released to anybody. [*In a whisper*] I was born in Brooklyn!
Now *nobody* knows that. [*Clears his throat noisily*] Yes, Brooklyn—a
stone's throw from here. Gee, do you think we blew the needle?

M.M.M.   I wouldn't be surprised if we are off the air, but please pay attention. I wanted to tell you, you're seven and a half years late on this program. I invited you just seven and a half years ago.

D.K.   Seven and a half years ago? Nothing interesting ever happened to me seven and a half years ago. Everything interesting that ever happened to me has happened in the past seven and a half minutes.

M.M.M.   Really? I don't dare ask what.

D.K.   Well, these books you say you've read.

M.M.M.   Your wife, Sylvia Fine, who came seven and a half years ago instead of you, said, "You and Danny will like each other." Now don't spoil it.

D.K.   I adore you—simply because you've read all these books.

M.M.M.   I didn't say I'd read *every* book—I said I've read *nearly* every book.

D.K.   Mary Margaret, may I conduct this trial? Ladies and gentlemen: Did you or did you not hear Mary Margaret McBride say, "I read every one of these books!"

M.M.M.   Listen—I'm known as having the most truthful program on the air.

D.K.   And the opening crack out of the bag you tell a lie. [*Laughter*]

M.M.M.   Couldn't we just change the subject?

D.K.   All right—I'll come back to it though.

M.M.M.   You're in a picture.

D.K.   *What* picture?

M.M.M.   Surely you want to talk about your picture. They all want to talk about their pictures.

D.K.   I don't want to talk about a picture. Any information you glean from me will have to be dragged out.

M.M.M.   Sam Goldwyn had me on the telephone this morning, and I told him he was very bad the last time he was on my program. I couldn't do a thing with him. He just kept getting in publicity for his current picture.

D.K.   Who? Goldwyn? Do you mean he talked about nothing but *Hans Christian Andersen?*

M.M.M.   No, this was about another picture. I thought I'd have *you* tell about *Hans Christian Andersen*. You like it, of course.

D.K.   I don't know. You know why? I haven't seen it. It's unfair to ask me if I like it, because when I sit in a motion-picture theater and

look at a picture I've done it's beyond my control. It isn't like walking
out on the stage—then I'm in control, but once it's in the can—it's beyond recall. There's nothing you can do about parts you'd like to speed
up or take out, so I just sit there and fidget and hope. I see a picture
much differently than you would. This one cost four million dollars—
and created an international incident—a protest lodged by some
Danish dame who asked Sam how can you let this idiot portray our
national hero.

M.M.M.  Meaning you?

D.K.  Yes. I don't look like an idiot to you, do I? [*In a quivering
voice*]

M.M.M.  Do I look like a liar?

D.K.  I'll say yes if you will.

M.M.M.  No, sir. You don't look like an idiot to me and I know you
aren't. Well, do I look like a liar to you?

D.K.  Have some water, Mary Margaret, please. Have a sip—it isn't
nice to drink before a lady does. Gurgle, gurgle, gurgle—cheers!

M.M.M.  Let's be serious. Let's talk about you.

D.K.  I'm the most wonderful fellow you ever met in your whole
life. I've never met anybody that's as nice as me.

M.M.M.  Your wife said you're unpredictable. On time for your appointments——

D.K., *interrupting*.  And read a lot of books.

M.M.M.  . . . but might not come home for dinner. If you did you
might sit at the table for a whole meal and not utter a word.

D.K.  The most honest thing to say about myself is that I'm a creature of whim. Most people would like to be. I'm just crazy enough
to be it.

M.M.M.  Were you when you were poor?

D.K.  Oh yes. You know, with added responsibility the impulsive
things you did when you were young are stifled—and to be aware of
any position you might have attained, weighs heavily.

M.M.M.  What kind of crazy things did you do?

D.K.  I was once supposed to sing in a choir. It was during Easter
vacation. A friend of mine said, "Dan, how would you like to take a
trip to Florida?" I said, "All right." And thirty minutes later we were
on our way. Hitched all the way to Florida and back.

M.M.M.  How did the choir get on?

D.K. They did very well without me. Once we were playing in Detroit—I was with Dave Harvey and Kathleen Young, my partners. The manager said, "How would you like to go to Japan?" We said fine. He said, "I'd like these two people—the redheaded boy I don't need!" meaning me. So I talked hard and fast and I went to Tokyo, Osaka, Nagasaki, Kobe, Shanghai, Canton, Hong Kong, Siam, Singapore.

M.M.M. You sound like a train caller.

D.K. They had a typhoon in Osaka while we were in the middle of a show. All the lights went out and there was a rumbling and rattling and the people were terrified. There was a boy on stage with me—Hershey Martin—and we got two flashlights, sat down on the stage with our feet dangling, and until the lights came on sang every song we knew to keep the people from leaving the theater.

M.M.M. Were you scared?

D.K. Yeh . . . Where are you from?

M.M.M. Missouri. Danny, when Bob Hope was on with me recently I found an old joke of his to startle him with. I couldn't find any of your old jokes.

D.K. I never told a joke—never told a gag, even. Well, maybe that's not quite true. I've been in show business going on thirty years, and the first time I ever told a joke in my life was a month ago on the stage—and you know who told it to me—a little girl named Jeanmaire.

M.M.M. Tell me the joke.

D.K. No.

M.M.M. Why?

D.K. Because I'm planning to tell it at the Palace when I'm there next week.

M.M.M. Oh, you dog—to lead me up to this point. I ought to put you right off the air!

D.K. I could get us off the air quicker than you could. No—if I were to tell you that joke it would take too long and I can't leave the air without talking about *Hans Christian Andersen*.

M.M.M. You already have.

D.K. Well, I can't leave the air without telling about the marvelous score, the music, the dancing, the costumes—now, can I?

M.M.M. I could bear up. I want you to talk about yourself. Why won't you?

D.K. Ask me anything.

M.M.M.   I could ask why you suppose Princess Margaret thinks you're wonderful. There's a poser for you.

D.K.   Well—*Hans Christian Andersen* is the kind of picture——

M.M.M.   What good are you to me? You could be such a wonderful guest.

D.K.   I'm not being good to you, am I?

M.M.M.   You're worse than Samuel Goldwyn, that's all.

D.K.   Well, I'll tell you. In 1948 when the royal family came to the Palladium it was the first time in the history of the variety theater in England that reigning royalty sat in the first row of the theater and not in the royal box. After the show was over I met them and spent an hour with them—we talked and laughed about a great many things— I absolutely forbade any photographers to be there. . . . It was a great honor royalty had shown me by even coming to the show.

Well, the next day there were some who wanted to know what I said to the princess and what the queen said to me and what the king talked about. I answered to all those newspaper people, "Look, I'm not going to tell you anything about it. Rather than have the royal family feel I'm making capital of their visit I will not discuss it. Rather than run the risk of anybody misquoting anything I say and thereby embarrassing the royal family who did me this honor, I'd rather not discuss it."

M.M.M.   I see your point, but I don't think it's that much more important what a queen or a president says than just an ordinary person. Try this instead—what is success?

D.K.   I don't know. Some people think it is being very happy or very productive, or accumulating a lot of money, or being famous. People say to me, "Isn't it wonderful to bring so much laughter and gaiety? Doesn't it make you feel good the whole day?" And I say sure it does, but once you stop being an entertainer after the hour and a half, you have to function like a human being for the other twenty-two and a half hours, and if you can't find some measure of happiness in your ability to be a human being, then your success as an entertainer isn't worth much, is it?

M.M.M.   I don't know whether I've been a success or a failure in this interview. I don't know what kind of Danny Kaye has emerged. What is important to you? Work? And does your work ever satisfy you?

D.K.   Sometimes. I think I would be a little bit untruthful if I said

I wish I could do everything all over again—but what I do never *quite* pleases me. I'm not a perfectionist though. When somebody says he's a perfectionist I say, "By whose standards?" He creates his own standards and by his standards he's a perfectionist, which means that everybody else's opinion is no good. I sound brilliant, don't I? Am I making a good impression?

M.M.M.   Are you saying all this just to make a good impression?

D.K.   No, I'd like to know whether people want me to sound like this or tell jokes.

M.M.M.   It's my job to make people talk about themselves.

D.K.   Well, you've drawn me out if that's what you want to know. Now I'm going to stay here and read every book.

M.M.M.   Before you go I want you to write on my celebrity screen. Now I have to get on with the products.

D.K.   You're inconsistent. You want me to tell all about myself, and now just as I'm getting warmed up and am about to tell my life story you chase me out. You know what I'm going to do—change every one of those books around and put each in a different place.

M.M.M.   Please don't. They're all listed in the files.

D.K.   And you'll come to see the picture?

M.M.M.   Yes.

D.K.   What picture?

M.M.M.   *Hans Christian Andersen.*

While I did my products Danny wandered round the room, at intervals shouting, "I'm not a comedian, I'm an entertainer," and finally, as he wrote on my screen, sing-singing what he was writing: "Mary Margaret McBride is a liar."

At this distance from the events, I can't quite decide which I had more trouble with, Danny Kaye or Bob Hope. At least Danny was on time for the broadcast.

"One o'clock and here's Mary Margaret McBride," intoned Vincent. I was watching the door for the man who wasn't there. I could see Stella on the control-room telephone undoubtedly trying to locate the missing Bob Hope. And I thought frantically, as I always did when somebody was late, "Were we definite about the time? Did he really understand? Or does he think it's tomorrow?"

"The guest today is one of the most famous men in the world," I told my listeners more gaily than I felt. "He's not here yet, but I'll give you a few clues so that maybe you can guess who he is. He's traveled more than a million miles during World War II. He owns part of a major-league baseball team."

The women in the studio murmured and rustled. I did a few commercials. I described a tea party I'd gone to for a new brassiere account, and a luncheon for Mrs. Roosevelt. Still no guest. I decided to try another clue. "He wrote a book—in fact, he's written two books—and here he comes!"

Bob strolled in as casually, as if he weren't twenty-five minutes late. "That's what I call making an entrance, Bob Hope," I remarked, acidly, when the applause died down. He sat opposite me looking sleepy and explained: "This is morning for me. I'm on before the acrobats here. And what have you got in this studio, anyway—the YWCA?"

"No," I said, "they're friends of mine, and when I told them before the broadcast that you were coming, they squealed."

"Who'd they think I was—Sinatra's father? . . . Got any coffee around? My taxi must have gone underground on the way. How late am I?"

"Twenty-five minutes," I replied grimly.

"And what did you do? Don't tell me—I know! You ad-libbed. You see, I've heard a lot about this little program. What am I saying, *little program?* I'm ruined before we start . . ." All this delivered in the familiar Bob Hope style with pauses for laughter which obligingly came from the studio guests.

"For one thing," I interrupted, "I've been giving our listeners clues about you and if I'd gone on, I'd have said, 'He's a statuette in the Smithsonian Institution—and he's head of a plumbing concern.'"

"Why don't you just tell them I'm Crosby's son?"

"Now listen, Bob. Do you know the answer to this one? Why is a little pig's tail like getting up at five in the morning?"

Bob looked absolutely blank. "Why is a little pig's tail . . ." he muttered.

"Yes—why is a little pig's tail like getting up at five o'clock in the morning? . . . Twirly! Too early! And it's your own joke."

"No," Bob moaned. "No, I couldn't have. Did I really? Twirly, twirly. How awful!"

By now my studio audience was in mild hysterics. Bob rallied. "All right—it's my joke from thirty years ago. What did I pay my writers then, I wonder? . . . But," brightening, "it might not be so bad at that for the early audience at the Palace. Always keep your writers' jokes, even the bad ones—you paid for them. I've had ten writers in the past twelve years and never thrown a single joke down the incinerator."

The audience laughed again and Bob Hope stared at them incredulously. "Hey, Mary Margaret, would you rent this audience out? Listen to them. What do you hustle on this program anyway?"

"I've already hustled them. Now let's talk about your command performance in London when you presented your album to Princess Margaret Rose. And the King of England played your straight man."

"Yeah—but he's pretty good himself. I was careful. You could get killed for topping the King of England. He asked about Bing Crosby. I said Crosby's middle name is Fort Knox—you know, parlor stuff. Fun, though."

Bob Hope couldn't get over the fact that our show was really ad lib. "Mary Margaret, you just flip it. I'm a script man myself. But gee, it's really something just to sit down like this and go easin' along, Miss McBride."

"You called me Mary Margaret before—you can keep right on."

"I can? Let's dance."

"Bob Hope, I don't care whether you say one single funny thing today—this is an interview. I want to find out about you. I like you even if you *were* twenty-five minutes late."

"You have to like people, Mary Margaret—or you can't stay in show business. And I do like people. In Springfield yesterday a fellow came backstage, and he turned out to be a Danny O'Brien who remembered me from a show in New York called *Sidewalks of New York*. Ruby Keeler was in it—and Al Jolson, Eddie Dowling, and that little girl he married, Ray Dooley. So I took Danny on stage and introduced him, and he told how Jolson always gave Ruby Keeler a big kiss every night—I added that in those days of course Jolson was doing his own puckering."

The studio audience roared and so did my announcer, who never laughed at *my* jokes. I didn't think it was that funny, but I waited and finally got back to what I hoped was going to be an interview (the clock said it never could be). Before I could ask a question Bob Hope observed, "You're trying to tell my life story, Mary Margaret—and I think it's awfully jolly, really."

Thoroughly frustrated, I began again. "You do have children."

"Yes, four—talked to them an hour and a half ago, and they're as sassy as ever."

"All the pictures I could find of your baby show just her back."

"Sure, she's a backward child."

My audience again shrieked with laughter, and Bob Hope looked at them fatuously. "I want to wrap up these kids of yours, Mary Margaret. I may need them at my opening Tuesday night!"

Gratified laughter while I returned doggedly to the Hope life story. "Remember when you clerked in a store?"

Bob, amid hoots of laughter, noted, "This girl Mary Margaret is part of the FBI."

"Bob, please."

"I know—there's a lot of ham in me."

"Bob Hope, time's almost up, so do be serious for a moment."

"Well, here's a serious thought—we're living at too fast a pace. Bombs, jet planes. Wouldn't it be awful if the Republicans had got in just as the world went out? Sorry—I used that once before—I have a little Milton Berle in me. You gave me a straight line and I pointed."

"It's too late now—only a few seconds left before Vincent puts us off the air—but I've been trying for a long time to find out how a person like you feels about being famous."

"I don't feel famous. I don't know—I think you have to try to keep your balance. As for work, you have to do the same things you did while you were on the way up only, I guess, more so."

VINCENT   Mary Margaret McBride returns at this same time tomorrow.

And that was the first time I was a straight man for Bob Hope.

I tried again—and again, but it always came out the same way. That's why I say that comedians are the hardest people to interview. They can't help it. They are always on.

Years after that on Jack Paar's television show he allotted twelve minutes for me to ask him about his life. I dug up all the information I could about him. He had a bad illness when he was young, frustrations here and there, and I felt his listeners would like him the better for knowing some of this.

It turned out I was right. There was lots of mail, and some people said they hadn't been sure whether they liked Jack or not but after hearing him talk seriously about himself they knew they did. But the interview was the same old agony for me. Jack tried, I know, but the audience didn't expect a funny man to be serious. It laughed all the way through. I cried afterward, which reminds me that Jack, introducing me one time, said we were the two cryingest people in New York. Which could be true. But all funnymen I've known can go from wisecracks to tears in the blink of an eye.

Jimmy Durante is a prime example.

"Something inside kept him good and honest and kind." I read that quotation from Gene Fowler's book *Schnozzola* as Jimmy sat across the microphone from me. "When you come near him, it's like warming your hands at a fire."

The tribute was Lou Clayton's, long-time partner of the great comedian. I thought Jimmy, listening, seemed about to cry, and since that's just what he had done the first time I interviewed him (we got off on our childhood memories), I switched abruptly to his nickname, Schnozzola. Jimmy explained: "The kids used to yell at me, 'Big Nose!' They'd turn around and stare at me, and I was always having fights. The greatest thrill I ever got was when I made my first picture, *Get Rich Quick Wallingford,* and got letters from thousands of kids all over telling me they didn't mind any more about their noses. In fact they were tickled to death when some other kid yelled 'Schnozzola' at them."

Jimmy looked pensive. "I guess it's because I was hurt that I never like to make fun of anybody. I keep away from a joke that's got anything to do with afflictions, like stuttering, or hospitals."

I told him Eddie Cantor and I had been talking about the old days when Cantor and Durante were at Coney Island.

"Yeah—we bragged we knew any song and could sing it. Anything to get a dollar. Eddie'd come over to me and say, 'A guy just gave me two dollars to sing "Kentucky Hills" and I don't know it.' I'd start improvising on the piano and Eddie'd start singing:

> *'Way down in those Kentucky Hills*
> *Far, far away in those Kentucky Hills*
> *Oh those Kentucky Hills, great Kentucky Hills . . .'*

"Of course the guy would say, 'That ain't the song,' and he'd want his money back. But two dollars was a lot of money in those days and so we'd keep right on doing 'Kentucky Hills' until the fellow would give up."

Jimmy didn't sing then, just played the piano. "But back in 1912, when we opened up the Club Durante, Clayton and Jackson used to walk around like bosses—and there I was, the owner, sitting and playing the piano until five or six in the morning. So I said, 'I want to be a boss, too,' and we hired a piano player and I started singing. I was scared but I got on the floor with Clayton on one side and Jackson on the other and we picked up some routines."

I asked if he had really played piano for the great Albert Einstein. Jimmy nodded. "Yeah, it was at the Mirador in Palm Springs. The owner called me up and said, 'Jimmy, Einstein is down here and he's playing violin and his wife is playing piano. Gee, it would be great if you came down and played piano for him.'

"I wanted to know who Einstein was—did he come from the East Side where I was born? The guy said, 'Are you kiddin'?' 'Yeah,' I said, 'I'm kiddin'.' Because he thinks I ought to know Einstein. Only I didn't. But down I come.

"His wife spoke English and said, 'Mr. Einstein would like to play with you.' So they give me the music—it was some Jerome Kern melodies and it was just the accompaniment. You know, the violin plays a few bars and then you come in and hit a chord and a little later another chord or maybe an arpeggio. So I sat down at the piano and he give a wave of the wand. And I didn't start. So he give another wave. Then I came in with the wrong note at the wrong time. We started again and I hit another bum note. Then his wife said, 'Perhaps—if you don't mind—Mr. Einstein is a little tired today.' And that ended the concert."

Jimmy looked disconsolate, like a small child who doesn't know quite what he's been punished for, and all I could think of to do was to reach over and give him a hug. I love Jimmy Durante.

For that matter, I love Eddie Cantor, who swapped quips with me often through the years. There was one Eddie Cantor day I remember especially, because the night before had been Eddie Cantor Night in Carnegie Hall. In the programs before, Eddie had been funny and sad, corny and pretty wonderful. But this time I had backstage news for my listeners because I'd been at Carnegie Hall the preceding night to present Eddie with the One World Award. As I began describing the award which chronicled his services to humanity Eddie minimized it to the applauding studio audience.

"Service? That's the rent we pay, isn't it, for the room we take up on earth—and I merely try to be a good tenant."

I went on to detail the frantic moments of the night before when Ida, the wife he's made famous, was sewing a button on his best suit and I was worrying about how to pronounce "status" and finally said it as in "statue." But after I'd said it I was sure it should have been as in "state." Vincent, with Princetonian aplomb, ruled that either was permissible, and Eddie Cantor grinned:

"Don't worry about grammatical errors with me on the air."

*He'd* been worried about his grammar the night before, though. A darling little woman had come backstage, put her arms around him, and hugged him tight. She was Miss Katherine Luddy, once Eddie's eighth-grade teacher. "I was scared she'd get up in the middle of the performance and correct my grammar," Eddie admitted, and I think he really was.

I asked him how he felt just before he went on to be introduced as a man who'd raised $150,000,000 at benefits during his years in show business. "I'll tell you, Mary Margaret—I said to myself: 'Well, Eddie Cantor, the kid from Henry Street, is in Carnegie Hall. He has Toscanini's dressing room. There are photographers everywhere—and flowers and telegrams. It's a switch.'"

I described the fantastic cake that arrived at Carnegie Hall—done in flowers made of icing—with figures of the famous five Cantor daughters, their dresses made of icing too.

"Yes, it was beautiful," Eddie agreed. "I wish I *could* have had my daughters' clothes made of icing—it would have saved me a fortune."

I was curious about the enormous repertoire of songs and gags which Eddie had managed at Carnegie Hall for over an hour, without a note. He explained that any song he'd ever sung, any bit of reading he'd really liked, he could recall letter perfect without an effort.

"I remember all the nice things, the unpleasant things I forget immediately."

But Eddie does remember, and tells graphically, about his childhood on the Lower East Side, when pennies were hard to come by.

His parents died when he was young, and his Grandma Esther, as he called her, brought him up. "We lived in two rooms," he went on. "Grandma Esther ran an employment agency, and so all the unemployed would sleep in our two rooms. I'd ask where could I practice and she'd say, 'Oh, go out in the hall.' If she knew that last night I played in Carnegie Hall—— But I think Grandma Esther was there."

Once Eddie Cantor invented a father. "All these kids were telling about the presents their fathers were bringing home, so I made up this character. I said, 'My father is a fireman.' They asked where and I said, 'It's out of town—it happens to be he's in Newark—that seemed very far away—he's been at a lot of big fires and they've promoted him.' Then one time they all chipped in and said, 'Let's go to Newark and see your father,' so I had to tell them the truth."

In those days Eddie Cantor bought broken crackers which were sold on the Lower East Side from a barrel for a penny a pound. "I'd eat a broken cracker and a piece of pickle and a hunk of cheese even the mice had given up."

It was getting a little too sad for a comedian's story, and besides, I suddenly remembered that I wanted to ask about one of last night's telegrams that was addressed "Dear Sam."

"That," snorted Eddie, "was from Georgie Jessel. He never calls me by my name. He'll telephone and say, 'Peter, this is Fred,' and I'm supposed to know it's Jessel. He's going to be narrator at Carnegie Hall next week for a Gershwin memorial and so this telegram of his said: 'Dear Sam, don't worry about yourself tonight. Just go outside and see how is my billing!'"

Hardly any comedian ever seems to get places on time. Not to my broadcast, anyway. Eddie Cantor was always late, Bob Hope was late, Jimmy Durante was late. So were Jerry Colonna and Frank Fay. Also Georgie Jessel.

Georgie was commuting to Hollywood twice a week just then, so I couldn't blame him too much for oversleeping. This day he arrived just as I was wondering aloud whether it was true that he and Eddie Cantor once had six benefits scheduled in one night.

Georgie said yes, but the pay-off was: "Eddie and I rushed through five of the benefits and by then we were pretty good. We'd worked up a real snappy act. It grew from five minutes to half an hour, so when we got to our sixth benefit and found the theater had closed for the night—well, we did our act, anyway, for the doorman. Four months later we were booked in at the Palace—with that act. Stayed three months too."

I opined that three months at the Palace must have brought in a lot of money.

"That's right—and Cantor still has his share—I lost mine."

Before anybody could work up tears of sympathy I brought out a rumor I'd read that George Jessel often got as much as $2500 just for emceeing a dinner.

"Well, some places I get $5000 to make a speech."

"Honest?"

"I wouldn't say it's quite honest—no—but then there are lots of times I make two and three speeches a week and not only I don't get anything, but three places somebody spilled soup on me and four places I tore my pants—so it isn't quite as good as it seems."

Georgie made his first speech at the age of six. "I went to a wedding, and my mother had bought a suit for me that had little rhinestone buttons and I thought they were diamonds and I made this speech —maybe I heard it somewhere but anyhow, I said it: 'Here's to the bride and groom, may their future be as bright as my three diamond studs.' I was a bigger hit then than any time since."

George Jessel speculated about the great demand for him as a speaker and concluded it was simply because ad-lib speakers are getting rarer every year. "The theater isn't big enough any more to train them. Arnold Daly, Frank Daniels, George M. Cohan, Nat Goodwin, Sam Bernard—all these men were students of the theater. They were literate and they looked forward to making curtain speeches. People used to say, 'Maybe we'll be late, but we'll be in time for the curtain speech.' Now nobody learns the art of public speaking. I'm not against advancement—no buggy is as good as a fast car—but I do say that this younger generation becomes successful so quickly, they've never heard or had to say, 'Ladies and Gentlemen.'"

Georgie claims Groucho Marx once declared: "Jessel is the only man I won't interrupt."

"A nice compliment," added Georgie, "from a fellow who heckles his own child."

Groucho heckled me once, in a manner of speaking—but I am used to that from comedians. One night a friend at whose house I was dining asked if I wanted a certain television program. I said no, I preferred Fred Allen, and she turned on just as he was saying, "Well, it's not Mary Margaret McBride, kiddies."

Nothing would convince my friend that I hadn't been told he was going to do it. But the truth was that I never knew when I listened to a comedy program that my own name or a reasonable facsimile mightn't come popping out. And I didn't understand why. I knew that as a person I lent myself to kidding and even caricature; overweight, unmarried, with a reputation (really undeserved) of babbling on and on forever like the famous brook. But what was funny about my name? All this perplexity and what light I could get on the matter I put into an open letter to Groucho Marx in a column I did for Associated Press.

"Dear Groucho Marx: People keep telling me that you said, not once but several times on your television program, that you have written me five letters asking whether to put raisins in bread pudding and that because I have never answered any of them, you have decided that I don't exist.

"I don't like to doubt you, Mr. Marx, but I have a funny feeling that you were joking when you said you'd written me all those letters. In the first place, I answer every letter I get practically the day I get it. There have even been complaints about this. In fact, one of the kind friends who always tells you horrid things informs me that some people threaten to stop writing to me because it makes them nervous, always owing me a letter.

"Of course there is a possibility that you wrote and the letters never were forwarded. What address did you use, may I ask? In care of the paper in which you read this would be a sure-fire guarantee that you'd be happily eating bread pudding with raisins, made the McBride way, in no time at all.

"It just happens, Mr. Marx, that I have a cookbook coming out next spring that tells about how to make bread pudding 127 different ways, one of which doesn't include bread at all. That one is called Mock Bread Pudding. It does contain raisins, though, and if you'd like me to, I'll name it Marx Mock Bread Pudding for you. Wouldn't that be nice?

"Now that we've disposed of the subject of bread pudding, I think I ought to assure you that I really do exist—and far too solidly. Moreover, you are not the only radio or television personage who bandies my alliterative name around. Fred Allen started it, Bob Hope and others—most recently, Tallulah Bankhead—picked it up.

"The lot of you got me into trouble in my home town, too. The last time I was there a lady who is very nice but sometimes puts a little sting into her approach said, 'What do these comedians mean by making a joke of your name? I think we ought to write them and say Our Mary Margaret doesn't have a funny name at all.'

"Well, I assured her that you meant no harm and that I rather liked it, but she looked politely unconvinced. So then I asked a very amusing man I know, named Henry Morgan, who has also kicked my name around a little, what is back of it.

"I've felt better about the whole thing ever since, for Henry was very comforting. He answered me on his radio program, sort of the way I'm answering you in this column. He said that in the first place it's a nice long name with a lot of Ms that give it a kind of rolling rhythm. Then he added that since I've always been associated with home and mother and sentiment, it makes a funny contrast to drop my name into the middle of horseplay or slightly raucous fun. To tell you the truth, Mr. Marx, I think Henry Morgan was just explaining in a nice way that I'm considered somewhat corny. But I don't care. I think all of you are corny, too—if you weren't, people wouldn't like you so much.

"So now I hope you will realize that I do exist, Groucho, and many happy dinners with bread pudding to you!"

In reply Groucho declared (which of course I knew) that he was just being mildly humorous about my name and meant no harm even though he connected it with bread pudding which, he now confessed, he "loathes, with or without raisins."

"I do like rice pudding with raisins," he added, "but outside of Dinty Moore's in New York, I rarely encounter one that is worth eating. Bread pudding is a confession of failure. When people have fresh bread, they eat it. When they have stale bread, they either stuff it in a turkey or pretend it's a dessert and make bread pudding out of it. Why don't they just throw it out? Somebody once told me that stale bread is good for cleaning windows. Perhaps that is the solution.

"At any rate, I love you madly—and if I wasn't a married man with a number of children, I would ask for your hand—but not the one you use for making bread pudding."

So now, though I often listen, Mr. Marx never mentions me any more.

I'm pretty sure Groucho's mustache is real but for years I'd been wondering whether or not Jerry Colonna's was a fake, so when he arrived for our broadcast (late, of course) I reached across the table and pulled it.

"I thought it was false maybe."

"I thought so, too, for many years," agreed Colonna, unabashed, "but I pulled it myself one day and sure enough, it wasn't."

I'd have liked to have had television then, but next best I tried to tell how the Colonna face kind of turns up—mustache, mouth, even eyebrows.

In keeping with such a face, he boasted: "I just have fun—all day long. Nothing but fun."

I asked a silly question and got what I deserved: "How did you get to be funny?"

"My mother woke up one day and saw me and blew her top. I looked funny—she named me Jerry Convertible Colonna. I sang in St. Mary's choir in Boston—but there was even something funny about my voice. I managed to sing barbershop tenor, and as soon as Father Collins located where the tenor came from I lost my job. So I went out on the road with an orchestra of my own. I played drums and the trombone."

"Jerry Colonna, I've been hearing about a man in a book who had a tooth pulled at Tarawa, crashed in a plane in Australia, had a betel-nut hang-over, gave a command performance for a sturgeon, and made a perilous escape from an ice-cream freezer."

Jerry beamed. "All true. I'm that man—it's all true!"

"Just start with the ice-cream freezer, please."

"Well, it was a South Pacific island. The Navy was the only service branch that had refrigeration down there, and I got in the refrigerator because I was terribly hot and it was nice and cool inside. Then I heard a snap—and it locked. I pounded and hollered but nobody heard. Luckily they were making ice cream and hours later they sent someone down to get ice to freeze it—and they let me out."

I thought the story came off better in his book. I decided to try the sturgeon.

"It's just that I was swimming around out there and saw quite a few fish, that's all."

"That isn't all—not the way you told it in the book, Jerry Colonna."

"Well, one of the fish happened to be a sturgeon, and I don't know how he got way down south there from Siberia."

"And what did *you* do?" I tried again.

"I got back on the ship as fast as I could."

I decided to end that. "Jerry Colonna, you're a nice guy," I told him, "but I guess you're a script man. Bob Hope says he is too. Next time we'll break our rule. You put your writers to work, and I'll let you use the script."

Phil Silvers, I'd say, is one comedian who can take a script or leave it alone. But then I'm partial when it comes to judging this man. When he and Nanette Fabray were playing in *High Button Shoes,* I got stuck with a broadcast somewhere in New Jersey. Stars, especially when they're playing in a big success as these two were, don't like to take long rides out of New York, but Phil and Nanette promised to go. However, on the morning we were to leave at nine o'clock they were both sick to the throwing-up stage from something they'd eaten after the theater the night before. I was desperate but I said of course— if they felt too awful . . .

"Certainly not," they both protested. They went along with me (three hours there and three hours back) and were delightful. Nobody could have guessed how they felt. Another reason I have a special soft spot for Phil is that he didn't once evade a question or pull a wisecrack or try for a laugh in the interview.

He said: "Yes—I came from a pretty rough neighborhood—Brownsville in Brooklyn. That was where they had Murder, Inc., you know. I guess it's still pretty well publicized as a bad spot for juvenile delinquents and goons. I might have been one of those kids, but I was raised with a lot of affection. Sure, my folks were against my going on the stage. But since the age of three I had that desire. For my mother and father being an actor was next door to being a leper—but finally they saw I had to do this and they kind of went along and so I stayed on the stage, even though they hoped I'd go back to school. I guess my greatest ambition was always to be top banana. You know, a top banana is the top person in burlesque."

When I saw Phil Silvers some time later, he began to talk about his performance for the President just a few days earlier.

"That was the highlight of my professional life. We entertained the President. I got real tensed up. Every place you looked there was a secret service man—I guess they knew me but there was a possibility I look like another fellow who looks like me—you know? Anyway, there was a last-minute emergency and one of the acts was canceled, so I said, 'Give me a clarinet.' See, I had this thing I could do and I offered on impulse. It was a big moment. I got real butterflies. And when I walked out in front of the crowd I shielded my eyes from the spotlight and looked round and there was everybody—just everybody in our government. I stayed there for twenty seconds perfectly still— it took a little guts, too, Mary Margaret—but I simply stared at all those important people and finally I said: 'My goodness, who's minding the store?'

"That first laugh kind of took the butterflies away. There was another wonderful, happy accident. In the Statler ballroom in Washington where this affair was held the telephone rang accidentally and secret service men immediately jumped on it—might be a bomb or something, I guess. Well, I felt the distraction—everybody looking toward the telephone—but I kept on playing the clarinet and telling the things I was supposed to tell. Then I stopped, looked off stage as if I was listening to somebody talking, and I turned toward the President and said: 'There's a long-distance call from Mr. Dulles—he says he'll talk to anybody.'

"Later, when I came to the President in the receiving line, he told me—'Son, you've given me some laughs I need very badly right now.' And that great ad libber, Phil Silvers, just looked at the President— and froze. Ten seconds later I thought of the sweetest things I could have said—too late!

"When you see the President—Eisenhower, Roosevelt, whoever it is—*the* President, it's something. Like during the war we did USO entertaining and we knew about the bombings. But when we walked among the ruins and rubble of London—you could smell it and feel it, then you knew. And when you see the President in wartime, you realize what he's up against and you don't think of yourself and how good you want to be. You just want to make that man laugh and forget his troubles for a while."

On another broadcast with Phil Silvers we'd had some literary guests, too, and the talk got round to Henry Morton Robinson's best-selling novel, *The Cardinal*, which Phil said he'd read in a paperback edition.

"As a matter of fact, the head man is a very good friend of mine," he commented.

I didn't know exactly what to say. Cardinal Spellman, did he mean?

Phil bubbled on. "The Pope—we had a private audience, Frank Sinatra and I. We were in Rome and Frank just lifted the phone and half an hour later we were in the Vatican. I bought some rosary beads from a little old lady outside. I'm not a Catholic, you know, but I thought of Crosby—and asked His Holiness if he knew him and he said yes. I guess *Going My Way* didn't hurt Bing at the Vatican. Sinatra was explaining about not singing opera, and the Pope said, 'You're a great singer and you don't sing opera?' That was a joke to the Pope. Anyway, I asked if he'd bless these rosary beads for Crosby's sons, and I put them in a little can so I could honestly tell Bing that the last hand that touched the beads had been the Pope's. We talked a while longer and he gave me a mother-of-pearl Vatican-stamped rosary and a prayer for the family, a great lesson in—I hate the word—tolerance. But here's this little Jew from Brooklyn and the Pope gave me all that time. But the blackout for the humorous part of this story is we're walking down the steps and Sinatra hits me in the arm full strength—like a fly lighting on me—and he said: 'You silly slob. I take you to see the Pope and you plug Crosby!'"

And that's the way Phil Silvers, funnyman, is when he's not on!

# 14. ADVENTURERS

*"My whoop of joy when I found a cookbook was so loud in my ears that I was embarrassed. In twenty days it was the first sound that had passed my lips." Admiral Richard E. Byrd, explorer, was telling that day about his incredible stay all alone for months at a weather base in the Antarctic where the thermometer sometimes registered 74 below zero.*

Those were my favorite programs, the ones in which I talked to men and women who had been to faraway places. One brought in a dinosaur egg that looked like a baked potato. Another jangled an ancient emerald necklace in front of the microphone and tried it on me. It had belonged to Cleopatra, he said, and there was a curse on it. I hastily took it off. A third was escorted by a myna bird which started singing "The Star-Spangled Banner" just before time to go off the air, delaying our exit thirty seconds.

But their stories were the chief treasures the adventurers brought me. Sometimes their memories almost overcame them. Admiral Byrd stared straight ahead, not at me or the microphone, but at some vision out of the silence and solitude of his frozen Antarctic. The pauses in his narrative showed he was at times deeply affected. His decision to go it alone at the weather base was motivated, he confessed, partly by a desire to look in on himself. Perhaps he was still doing it.

The experience was so personal, he said, that it was years before he could write about it, and writing about it so painful that sometimes he put his manuscript aside for months.

"Though I marked off the days on my calendar I was not bored by the endless time on my hands," he told me. "The silence had a rhythm and I was part of it. I felt one with the universe."

The cookbook incident to which Admiral Byrd seemed to turn with relief from graver matters had figured earlier in a problem at the main base. All their flapjacks stuck to the griddle, and the cookbook didn't say how to prevent it. Finally Admiral Byrd sent an S O S to Oscar of the Waldorf and back to the Antarctic came instructions about batter consistency and hot skillet. Now the cookbook turned up in the gear that had been packed for his solitary experiment.

The explorer let his hair grow long because it kept his neck warm. He shaved once a week, not for looks, but because otherwise his beard would ice up and freeze his face. He took a daily bath because he liked to feel clean. At first it was a wonderful luxury to take an hour if he pleased to read a single page of a book. Everything he did was in slow motion because there was no reason to rush. Then came the polar night—the temperature went to 65 degrees below, then 72, then 74.

The ink in his record keeper froze, though it was diluted with glycerine. The air in the fuel tank expanded and oil went shooting all over the place. The fuel wouldn't pour from the drums. He had to keep Primus stoves burning in the tunnel that connected his quarters with his work and supplies.

One day he found he couldn't see. Then he fell into a stupor. Finally roused to half-consciousness, he realized that the fire had been out for twelve hours, that he hadn't eaten for thirty-six hours. He was probably dying.

Then came the miracle. The explorer tried to explain it: "Somehow I deliberately took hold of my thoughts. If a pessimistic idea tried to get through I suppressed it. I knew that confusion and despair would finish me off, and I just didn't let them!"

Admiral Byrd really came on my program not to talk about himself but about a cause close to his heart—moral rearmament. He had come to certain firm conclusions during his stay alone in Antarctica.

"After I was poisoned with carbon monoxide," he said, "my eyes got bad and I wasn't able to read any more. For two and a half months I was under the snow, in darkness. I thought a good deal about the world I really believed I'd left forever behind me. I reflected on all the foolish things people do, the most foolish of which is to settle disputes by killing one another instead of meeting in godly arbitration.

And I decided if there was to be a world left, people would have to change their thinking."

The strategic area in the world, Admiral Byrd believed, "is the North Polar Sea and the North Pole." Any future war, he predicted, will be fought across that expanse.

Peter Freuchen had the same conviction. A newspaper dispatch reported that a winner of the $64,000 quiz had been hit by a taxicab in Paris. I was shocked to hear Peter Freuchen, scholar, explorer, and historian, identified as a quiz winner. It seemed to minimize him and to be a sad commentary on our times.

Peter came closest to looking like an explorer of anybody I ever interviewed. He was a tall viking of a man, with a wooden leg, a swinging beard, and a delicious sense of humor. His curiosity first showed itself when he was very young. He and his brother, then in school in Denmark, decided to find out whether hair would actually stand on end.

"We experimented on our teacher," Peter told me. "She had beautiful hair, and we thought it might stand on end if we put tacks on her chair. Alas, *she* stood, but did her hair? We never knew!"

Though it was such a grim story, the explorer talked calmly about the loss of his leg. He was alone in a polar storm with his dogs, and when the snow became too blinding for travel he decided to try building some sort of shelter.

"But the snow was coming down too hard, and all I could do was dig a kind of trench and use the sled as a roof and one of my clothes-bags as a door. The snow went on piling up and up. Finally I fell asleep.

"In the Arctic you're all right as long as you can feel the cold. I woke and realized I was in danger because I felt nothing. I knew I must somehow rouse myself, start moving. I got myself dug out, but I couldn't walk." So he crawled back to the camp base, and an Eskimo woman put him to bed. Then she killed some lemmings, applying the still-warm skins to his numb toes.

"My toes looked green and gray, and it was horrible when she lifted off the lemmings' hides because my flesh came off too," he remarked unemotionally. "Finally I simply took a chisel and sawed off the toes of my left foot."

Later in a hospital in Denmark the whole leg was amputated—a drastic loss for a man whose lifework depended upon strength and stamina.

"But he was a wise doctor," Peter Freuchen went on. "He kept me in his office while other amputees were coming in for postoperative treatment. Watching them, I realized there is almost no loss from which you cannot recover, almost no situation you can't adjust to unless you prefer making a big thing of your disability; and I didn't prefer that."

So Peter Freuchen went on other expeditions and recorded them in valuable books. Full of years, esteemed and wise, he died of a heart attack on his way back to the North.

Peter Freuchen said that "risk has no real part in true exploration" (though his experiences seemed to prove that he didn't practice what he preached), but Vilhjalmur Stefansson, serene blue eyes smiling, long before that had tried to correct what he said was my mistaken notion that scientific expeditions had to be full of hazards.

"A narrow escape is interesting enough in retrospect, especially to the person who didn't have it," he commented.

Mr. Stefansson, whose Arctic explorations, studies of the Eskimo, and experiments with diet have added so much to the world's knowledge, believes that the how-I-escaped-death stories are actually "a sign that someone is incompetent—something has been bungled."

I reminded him of an encounter I'd read about between him and a polar bear. He grinned. "That was due to the incompetence of the bear. He outwitted me at the start, but he let his love of a grandstand play lose the game. I'd been trying for hours to track that bear. As I was climbing down a steep ridge I heard a noise behind me, looked back, and there he was not more than twenty feet away, hissing at me as if to say, 'Now I've got him.' If he'd come along silently as polar bears should, instead of warning me, I wouldn't be telling this story."

I suggested that maybe the bear was playing fair. The explorer thought not. "Why should an animal try to warn a human? Has the man with a gun ever played fair?"

The Stefansson theories of living off the country, of an all-meat diet, of learning to exist in the most brutal of climates caused great controversy in his early years, but he has had the satisfaction of being proved right in his own lifetime.

When he and a group of Eskimos were stranded in what he called
"the most desolate place in the whole region—no people and no game"
he used the time to talk in their own language to his companions. In
those months he found out much that was strange about their customs.

"Eskimos always pour a dipperful of water into the mouth of a seal
when they catch him," he told me. "That's because they think that
seals allow themselves to be killed when they are thirsty and since they
live in salt water, man is their only hope of a fresh, cool drink. Polar
bears, the Eskimos instructed me very solemnly, have great need of
knives and drills. The female polar bear also wants women's skin
scrapers and needle cases, so when a polar bear is killed his skin is
brought into the Eskimo's house and beside it are hung the tools the
bear wants. After four days for the male and five for the female the
Eskimo uses a magic formula to drive out the soul of the bear, and
the souls of the tools go along at the same time.

"If the soul of the bear has been properly treated, the report goes
back to the land of the polar bears and other bears are then anxious
to be killed. But if the hunter or his wife has behaved badly to the
'soul-skin,' that hunter may not be able to get any more bears. And
his wife, if she is known to be careless in treating the souls of animals,
doesn't have a very good chance of acquiring a second husband."

I'm not sure I could survive in Eskimo-land even with training,
but for a while after a visit from explorer Stefansson, I would go about
trying to become a seal.

"To successfully hunt a seal you must become a seal," he had explained. "You needn't worry until you are quite close, as seals have
very bad eyesight. But at about three hundred yards you must begin
to move when the seal is asleep, stand still when he is awake, and
travel on all fours. At about one hundred yards the seal will be quite
awake and staring at you. A seal does not sleep more than four minutes at a time, so if you make the mistake of keeping still for longer
than that he will know you are not a seal and slip quietly into the sea.
When the seal has stared for thirty seconds or so, you must raise your
head and scan the horizon, then drop your head back down on the
ice, seal-fashion. After that, it is no trick at all to shoot the seal."

Mr. Stefansson observed that fresh rawhide is good eating! "We ate
our snowshoe lashings and lots of other rawhide. When boiled it tastes
something like pig's feet. In an emergency the skin clothing worn over

regular wool clothes can be eaten or fed to the dogs, and thus put off starvation by a week or more."

Vilhjalmur Stefansson loved the Eskimo people. He came to one remote group, still in Stone Age civilization, as the first white man they had ever seen. And he was to establish connections with them because he had taken the trouble to learn their ancient language, not easy to do, either.

Another man of the North, Commander Donald B. MacMillan, brought his winsome wife, Miriam, to our program to talk about their pet polar bear (Miriam had written a book about it) and their magazine-story romance. As a small girl she had sat on the knee of the young explorer, listening raptly to his tales of the Eskimos, and had said earnestly, "When I grow up I am going to marry you."

This determined little female, having become Mrs. MacMillan, announced that she wanted to go North on his next expedition. Indulgently he told her very well, she could go as far north as the train would take her. The indomitable woman reached an Eskimo village where her husband's icebreaker was due to stop.

"When we got there Miriam met us, all dressed up in Eskimo clothes," the commander related proudly. "I explained that our boys did not want any women on board. And then the boys double-crossed me. They took a vote, signed a petition, and Miriam came on as a member of the crew. She did all right. I'd wake her at three-thirty in the morning and at four she would take the wheel. At five she went on watch, and in addition she swabbed down decks and helped the cook."

A veteran of thirty North Pole trips, some lasting three years, Donald MacMillan was still as excited about his work as on the day he took a leave of absence from a teaching job in 1907 to go north with Peary. He was still on leave forty years later.

The spot where the ill-fated Greeley expedition had built a hut and lost most of its men in 1883 was the one Commander MacMillan remembered best of all his wanderings.

"It was a tragic mistake," Commander MacMillan explained. "The government decided to build two scientific stations in the North, but one group of twenty-five men was taken so far—nine degrees from the Pole to Lady Franklin Bay—that it could never be rescued. The men were left with lumber and food and told that the ship would be back next year. Next year came and another year, but no ship. The twenty-

five proceeded south in the boat to the place where the ship had
been. After a terrifying tempest-tossed 250-mile trip Greeley led them
ashore and there under a pile of rock they found a note in a bottle
telling them the ship had been wrecked and its crew picked up and
taken home.

"It was then October, the sun had long gone down, the long winter
night was coming on. Most of the poor fellows never had a chance.
They turned their little boat upside down, built stone walls around
it and, one by one, eighteen died.

"The whole nation was aroused when the story of the deserted men
got out, and a searching party was organized which was greeted by a
man feebly waving a flag, muttering, 'A hard winter, a hard winter.'
The feet of one of the seven other survivors had dropped off at the
ankles and his hands at the wrists. He died on the way back to the
United States.

"Pieces of blanket we found after all the years still stuck in the
cracks of rock where the men waited told a tragic story. Those bits of
blanket meant one of the men at least had crawled away to be alone
rather than stay huddled in the boat quarreling with the others. That
is one of the hazards of exploring—the fierce irritation that develops
among men who see too much of one another at too close range."

"The most important thing is for the men to be matched together."
The young Norwegian Thor Heyerdahl told me that, and I remember
a submarine officer saying the same after a shakedown cruise where
discord had developed.

"We were in more peril on the *Kon-Tiki* from one another's nerves
than from the elements," Thor declared.

The model of his raft, a gift from him, stands on my living-room
mantel. He with five companions sailed forty-three hundred miles on
the actual raft from South America to the islands of the South Pacific.

Heyerdahl's adventure—for it certainly was that even though he
undertook it to get information on weather, currents, and the like for
science—had its beginning in a story told by a leathery-skinned old
man on a South Pacific island; a story about Tiki, who had led his
people across the ocean to that island. The dream took hold of Thor.

He and his companions flew to the Andes, drove by jeep to the
deep jungle, cut the balsa wood they needed, and the enterprise was
on. They were a hundred and one days afloat. Masses of seaweed

grew on the bottom of the raft and barnacles dangled in garlands—
"so that *Kon-Tiki* looked like a bearded sea god tumbling among the
waves," declared Thor poetically. He was as graphic but less lyrical
about whales and dolphins.

"Our first whale," he reported, "steered straight for us. Seven or
eight more then began making for us. The first came at us and a few
yards away sank quietly under us. It was a moment of suspense. The
whale was bigger than *Kon-Tiki*. But then we saw him sink deep
into the bluish water and vanish. All morning the whales played and
puffed and blew and sometimes even hit the raft. Suddenly at noon,
as if by a signal, they all disappeared."

Dolphins, which I always thought of as endearingly fun-loving, play
only when they are happy, according to Thor. When they are angry,
as when hauled aboard the *Kon-Tiki*, they bite.

"Sometimes they eat people," the master of *Kon-Tiki* said darkly.
"Evidently we were not appetizing enough. They nosed at our toothbrushes, though, when we dipped them over the side. I guess they
thought the toothbrushes were flying fish, which they adore."

To avoid being sampled by sharks, Thor and his men contrived a
leg basket. They had to get under the raft daily to be sure it wasn't
coming apart. Sharks, waiting for something to be thrown overboard,
were all too likely to decide that a pair of legs had been discarded.
However, in a bamboo-lined fruit basket a man could get feet and
legs under water safely, and by the time the rest of him arrived the
sharks, instead of attacking, lurked in the background, curious to see
what was going on. Or at least so Thor assured me. I always felt about
Thor Heyerdahl that if he had time he could explain many mysteries
to me.

There was a secret air about Ruth Harkness, too, as though she
had found out a great many things she couldn't or wouldn't reveal.
She was known all over the world as the Panda Lady. When her husband died on their expedition to bring back a baby giant panda from
the outer reaches of China, Ruth kept on alone.

On the day I saw her first, she wore on her straight hair a coronet
of brilliant tropical feathers that lighted up her dark eyes. Right away
I felt she was impatient of the city, restless to be off again. However,
she was a walking case history for the doctors, and so she had to stay
within hospital reach as they studied the five or six types of malaria

she'd managed to acquire. She was manna to me, for she was full of odd facts. She told me that a curator of birds had once estimated that during her three expeditions she had eaten more than $20,000 worth of pheasant. That stuck in my mind.

She succeeded in bringing back three pandas, whose masked faces and clown antics delighted millions of people, but the poor pandas themselves did not get on too well in the civilized world. Ruth was sympathetic about that. She, too, preferred jungles to cities.

Her first and most famous panda was Su Lin, a female, Ruth believed. But when she returned to the jungle to find a husband for her charge she discovered that Su Lin was really a male.

Ruth had lived in many odd places—once in a cave during a rain which lasted a whole week, another time in a ruined Tibetan temple that had been ripped apart by a Chinese army. The priests, fleeing, left their prayer wheels, beads, and holy pictures painted in vegetable dyes. Ruth set up her kitchen in a small shrine. Again, miles into the interior of French Indochina, she lived in a series of tumble-down ghost temples. One of the nicest memories was her house in China that had a moon door and came equipped with a small boy named Flower-flower and a tame goose that followed Flower-flower like a puppy.

In the jungles of South America, Ruth Harkness found primitive cures and remedies which, centuries old, approximated some of our modern medical discoveries. She told me about an insect with bright green wings and red eyes. She'd found children practicing witchcraft, and learned of a chief who died because of a child's curse. She herself was accused of witchery, and an old woman who had taken a dislike to her threatened her with a plague of bats . . . which came right on schedule.

"There are so many strange things I cannot understand," Ruth said thoughtfully. "There are people who actually seem to know what's happening to you before it happens. How? I'd like to learn what it is they know that we don't."

Something of a mystic was Ruth—and so was the lean French count, Byron de Prorok, who brought Cleopatra's necklace to the program. He told me the ornament was originally found by him during the excavation of what was believed to be the ancient queen's summer palace. But it disappeared from the digging site and the next time he saw it, it was on the neck of the guest of honor at a Boston dinner party.

Byron shrugged his shoulders. "What could I do? I had to go up to her and say, 'Madame, that necklace was stolen.' It turned out that her husband had bought it from one of those under-the-counter dealers in Cairo. He'd been told that he was buying Cleopatra's necklace—and for a change he really was!"

Byron agreed that thrills and narrow escapes are avoided by well-organized expeditions, but, he contended, accidents do happen.

"Like getting lost in the desert in a sandstorm that lasted a week," he cited. "Or the night we crashed in the jungle of Tabasco in Mexico and were six weeks cutting our way out. Or the day I was deep under the Mediterranean, hunting a buried city, and my life line got tangled in the ruins a hundred and twenty feet down. I remember seeing a huge octopus just before I passed out. They had to pull me up so fast I was bleeding at the mouth, ears, and nose; and I'd crushed my helmet, smashing into the bottom of the diving boat."

There was another near accident when he was opening the tomb of the so-called Eve of the Desert, an Amazonian queen, and superstitious natives gathered in a silent, menacing mob. That time the count shot it out with fireworks—rockets and flying snakes—and the mob ran away.

I was collecting Shangri-las when I talked to Byron first, the few strange far places left in the war-weary world. The count added one: the colony a French doctor had set up in the Sahara after World War I.

"He was one of the happiest men I've ever seen," Byron commented, and added that I would also like the Tuaregs in the desert, who have fresh air, the gift of contemplation, calm nerves, no wars, and live to be a hundred. Tuareg men go veiled (I'd heard that) and the women do the courting.

"I saw one woman," recounted Byron, "who had ridden six hundred miles by camel and camped outside the tent of a very tall, rugged Tuareg. She had a sort of banjo, on which she played melodious serenades, rather like Hawaiian music. Finally the man came out of the tent and joined her, which meant he was saying yes."

One day Byron de Prorok brought a recording he'd made at the court of a sultan whom he described as the bravest man he had ever met and enlarged on that with: "He had six hundred wives! At New

Year's his mother picks for him the wife who is to be his favorite. It is her choice, but she knows well what pleases him."

He also made a recording of the sultan's six hundred wives dancing to shrill, commanding rhythms. "That dance lasted twenty-four hours," he recalled. "The women were in a great circle around a fire, and before the dance began they ate a dinner of sixty courses."

Byron's recording sounded too strange and barbaric to be a lullaby, but the explorer claimed men, camel riding across the desert, could sleep to the music of the flutes and drums as comfortably in their saddles as they could in their own beds.

Last time I saw Byron de Prorok he was walking painfully with a cane because of bad arthritis. He had been warned never to go back to the Sahara. But of course he went back, and that is where he died.

Of all absurd articles (next to an emerald necklace) to mislay, a dinosaur egg would seem to head the list. But our program actually lost a dinosaur egg—at least temporarily.

Dr. Roy Chapman Andrews, head of my beloved American Museum of Natural History, brought the egg to the program and because he had to rush off forgot the ancient trophy. When it was missed a frenzied but fruitless search was made for it. After hours of this, Stella, who had been at a luncheon and a business conference, came back and calmly pulled the missing object out of her capacious handbag where she had thrust it for safekeeping. She called a messenger who got the ancient treasure back to relieved museum officials just at closing time.

Dr. Andrews fell in love with the Natural History museum as a small boy and later, just out of college, begged a job scrubbing floors there. He was willing to do absolutely anything so long as it was on that, to him, sacred ground.

Eventually he became director of the museum, but long before that he began to go on expeditions to the far corners of the world. He found dinosaur tracks and dinosaur eggs in Mongolia, where he unearthed great fossil fields and remains of the Baluchitherium, largest land mammal yet known to have existed. Back home, after all the thousands of miles he had traveled and the hundreds of thousands of dollars spent on the search for dinosaurs, the scientist found such traces on his Connecticut farm!

Dr. Andrews predicted that in half a million years from now, we'll have heads like billiard balls and only four toes. "Actually the foot has come more and more to depend on the big toe and the little toe is of less and less use," he pointed out. "It wouldn't make much difference if it were cut off, and so it's getting smaller and smaller."

Dr. Andrews had encountered jungles in Borneo "where the hum of insects is so maddeningly loud—all day long—that your eardrums ache and you pray for one instant of silence."

He awakened in the jungle more than once to find the bedclothes bloody. "The work of vampire bats," he explained calmly. "They like to get in and hide under your pillow."

You never knew what those adventure fellows would come out with!

Deep-sea diver Hans Hass stated calmly that if a murderous-looking shark approached him deep under the Red Sea he just shouted at it "and it went away." This handsome Viennese had stopped off at our studio on his way to Hollywood, where he worked out a plan for his stunning motion picture of underseas adventure, exploration, and photography.

Talking of the deep underseas world, Hans Hass made you feel his own excitement. I think he must have inspired a lot of the subsequent skin-diving craze. He described swimming among a shoal of giant manta rays, some pitch black, their terrific jaws snapping up small fish as they went, flapping like monstrous undersea birds.

Hans Hass found that the terrifying manta rays seemed to recognize him after the third or fourth encounter—something that never happened with fish, although it seemed to with certain sharks.

I noted that I'd rather have sharks and manta rays forget me completely. He agreed.

"But it was interesting, all the same," he insisted. "I felt that their mental reactions were higher than those of fish. Sometimes it seemed to me that I must be dreaming. When I swam along with the fantastic creatures I felt no fear—only a kind of exaltation. It was almost as if I were a manta ray myself!"

That was odd enough, I thought, but I hadn't heard anything yet. He went on about small fish that act as toothbrushes for the mantas, and produced photographs of a manta's gaping jaws with the little fish swimming around at their work.

Sometimes I wonder. Am I perhaps a little too credulous?

On another visit to my microphone Hans Hass brought his beautiful young bride. She'd gone on an expedition before they were married, and when she succeeded in getting within inches of a huge shark for Hans to photograph her, he promptly proposed. She'd passed his wife-test!

Author Hassoldt Davis was not much interested in tests of a scientific nature. He went to distant places simply because he was curious about them.

When he was twenty-one and in love with a golden Polynesian girl he said enviously of an old American Negro he'd met in Tahiti, "He had been everywhere and done everything." When Hassoldt Davis died at just past fifty, he, too, had been everywhere and done everything.

I had him often as a radio guest just before he went roistering off to some remote speck on a map, or just after he came back. He was reckless with his life, even to stubbornly refusing to move, when his doctor urged it, from his five-flights-up apartment where he served a mysterious indigo-blue cocktail to apprehensive guests and kept two black devil-cats that prowled like jungle creatures among the carved chests and chairs from all over the world. There was also a green ghost in that exotic apartment which the cats could see—or so Hassoldt declared.

Some of his best stories came out of an expedition to Nepal with Armand Denis and his wife, Leila Roosevelt, two other world girdlers who were pet guests of mine. Typically enough the hotel the three chose in Calcutta had a sacred bull which liked to ride in the elevator. The animal had moved into the hotel years before and, being sacred, could not be disturbed, even when he upset guests.

In the then forbidden kingdom of Nepal the brash Americans photographed the head man in what Hassoldt irreverently called his million-dollar hat, made entirely of rubies, diamonds, and emeralds.

"We saw many terrible and beautiful things that trip," Hassoldt asserted, "some that I remember like scenes in a nightmare. One was a temple ritual, a blood festival, literally thousands of buffaloes slaughtered to honor a goddess. My stomach kept churning like a washing machine as the flower-garlanded beasts were knifed to death."

I was to read a description of that scene after Hassoldt Davis' death, in his autobiography, *World Without a Roof*. I didn't realize until then that all the film he and the Denises took in Nepal, when sent back for development, turned out to have nothing on it! They'd spent a fortune to get it, but all that came out of the trip was the vivid diary Hassoldt kept.

It was on the same expedition that he picked up the strangest of all the strange stories he told me. When they were buying gold leaf in a dirty little pharmacy in Cairo (he and Leila planned to stir it into a bottle of vodka as a special gift for their host) the proprietor invited them to go into the garden.

"There, back of that malodorous shop, was the loveliest sunshine-filled walled patio with fig trees, orchids growing in baskets, a silvery fountain, and a life-size statue of a young girl, apparently of copper. Only the copper was a coating for the actual body of the pharmacist's beautiful Indian wife. He had vowed always to keep her with him. And so he put her body in his garden and covered it with copper."

Perhaps that tale was a little less fantastic than the saga of a haunted lake where an odd breed of eel with big ears lived. Hassoldt brought one of the eels back to his hut where a Tahitian girl, terrified, bade him throw it into the sea. She said he would be punished for capturing it. And this is what Hassoldt said happened that night:

"I wakened to the sound of music—strange whining music such as sailors reported hearing long ago when Tahitians played little nose flutes. I bounced out of my hammock and the music vanished. Then I found I could hear it only by putting my ear to the hammock. I went outdoors and there were two moons, a full moon in the sky and a second full moon coming down the mountain along the path I'd taken with the eel.

"Doubting my sanity, I ran half a mile to the next hut and dragged a sleepy Australian friend out of his bed. I made him come back with me, and he, too, saw the second moon, now sliding down the trunk of a tree and gliding so close to us that we could examine its bluish, luminous composition. Then we both heard the music. It came close, close, and was almost like breathing. Then suddenly it went off up the mountainside. Bobby, my Australian friend, had seen one of these —he said it was a *tu-paupau*—a month before."

I'd rather like to meet that Australian sometime, but I suppose it's not any more likely I'll do that than that I shall see a moon sliding down the trunk of a tree.

Though come to think about it, when Carveth Wells first came back from some outlandish place and told me about a fish that climbed trees, I didn't quite believe *him*. But years later I found the tree-climbing fish was in good and regular standing in the piscatorial world. So one never knows.

Zetta and Carveth Wells owned a delightful and mischievous myna bird named Raffles which they had brought back from their travels. From the first time I met him, neat and tailored in his shiny black feathers, I entertained a notion of having a myna bird of my own. Years later, Henry Trefflich, collector of strange beasts and birds, gave me a myna and I dreamed of teaching it to help with my commercials. But by the third day, when it still sat silent and dejected in its cage, I decided that I'd probably never have enough time and patience and maybe not enough love to train it (Zetta said you need lots of all three), so sadly I sent the bird back to Mr. Trefflich.

Recalling the first broadcast with Raffles, though, I think I was wise to give up my idea of a myna-bird assistant salesman because Raffles walked straight up to the microphone as I was midway through a gingerbread commercial and produced a large Bronx cheer. That seemed funny until he made the same rude noise during a cat-food plug. Zetta said he was allergic to even the word cat.

He whistled wolf calls, talked about pretty girls, and imitated a door buzzer so well that one or the other Wells was always running to answer the door when it was only Raffles.

As we were going off the air that day, the demon bird, who'd refused to sing a note during the hour, suddenly embarked on "The Star-Spangled Banner." Protocol says our national anthem must not be cut, so NBC stayed with us while Raffles sang on in a slightly off-key bird baritone, from "Oh, say can you see" to "whose broad stripes and bright stars." Here he stopped, and to everyone's relief said in as smug a voice as ever I heard, "Good-by—good-by."

I never intended to feature Raffles like that in this chapter, though he traveled widely and even climbed at least one mountain, which is more than I've done. I haven't even climbed the modest Catskill specimen back of my house. But along with a large part of the world, I've been fascinated by men who face the challenge of high places.

Young Maurice Herzog, en route from France to Hollywood, made his radio debut with us, talking in halting English about climbing Annapurna, then the highest summit yet attained by man.

That great mountain in the Himalayas—26,943 feet—almost killed Maurice.

"The marks of the ordeal are apparent on my body," was the way he put it (the ends of his fingers had been amputated).

"I had overstepped man's limitations—touched the extreme boundaries of man's world and had come to know something of its true splendor."

Trapped all one night in a crevasse, with ice and darkness closing in, Maurice Herzog had been sure he was dying.

"Then I didn't die—I was saved. I am not sure how to tell this, but I was coming to know a deep significance of existence of which until then I had been unaware."

I spoke of his triumph. He said thoughtfully: "It was triumph—yes —to achieve at first attempt this conquest of the unknown. But for me it was something else. In it I won my freedom. It is a freedom I shall never lose—an assurance, a serenity of a man who has fulfilled himself; who has had a new and splendid life open out before him."

I asked James Ramsey Ullman, courageous mountain climber and fine novelist, why men chose to risk their lives to conquer Annapurna and Everest.

He said I reminded him of his son. "When the boy was about six I took him to Bear Mountain one day and we started climbing. It was summer and hot, and when we'd walked an hour or so he suddenly put down his knapsack and said, 'Daddy, what are we doing this for?' What to say, how to answer, I didn't know. I suppose the only answer is the one given by Mallory when someone asked why he wanted to get to the top of Mount Everest. Mallory said, 'Because it is there'— or that's the oft-told legend, anyhow."

James Ullman said sadly that although Everest was his own pet dream, he'd reached an age and stage where "the most I could hope for would be to get on such an expedition as cook and have a hot meal ready for the boys when they come down."

After Edmund Hillary and Tenzing Norkay stood for fifteen minutes on the summit of Mount Everest on May 29, 1953, James Ramsey Ullman went to the tiny Himalayan village, only a day's march from the foot of Everest, to write the story of the Sherpa Tenzing, who could tell it but could not write it because there is no written Sherpa language.

Ullman told me: "I asked Tenzing would he ever climb again and he said, 'Yes, but on smaller mountains. In 1953, I felt I must either get to the top of Everest or die. I am forty, which is not so old but neither is it so young, and I do not long for any more tops of the world. I am a lucky man. I have had a dream and it has come true.'"

The dream—that is what all these men had in common. And when it came true, they were lucky.

## 15.  FOUR-STAR STORYTELLERS

Bennett Cerf once gave our listeners rules for successful storytelling, the most important of which was "don't try to establish a monopoly. Give the other fellow a chance."

I was delighted, however, when Bennett or some other good storyteller came to my microphone, to let him monopolize as long as his stories were good. With Bennett or Harry Hershfield I had only to suggest a subject and they were off.

Bennett's most famous story as far as my listeners were concerned was not funny at all—just the opposite. It was about a poor orphan girl, ugly and entirely unequipped with any of the graces that make most children lovable. She had been passed about from one institution to another because everything she did got her into trouble and nobody cared enough to help her. When she had been for some weeks in her current "home," those in charge were also longing to get rid of her. One day a supervisor came to the head with a note he had found in a tree.

"Griselda left this in the tree and since it is absolutely against our rules for the children to have unauthorized communication with the outside world, now is our chance to expel her!"

They opened the note and it read: "To whoever finds this, I love you."

Bennett had emphasized that the story was not factual, but in five minutes after he had told it ten women were on the telephone wanting to adopt the little girl.

I have told the story from memory and probably illustrated a sad truth—that I am not very good at it. But if I do say so myself I *was* good at picking those who could make masterpieces of their own and other people's experiences. And here they go—my four-star story-tellers!

I said to showman Billy Rose: "Your life has been full of surprise endings."

"Yes," answered Billy. "I've lived in a world where the usual thing was the unusual, so when I went to work on a plot it was natural to grab it by the tail and try to give the tail a twist. Of course sometimes it came out like a pretzel."

"One of my favorites is about the time you dictated some words to the President of the United States."

"That was way back in 1918 when I was working for Bernard Baruch, then chairman of the War Industries Board in Washington. One day I was sent to the White House with a letter to deliver to Woodrow Wilson. I handed the letter to one of the President's secretaries, and he asked me to wait. This happened to be a few hours before the Armistice in the First World War, and the waiting room was full of cabinet ministers, important brass, journalists, and tension.

"The secretary came back in a few minutes and said, 'This way, Mr. Rose, the President wants to see you.' I was eighteen, fresh out of the East Side, and just plain fresh—and the only presidents I'd ever met were the ones on dollar bills, so I was trembling inside.

"President Wilson looked up and said, 'Mr. Baruch tells me you're quite a shorthand writer!' At the time I *was* quite a shorthand writer and I had won medals and contests which made my mother happy, so when the President said that, my fears disappeared. 'Mr. Baruch tells me you can write two hundred words a minute!' said the President. 'Would you mind giving me a little demonstration?' And he began dictating to me.

"Well, I'd been writing in contests at approximately two hundred and fifty words a minute, so when he finished and said, 'Will you read it back to me?' I read it back a lot faster than he had dictated. And, being a show-off even then, I read it to him backward, then upside down. The President chuckled. He asked me some questions about Gregg shorthand, and by that time I was patronizing him a little.

"I knew he could write shorthand but not very rapidly, so like a caddy who can go around the eighteen holes in sixty-nine and isn't impressed by a Rockefeller, I said, 'Mr. President, I understand you write some shorthand. Would you mind writing for me?'

" 'I'll try,' he said, 'but I'm a little out of practice.' He rubbed his glasses on his coat sleeve, I handed him my notebook, and dictated quite deliberately at a hundred words a minute. The President read it back, and when I told him he hadn't made any errors he sighed like a kid who had just played the 'Elves' Waltz.' Then he reached for my notes.

"I said, 'O.K., Mr. President, if I can have yours.' So we traded notes, shook hands, and I floated out of the White House back to the War Industries Board. When I got there a girl said, 'Mr. Baruch wants you.' And I thought—pretty good for an East Side boy. In one hour Mr. Baruch and the President of the United States! But Mr. Baruch let me down. The girl said, 'Mr. Baruch would like you to get him an ice-cream soda!' "

My other favorite among Billy Rose's stories was the one about the time in 1936 he was producing an exposition in Fort Worth, Texas, and engaged Sally Rand to do her famous bubble dance.

"One evening Dave Schultz, governor of Florida, came and wanted to meet Sally. We found her stretched out on the floor in her kimono, reading, believe it or not, the Bible! Sally was always reading something, and that year it was the Bible from Genesis to Revelation. The governor said, 'There's a chapter here always gives me great comfort,' and he turned to one of the Psalms. The orchestra was already tuning up so I had to go and get the show started. I began introducing some of the visiting celebrities, and someone at Governor Shultz's table called to me to introduce the governor of Florida.

"I said, 'I'm sorry but the governor is talking long distance to Tallahassee.' I wasn't going to stand there and tell four thousand people that the governor couldn't show up because he was in Sally Rand's dressing room reading the Bible!"

I was always glad to have super-storytellers along when I had to broadcast before crowds.

At a great gathering of women in New Brunswick, New Jersey, I introduced Willie Snow Ethridge, wife of Mark Ethridge, editor and publisher of the Louisville, Kentucky, *Courier Journal*, as the funniest woman in the world. And I believe she is. She started writing about her own family and Louisville, and then she took to traveling.

Her husband was the United States Delegate on the United Nations Commission to study Greek frontier incidents, and the State

Department said she could join him in Greece if she would pay her own way.

"That rocked me for several days, but then I remembered I had a piece of land down in Georgia on which I intended to be buried someday so I decided I would rather be buried in a pauper's grave and go to Greece so I telegraphed Georgia and said: 'Sell my land quick.' And when I got to Washington, Mark said he wasn't surprised to see me. He knew I'd always go anywhere I was invited. He said he was going to put on my tombstone: 'The Lord called her—and she could go.'"

The women were shrieking with laughter by this time, and they never stopped for about half an hour.

"I was traveling around in Greece, and the powers that be in Washington got worried about me; they thought maybe the guerrillas would get me. They warned Mark but he just said, 'If the guerrillas get her, they'll have to look out for themselves. I wash my hands of it!'

"I wanted to get to Delphi to ask the oracle who was going to win the next Kentucky Derby. I thought if I could only find out ahead of time who was going to win, I'd never have to write another book. So the chief of police said the guerrillas were active, it was dangerous to travel. He said they were traitors to the country, they were barbarians, they had no morals whatsoever—they took what they wanted. Then he looked at me—at my thinning gray hair, my wrinkles, and my sagging jaws—and he said: 'Yes, Mrs. Ethridge, the guerrillas take what they want, but I think you will be safe!'

"I was called up and asked to tea at the palace. So I went and there was a low tea table in one corner of the room where people were sitting. My hostess came across the room and greeted me very cordially and carried me back—that's an old Virginia word—and began introducing me to the people at the table . . . first to the man at the right, but she didn't call his name—just said, 'This is Mrs. Ethridge,' and I thought, 'Poor soul, she's forgotten his name,' and I was full of sympathy because I'm always forgetting my guests' names. So I wanted to cover up for her and I was very cordial. I said, 'How do you do?' and went around and met the other guests, then landed back next to this man.

"I wanted to get on a friendly basis with him so I leaned over and said, 'Are you visiting here in Greece as I am or do you live here?'

And he looked at me as if to say, 'Are you trying to be funny?' Then he saw that I was serious and his eyes crinkled as he said, 'I live here when the people let me.' He was the King of Greece.

"He had already been banished three times, so my question wasn't very diplomatic. We got to be real good friends though. We went out once to a movie, and another time we were at a party and the hour got late and the hostess had her arm in a cast and looked very tired so I turned to the king and said, 'Don't you think we should go home?' That caused real consternation. It seems nobody should say anything to the king about going home. He must say it first. But anyway, we went.

"In Bulgaria, I got behind the Iron Curtain—though I wouldn't have known it if they hadn't told me. I was on my way to Sofia but stopped one night in a monastery which dates back to the ninth century, and I, being the wife of a United States delegate, was given an honorable place next to the abbot. He was big and round with a long black beard and black hair wound up in the middle of his head in a little knot. Suddenly it was discovered that the abbot knew French and Bulgarian but didn't know any English and of course I speak only *this*, so there was considerable consternation until someone said he understood English and could translate it into French.

"He came over and we began talking, but suddenly the muscles on his neck began puffing out and his eyes to extend from his head and he said, 'Stop, stop—you speak a brand of English that I have never heard before!' So then they had to scout around everywhere and find somebody who understood the way we speak English in Georgia. When they found him, all this man had to do was just translate me from Georgian into good English. I can't tell you how humiliated I was.

"But just the same, that night in the monastery I was given another very honorable spot—I was allowed to sleep in the exarch's apartment. Now, the exarch in Bulgaria is as important as the Pope in Rome—he's head of the whole Greek Church of Bulgaria—and to be allowed to sleep in the exarch's bed, that's a tremendous honor. I reckon I should mention that the exarch was away at the time.

"That night when I started to go to bed I decided I must have a shower. I'm not one of those people just crazy about showers—I can do without a bath as well as anybody—but I had been traveling all day in a jeep—no sides, no top, and scarcely any engine—and in Bulgaria it's very dusty so I was pretty grimy.

"I got under the shower, and the water came right off of the top of those mountains with snow—nothing but snow. It melted just long enough to come through the pipes and hit me, then it froze right back to snow and when I climbed into bed I couldn't get warmed up.

"So I put on some snuggies and a flannel robe and then some old red bedroom slippers. They had leather soles lined with sheep, terrible-looking slippers, about a foot wide and two feet long, but they were cozy.

"Of course after I got to feeling warm and drowsy I should have put them out of the bed but I didn't, and I never thought of them again until I was in Sofia and remembered I had left those slippers in that exarch's bed. I confided in one or two people and they said I could write back, but I said, 'No, by the time the exarch gets into that bed he'd have forgotten who had slept in it last.'

"Next day there came a messenger holding the unwrapped slippers in his hands, and he went into the meeting of the Commission—a hundred and twenty men were there—and he walked right up to poor Mark and said, 'Mr. Ethridge, here are your wife's bedroom slippers. She left them in the exarch's bed.'"

For her final story that day, I asked Willie to tell about her entrance into the life of Louisville's hunting set.

"Well," she obliged, "I was invited to go beagle hunting and, being new, wanted to go correctly attired. If you were supposed to wear a pink coat, I wanted to wear a pink coat. So I went down to a big department store in Louisville and I said, 'I would like to get a beagling costume.' First the clerk and then the floorwalker asked, 'Did you see something like that advertised?' And I said, 'No, it's my own idea.' So he said he didn't know about beagling costumes but to go to the Town and Country Shop.

"They didn't know anything about beagling costumes there either, but they were sure that the thing to wear at all times of uncertainty in any sporting event would be a black and white check, lined in a warm sort of fur that would keep me cozy on the coldest day.

"Well, the day came and we went beagling and we got out into the field and watched tiny little dogs running around and I kept thinking, 'Why don't they go out and hunt the beagle?'

"Finally I asked somebody: 'Don't those little-bitty dogs have trouble hunting big old beagles?' and the person looked at me, shocked, and said, 'Those are the beagles!'

"Those little dogs! I was simply amazed.

"But instead of the beagles running around hunting rabbits like they were supposed to do, they kept getting between my feet, and the more the hunter kept blowing his horn and the people kept saying, 'Come on, beagles,' the more no beagle would come. They just kept running around my feet, and everybody got to looking at me and I became very confused and hot so I took off my coat, and do you know what? It was lined with *rabbit!*"

Later I really had my hands full when I interviewed Willie and Russian-born Nila Magidoff together. They had collaborated on a book about Nila's life. They talked at the same time, argued and interrupted until I was in hysterics. One of Nila's funniest tales was about a luncheon at the White House with Mrs. Roosevelt.

She had expected to be alone with Mrs. Roosevelt and was upset that there were a number of wives of cabinet members on hand.

"So I'm bitterly disappointed and you know me, I don't try to hide my feelings. I don't mingle at all, I just look round in the bored way. Finally we go into the dining room—it's so much silver you'll be surprised. The first course is tomato juice. Then on a very beautiful huge platter there comes scrambled eggs. Nothing else, just scrambled eggs.

"I look at the platter and say to Mrs. Roosevelt: 'If it's the scrambled eggs, why so many knives and forks?'

"Mrs. Roosevelt answers: 'No matter how simple the meal, we set the table as if for a dinner.'

" 'But which fork?' I ask. 'I'm not accustomed to so much silver.'

" 'Any one you like,' Mrs. Roosevelt answers. She tried to make me talk, but I am so upset I am horrid. Then she asks me what impresses me most in America and I tell her: whistling.

"I tell her it took me three or four hours to come to Washington by bus, and I sat in front of a sailor who kept whistling *Carmen*. Finally I turned round and I said to him: 'Citizen, you're not alone in this bus, and your whistling is going on my nerves.'

"Then right away the whole bus is divided—pro-whistling and anti-whistling. One woman says she has two sons who are sailors and this is a free country where anybody can whistle or do what he wants, but

I explain I feel that a free country means everybody respects everybody else's rights so that if a person desires to be quiet, he can be. Next day Mrs. Roosevelt wrote a column called: Citizen, you're not alone."

Trying to describe to Willie, her collaborator, the hard time she had to find a place for kissing and hugging when Robert Magidoff, American correspondent, was courting her, Nila said:

"Robert could only have his room as long as he never bring a wife or somebody to live with him. I had no room of my own, and they would not let you love in the park. Then I got the idea. At the station trains come in every few minutes so we went there and when a train came in we would kiss and kiss. Then we would wait for the next train. Only one day the what you call policeman came and say: 'You've met enough trains now. Go home!'"

Willie and Nila, consciously or unconsciously, took advantage of the fact that the anecdotes that make an audience laugh loudest nearly always concern the mishaps of the narrator.

Even when the incident doesn't provoke uproarious mirth, a story that makes a fall guy of the teller is sure to delight the hearers, especially if the fall guy is as distinguished as the French writer, André Maurois.

"During a lecture trip to Atlanta, Georgia, I was invited to dinner," he related. "The woman on my right talked quite a lot. The one on my left was very quiet—she wore spectacles and had the look of a shy little girl.

"Toward the end of the meal she ventured: 'Aren't you going to speak to me at all? I'm a writer too.'

"'Oh,' I asked indulgently, 'and what have you written?' The small woman explained apologetically that she'd written only one novel.

"'And what was that?' I inquired.

"'*Gone With the Wind*,' answered Margaret Mitchell."

Sometimes the people I longed to meet but never did came alive on my program—Gandhi, Churchill, Albert Schweitzer—when guests began spinning stories about them.

Louis Fischer, reporter and analyst of world affairs, talked often about the man both he and I admired most, Mohandas Karamchand Gandhi. In 1944, Louis, back from India where Nehru had arranged for several long meetings with the Mahatma, was as excited as a cub reporter after his first successful interviewing job.

"It was my most thrilling experience," he admitted. "Because I didn't want any pretense, I explained that I was strongly in support of the war. It didn't faze him. He just went on talking quietly of his own philosophy—not arguing, just talking. I felt somehow that he was more than man."

"Saint," I suggested, but Louis wasn't quite ready to concede that.

"Oh, he had very human qualities—he could change his mind and admit he was wrong. And he didn't take himself altogether seriously. He was amused when I said I'd talked to Lloyd George on a visit to England in 1938 and he'd described how Gandhi sat cross-legged on the sofa at 10 Downing Street and suddenly, out of nowhere, a black cat appeared and perched on the Mahatma's lap. Gandhi remembered, but what he didn't know was that, according to Lloyd George, the cat had never been seen in the house before and, after Gandhi left, was never seen again."

Louis Fischer shared walks, prayers, and meals with Gandhi. Once, on a walk with the frail, tiny leader, wearing his usual homespun dhoti and carrying his staff, Louis, who is more than six feet and not thin, felt a hefty prod in the middle of his spine. It was Gandhi, saying, "Come on, get along with it."

On the third day Louis refused his bowl of vegetable mush. Gandhi asked why. Louis said it hadn't any taste, and Gandhi suggested adding lemon and salt.

"To kill the taste?" inquired Louis.

"No, to enhance it."

"You're such a pacifist, you won't even kill a taste!"

It was wonderful to be with him even though the temperature went to 110 with no trouble, there were no cold drinks, no fans, no ice— only a water girl of about sixty who brought a tepid bath you could pour over yourself five or six times a day. Every meal began with a chanted prayer for peace and ended with "peace, peace, peace."

Four years later, when Mahatma Gandhi was assassinated, Louis Fischer said, "He was just an old man in a loincloth in distant India, yet when he died humanity wept."

I asked Madame Pandit of India once about her first meeting with Gandhi. She answered, "It's very curious your asking me that; nobody

else ever has and I don't really remember it—it was probably brief
and in my father's home. What I do remember is the second time
I saw him.

"I was about seventeen, and Gandhi had come to my home town
to start his nonviolence movement against the British government.
Very few people knew of him; he was just beginning and his name
had come into prominence in South Africa but not much in India.
All sorts of humiliation had been heaped upon us, and there was a
spirit of revolt in the country which he took advantage of. He spoke
at a very big mass meeting, and my mother was averse to the idea of
my going because in those days my family was rather conservative—
young girls didn't knock about at such meetings.

"However, I went and was absolutely enthralled because here was
this little naked man, something entirely different from anything I
had seen, and he spoke about things of which I had no knowledge.
He talked about suffering, humiliation, and the need for freedom.
At the end he made an appeal.

" 'Until the people of this country are united for freedom,' he said,
'they can't get freedom. Freedom is difficult and it requires renuncia-
tion and a complete dedication of self. You can't continue your life
of ease, taking from the British and then thinking that somewhere,
sometime the gift of freedom will drop down. Money also is required
for this in order to sustain and support those who may become victims
of the ruling power. I make an appeal to all women here to give me
their ornaments.'

"Indian women, you know, used to wear a good many jewels. A
young woman would always have gold bangles and something on her
neck and a few rings. To take off an ornament in India is inauspicious.
Only widows are unadorned. So there was a little ripple of horror
among the older women. He asked his volunteers to go around with
caps and I wasn't conscious of what I was doing, but suddenly I found
myself struggling with the bangles I was wearing, trying to pull them
off. By the time the collector came, I had managed to get all those
on my left hand off and so I gave them and then was filled with
terror. What was Mother going to say?

"When I got home I tried to hide my hand for a little while, but
what I had done was discovered and my mother told me people of
breeding did not act that way, little thinking that in the very near

future she was not only going to give all her bangles but dedicate her whole life to that same little naked man whom she was criticizing that evening.

"She had not gone to the meeting; she knew about him, of course, because my father had already been drawn to him and my brother was almost his disciple at that stage. But Mother was a very practical woman, and I suppose she had a stronger fight with herself to give up what a woman of that age values—a settled home and all the rest of it—but once she did, right up to the day of her death there was no turning back. She entered into the thing joyfully and, in fact, suffered far beyond what she should have at her age as a result of her beliefs.

"She went to prison for a few days; she was caught up in a procession and badly beaten up by the police and brought home in a state of collapse. My mother was a tiny woman, like a Dresden-china figurine, delicate and very beautiful, and to the last day of her life she was like that. It seemed terrible that this scrap of a woman should have to stand up so belligerently for what is so obviously right—the freedom of one's country."

Madame Pandit wrote a poem about Gandhi. Most talented people write poetry.

I said to Vincent Sheean: "I have the strangest feeling that the first thing you ever wrote was a poem. Don't tell me I'm wrong."

"No, I don't think you are wrong," he answered thoughtfully. "I used to write a lot of poetry as a kid."

Vincent Sheean had come that day to talk about *The Indigo Bunting*, his memoir of Edna St. Vincent Millay.

"She died on the stairs between her poets and her birds. The poets were at the top of the stairs in what she called her poetry room—and her birds at the bottom. I came to her house—Steepletop—and there was this bird, the indigo bunting, blue all over, at the window. The blueness of the bird is startling when you first see it. It's five inches long and the only bird in North America that's blue all over.

"Edna St. Vincent Millay was a difficult and retired and shy person and the first few years I knew her, I had very little communication with her. She was always so frightened of other people she made them frightened of her. She was a complex personality—in her youth she'd had enormous worldly success which had worn off, and also her liking of the world had worn off. She preferred to stay at Steepletop and see nobody, and I don't know how many times I met her before I was able to talk to her at all.

"The weekend when I did succeed in finally talking to her, we didn't stop for three days. She took me up to her poetry room. It was a library, really, but among her books were many on poetry in all languages, because she was a formidable linguist; she read Latin all her life, read the Greek poets. She showed me editions of Italian poets and up there we talked only poetry, but otherwise her conversation had endless range. We had a long talk about cooking. She didn't eat very much but loved the taste of food.

"She wasn't much interested in politics; it left her rather cold. She would dry up and be silent when the talk got on to it, but she was troubled about the situation in the late thirties when the Nazis were trying to take over the world. That she considered a deep evil, and it concerned her. She didn't read newspapers very much, and when she went to Ragged Island she didn't have a telephone or radio. She didn't even know when the war was over. She and her husband used to stay on the island for two or three weeks at a time and would only get news when they went to the mainland for provisions.

"She never talked about work she was doing, but she would say aloud poems she had already written and published. The range of her voice was very great, and once she did two long poems by Shelley that I wouldn't expect anybody to know—in two quite different voices. One was the 'Ode to the West Wind' and the other the 'Hymn to Intellectual Beauty.'"

I shall always see in my imagination Edna St. Vincent Millay reciting Shelley, and I shall always remember what Paderewski told Olin Downes, distinguished music critic of the *Times,* about success.

Olin, who proved to be warm and human and not formidable as I expected, was just getting started on his career when he met Paderewski for the first time. The pianist was so cordial that the young stranger felt perfectly at ease and put one of these indiscreet questions that only the young ever dare to ask.

"You're now by common consent the leading pianist of the world." (He had just told Downes how he never practiced less than seventeen hours a day when his first chance came and had suffered neuritis from excessive practicing and had had various other setbacks.) "I know your eminence has cost you dear. And what I want to hear is do you think the reward has been commensurate?"

Paderewski thought the question over for a moment and then he said, "Well, my boy, I'll tell you this. I've fought some good battles."

Much later in his life Downes went to Finland to visit composer Sibelius, and since he didn't get to see the aging composer until nine in the evening the two men talked from half past nine to half past three in the morning. Sibelius was then nearing ninety.

Olin Downes told me: "I kept awake with alternate cups of coffee and cognac. Sibelius took them, too, but I don't think he needed them. He was having a wonderful time. He said: 'I'm an older man. I love my Finland, I love my friends. I love my scores, I love my whisky. It goes on this way, and as you grow older it gets better, so don't be too serious. Take it easy and realize there is some happiness in life!'"

Although he was nearer to my base of operations than some of the others people told me about, Henry Luce, publisher of Time Inc., was almost as inaccessible to me. He doesn't much like to be interviewed. Novelist Laura Hobson was working for Mr. Luce, not interviewing him, at the time she talked about him on the program.

"We were just starting the *March of Time*—remember? I was ready to leave the office one day when Mr. Luce sent for me. He showed me a big double-spread promotion which was to run in *Time* and asked what I thought of it. I read it and asked, 'Do you really want me to tell you what I think of it?' He assured me that he did. I declared emphatically, 'It's stuffy and pompous and dull—just dreadful. It isn't good promotion.'

"There was a pause. Then, 'I wrote it,' said Mr. Luce.

"My first thought was, 'Well, I'm fired.' Instead he said quite amiably that since I felt that way would I take the advertisement home and rewrite it. I stayed up until six in the morning and do you know —it ran as I'd written it. I've often wondered whether that was because they hadn't time to change it."

Judging from Laura's writing, I'd say it ran because Mr. Luce is a good editor and knows superior material when he sees it.

I knew Franklin D. Roosevelt a little, but I knew him better after listening to others talk about him. I was happy to hear from his son,

Elliott, that he was not a very good speller. It is always comforting to find your own faults shared by the famous.

Said Elliott: "His early letters were something and he and his mother had quite a tussle over them, especially the word 'disease,' which he persistently spelled 'desease.' Finally when he went to Groton came a letter with 'disease' spelled correctly, and his mother wrote, 'Thank you at last.' Groton improved him and he spelled most things right but not sandwich. He *would* put in a 't' or even spell it 'sandwidge.' "

Elliott Roosevelt said that his grandmother, the *grande dame* Sara Delano Roosevelt, believed from the day FDR was born that he would be an important world figure.

"She saved all his letters, tying them together at the end of each year with pink ribbon, carefully keeping them for posterity. There were indications that Father expected the family letters to be published some day because he kept all the letters she wrote him, and those from my mother. Mother saved the ones he wrote her, but this may have been only because in their generation and in that kind of up-bringing it was considered a good idea for family reasons, to keep such letters.

"I remember Theodore Roosevelt coming to our house when I was about five years old. He put all us children on his lap and took a very large, gold watch with a heavy gold chain out of his pocket and held it up to our ears so we could hear the chimes it played. Then he roared with laughter because we were so puzzled at a watch playing chimes."

Elliott told that day about the last Christmas he shared with his father at Hyde Park.

"There was a tall Christmas tree, piled up presents, a blazing fire, and Father in his favorite rocker about to open the familiar Dickens at its Christmas Eve place. We were once more one family together. I lay, as I always did, on the floor in front of the fire and the reading of *A Christmas Carol* began. Suddenly Chris, one of the grandchil-dren, noticed that his grandfather had forgotten to put back a false front tooth. He said so in a clear childvoice, and Father, ignoring him, read on. Chris bore it for a bit, then he marched to the chair, pointed within inches of his grandfather's nose, and again announced: 'You've lost a tooth.'

"At that Father gave up. He said there was too much going on for reading aloud. But for me that evening was a time of peace and contentment—the war, the world were for a brief moment shut out."

Another Roosevelt son, James, asked Van Heflin, the Hollywood actor, who was my guest during the Democratic convention of 1948 in Philadelphia, to tell a wartime story at an FDR memorial.

"This happened when Roosevelt died and I was in the Army, stationed in Italy," Van explained. "Franklin D. Roosevelt made a lot of friends there. An Italian came up and tried to say how sorry he was that we had lost our president. 'He was a good man,' he said in his halting English. 'He was a wonderful man—and a good Catholic.' President Roosevelt had seemed so close to that simple fellow that of course he thought of the American president as a man of his own religion."

Since I last talked to him, *Life* magazine's extraordinary photographer and equally good storyteller, Philippe Halsman, has had his *Jump Book* published. I suspect he gave us a preview of it years ago when he told of photographing the wife of that headline-making artist, Salvador Dali.

"I wanted everything in suspension in that picture," he explained. "She was suspended over a sea which was suspended from the land and I then suspended an easel and asked Dali to jump. We needed a subject for him to paint in mid-air, so we got three men to toss up cats and a fourth to throw water at them. It took twenty-eight throws and five hours and Dali jumped and painted the whole time.

"The cats," Halsman added, "didn't like it at first. But they got sardines afterward and they still talk to me."

Was Dali the first of a long line of celebrities to jump for Halsman's camera? I'm sure, anyway, it was the first time camera-jumping was described on the air. By 1960 everybody he photographed was jumping.

Judy Garland's first divorce almost wrecked a Halsman *Life* cover.

"When she arrived she was crying, and I very much wanted her to stop so I said, 'The first divorce is always the hardest.' She was furious at me, but she stopped crying and I got my cover picture.

"Gloria Swanson cried too. She explained that she'd fired her maid that morning and everything had gone wrong. So I put away my equipment and we went walking in the park. She talked about her youth, and by the time we came back she looked twenty years younger."

Winston Churchill, he said, was grouchy and un-co-operative.

"Before each shot he made me count three-two-one. But afterward he wrote me a nice letter."

When the actress Lilli Palmer came for a sitting she told Philippe that *Life* magazine had photographed her once before.

"And instead of me, I found a dog on the cover. Could anything be more horrible?"

"Yes," Philippe answered. "Another actress."

He had difficulties with the Duke and Duchess of Windsor, who sat down and looked at him in stern silence.

"Finally I begged: 'Don't look at me like that. You're the most romantic couple in the world. Every man who has difficulty marrying the girl he loves thinks of you who gave up a throne to marry the woman *you* loved.' Suddenly the duke began to smile and their heads came closer and it was a very lovely double portrait. If you look at that first picture, then at the second taken perhaps one minute later, you'd be astonished. In the second they look younger, they glow— they're proof of the importance of what a person is thinking and feeling when a photograph is taken."

Mercifully, Philippe did not tell the name of a famous woman he took for a magazine cover.

"She had interesting eyes," he explained, "so I photographed just her eyes peeking out of a curtain. She never looked better in her life, but unfortunately she couldn't always carry a curtain around with her."

Prince Louis Ferdinand, called the rebel prince and reported to have been the Kaiser's favorite grandson, if not a storyteller extraordinary was interesting about his grandparent. I suggested that he was his grandfather's favorite.

"I don't think my grandfather had a favorite, but he was very nice to me. When I came back from the States where prohibition was going strong, I had developed into a bit of an alcoholic. Grandfather said: 'You'd better come to my place and I'll cure you.' So I went to him at Doorn and he cured me. He called me his patient, and in those months we were alone I got to know him intimately. He was very human, a bit of an adventurer, and misunderstood by the world."

The rebel prince was once addressed individually by Hitler.

"He worked himself up into a lather as if he were talking to a group big enough to fill Madison Square Garden. He was talking about Ford cars and how much he admired them and Ford. He wanted me to tell Mr. Ford what he had said because he knew I had worked on the Ford assembly line."

Later the prince took part in the plot against Hitler which failed.

When I could get them started, actors had wonderful tales that they often did with gestures. A pet Christmas story of mine was the contribution of English actor Cecil Humphreys.

"I was touring with a repertory company of *The Little Minister* in Scotland," he began. "It was Christmas Eve, bitterly cold, and the company was broke because the manager had skipped with all the money. There we were, no food, no way to pay our rent or get back to London. I was recommended to see a bailiff named Angus Mac-Pherson about what could be done to trace the manager. I was told Angus did not approve of anything about the theater, but we were desperate and he was a last resort.

"He began with a lecture about the evils of the stage and then asked if we were all Christian folk. I said I thought so. Then he instructed us all to appear at kirk the next morning—Christmas Day. Afterwards he took us back to his house. In a sort of workroom outside, he'd laid long trestle tables with two enormous joints of roast beef and Yorkshire pudding, potatoes and vegetables. We ate and ate and ate. [Only Cecil Humphreys said 'et.'] Afterwards Angus made a speech advising us to give up this sinful life, but took all our bills, paid them, and not only bought us third-class tickets back to London but gave us each ten shillings. Three years later, when I was doing a little better, I mailed him five pounds. I got a post card back saying 'You're an honest man'—Angus MacPherson."

Ray Bolger became one of my favorite storytellers when he sat opposite me and spoke about liking to do clean plays. He came right after the first matinee of *Where's Charley?*, and the audience had laughed and screamed. And said Ray Bolger: "Looking out over those young faces, I thought, 'This is really worth-while. This is good—having a play you aren't ashamed of children seeing and hearing.'"

Some time later, I asked Ray what was his pleasantest experience in the theater. He didn't have to think.

"The nicest thing that's ever happened to me was taking *Where's*

*Charley?* back to Boston after it was a success. You don't know what a wonderful feeling that is—usually we go to Boston to break a show in, but here was a show that had played 792 performances on Broadway and to be able to show that to your home town—a show that had reached its peak of performance—was a treat to me. The Boston audience took us to its heart and after it was over wouldn't leave.

"One fellow yelled out: 'Come on, Ray, let's sing some more.' I said: 'Wait a minute. I never had this happen before but you paid your $6, and if you want to sing, we'll sing.' So we sang 'Amy' and we sang 'Should Old Acquaintance Be Forgot.' It was so beautiful, tears came to my eyes. I finally said to the audience: 'Now you know how things are these days, ladies and gentlemen. After a certain period one must finish one's work because overtime starts and you wouldn't want to cause me any expense, so why don't we all go home and go to church tomorrow and say a prayer for each other—and now good night!'

"The president of the First National Bank of Boston came back after one performance, and when he walked into my dressing room I said: 'I'm very sorry but I refuse to come back to work in your bank.' He said: 'Well, I'm the man who fired you!' He let me see the employee's card they kept on me in their files. On it was noted: 'very young, very bright, very fresh, probably will outgrow it!' "

Music critic Deems Taylor, who wrote a book about the Rodgers-Hammerstein composing team, knew Dick Rodgers when a Rodgers and Hart effort called *All Points East* was produced in Philadelphia by, of all people, Leopold Stokowski. "It was a curious contraption that ran about fifteen minutes," said Deems, "a soliloquy by an old gateman who finally gets shot—I forget why.

*"The Light,"* Deems added, "was an early Hammerstein attempt of about the same merit. It lasted three performances, and at the second, a Saturday matinee, there were only six people in the audience. The ingénue came on and her first line was, 'Now everything is coming down,' and promptly lost her slip. Oscar told me he didn't wait for the laughter—he just ran out of the theater and sat on a bench in Central Park and there got an idea for a new show."

The Rodgers and Hammerstein *Allegro*, favorite of mine and of theirs though it was not a hit, made a star.

Dick told about her on the program. "Lisa Kirk had one song, late in the show. During the tryout in New Haven she got a little too close to the audience, lost her balance, fell into the pit, but never stopped singing. Two cellists lifted her back on the stage, and she went on to the finish, stopping the show. She's been stopping shows ever since."

Dick Rodgers likes to tell, and I do, too, about the advertisement Oscar Hammerstein took in *Variety*. The ad said: "I've done it before and I can do it again," and it listed Oscar's six or more flops.

Oscar, who is shy in spite of his great success, revealed a secret ambition to me one day. He was telling about rehearsing *Show Boat* and trying to find someone adequate to play opposite Helen Morgan. Suddenly Helen turned to him and asked: "Oscar, why don't you play the part?" He'd been directing but also filling in by reading the lines of Steve, the actorless role.

"I like to tell that story," Oscar added. "It makes me sound like a good actor, which I've always wanted to be, but nobody will give me a job."

David Belasco, pioneer Broadway producer, with his dramatic white hair and turned-round collar, became a recognizable celebrity without the aid of motion pictures, fan magazines, or television. Everywhere he went people knew him.

P. G. Wodehouse, creator of the hilarious English valet, Jeeves, told me of an encounter with Belasco back in the early days when Wodehouse and Guy Bolton had begun to collaborate on plays.

"Guy Bolton had just finished, with George Middleton, the script of *Polly with a Past*. They went to that fabulous studio of David Belasco's over the theater, and as always Mr. Belasco was changing things around, tacking up hangings, taking down prayer rugs. This day his secretary was putting hot compresses on her face—she had neuralgia. Valiantly the playwrights began to read *Polly*. Every sentence was punctuated by the bang-bang of the hammer, the moaning of the secretary, and Belasco, at the slightest pause, shouting, 'Go on, go on, I'm listening.' Finally they gave up and went quietly away, defeated.

"To their astonishment Mr. Belasco telephoned that he was going to do *Polly* on Broadway. He had taken it all in, and *Polly with a Past* was a gold mine for everybody connected with it."

Henrietta Nesbitt, White House housekeeper for the Roosevelts' tenure, could not be called the conventional storyteller, but let her start on diets and she could be eloquent.

"When Governor-General Tweedsmuir of Canada came visiting a memo was sent ahead listing the items of food that must not be served him," she told me, half resigned, half indignant. "They totaled twenty and went from soup of any kind through fish, meats, salads, savories, ice cream. What was left to give him, I wondered!

"Then there were the diet lists of our regulars—Jimmy Roosevelt (ulcers, he had), Secretary Henry Morgenthau, Secretary Hull, Louis Howe, and even Fala, the dog.

"When we had filet mignon on Mrs. Roosevelt's birthday, I had lamb chops served inconspicuously to Secretary Morgenthau. He tried to keep his diet unobtrusive—not like some who treat it like a religion and want to talk about it all the time.

"With Harry Hopkins' diet I had to watch out for forty-eight items. He was virtually not allowed to eat anything or drink anything—but he did. Puréed banana was the only fruit permitted him. I sometimes think history might have been different if it hadn't been for those forty-eight items."

A story that amused Mrs. Nesbitt much more than the diets (they were serious business) was about the time the committee in charge invited President Roosevelt to his own inauguration.

Gleefully she commented: "The President was a tease, and he had our social bureau send back a reply, in formal script to the effect that the 'President regrets that due to the rush of official business, he is unable to accept the courteous invitation to be present at ceremonies attending the inauguration of the President of the United States.' Underneath in his own hand he wrote a P.S. 'I have re-arranged my engagements and think I may be able to go. Will know definitely January 19th. F.D.R.'"

## 16.  THERE WERE GIANTS

The most fascinating and at the same time exasperating guests I tackled in my early days were stage people. They would freeze right up because they were used to lines and felt helpless in a public appearance without them. Sometimes the broadcast was almost over before I thawed them out.

But what glorious performances they gave when I did manage to find the key to unlock them. They sang songs that went back to their beginnings. They revived roles they thought they had forgotten, they preened themselves and strutted a little but with a kind of open innocent delight in the success with which they had negotiated a long road through poverty, discouragement, and hard work.

Sometimes, compared with present-day standards or lack of them, their record of effort sounds almost unbelievable.

Dignified Walter Hampden, for instance, whom Edwin Booth's grandson, presenting his illustrious grandfather's jeweled girdle, hailed as the greatest Hamlet since Booth, studied for twelve years after his first appearance as the melancholy Dane before he felt he was ready to do the part again.

"At twenty-five I was playing Laertes in Henry Irving's *Hamlet* and kept feeling that Mr. Irving was straining his voice, so I studied Hamlet's lines day and night. Sure enough, one afternoon the director told me that Mr. Irving had lost his voice and I was to go on."

The day after one critic said Hampden's Hamlet was the greatest thing that had happened in the theater since Booth.

"But I wasn't satisfied, and I did truly study *Hamlet* for twelve more years before I was willing to play it again," Mr. Hampden told me.

"I lived and breathed only theater from the time I was a senior in Brooklyn Polytechnic and played Shylock. I saw Modjeska do Lady

Macbeth at least twenty times. I knew every word of the play by heart.

"Later when I went abroad I read *Hamlet* and learned that, too, in a little rented room in London. In France, I studied acting, singing, fencing—anything I thought would help me in the theater because I knew that was the only place on earth for me."

All his life the actor fought to keep Shakespeare part of the living theater. When Broadway managers in 1918 believed that even *Hamlet* spelled box-office ruin, he used his salary from a hit play to hire the Plymouth Theatre and produce the Bard of Avon there in off-hours.

"And I proved my point," he declared triumphantly. "People did want to see Shakespeare. They even came to the theater at ten-thirty on Saturday mornings."

Another long-time dream of his was to do *Cyrano de Bergerac*.

"I saved my money and risked it all on a Broadway production," he said. "The reviews were everything we could have asked, and we seemed headed for a good long run. Then one night the trapeze which simulates a tree branch on stage broke and I fell. We rang down the curtain for two minutes and then I managed to hobble my way through the rest of the performance. But doctors found that my foot was badly fractured; we would have to suspend performances for several months. It nearly broke my heart.

"Then I got thinking, and I said to my wife: 'Accidents do not happen of themselves. Perhaps this was my fault. Perhaps I'd been thinking too much in terms of my own personal success and fame. And that, as Cyrano says, isn't in the story.'"

I doubt if Walter Hampden, reverent as he was about Shakespeare's genius, ever tampered with his idol's immortal lines. But Margaret Webster confessed with a chuckle that she wrote in dialogue for *The Devil's Disciple*.

"I know George Bernard Shaw objected violently to a single word of his plays being changed, but he didn't put any dialogue into the crowd scene," she explained, "and since I can't stand crowds that just mumble I inserted some talk."

One of my favorite interviews of all time was with Margaret and her mother, Dame May Whitty, then eighty. Dame May was starring on Broadway in *Therese* at the time, and Margaret was directing her. After we had explored the uniqueness of a daughter directing a mother —I was the one who thought it remarkable, not they—they began to reminisce with affectionate raillery about their years in the theater. Dame May had then been acting sixty-five years.

She had pushed Margaret on stage with Ellen Terry in *The Merchant of Venice* one night so that the girl might have the experience of being on with such a great actress. Margaret carried a spear.

"Ellen Terry was at least seventy years old at the time," she recalled. "Her eyesight was failing, and she was rehearsing in an outdoor theater on a stage that had no footlights. She was frightened of stumbling, and it was sad to watch her in rehearsals.

"But when the night came she swept on stage in Portia's fair wig and scarlet robe and suddenly she was all youth and beauty. It took my breath away.

"Then there was the time she was playing Beatrice in *Much Ado About Nothing* at the Temple Gardens in London. There is a line— '. . . look where Beatrice, like a lapwing, runs close by the ground'— and from a distance came Ellen Terry running from behind a tall hedge close by the ground, exactly like a lapwing.

"Margaret was fortunate to see Ellen Terry like that; it's a great possession for her to have," Dame May Whitty commented contentedly. "I of course knew Ellen Terry and played with her for many years. Once I was doing the gentlewoman in *Macbeth*. Ellen Terry, as Lady Macbeth, came to those lines—'To bed, to bed'—and took up a little Roman lamp. Instantly one of her long, loose braids of hair, half undone, caught fire. I was close so I stepped nearer and wiped out the flame with my heavy cloak. Ellen Terry went on with her lines, those wonderful green-blue eyes staring out over the footlights, and finished the sleepwalking scene as though she had no knowledge that she was dangerously close to being burned alive. She was for all time—a great woman, a beautiful actress."

Grace and enchantment—all the great actresses have those qualities and they spread a special aura, as they did around Laurette Taylor when she returned to Broadway as the star of *The Glass Menagerie* —the last role she ever played and surely the most triumphant.

I invited her to our microphone to celebrate her triumph, but mostly she wanted to talk about the years after the death of her husband, Hartley Manners, who'd been very close to her in her theatrical life.

"I went on a wake," she told me, "and it lasted eighteen years."

She was young, beautiful, talented, and every producer on Broadway tried to give her a chance. But always her drinking spoiled everything. Toward the end of the eighteen years Eddie Dowling read a script by an unknown young playwright. The play was called *The Glass Menagerie*. Eddie, telling me about it said, "Nobody on Broadway had enough faith to put money into this somber drama of a decadent Southern household, not until Tennessee Williams brought it into my office. I knew the instant I read it that here, finally, was the perfect vehicle for Laurette Taylor."

He could not foresee the perilous weeks in Chicago when all the money he had in the world seemed about to go down the drain. Or perhaps with his Irish feyness he did half foresee the fact that critics would not understand *The Glass Menagerie* and he would face ruin. What he did feel certain about was the play, and in spite of the critics the public began to agree with him and buy tickets. Eddie decided to ask the reviewers to come round for a second look. When they did they, too, backed Eddie's opinion.

"I felt sure," said Eddie, who was playing the male lead as well as producing and directing, "but rehearsals were tough. Laurette just went through the motions. She seemed to be sunk in a sort of lethargy. But on opening night, the instant she walked on stage, the theater came alive."

However, the Broadway first night that would make or break the play was still to come. Eddie and his wife, Ray Dooley, went off to supper a few hours before curtain time. He recalled, shuddering: "When we came back to the theater it was raining and dismal, and the doorman asked anxiously whether Laurette had been with us. He hadn't seen her for hours.

"Opening night on Broadway and no star! Ray and I hurried to all the nearby restaurants, fearing she had suddenly decided to take a drink, praying she hadn't. We couldn't find her. Ray insisted that I get into make-up and, half frantic, I did.

"Thirty minutes before curtain time Ray came to my dressing room to say she had found Laurette. Our star was sitting on a fire escape in the rain. She was crying and she said to Ray: 'It's no use. I can't do it. Tell Eddie I'm not going on.'

"I gave her the old pep talk of course. 'Do you want to let your public down? Are you going to give the critics a chance to say I told you so—Laurette Taylor will never make a comeback.' No answer.

"So I told her sadly, 'All right, I'll tell your understudy to get ready.'

"With that I went back in the theater. Laurette, soaking wet, followed me—and as everybody knows gave one of the great performances of all time."

The theater has been Eddie's love all his life. He has made several fortunes and lost several serving this capricious mistress. Eugene O'Neill's *The Iceman Cometh* was one of his loves.

"It was a long, exacting play, and one day we rehearsed all afternoon and evening with a short supper break about five," he told me. "Nobody bothered to wash off make-up or change clothes. With Eugene O'Neill and me in the lead, the cast proceeded up Broadway, all looking like the down-and-out characters they played on stage. Broadway bums on the look for a handout, spotting the little procession, tagged along, too, and the cast of nineteen doubled along with the bill for sandwiches and beer.

"I was just instructing the restaurant manager to throw out the bunch of free loaders when Eugene O'Neill stepped in. 'No,' he said gently. 'It isn't costing that much. Let them stay. I know what it's like to need a meal.'

"Late at night, after rehearsals, I would walk home with O'Neill. He lived up in the Seventies. He was frail and sick and I'd try to get him to take a cab, but then I realized he just wanted to talk. He told about his boyhood and his family, all the heartbreaking stories he'd put into *A Touch of the Poet*. Maybe he'd already written it then, but it wasn't published."

Another of Eddie's poignant memories was of the day a tall, shy young man stopped him outside the theater and asked whether he might sneak into the balcony and watch a rehearsal of *The Iceman Cometh*. "It was Eugene O'Neill, Jr.," said Eddie. "Relations with his father were strained at the time, and he had not been invited either to a preview or to the opening. Afterward I found him waiting in the shadows outside the stage door.

" 'I want to thank you,' he said. 'Dad's play is really good, isn't it?' Eugene O'Neill never knew that his son had been there."

Eugene O'Neill, Jr., came on our program first through Stella, who had a talent for becoming involved with people with problems. Stella met young O'Neill, then one of the world's most promising Greek scholars, and he was broke. Stella took him on as a cause. She badgered people, including me, into giving him engagements with pay, and herself quietly wrote checks—heaven knows how many.

O'Neill, Jr., didn't want to talk about O'Neill, Sr., on the air and Stella said he needn't—he could talk about classic Greek or anything he pleased. She said he not only needed the money, he needed kindly understanding—he was unhappy. She was right. Some time later this really brilliant young man hanged himself in a mountain resort near Stella's farm.

Tennessee Williams once said on the program that his second Broadway hit, A *Streetcar Named Desire*, came close to not being written at all.

"I started working on it while *The Glass Menagerie* was playing in Chicago," he related. "But after two or three weeks I decided to give it up, thinking it was too violent for the theater and that if I did it at all it would have to be a novel. I began writing a quieter sort of play, but then I'd find myself in a mood of violence and back I'd go to *Streetcar*.

"The idea haunted me ever since I saw the two streetcars that run along one track down in New Orleans. One is marked Desire—it goes to the Desire section of the city. The other has its destination marked too—Cemetery . . . and they sum up all of life."

This was in 1947, and I introduced Tennessee Williams as the most gifted young playwright in the theater.

"I don't know about that," he demurred, "but I do know we've got the most gifted young actor of the day in this play—Marlon Brando."

We were both right.

"I was once described as having a shape like a battered coal barge and a face like a bulldog," Josephine Hull, for whom no glowing future was predicted in the theater, told me, chuckling. She could afford to make merry about criticism, for she was the biggest success just then on the street of bright lights. She was starring in *The Solid Gold Cadillac*, and everybody was talking about her masterly spoofing of big business.

Josephine Hull is the only actress I can remember who professed to like getting older. What was tragedy to most of her profession was prosperity and acclaim for her.

"I've had much the best parts of my career since I've been older," she exulted, and added thoughtfully, "I never was glamorous anyhow.

Maxine Elliott—now, *she* was glamorous—once took me in hand and taught me how to dress so that my figure didn't look quite so awful, but I never got a part because I was beautiful."

Although she enjoyed her own aging, the veteran actress did not think the good old times were necessarily the best.

"Richard Mansfield used to insist that no lesser actor—and they were all lesser, to his mind—ever speak to him until spoken to. I don't think anyone in the theater acts like that now."

It was back in those days that Josephine Hull had a small part in a melodrama which she remembered vividly because of one episode.

"The big moment came when the leading man committed suicide by leaping from the top of a tower. Backstage they had a rubber mat for him to land on. On this particular evening they'd installed a new mat. He made his suicide jump and, to the joy of the audience, bounced right back."

I commented that in *Arsenic and Old Lace* critics had called Josephine Hull "the duckiest little murderess in the world."

"I'd think that play would have given you goose flesh—killing thirteen old gentlemen and burying them in the cellar," I added reproachfully.

"No, Mary Margaret. At the very start our director said: 'Now remember, these are happy old ladies who think they're doing the kindest thing in the world.' So we went at it in that spirit."

"Well, all I can say about you is that no matter what diabolical plot you're weaving, you behave as if you were presiding at your favorite nephew's christening."

"Somebody has suggested," she answered to this, "that our government send me to interview Stalin."

She could have done it, and so could May Robson. At seventy-seven, May told me deprecatingly that her comparatively recent success in Hollywood was only her second career out of a half dozen she had planned.

"My first was the stage," she explained, "and if Hollywood doesn't pay as much after a while as I think it should, then I'll go on to my third career."

"And what will be your third career?" I prodded.

"A cook, I think," answered May. "I'm a very good cook and almost more proud of it than of my acting. I'm never so flattered as when people say, 'This is the best pie I've ever eaten.'"

"What kind of pie?"

"Aha." The actress fixed me with a mischievous eye. "You're going to try to make me do a commercial for you and say the best pie is made with Florida fruit. But I won't."

I steered hastily away from cooking and told her I thought she was brave to work without a stand-in in Hollywood. "That time you took the ninety-mile-per-hour ride hanging on to the driver's leg—wasn't it rather frightening?" I asked her.

"I didn't know it was dangerous until it was all over—you do those things without realizing—and then the poor director was in a fainting condition. 'Do you mean to tell me that was *you* in that car going on like that?' I said: 'Of course it was.' He said: 'I wouldn't even have had a camera click if I had known.' He was frightened but I wasn't."

And on the subject of landlording, she was proud of the fact that she refused to rent to childless people.

"It came about like this," she told me happily. "One day a few years ago I saw a little boy sitting on the curb, looking as though he was about to burst into tears. I asked what was the matter and he told me: 'My mummy's trying to find a house and she can't.' Why can't she? 'Because they don't want children.' Well, I went straight to the real-estate agent, who handles the little bungalows I own, and I informed him that I would not rent the bungalows to anyone who hadn't a child. He was very much upset. 'You're crazy, Miss Robson,' he accused. I said with finality: 'That's settled. No tenants without children.' And that's how it is to this day."

A syndicate asked May Robson to write five hundred words on her philosophy of life. What had her fifty-eight years on the stage taught her?

"I told them it didn't take five hundred words, or even fifteen," she snapped. "I just try to be what those who love me think I am."

Before me as we went on the air November 18, 1947, was a two-page magazine spread featuring the photograph of a little girl with golden curls. The caption read like a threat: "If there is a human being living who doesn't know who *this* is!"

I said on the air: "The picture that needs no name to identify it is of our guest today—and who is she?"

My audience roared back: "Mary Pickford."

Mary Pickford smiled at the wildly applauding audience, eyes as clear and blue as those of the little girl in the picture, and told how her fabulous career really started—"With Mr. Murphy, who hired our front bedroom after Father died. I was five and my sister Lottie was four and one day Mr. Murphy, who was a stage manager, asked Mother whether she'd like us to be in *Silver King,* a play he was doing. Mother was horrified at the idea of her innocent babies in the wicked theater.

"But Mr. Murphy said, 'Why, I'm sure that if you come backstage you'll find the ladies and gentlemen of our cast as well behaved as any of your friends.' Mother went backstage and was charmed with everything and everybody.

"The next week I played a villainous little child. In one scene I told Lottie and the other little girls not to speak to the leading child. My line was, 'Don't speak to her. Her father killed a man,' whereupon Lottie was so sorry for her, she ran across the stage and gave her a stick of candy. Those were our first parts."

And the first salary check when Mother and Brother Jack joined the two little girls in a stock company was twenty dollars!

Mary Pickford adored her mother. "She was a great woman. When I think what she did to keep our little family together I could cry. My grandmother was paralyzed, and my mother took care of and supported her too. Somehow she always made a living for us. I feel sorry for rich little children who've never had that close, intimate contact with their families."

Mary told that day about going to audition for David Belasco.

"I was terrified. They put me on the stage with the lights on and all I could see of Mr. Belasco down front was his white hair. I did the role of Patsy Poor begging a kitchen chair, representing a policeman, not to take me to jail. Afterward I told Mr. Belasco that the scene wasn't worthy of him. But he was sweet about it. He asked whether I wanted to be an actress. I said, 'No, sir.' I was thirteen then, and I'd been acting for eight years. 'No, sir, I want to be a *good* actress.'"

That was when they changed her name from Gladys Smith to Mary Pickford.

"When I first went into motion pictures I didn't want anybody to know. It was disgraceful for a legitimate actress to be in the flickers, or the five-cent shows, as they called them then. So I was Goldilocks or the Biograph Girl."

But the Biograph Girl's blond, pink-cheeked beauty achieved too much popularity for her to remain anonymous. She moved to the Essenay Studios and remembers her mother bargaining over salary. Essenay offered $45 a week, Mother held out for $55.

"I didn't say anything, but I'd made up my mind that unless I got $500 a week by the time I was twenty, I'd be a failure."

Long, long before that, newspaper headlines announced that Mary Pickford had signed a new Hollywood contract at $10,000 a week. She'd come quite a way from the little girl who landed in Baltimore with her family at three o'clock on Christmas morning with no Christmas tree, no presents, no festive holiday dinner.

"But let's not cry about it," Mary comforted herself. "I've had wonderful Christmases since. And even then, we had one another."

Her only expression of bitterness was about the famous curls!

"I never had a hairdresser. I had to wash my hair myself and then every morning Mother would spend forever brushing and fixing. I was a slave to those curls."

I remembered that it was regarded as a national calamity when Mary Pickford decided to put up her hair.

"Yes, they kept me from doing it for a long while. I said it was ridiculous to have long curls when I was really grown-up—that either I was an *actress* or a make-believe child and I intended to find out which."

At the time we talked Mary Pickford was interested in philosophy, religion, and the fourth dimension.

"No, I don't understand the fourth dimension," she confessed, "even though Professor Einstein came to dinner and tried to explain. He illustrated with forks and knives and spoons and a plate. I couldn't comprehend the Einstein theory so how can I—how can anyone—hope to understand the Great Creator of all? I believe that since God gave me my mother and brother and sister, whom I dearly loved, He will give them back to me. I know that life is eternal. It's just that you have to say good-by for a little while.

"I think there is little excuse for any of us to be here unless we are willing to learn and progress—to be more tolerant, more loving, more kind to one another . . . and sometimes to ourselves. All my life I have had a tendency to condemn myself. Mother used to say, 'Mary, you can forgive other people but you don't seem able to forgive yourself. You must try.' So now I do. I say to myself: 'All right, Mary, I forgive you. Now be a good girl and start all over again.'"

I never heard Gloria Swanson worry about her own behavior, but she was always trying to find domesticity. She was late one day at our broadcast because she'd eloped the night before, and came into the studio on tiptoe, explaining to an enthralled audience that she was wearing a silver sixpence in her shoe for luck and that she intended settling down to be a nice little housewife.

She looked then and always like anything but a nice little housewife. She had the figure of a lucky seventeen-year-old, although blithely admitting that she was fifty-four. Her skin glowed, her eyes shone. I complained that she was unfair to American women.

"I don't somehow see you in a gingham apron, making jelly."

"Oh yes, Mary Margaret, with geraniums at the kitchen window and everything."

I said maybe, just maybe, in another incarnation she might be a clinging vine.

"That's what I hope to be now. I've worked since I was fourteen and a half. That's a lot of work, and I've had children too. I'd simply love to settle down and be petted and pampered and have all the responsibility taken from me."

Anyone following Gloria's recent commuting trips to Paris and Rome and her career as a fashion designer and promoter knows that particular dream died quickly. This day we began talking about Hollywood in the days when the great stars and producers occupied lofty pinnacles.

"Cecil B. De Mille used to call me 'young fellow'—I don't know why. He'd argue: 'Now, young fellow, you've got to be more careful.' You see, we did some pretty violent scenes, and I had many a cut and bruise. But youth doesn't notice.

"We had a scene in a den of lions. I remembered a picture in my grandmother's parlor—The Lion's Bride—pathetic, with this young girl coming to see her pet lion to say good-by because she was to be married and had to leave the lion behind. Well, the lion ate her— and of course as a child this fascinated me. When it came to our own lion scene I insisted that I'd go into the den myself—no stand-in for

me. Mr. De Mille said: 'Very well, I'll go in with you.' And he did.
I had on a gown trimmed with peacock feathers. Peacock feathers are
supposed to be bad luck. Well, we were in the lion pit, and when the
trainer cracked his whip the lions roared. You've no idea how it
sounded, close up. One lion was about ten feet away, and I could feel
his hot breath. The finale was when I was lifted out and tossed bodily
to one and another of various people standing round the pit.

"I got back to my dressing room, shaking, and word came to get
ready to do it again. Suddenly I rebelled. I ran to Mr. De Mille's
office in tears.

"He said: 'Young fellow, come over here,' put me on the arm of
his chair, patted me, and said: 'At last I know you're a woman.'"

Lawrence Langner once asked Gloria, "What do you imagine you
would have done if not for that wonderful invention, the motion-picture machine?"

"And I answered," reported Gloria, "'Mr. Langner, if I had been a
telephone operator I would have been the best darn telephone operator in the world—or the best darn whatever else I undertook!'"

Lawrence Tibbett had the same idea as Gloria.

"You rise to the occasion or else you miss. And, depending on this,
you are a success or a failure."

His first efforts were spectacular, too, if not always successful. He
was to sing "Jesus Wants Me for a Sunbeam" at a church social. His
mother had taught him and coached him.

"But when I got on stage my mind went blank," he took up the
story. "I could hear my mother off stage trying to give me a cue, and
finally quite audibly she commanded, 'Sing *something!*'—so I did—
'The Star-Spangled Banner.'"

He was turned down by his high school glee club. In his first professional role, Pish-Tush in *The Mikado*, he says he was "as stiff as a
ramrod."

In his first audition at the Metropolitan Opera he "cracked wide
open on the first F sharp of '*Eri tu*' from Verdi's *Masked Ball*."

"But that fine singer Frances Alda, married to Gatti Cassaza, believed in me," he recalled, "and pleaded with Gatti to give me another
chance. He finally agreed, offering $50 a week. Frances Alda got it up
to $60, and the fifth year I was raised to $150."

Tibbett applauded Madame Alda's sportsmanship because once

when he appeared with her and had to throw her about, out of inexperience and excitement he gave her a shove so that she went flat on her face through the door and was black and blue with bruises.

Lawrence Tibbett's big chance came, as it so often does on the stage, when another performer was sick—the singer who was to do Ford in *Falstaff*. There's a spectacular aria in the second act, and as Lawrence Tibbett finished it he heard that intoxicating sound—an audience on its feet shouting "bravo" and applauding thunderously. The curtain was held up fifteen minutes while the newcomer, in stunned disbelief, heard them shouting his name.

"It was the most exciting moment of my life, one of those Horatio Alger bits. It happens only once in a lifetime and it's thrilling."

When I met Billie Burke I expected her to be exactly like the parts she always plays. She doesn't flutter like her characters, but she does look innocently expectant like them—and people treat her accordingly.

She got into a taxicab that day, gave an address, and the driver said, "First I'm going to take you over to Central Park and show you the cherry blossoms."

Billie's real name is William Ethelbert, for her father. She was christened at ten in Westminster Abbey. Her mother wrote poetry and was determined that William Ethelbert should go on the stage. So the girl obligingly did.

Enrico Caruso was one of her great fans. He would come to watch her in the theater and throw on the stage great bouquets of violets or long-stemmed American beauties tied with enormous bows.

Another of her admirers was Mark Twain. "He had a weakness for redheads," she explained modestly. "I used to come down from Boston to dine with him on Sunday nights. He would walk up and down in his white suits with his great shock of silver hair and talk about everything. I remember he said once, 'Truth is so rare we must use it discreetly.' He probably tried out on me some of the wise sayings he later used in his writing."

Billie herself is inclined to philosophize. "Charm," she said, "makes old age possible." Beauty she considers rather dangerous. "One learns to depend too much on it. I've known such tragedy among the beautiful Ziegfeld girls. Anyway we can do such awful things to ourselves. I knew one person who died just from not caring to live. If you can get past the bad corner, life takes an up and you can't imagine how you could have felt as miserable as you did."

Life took an up for her when the lovely young actress met a slim man "who looked a little like Mephistopheles." He had the orchestra at a party play a Paul Jones and told the caller to blow the whistle at the right point for him to dance with Billie Burke. She didn't know who he was, but somebody called him Flo and then she realized it must be Florenz Ziegfeld. She couldn't believe it because, she said, she'd expected him "to be a bearded lecherous old man."

Daniel Frohman called her next morning to say, "That man Ziegfeld is buying up all your photographs." Frohman was frightened for her career and he was right to be, for as she put it succinctly, "It went. I thought making a home was more important than any career."

At the end of the interview she told me: "I've never spoken like this before, and it's an odd experience."

My listeners and I found it an enchanting one.

It's difficult to put down in cold print the enchanting quality of these talented creatures talking frankly about themselves. Probably no actresses in any medium ever had more adjectives lavished on them than the lovely Gish sisters—Lillian and Dorothy.

I read one such description of herself to Lillian: "She is the fragrant April of man's hopes; her eyes are butterflies, fluttering softly to their object."

"That has nothing to do with me," declared Lillian shaking her head vigorously. "The silent screen was a medium in which people's imaginations did most of the work. We could never do the wrong thing and we never said the wrong thing because we never spoke. The audience brought their own imaginations to the shadows they admired and supplied what we lacked. I really shouldn't tell you all this, but it's true!"

"Well, somebody else—male of course—said you had a mind like a man's."

Lillian: "No comment."

I read to Dorothy: "She is radiant, exquisite, fragile, gossamer, dew-drenched youth."

"At least I was young," commented Dorothy dryly.

She was a male impersonator at four—Little Willie in *East Lynne*. Lillian cried because she wasn't in the play and Dorothy cried because she was ashamed to appear in trousers before the public.

"It marked me for life. I can't bear slacks to this day," she commented.

Their mother, who, Lillian and Dorothy claim was the beauty of their family, was a saleswoman in a Brooklyn department store and to add to the family income rented out two rooms in their railroad flat to actresses. The actresses noticed the attractive children, and soon Dorothy was playing Little Willie.

In an interview with the combined Gishes each preferred to talk about the other.

Thus Lillian: "The time Dorothy sat in the fire? Well, she loved Fiske O'Hara, who'd promised he'd marry her when she grew up. She adored watching him from the wings, and one night when Mother sent her down a little early for her scene she couldn't see well, so she started inching her way on stage through an opening that was a fireplace in the scene. The audience giggled, and Fiske and his leading lady worried about what was wrong until suddenly Fiske saw Dorothy sitting plumb in the middle of the lighted logs, glowing red."

And Dorothy: "Lillian was a little girl playing in a quarry. The villain had put dynamite there, and when the hero found out he was supposed to swing a rope over, grab the child, and swing back. Lillian had a rehearsal, but nobody told her there'd be an explosion. The moment came, the hero swung over and grabbed a dummy made up like Lillian, the explosion sounded—and instead of lying unseen in the dark, Lillian jumped up and ran in the opposite direction, screaming!"

Added Lillian: "I got many more curtain calls than when I used to do it properly!"

Dorothy again: "Lillian played as a child with Sarah Bernhardt in *Froufrou*. The play was in French and she didn't have anything to say, so she always watched Sarah and thought she was singing; her voice went up and down so beautifully. She had vivid red hair with an aura about her, and sometimes she'd take hold of Lillian's tawny hair and Lillian would wonder why the beautiful lady was singing about her hair."

Once when she came to us Lillian was playing a character on Broadway who had been left ten million dollars.

Lillian said, "If I really had ten million, after a national theater in Washington was built, if any money was left I'd build the next one in New York and go on putting up a monument like that to the theater in every city. In France if they have a dispute about the pronunciation of a word or anything to do with language or their culture, they go to the Comédie Française to settle it. Wouldn't it be wonderful if we, too, had a national theater where English would be spoken perfectly and beautifully?

"And I don't think the theater should be called an invalid—fabulous or otherwise. It should be called something rare and lovely. There's nothing more stimulating in the world than seeing great plays. It's like collecting first editions or surrounding yourself with beautiful fresh flowers. How can you enrich your life in a better way than seeing all the wonderful plays there are?"

Good actors are always stagestruck, I suppose, the Gishes only a little bit more than most. Gertrude Lawrence told me she had to be stagestruck to make a living, but a look of pleased remembrance came over her face at my question about her earliest stage success and right there on the air she began to sing the words of a song that had enchanted an audience when she was six: "Oh, it ain't all honey and it ain't all jam, walking round the 'ouse in a three-wheel pram."

I thought of that time when after her death I read Richard Stoddard Aldrich's *Gertrude Lawrence as Mrs. A.*, for it was one of my few firsthand glimpses of a woman with (her husband's tender and touching tribute had convinced me) rare ability to put herself into another's skin.

To prove it there is Richard Aldrich's story about the lean time his sister Barbara and her husband were having and the Christmas they got the practical food and clothing type of Christmas presents from the Aldriches. But there was one exception—Gertrude Lawrence Aldrich's gift, delivered on Christmas Eve and requiring two men to carry it, was a six-foot orange tree in a tub.

"Just think," marveled Barbara to a relative bringing a hamper of groceries and a check, "we can't even eat those oranges—you don't know what that tree does for me. What hunger it feeds. But Gertrude understands because she has hungered too—not only for food but for a touch of brightness and beauty without which life can be so drab and empty."

The same understanding was shown in Gertrude's relationship to an old vaudevillian, blind and ailing, who years before had found her a place in the chorus of *Charlot's Revue*, thus helping her get started in the theater. The actress had arranged board for the vaudevillian with a family in his home town and she sent him an allowance. But it was her frequent gifts—Sulka silk shirts, for instance—that he liked best and that her husband found mild fault with.

Gertrude was determined: "Not used clothes. And not useful ones. He will feel the silk shirts and they will remind him of old times. They are what he used to wear. Besides, think how he'll enjoy showing them off."

Just after *The King and I* opened so triumphantly, Gertrude came to us again. She was very gay that day and full of talk about her childhood.

"At Brighton when I was eleven, I put a penny in the slot to weigh myself and a pink card came out with a fortune on the other side: 'A star danced when you were born.' My grandmother said it was a prediction.

"My stepfather eked out a livelihood backing horses and giving tips, which was exciting when he was successful but dreary when he wasn't. We were constantly furnishing new homes on the installment plan when he was hitting the winners, and I remember one time when we moved two blocks away because we couldn't pay the rent. We did it by what we called 'The Moonlight Flit'—in the light of the moon. Mother put most everything we had left in a barrel (they'd taken away all the furniture), Dad and I followed with our mattresses and a few kitchen utensils. We'd lie low until Daddy got another lucky streak. Then Mother would give a party for the neighbors and maybe make me a new pinafore, and that would last until we were turned out again.

"I don't think I'd want my life to have been different. I'm no fatalist, but I do believe things are mapped out for you. I believe it's essential to have to earn your own living. I never had any intention of achieving stardom. It happened during the years I was taking care of my responsibilities and learning as I went along."

I asked, "If you ever did retire, Gertrude Lawrence, what would you do then?"

"Oh, I'd paint or learn to play the piano or maybe study some languages—and I've always been interested in medicine and law. I simply couldn't stay idle."

I said, "Very likely *The King and I* will run for years, so we shan't have to worry about your retiring!"

Gertrude Lawrence felt she owed a lot to Beatrice Lillie, for once when Miss Lillie was ill and another time when she was in an accident, Gertrude, who was her understudy, went on in her place.

"Gertrude and I were always up to some prank," admitted Beatrice. "Charlot once exiled us to the provinces because we bobbed out as ducks when our parts called for something quite different than quack, quack. Another time I went on, saying, 'Pardon me, you're wanted on the gramaphone,' which I thought was wonderful but I got expelled for two weeks for it."

When Beatrice Lillie came in for that first interview she said: "Speaking about myself terrifies me." But soon she, like Gertrude Lawrence, was singing delightedly and delightfully number after number from her old repertoire—an organ-grinder song she had learned with Harry Rich, followed by "Everyone Is in Slumberland but You and Me."

"I think I'll work them up again, and the costumes too—this is such fun," she decided.

I said, "Sometimes I'm sure you're the funniest woman in the world."

"If I'm not having fun, then I'm not funny. My first memory is of being vaccinated and my father and his brother leaving Canada— where I was born—for Ireland. I wanted to cheer my mother, who was crying, so I dipped a linen handkerchief in ink, smeared it all over me, and sang a song in blackface. I got a whipping, which I thought very unfair. All I wanted was for my mother to be happy and to laugh."

Beatrice Lillie even made people laugh when she sang in the choir. "It was the first time I became aware that I could do it and I hadn't even meant to," she commented thoughtfully. "I was using a palm-leaf fan because I was warm. My mother was the choir leader and my sister the organist. I thought I was very grand waving that palm-leaf fan, but it upset the minister and the choir and the congregation laughed so the minister asked my mother not to bring me again."

As we neared the end of our first broadcast together I asked Beatrice Lillie a question I often asked celebrities: "Have you ever felt famous?"

The answer wasn't unexpected. "Not at all. I'm always surprised when I pull it off again. I always think they'll rumble me, find me out, you know."

Miss Lillie and I once painted a picture apiece to be sold for the benefit of the Urban League. Artist Neysa McMein persuaded us to do it, just as she did fifty-odd others in Manhattan.

Beatrice Lillie was a veteran painter by comparison with me. But she began painting, of course, in a thoroughly improbable manner. "It was doorknobs," she explained, "imitation antique doorknobs. I wanted the real ones but I couldn't afford them so I got some wooden ones. Then I got some black lacquer and painted like mad. In the morning they were hard and shiny—just like china—and so I put on a few flowers. Then a friend of mine said the flowers actually looked like flowers so why didn't I paint some, not on doorknobs, but canvas. So I painted a whole bowl of flowers on canvas—at night of course. I never paint in the daytime. I'm frightened I'll see what I'm doing. I paint at night, lying on my stomach, and hope for the best in the morning. Sometimes flowers seem to grow while I sleep. For this Urban League thing Neysa wanted me to paint my hat. I thought that would be very dull, but she insisted so I painted my hat which looked like anything but my hat, so finally I did some flowers."

I was in New York in the twenties when *Charlot's Revue* came to Broadway and America first reacted to the charm of Beatrice Lillie and Gertrude Lawrence.

Beatrice Lillie said, "We took the revue to Hollywood after New York, and every night the audience was full of stars. But on the last night we didn't know what had happened. The front rows were suddenly empty. Charlie Chaplin, Valentino, and the others had all sneaked backstage and got into make-up and the Scottish kilts we wore in one number, and they all came on stage for the curtain call. It was wonderful."

Just as we were about to go off the air and had had the fifteen-seconds signal, Beatrice Lillie was going so strong that she said, "Have I time for one little thing? A little mistaken-identity thing?" And she sang: " 'I was standing at the corner, as quiet as quiet can be; when a great big ugly man came up and tied his horse to me!' Thank you!"

The program's first encounter with Eva Le Gallienne, that very great lady of the theater, was also a performance. There is no recording of it, and neither she nor I remembers what poem she read that day in 1934. It is true that I do not know what words she was saying, but I can hear now that voice, like rich cream pouring out from a jug.

Eva Le Gallienne's life has been one long love affair with the theater. As a little girl in London she was taken to see *The Water Babies*. That night she insisted hysterically that she was going to be a water baby and was only quieted when her mother said the play manager would ask if she could read and write. She stopped crying at once and set fiercely about learning to read and write.

She met her mother's theatrical friends—Constance Collier, Forbes-Robertson, Maxine Elliott, William Faversham—and finally was taken to see Sarah Bernhardt in *Jeanne Doré*. Backstage afterward she kissed the divine Sarah's hand, and the actress raised the little girl to the seventh heaven by leaning over and embracing her.

Always fine acting threw her into a kind of delirium of happiness. Most exciting of all was Eleanora Duse.

Said Eva Le Gallienne: "One of the most important events in my life was seeing Eleanora Duse that first time. The curtain rose on *Cosi Sia* and on a new epoch in my life. At the first sound of Duse's voice, at the first glimpse of her face, tears came into my eyes, tears of wonder, tears of exaltation. For the first time in this world, I felt I was looking upon perfect beauty. After the first act, I got permission to sit on the floor in the first-row aisle; I could not bear to be so far away. And after the final curtain I was in a sort of daze. I lost all my belongings: hat, coat, pocketbook. My one thought was to get away from people and enjoy in solitude the tremendous ecstasy with which her performance filled me."

Of course such fervent longing combined with real talent and that heart-stirring voice of hers won the young Le Gallienne her chance and soon she was a success on two continents.

But fulfillment for herself alone wasn't enough, as it is for some, maybe most, actors. It was the theater that she cared about—that all people everywhere should know an ecstasy like her own when she saw fine acting of fine plays, that young eager dramatic students should be given their chance.

Her Civic Repertory Theater in New York brought her dream gloriously to fruition for a time—young people got their opportunity, men and women saw good theater at a price they could afford.

As soon as the Civic Repertory Theater seemed established Miss Le

Gallienne added a free school and library. At the end of five years the curtain rang down on *Camille*. Eva Le Gallienne had announced that the company would take a year off to rest and get renewed energy.

Said Miss Le Gallienne: "The audience that night gave an extraordinary demonstration of their appreciation. From all over the house they shouted to us: 'Come back! Be sure to come back! Don't go away!' Those in the gallery and the back of the orchestra fought their way down the aisles to get a closer view.

"The entire Civic personnel—office staff, stagehands, and actors— stood on stage with tears in their eyes as the curtain rose and fell to the seemingly endless applause, and when I came out to take a final call alone I suddenly found myself ankle-deep in flowers, thrown singly and in small bouquets from every part of the house. It was 1 A.M. by the time the crowd dispersed. I stood at my dressing-room door, shaking hands with these unknown friends as they filed past.

"As I started upstairs to my apartment on the top floor, exhausted by the emotions of the evening, the porter told me there was still an immense crowd at the stage door. They refused to go away without a final glimpse of me, so I hurriedly threw a cloak over my *Camille* nightgown and went out to wave farewell. Again came the shouts: 'Come back! Be sure to come back!' I was tempted then and there to abandon our year of respite and go on working, yet I felt we needed the break.

"A few weeks later, when I found myself painfully struggling through my unexpected ordeal [she was seriously injured, especially her hands, in a terrible explosion], the memory of this demonstration of friendship was a potent factor in my fight for recovery. I felt that, like the legendary salamander, I must somehow emerge from the fire unscathed and keep my pledge to come back."

And she did come back with her dream untarnished.

# 17. STRANGE STORIES

*"There are more things in heaven and earth . . ." Shakespeare, quoted by Henry Sell on my program.*

Though I don't exactly believe in ghosts, never having seen any (except a light I couldn't account for over my bed in a Greenwich Village apartment), I am always interested in hearing about them from people whose contacts have been more substantial. If, of course, one could call any contact with a ghost substantial. Sometimes the most unlikely prospects have furnished me with the most likely stories.

One of the last people I'd ever had picked to be living a ghost story is Henry Sell, editor, gourmet, world traveler. What Henry really believes about all this, I'm not sure, but here is how he told it to my listeners and me.

"I was sitting beside novelist Elinor Glyn at a dinner at Elisabeth Marbury's. Elinor said: 'Henry, you were a marquis at the court of Louis XIV. You were sent to Venice on a mission by the Sun King and you were murdered. Your body was thrown into the Grand Canal. Later it was recovered and taken back to France.'

"Then she went on eating prime ribs of beef. Impulsively I pulled out my pocket piece, an old louis d'or, and dropped it on her plate to pay her for the fortune. She smiled, put the piece into her handbag, and the incident was over.

"Years later I went to Venice for the first time. I was dining at the Danieli hotel when I remembered Elinor's remarks. I told the story to my two hosts. One said: 'That's not so funny. A Frenchman was murdered on this very spot in 1591 when this hotel was the home of the doges. Your room may well be the one he slept in—even the bed may be the same, for the furniture has all been preserved. Where we are now could have been where the doge entertained the marquis.'

"I laughed but the tale haunted me, and for the next three days in Venice I searched as if compelled by an outside force for a gold Louis XIV coin dated 1591. I had no luck. Then on the Orient Express, going toward Paris, I had the strangest feeling that the coin was there and that I'd find it. When I got off the train I sent my bags to the hotel and went straight to the Bourse where I knew I could find old coins. The first shop I went into I said to the clerk: 'You have a Louis XIV coin—a louis d'or—and it's dated 1591. Please find it for me.'

"He reached back into the vault, took out a tray, and there it was—my coin, the one I'd given Elinor Glyn a quarter of a century before. I knew it by the small marks on it where it had once been set in a brooch. But I wanted to be sure of its authenticity, so I took it to an authority who vouched for it and didn't even look surprised when I said, 'I'm glad it's genuine because it's from another life when I was a marquis in the court of Louis XIV.' "

New York City is not a very good ghost town, according to Eileen Garrett. There is too much concrete, metal, and stone, Eileen said, and ghosts are partial to old, seasoned wood. Mrs. Garrett made a considerable reputation for herself in England, where they have a lot of old, seasoned wood, for her ability to de-ghost ancient houses.

"I've done *some* de-ghosting in New York," she told me. "Once in a big Manhattan hotel I was called in because there was a rocking chair which had been bought at auction and it was creating a lot of disturbance. People who sat in it found themselves suddenly dumped on the floor or else they got unexplained pain in shoulders or knees."

In order to de-ghost the chair Eileen looked up its history and learned that it had belonged to a Mississippi River boat gambler who'd committed suicide. How she proceeded after that is a trade secret which she never explained to me. She did say, and Stella Karn maintained it was true, that she was born with special powers. The British Institute of Psychical Research certainly thought so.

One of my favorites among ghosts inhabited Nyack, a Hudson River town only half an hour from New York City where a lot of high-salaried people from Madison Avenue and from the upper echelons of the theater have homes.

One such family bought an ancient farmhouse and did considerable remodeling, including the installation of a modern bathroom. They were somewhat upset by sudden slammings of the bathroom door when they knew nobody else was in the place and even more puzzled when the shower was heard to run vigorously.

Danton Walker, Broadway columnist, who told me about this haunt and has done a whole book on fascinating ghosts, speculated that this was a colonial type who was so charmed by modern plumbing that he (or she) couldn't resist dabbling in the new magic.

Danton told of visiting another Hudson River home in which the century-old shade was a lady who objected to radio and television. "If the family turned on either, a deadly chill would settle over the living room and they would hear soft footsteps and a swish of silk," he insisted solemnly. "The ghost was coming down the stairs. As soon as they gave in and switched off the set the soft footsteps retreated and the room returned to warmth and normalcy."

I'd like to be luckier about seeing ghosts. When I slept in the Lincoln Room at the White House everybody asked whether I'd seen Lincoln's ghost. I had to say no.

When I stayed at Government House in the Virgin Islands I *did* once imagine I heard a soft voice calling in the night. I had been assured that the house has a ghost who nightly summons her carriage. First you hear her voice, then the clatter of carriage wheels. I certainly didn't hear the wheels.

The house in Greenwich Village where the strange light used to hover over my bed was later occupied by the mysteriously murdered Starr Faithful, and subsequent occupants claimed she came back at intervals.

I don't mean to sound frivolous about the supernatural. I agree with Eileen Garrett that when "you deal with the mind you are dealing with the divine, so you ought to be careful."

Eileen never wanted to use her gift for money. She makes her living as writer, editor, and publisher.

"I've been a guinea pig for years, with scientists poking at me and questioning me," she says a little plaintively. "I know that what I can do is real—it is called supernormal only because we have not studied enough, not tried hard enough to reach a complete understanding of it. I believe that man has a terrific potential power within him that has not yet been realized."

But what I envied Eileen Garrett most was her ability to hear the growing world around her, to put her ear to the ground and listen to the small sounds.

"I can hear spring coming," she declares. "It's a lovely, silvery, tinkly whisper, and then I know I must go into the woods and poke under the brown leaves for the first violet."

When Eileen said that New York's steel and concrete buildings were inhospitable to ghosts I forgot to remind her of the swank Persian Room at the Plaza Hotel. This ghost is more of a snob than the people who go there for expensive food and entertainment. He limits his appearances to opening nights!

Folk singer Burl Ives knew all about this first-night mischief-maker.

"Earlier this season," Burl told me just after he'd had his own gala opening, "Tony De Marco, the dancer, slipped and skidded toward the end of his third number. Singer Lisa Kirk stumbled and fell head over heels on her opening night. Tito Guizar fell, too, and broke his favorite and most expensive guitar."

I asked Burl how he'd got through. "Well, I was on the lookout and I spotted the ghost coming out of the little entrance door, so he didn't get to knock me over. I thought I was keeping close tabs on him, but he must have wrapped the microphone cord around my foot because when I stepped back for a bow—wham, over went the mike, smashed to bits."

Europe is more accustomed than America to ghosts. In fact, ghosts, actress Sarah Churchill told me, play a prominent part in the lives of the English and in the English landscape.

"I had an Irish grandfather and a Scottish grandmother, and I was often near Castle Glamis, the queen mother's home before her marriage. There as a child I heard all sorts of stories of spirits who lived in the big houses of the region. They didn't scare me, not the way you'd be scared of a burglar you thought was in the pantry. But they did give me an extraordinary sensation—a strange feeling of someone who's been there, or something that's happened. It's a sort of atmosphere.

"Once in autumn my cousin and I went for a walk down a lovely narrow glen with a river at the bottom. Halfway down both of us were suddenly seized with an uncontrollable feeling, not fear, but we didn't want to go a step farther. We ran home and later, when our great-aunt was giving us tea, we told her about it.

"She said, 'That's not an unusual occurrence at all. None of us ever dares walk in that glen. It's unlucky.'

"And it proved unlucky for us too—at least we thought so. Two boys who were to take us to our first dance—we were so excited about it—had an accident on the way to get us and we were without beaux for the party!"

As Sarah intimated, the Scottish and the Irish are best at ghosts.

Blue-eyed Paddy the Cope, otherwise Patrick Gallagher, came from Ireland to explain his co-operative organization, formed to help Irish farmers "born in debt and never out of it." He was telling about Cleeandra, where he was born, a townland on a mountain.

"Our house was one room," he explained in his soft Donegal voice, "thatched with straw, and it had a small window of one pane. Of our twenty-three acres, eighteen were wild mountain. We were careful not to improve our cottage, for like as not the landlord would raise the rent."

Here is one of Paddy's ghost stories: "One night I and my Cleeandra friend Charlie started home late from a pub in a nearby town. On some occasions we drank more beer than we should and this night it was late, so we took the fields for a near way across the glen. When we came near the fairies' home we heard a fiddle up in the glen playing the most beautiful music. I had no ear for music, but I knew this was something great—music like no earthly sound I'd ever heard. We sat on the gravestone to listen, and then a hornpipe began and Charlie jumped to his feet and began to dance. Such dancing—I thought he'd kill himself and I kept calling out: 'Stop, Charlie, stop.' But all he did was say, 'Can't—can't.'

"I was frightened and made for Peggy Manus' house, which was the nearest. I told her I was sure the fairies were playing and Charlie was killing himself dancing. She said to hurry back and tell Charlie to thank the fiddler. 'Because if he didn't,' said Peggy, 'when the sun rose the wee people would take him into the glen and it would be the end of him.'

"I ran back. There he was, still dancing, and I shouted, 'Charlie, say "Thank you, fiddler."' Charlie did, the music stopped, and we walked on home. We never heard the fairy music again. Peggy Manus sat us on two turfs by her fire and told us about the misfortunes of a farmer and his family who'd been so absent-minded as not to put out a pot of praties, and we all cried a little and ate praties dippity.

"Dippity means a drop of milk in a saucer with a pinch of salt in it, and you dip the potato for each bite."

If it hadn't been for his co-op Paddy might have become a storyteller in the grand tradition of Ireland, like my friend, Seamus McManus.

Seamus seemed to carry about with him an aura of turf smoke and mellow tobacco. He, too, came from Donegal, pockets filled with smoke-stained copybooks containing his stories.

"I got off the boat and asked what was the best magazine in America. I was told *Harper's*, so I went to see old Mr. Alden, the editor there. He was taken with my homespun suit—it was tweed woven by the mountain folk in Donegal and I guess it had cost me five dollars. It was a good introduction, for when I got out the notebooks he liked my stories too."

Seamus was in his seventies when he used to come to my program, but he looked at least twenty years younger. He went back every summer to walk miles through Ireland, talking to the storytellers, gathering whole villages around the pump to listen.

"When I was a child every glen and every hillside in Donegal had a great storyteller. Now I am the last, and the last of the great *shanochees* [a Gaelic word—he said it like "shawnohshee"].

"At wakes, after the prayers were said at midnight, the neighbors would remain for the whole of the night. For three days and nights, while the corpse was in the house, someone always stayed and the long nights were passed telling stories of the old Finnians and of the Red Branch Knights that flourished in the time of Christ."

I've always been convinced that restaurateur Gene Leone was fond of me because I reminded him of his mother. If that is true it is very pleasant to remind a man of his mother, for Gene used to send me extravagant long-stemmed roses of the American Beauty era flown in from South America. He would also bring by taxicab from his restaurant hampers of vintage wines and shrimp and lobster concoctions, always with my favorite, *fettuccine*, which I first ate at Alfredo's in Rome when I was young and in love.

Gene was often on my program telling good yarns about his illustrious clientele, but this one about his mother belongs in a collection of strange stories because it seems to indicate a premonition.

"Will Rogers was in New York for five days before his ill-fated trip with Wiley Post," said Gene. "Four of those nights he came to Mother Leone's—we were down in Greenwich Village then—for dinner. The last night, he arrived with his wife and some friends and asked Mother to come and sit with them. While she was at the table another of the famous early fliers, Colonel Roscoe Turner, came by and yelled over to Will Rogers, 'Hey, why don't you let me fly you on this trip?'

"That stirred Mother up. She never believed in flying, and even after I'd been doing it for thirty-six years she used to close her eyes before every trip and pray that I'd get back.

"On this night she absolutely pleaded with Will Rogers: 'Please don't go! Why do you want to take this trip way up there to the North? It's dangerous. You might get killed.'

"Will Rogers answered: 'Mother, if I'm going to get killed I might as well get killed at the top of my career.' And he was."

A startling demonstration of mind-guiding was put on in my own studio-living room by Franz Polgar, authority on hypnotism, telepathy, and memory.

He gave one of us a match folder. Then he went out of the room with an escort and the folder was hidden in the jacket pocket of Associated Press reporter Cynthia Lowry. Everyone in the room knew where it was. Dr. Polgar returned and asked Janice Devine to hold one corner of a handkerchief while he held the other, very loosely—just a link between them.

"Please do not say anything. But as I walk tell me in your mind whether I'm right or wrong."

Janice says, "He took three steps forward, toward the bookcase, and in my mind I said, 'Not the bookcase, the girl.' He put his hands on Cynthia's shoulder. Then again in my mind I said as she moved away, 'Yes, you're right.' He touched her hat. I thought intensely, 'Not there, her pocket.' I could almost hear him asking, 'Which pocket?' 'Jacket upper left,' I told him. And he reached in and pulled out the matches."

There's an answer, of course, but what is it? Thomas Sugrue, who was not like anybody else, said we need wonders. He was confined to a wheel chair because he was paralyzed, but his spirit knew no limits. A while before he died he had himself and chair bundled aboard an airplane and went to see for himself the emergence of the nation of Israel. He was interested in all philosophies, all ideas. Of the remarkable people he knew and talked to me about—jazz musicians, priests, presidents—I was most interested in Edgar Cayce.

"What first excited me," Tom said, "was learning from his son that Edgar Cayce believed the subconscious mind of any person is capable of getting in touch with the subconscious mind of any other person. He said it was as simple as calling on the telephone. The trouble is our conscious minds set up barriers against this communication.

"Edgar Cayce was a shy humble man, eager to be liked. He hadn't gone beyond the ninth grade in school. And he had been a poor student—that is, until one night when his father wouldn't let him go to bed until he mastered a spelling lesson. Edgar begged to be allowed to stick the book under his pillow and take a nap. When he awoke he knew every word in the entire spelling book, even knew which page the words were on. That was the beginning of his conviction that he possessed a strange power.

"When I met him, he had begun the business of going into a sort of trance and having the names and addresses of patients read off to him. He would give diagnoses which baffled the doctors because they were correct. After a diagnosis he would prescribe, and this upset the doctors even more because his prescriptions were often radical, ranging from the most modern medicine and technical treatments to herbs and primitive cures. Edgar gave his readings for forty-four years and in all helped more than thirty thousand people, most of whom reached him through letters when they'd lost all other hope."

I asked why Tom didn't ask Cayce's help for his crippling arthritis.

"I did and he advised me *not* to take the fever-cabinet treatments. I did take them, as you know, and they nearly killed me."

Tom himself had a strange experience during his illness, when the hushed voices of his family, friends, and doctors told him all too surely that they expected him to die.

"I expected it too. Then at the lowest point in my sickness that alter ego, the other self whom I called Joseph and who was lost to me for so long, Joseph came back. I felt sure the odds were against me, but Joseph said no, we would win.

"Then I saw the walls of my room recede and light reached across the bottom of the bed and touched my feet. Outside I could hear the chatter of birds, the hum of insects, could smell the fragrance of the full summer earth, could see a maple in sunny green leaf across the window, and I found myself rubbing the sight of the greenness into my eyes. And so I won the fight against death."

Strange stories of cures were often brought back to me by travelers among primitive peoples.

Author John Collier, student of American Indian tribes, told of the nine-day Curing Sing of the Navajos.

"The whole tribe participates. It is a strange ceremonial, but it seems to work. I was a chronic sufferer from insomnia, and they offered to do a Curing Sing for me. At the end of the nine days my insomnia was gone. It never came back until I returned to civilization."

Gem collector Russ Anderton, who went to South America for emeralds and to Ceylon for rubies and sapphires, told about a Ceylonese worker whose arm was fractured while he was on a war project.

"A friend of mine who was a navy surgeon X-rayed the man's arm and told him he'd have to keep it in a plaster cast for several months. The man said he couldn't. He needed his wartime pay. So he went to his native doctor. In three days he was back on the job. My friend X-rayed the arm again and found nothing, nothing except what looked like a few needle scratches on the skin."

I asked Russ whether he'd learned any magic in Ceylon.

"Yes," he said. "I know three magic words which will stop a raging elephant, but I doubt if you'll have much use for them here in Radio City."

My nomination for the most macabre story of the year was one told by Hans Reusch, after a trip to the regions around the North Pole.

"An Eskimo lost his sledge during a snowstorm," said Hans. "All his food and supplies were gone and there he was, with only a knife, in the heavy snow. After a while he realized that his feet were frozen. Having reached the simple decision that his feet were of no further use to him except as food, he ate them—and thus saved his life."

Carl Carmer is a teller of strange tales of the Hudson River country and my own upstate region. People up our way a few years ago were forever finding new prophets or predicting the end of the world.

Long before Bridey Murphy's story came out Carl told about a woman who died twice. Her first death was as Jemima Wilkinson. Then someone called the Public Universal Friend invested Jemima's body and returned as a prophet. She did pretty well, too, collecting a large number of followers whom she led through the Genesee country to a spot called Crooked Lane on Lake Cayuga.

"She was a beautiful woman and she ran her little colony like a dictator," said Carl. "But womanlike, she resented any other woman who attracted attention and she hated getting old and fat. Once she got hold of a portrait someone had done of her and promptly burned it. It showed her getting fat.

"When the Public Universal Friend died," Carl went on, "her followers left her coffin open. They were positive she would rise again. But she never did."

Another historian guest, Lloyd Morris, told about the Fox sisters, founders of modern spiritualism, who came from upstate New York. In New York City they gave the first séances with spirit rappings.

"James Fenimore Cooper went to the first séance the Fox sisters held," Lloyd Morris told us. "He'd made a bet beforehand that he could ask a question the sisters could not answer. The gathering included Horace Greeley and many other New York celebrities.

"Cooper questioned the rapping spirits about someone long dead. This person had died fifty years before, the spirits answered promptly, and not from a natural cause. Cooper said: 'What was the person's name?' The spirits named Cooper's own sister and said she had been killed in a fall from a horse.

"It was all true and Cooper never could figure any way the Fox sisters could have known. That séance started a vogue for the sisters which lasted about thirty-five years."

Another good storyteller, Edward Rowe Snow, told us about a most fortunate de-ghosting.

"During a storm off the Magdalen Islands in the North Atlantic a wrecked ship was washed ashore, and in the morning some of the native village boys ran to the beach to collect whatever they could from the wreckage.

"They were back in no time, wide-eyed and scared. They'd seen an awful monster stalking the beach. The local missionary took a group with him and went to investigate. They saw a huge, terrifying figure stumbling along the sand. The villagers were all for running, but the priest insisted upon going closer.

"And the monster was a man, a tall, broad man literally encased in ice from the freezing water so that he looked nine feet tall. Thawed out, he lived, sole survivor of the wreck, to become the first telegraph operator of the islands."

Intrepid reporter Helen Worden Erskine would never be frightened by a ghost, I'm sure of that. And by the time she finished investigating it I'm not sure how much of its ghostliness would remain. Although just the opposite of a hermit herself, she specialized in them for a time. And while hermits are not ghosts, they belong among these strange stories.

Her interest in hermits began one day when Helen passed a house that looked empty but had no For Rent or For Sale sign on it. An old lady told her, "Langley Collyer, the ghosty man, lives there." The reporter in Helen couldn't resist such a description. She found a doctor nearby who told her that the Collyer brothers (the other was Homer) had collected among other objects a Model-T Ford which they kept in the basement, a rowboat housed on the roof, and at least seventeen pianos.

"I went back at midnight and waited," Helen told me. "Soon a wisp of a man in overalls with hair tucked under a cap slipped out, dragging a box by a rope. I accosted him with, 'Mr. Langley Collyer?' Dignifiedly he asked, 'With whom have I the pleasure of speaking?' I explained that I'd always been interested in old New York houses and that was enough. He began talking.

"Hermits like to talk. He told me about that section of the city and about the piano Queen Victoria had given his mother. He offered to play for me."

When she did go into the soon-to-be-famous house as the first reporter to enter after Homer's body had been found, Langley was already dead and Helen Worden walked over his body without knowing it. He had been killed by one of his own booby traps.

Another of Helen's hermits was found dead with a wrist bangle which contained a squirreled-away fortune in large bills. This was Mrs. Coogan, who was a social outcast from Newport because of having married a Tammany politician. She became a hermit after she invited three hundred to a party in her Newport house with Delmonico to cater and a big orchestra to play—and nobody came.

"Next day," Helen told me, "she walked out, leaving the doors wide open, and lived the rest of her life shut up in a hotel room."

My favorite of Helen's collection was the old lady at the Plaza who kept binoculars turned all day on Central Park Zoo. If she believed some animal was being mistreated she called to protest. Once she said that a raccoon hadn't got his apple for lunch.

"Another time," Helen recalled, "she telephoned the superintendent of the zoo to inform him that one of his foxes had just walked into Bergdorf Goodman's Fifth Avenue store. The superintendent banged up the phone. But his next call was from Bergdorf's. 'Have you missed a fox?' the manager asked."

Dr. Maxwell Maltz, plastic surgeon, contributed a strange true story from his own practice.

"Most of the people who come to me want blemishes removed," he said, "but this woman, a countess, wanted a scar put on! Because of love. Her husband had a scar which was withdrawing him from the world. She figured if she could join him, she might save their marriage.

"Almost as strange was another woman to whom I wanted to give a new chin. As a memorial to my mother I went back to the section I grew up in and picked out people who needed my kind of help. This friend of my mother's refused the new chin because, she said, 'All of us want to belong somewhere, and I feel now I belong to the world of children who poke fun at me and call me Birdie. I have learned to be happy in my world. At least the children like me now.'"

## 18.  SIXTEEN TALK ABOUT THEMSELVES

*"I read the Bible with the children half an hour a day and try to get them not to take themselves too seriously, as I did myself for so long."*
*Joan Crawford*

A young secretary who overheard me on the telephone making an appointment to interview a famous actress asked eagerly, "What are celebrities like? Are they nice to you?"

Rather cynically I assured her, "Yes, they're nice to *me*, all right. I'm a reporter!" Then I added, a little to my own surprise, "Most of the famous people I've met really *are* smarter, more alive, and more fun to know than the rest of us. In the interests of perfection they make incredible demands upon themselves and accomplish the impossible. That's why they are famous, I guess."

The young secretary looked at me wistfully. She was feeling the fascination of that mysterious something that pushes heads above the crowd.

"Though, mind you," I warned her, "the illustrious ones are not always easy to take. The very vitality that makes them exciting often also causes them to be difficult." (I was thinking of the opera singer who walked out when I said *no script*, and the next one whom I circumvented by pulling a tantrum first so that she had her hands full soothing me!)

That very night I had an example of the aura of attraction that surrounds a celebrity. I went to the theater with Joan Crawford. We arrived just before curtain time. When somebody recognized Joan and called out, nearly everybody in the theater rose as if a spring had been pressed and began to applaud. She stood there and smiled, looking very tall and regal for a woman I knew to be only five feet four. It's the quality of stardom, I thought, that literally shines from her.

For years I'd been curious about this woman whose driving ambition took her into the rarefied atmosphere of Hollywood fame. I was especially interested because we'd both gone to school in Columbia, Missouri, and the place was full of stories about her. When I finally caught up with her and persuaded her to be interviewed on the air, we naturally talked about her days at Stephens College in Columbia—how devastatingly poor she'd been, how she really had worked as a dining-room girl and had been taunted by luckier girls. How, humiliated and angry, she finally ran away.

"And I'll never forget what Papa Wood" [he was the president of Stephens whom I, too, knew] "said when he came after me to the railroad station and hauled me back—'Don't you ever run away from anything or anybody in your life.'"

The ambitious girl worked in a department store and then in the chorus of a Kansas City night club where she danced too close to a table and spilled a man's drink.

"The man turned out to be J. J. Shubert," she said. "He promised if I came to New York he'd try to find me a job. I got to New York before he did."

Her name in these days was Lucille LeSeuer. "It was my real name but it sounded too made-up, so I chose Joan Crawford. It's a switch when your real name sounds too theatrical for the theater!"

We talked about her four adopted children. "I'm learning from them," she said. "I think they've helped me make an adjustment to life because with four lives to be constructive about, I can forget myself. I remember my own childhood and that children do not always want what their elders want them to have. So I try to bring them up for their own lives, not mine.

"We talk things over together, and their only punishment is for telling a lie. I read the Bible with them half an hour a day and try to get them not to take themselves too seriously, as I did myself for so long. I've finally learned to laugh at myself, and I try always to laugh first. That's important. It's also important to know people you can trust—and to trust them. When I find I can't trust a person I simply walk away."

I went back to the ambition that drove Joan Crawford to the top and keeps her there. "Well, I had a lot of fear," she admitted, "a far greater lack of courage than anybody believed. But I'm stubborn. I won't give up."

Another time when Joan Crawford arrived at my apartment for a broadcast she was mopping her eyes, and I thought something awful had happened.

"No," she reassured me. "I'm crying because I'm happy. Just as I was coming to your door a woman stopped me, and what do you think? She's one of my ten thousand correspondents. I've been writing to her for years. It's such joy when you've achieved a little of your ambition and there are so many to share your blessings. I love those people. This woman downstairs—I know all about her and her family and she knows all about me and my family. Right there at your door we had a good talk and a good cry. It was beautiful."

Joan has accomplished almost everything she planned to do. But is she satisfied? I think not.

Mary Roberts Rinehart, on the other hand, after years of great success as a writer, a husband she adored, worshiping sons, readily admitted that she was happy, though she added, "Success always surprises me."

A question to a guest about childhood often evoked odd, unexpected memories. Mrs. Rinehart recalled vividly how she and her sister made tiny paper carts and hitched them to caterpillars!

The young Mary Roberts went straight from high school into nursing. "Yes—twelve hours' duty, too, for two years. Once I had to sew up the throat of a man who'd cut it clear through the larynx to try to save himself from being hanged. Another time I was sent into an operating room to clean up—and had to carry out an amputated foot."

She learned about poisons, and it came in handy in her later career as a best-selling mystery writer.

"Even my son Stanley provided laboratory experience," she said. "When he was little he got hold of poison and drank it. I poured vinegar down his throat, and, while he got pneumonia, the vinegar saved his life."

Four days after she was graduated from nursing school the young nurse married Dr. Stanley M. Rinehart, then a surgeon on the hospital staff. "It was against the rules, and he had to face a board of inquiry as a result," she admitted.

"He was a violent man—and absent-minded," she went on fondly, "but he had a most delightful sense of humor. Once at night I heard him roaring with laughter. I went into the bedroom. He'd just discovered that he had thrown a lighted cigarette into the laundry hamper —and his best handkerchief into the toilet."

Her husband's practice also furnished Mrs. Rinehart with ideas. Her first best seller, *K* (1915), was inspired by the doctor's account of finding out just in time that a nurse had sewed a sponge into a patient's abdomen after an operation.

Mrs. Rinehart made up her rather formidable mind to go overseas in World War I and speedily got to the front lines. "I remember going across no man's land with a Belgian officer," she said thoughtfully. "We were looking into a German trench when the moon came out— made us perfect targets. I've wondered why they didn't shoot me. My son Stanley, Jr., who wanted to get overseas, sent a telegram to General Pershing: 'Please allow me to go to the front to see my mother.'"

Cornelius Vanderbilt, Jr., talked about *his* mother, that incredible dowager with the diamond dog collar who was queen of the opulent era she dominated. But what I, coming from a home where we saved the egg money for necessities like shoes, wanted to know was what it had been like to grow up in a family worth more than a hundred million dollars. He doesn't remember himself as happy but rather as the poor little rich boy who was never allowed to go anywhere without a bodyguard, "even at the age of eighteen," he declared, still bitter.

"That's when I became a rebel. I ran away to war, sneaked down a fire escape to do it! When I enlisted the officials thought I was an impostor using the Vanderbilt name, and when they investigated me Father and Mother heard what I'd done and were furious, but it was too late. I'd joined the Regular Army, and nothing they could do would get me out. I was gassed and had to have my jaw done over—I have a steel jaw—but when I got well I re-enlisted. Everybody thought I was crazy. Maybe—but it was the most interesting and exciting time I had ever had."

As a little boy, Cornelius Vanderbilt, Jr., didn't think it unusual that he was meeting practically everybody of importance in the world. Thus when he was six Andrew Carnegie lectured him on thrift. "And I used to feel sorry for one man who came to our house for dinner, because he'd look wistfully at the rich food he wasn't allowed to eat. That was Andrew Mellon.

"By the time I was sixteen I'd lunched and dined with all the crowned heads of Europe. There were a lot then and one saved my life—Kaiser Wilhelm, who pulled me out when I fell overboard from his yacht. Later, in his retreat at Doorn, Holland, when I pestered him for an interview, he said he'd better have let me drown!"

According to Cornelius, the kaiser promised the formidable Mrs. Vanderbilt never to go to war against England. "Because he broke his word she never spoke to a German afterward. Well, yes, she did once. She spoke to Baron Max von Oppenheim, who was helpful in getting me my first interview with Hitler. Mother spoke to *him* all right, in no uncertain terms—she showed him the door."

His mother's brand of society began to go into eclipse about the time McKinley was shot, Cornelius believed. "It was the end of the era of the robber barons. Let's say Uncle Sam began to get wise and to put up some barriers. I think things are much better now. It was ridiculous that only six or eight families should have most of the money of the world."

I don't remember whether or not I told Cornelius my little story about walking along Fifth Avenue one day with a woman I knew who abruptly said, "I have to leave you now. I want to go in here to see a sick friend." I watched her go into what I suddenly realized was Mrs. Cornelius Vanderbilt's Fifth Avenue mansion. And I walked on, thinking to myself, in the amazement that sometimes overcame me in my New York adventures, "Imagine. I know somebody who is an intimate friend of Mrs. Vanderbilt!"

I know I did tell that story to Mrs. Charles Dana Gibson, for as I suddenly looked across the microphone at her, I thought again, "Can this be I?" Because here opposite me was the face that literally had changed the appearance of a whole generation of young American women, the Gibson Girl herself—Irene Langhorne. Irene's high pompadour was copied by millions of females. Her starched shirt-waist was a fashion trend. All girls envied her profile and her air of well-bred elegance.

Beside her sat the portrait artist responsible for it all, her husband, Charles Dana Gibson; and alongside him was sculptor Jo Davidson, whose luxuriant beard long preceded the beatniks.

I asked Mrs. Gibson what it was like during the years her face was on magazine covers—*Life, Collier's Weekly, Harper's, Scribner's.* Silly question, but she didn't mind. "I liked it," she assured me with a warm smile. "Because, you see, those portraits were much prettier than I was. And that pleased me. I'm not being modest. Every artist flatters a little—and when it's your husband, of course he does!"

She asked Jo Davidson if he agreed. "No, oh no," he assured her with mock solemnity. "We sculptors tell the naked truth."

I wondered aloud whether it would be art if an artist did tell the naked truth. Wouldn't it be a photograph then?

Charles Dana Gibson looked at me sadly. "That's the tragedy," he mourned. "People have accepted the photograph as being the truth because it's mechanically made. But they are wrong. The camera sees with only one eye at a time. It can't see around a face, a head, an object. And the camera makes no personal comment; so it registers only a partial fact—and that is *not* what a portrait should be."

"The artist *does* make a personal comment?" I persisted.

"If he doesn't the picture is merely a map."

Then in their seventies, the Gibsons were beautiful—with their flashing eyes, unlined faces, silver hair, and patrician features. Mrs. Gibson said, "Being a Langhorne of Virginia was a good life. We had one of those southern structures with pillars. There were horses, dogs, and lots of music. It was a house filled with happiness."

Charles Dana Gibson interrupted to say that she gave up a promising career as a singer to marry him. "But maybe it wasn't a bad choice," he added with a laugh. "Her career in opera might have had its problems, whereas—if I say so myself—I have a beautiful disposition. I'm easy to live with because I never talk back!"

Feminist as usual, I opined that some of the lack of conflict might be due to Mrs. Gibson's good temper. She was delighted with that and crowed over him. "You see, darling, Mary Margaret knows that *I* am the one with the beautiful disposition."

Jo Davidson, not ordinarily a sentimental person, said softly, "It isn't true of very many people, Mary Margaret, but these two really would not be complete without each other."

I wish I could reproduce in words the glance the Gibsons exchanged then. I thought of it when I heard a year later that Charles Dana Gibson had died.

Jo Davidson agreed proudly that it was true he had made Gandhi laugh aloud. "We were looking at photographs of my sculpture and he said, 'I see you make heroes out of mud.' I said, 'Yes, and sometimes vice versa,' and he laughed. He had promised a friend of mine in London that he would sit for me, but he evidently didn't realize what he was in for. After I began working he talked constantly about graven images—and called the bust of himself 'that thing.' He never looked at it."

Jo Davidson picked from among his subjects some he said will survive in history as great—Gandhi, Woodrow Wilson, Franklin D. Roosevelt. "Time is a great critic," he continued. "Some have already been dropped by immortality."

Critic Time I am sure will be kind to novelist Edna Ferber, who has told so well the story of America in her fiction. But:

"I don't want anything big any more," she told me, explaining why she had sold her famous Connecticut estate. "That house was too big and the land too much; a big house and a lot of land seem to me a kind of vanity to prove that you're important—and I don't want to prove that any longer. I built it out of old stone walls on the place. You can see the whole Western Hemisphere out of every window, but now I don't understand why anyone should have any more room than he can use. Then, too, I was just pretending to be a farmer. I know now that what I want more than anything in the world is to keep on writing as well as I can. I really don't want to worry about whether or not the hay has been cut. I'm not a Maud Muller—perhaps because the squire never came riding by."

For years I'd been longing to have Edna Ferber on my program. *So Big* was a reading experience I couldn't forget. Seeing *Show Boat* —the original production—was one of my exciting theater memories back in the days when New York City was an adventure, a challenge, a love affair for me.

But when I began having guests on my radio program I was told NO every time I invited Edna. So the day she finally turned up in my apartment-studio overlooking Central Park I was apprehensive. She didn't help much by announcing right off that she had not wanted to come. She explained her belief (shared by John Steinbeck—I never did get him) that a real writer writes books and does not plug them on radio programs. Then she added: "I've been listening to you and you have a way of making people do things they don't want to do, so you ought to be in something bigger."

Nervously I asked what—but she didn't tell me. After the broadcast she wrote on one of the two screens autographed by my famous guests through the years: "You must get out of this. You must get into something bigger where you can be yourself."

Sometimes, looking at those screens, mostly full of the loving sentiments a pleased guest writes after he's liked what has happened to him on the air, I come on that bit by Edna Ferber and feel a horrible sense of failure. Because while I'm out of radio, I'm *not* into something bigger.

Edna Ferber's initial appearance on the program apparently cured her of radio-phobia because she came back several other times. Once, talking about *Show Boat*, she said with a lovely remembering light in her eyes: "One day Jerry came striding in [Jerome Kern the composer, she meant, of course] and said, 'Edna, I thought about a song today and—could I play it?' Mary Margaret, he sat down at my baby-grand piano and picked out the tune, humming it, of 'Smoke Gets in Your Eyes.' I sat and cried."

With true writer's skill, in the telling, she re-created for us that moment in her high-ceilinged apartment when a gifted maker of songs played for the first time a melody that was to become a classic. I envied her that, but most of all I envied her being what I had always wanted to be—a first-rate writer.

She said she felt sorry for all the people born since World War I. "They will never know," she pointed out, "the joy of living in a classic world. I don't even know how the young nowadays can take it. They've never known a normal moment; they've never been serene. This last quarter century has made people suspicious, jumpy, not able to care for anything outside their own little personal circuit. And, Mary Margaret, that is not good enough. People seem to be talking a lot about religion these days, but they talk about it as though it's some sort of medicine that works if you take enough of it. Well, my religion —and I suppose it sounds pretty silly—is contained in seven words, and they're from the Bible. I think that's the only thing that can get us out of this hideous situation. The Bible, I find, is a very interesting and sound book, and it says: 'God is good and good is God.' "

I could never be nervous with Edna Ferber again.

Looking back now, it seems to me I was often nervous before a broadcast even if not during. Certainly I was nervous before my broadcast with Tallulah Bankhead. People had been swearing on my program and NBC vice-presidents were agitated. Every day almost I got a note from on high to say that the swearing must stop. So I told Janice, "You'll have to go see Tallulah and tell her she must not swear!"

A few hours later Janice telephoned. She sounded worn out. Tallulah had behaved in her usual Tallulahesque manner. For forty-five minutes she had paced the floor talking and acting with gestures a scene from the motion picture *Lifeboat*; a few lines from a Broadway play she'd just seen; her feelings, with the telephone as a prop, the day she learned of the death of President Roosevelt; how she sorrowed and how she gave up daiquiris then and there. Then at one-half minute before Janice's allotted time was over, she sank into a chair, looked straight at my worried reporter, and said, "Now tell me about you, darling." All Janice had time for was: "Miss Bankhead, will you please not swear on NBC!" Tallulah shrieked, "The very idea! I wouldn't think of it!"

And then in the first minute on the air she told me sympathetically she understood all the trouble I'd been having about swearing—but she did want to tell me that a dear old great-aunt of hers down in Alabama had broadcast about the opening of a new bridge in the early days of radio and during the broadcast great-auntie had said "damn."

"I guess it's the first time anybody ever did swear on radio," added Tallulah innocently.

"And, Mary Margaret, one time at a party where I was, a grand old lady turned to Edmund Daly—she was wearing one of those diamond dog collars—they were both Boston blue bloods—and she asked him, 'When is Miss Bankhead going to do her stuff?' Daly said that I was behaving quite as usual and the old lady stiffened. 'Well, if that's the case——' I can't say *hell* on the air, can I, Mary Margaret?"

"No, you can't," I answered forlornly.

"'Well,' the old lady said, 'if that's the case then the so-and-so with it. If she's going to behave like everybody else, I'm going home!'"

"That's what it means to be a legend," I commented lamely. Tallulah grinned at me.

"Oh, not that I haven't turned cartwheels and hung from chandeliers when I felt like it, but I choose my time and place.

"I was born lazy about everything except the theater. Nothing would have kept me out of it, even if I'd had to walk from Alabama to New York. When I got here, I found all the pitfalls, anxieties, and disillusion as advertised.

"But when I made it, when I achieved what I'd set out for, it was only a beginning. Once you're on a certain level you've got to live up to it.

"I fell many times from grace, not always through my own fault—I'm not blaming anybody else because I like to take the blame for my own faults and a little credit for my virtues. . . . Anyhow, in my book I told nearly all, or at least as much as good taste would permit without besmirching the dead or offending the living; talked it into a dictaphone and tried not to mention any names simply because they were famous or infamous, but only when there was a story attached.

"Then when I saw the index I was appalled—nine pages of names: Thomas E. Dewey was one. I said, 'I never wrote anything about Dewey,' but of course I did. I quoted him. Then Nanette DuBose— she was my mother's maid of honor—you know my mother died when I was born. Well, her name was next to David Dubinsky's, and next to my beloved maid, Rose Riley—I hope she's listening—is Richard II. That's because my father read to me about Richard II. He always read to me, and I learned the Bible and the classics by ear."

At this point Tallulah began to worry about my commercials. She was familiar with the program because she'd been listening while trying to get a sun tan beside her Bedford Village swimming pool . . . "which I just finished paying for," she added.

"Go on with your beautiful products," she urged me. "I'm interested. I want to eat most of them right now, but my grandmother always said about me, 'You'll never get that child married—she's too fat.' Dieting has been the story of my life. Grandmother used to throw cold water on me when I had tantrums. I've always been pretty emotional and illogical. People can't understand how I'm that way and can still play bridge—any more than they understand why I like baseball. Well, what I like about baseball is my Giants."

Then she came back to me and my problems.

"But, darling, do go on, yours are the first commercials I ever enjoyed because you're telling the truth. Listen, you out there [*addressing the listeners*], she's not reading. She just has a few little notes she glances at."

Feebly I tackled a sponsor or two, and then Tallulah's attentive face spurred me on and I finally told her: "Tallulah Bankhead, you did quite a thing today. Often when I do commercials the person opposite me is so occupied with herself or himself that I get an awful feeling of an utter lack of interest. But not with you. . . . Let's go on about you now."

"You can ask me anything, Mary Margaret, after you finish your products—because it's making me nervous that you may not get them in and, after all, that's what we're here for."

So I continued and when I got back to her, Tallulah fished a note from her handbag and with small-girl excitement began to quote from it. It was from President Truman, thanking her for an autographed copy of her book, *Tallulah*.

"It is undoubtedly the most interesting book I've had in my hands since I've been President of the United States," the note began. I reminded Tallulah of the night she'd had the President's daughter, Margaret, on her NBC program and Mr. Truman had telephoned right after the show.

Told it was the President, Tallulah assumed it was the president of NBC and said airily, "Oh, tell him to call me at home." But Margaret interrupted to say no, she was sure it was President Truman.

"Yes," Tallulah remembered, "he just wanted to thank me for being sweet to his baby, so I told him that Margaret was on my program on her own merit."

As we neared the end of our time Tallulah confessed that she, too, had been nervous. "As a child I used to bribe God. Now, before every opening or any important event I just say, 'Dear God, don't let me make a fool of myself.' "

Judging by the engineers, production men, studio audience, and me —plus, subsequently, various vice-presidents and hundreds of thousands of listeners—God answered Tallulah's prayer that day.

Tallulah's signature on my celebrity screen is the biggest one. Gary Cooper, on another panel, takes up more space, but he drew a picture and his name is in tiny letters. Two admiring plumbers from the apartment right over mine surprised me as much as they did Gary Cooper when they appeared before the microphone in my studio-living room that day. We had often had doorbells, sirens, taxi horns, and ringing telephones producing ad-lib sound effects in the middle of a program, but we'd never had plumbers until the day Gary Cooper was my guest.

I was just getting him to the point of talking when I became aware that Stella and Gabe, our engineer, were agitated about a pounding overhead. I tried to ignore it, and Gary didn't seem to hear it. Then it stopped, and suddenly Stella appeared with two overalled men in tow. She escorted them straight to the microphone and interrupted what the guest and I were saying to explain that the two plumbers had agreed to stop pounding, provided they were introduced to Gary Cooper.

One plumber became so enamored of the microphone that he began to list every motion picture he'd ever seen Gary in, and every one his son liked. After about six minutes of that we all realized that we were going to end up by interviewing plumbers instead of Gary Cooper, so Stella managed to extricate them from the immediate microphone area and plant them, beaming, in two chairs.

Gary Cooper said, wide-eyed, "Nothing like this ever happened to me before. I don't even understand why plumbers should stop pounding to listen to me, because I don't think I'm very interesting."

I tried to convince him that people were always curious about a person much in the public eye. Gary Cooper complained, "That's one of our troubles in Hollywood. We are supposed to be something we aren't."

For the benefit of the plumbers I asked if Gary really believed, as I had heard, that most people work too hard. "I do believe it," he answered instantly. "You can't have a well-rounded life unless you leave time to play. I love to ski, to be in the open country, in deserts, in mountains, and on the sea. So I make sure I have plenty of leisure to do what I enjoy."

Gary admitted that a Hollywood career had never been his ambition as a young man. It was happenstance. He came back from school in England, moved with his family to Montana, got rid of his English accent, learned to ride. "Then friends of mine who were riding in rodeos said why didn't I come down to the Fox studios. I wasn't making much money and needed to so I went, and the first day I got ten dollars. The second day I got more—for falling off the horse. Nobody ever dreamed I'd make an actor—I didn't dream of it, either, but I watched Tom Mix and thought maybe I could do as well as he did."

A few years later Gary Cooper's agent took him to a conference where actors were being auditioned for a big Western. Gary said, "I didn't know what to do, so I just stood there—and that's how I got the lead in my first talking picture, *The Virginian.*"

Before we went off the air Gary Cooper drew me a charming little sketch of a cowboy for my screen and admitted he'd always liked to draw, though lately he hadn't had much time. Something about the shy candor of his face made me say, "You look to me like a man who never told a lie."

"Hmmmm," he murmured.

Not perhaps what Emily Post would have suggested for the retort courteous, but who was I to carp? The first time I called on Emily Post I forgot my gloves. The time I had an audience with the King of Norway—I forgot my gloves.

Yet at one time I must have felt that what Mrs. Post told me about gloves was important, because I put it into an article: "If you have clean white gloves you'll get along all right no matter how many other sartorial refinements you lack."

Recently in the state of Washington a hotel clerk reminded me of the article and assured me that she had brought her daughter up on that principle and added proudly, "She turned out fine!"

However that may be, the second time I was invited to the home of Mrs. Post I spilled tea. Worst of all, it was on her I spilled it. But Emily Post proved her own rules of etiquette by somehow making me forget my awkwardness—making me feel, in fact, quite poised and welcome.

I often lunched with her, and twice she had me pour tea at parties (it was at one of these that I spilled on her). I also broadcast from her home to describe her decorating scheme, and once we did an entire program just to tell the world she can't cook.

"I can't cook at all," she said at the beginning of the broadcast. *The Emily Post Cookbook* had just come out. "How would you plan a really special dinner for some special people you'd been putting off for a long time?" I had asked her.

"You'll have to ask Ned," she said, smiling at her son, Edwin. "It's his cookbook anyway. The publishers just used my name to make it sell better. If I planned a dinner it would be one I shouldn't like at all—it would be formal, and formal dinners are all of a pattern—oysters or clams, a clear or cream soup, fish, then meat, salad, ice cream."

I protested that Emily Post, coming from Baltimore, really must have some fondness for good food. She admitted that she did like terrapin. I said I was certain they'd had terrapin and champagne at Emily Post's coming-out party. But Mrs. Post remembered much more vividly the number of her beaux, her wonderful white tulle dress, her fifty bouquets.

"I wore a different bouquet every time I made an entrance," she boasted. "When a young man asked me to dance I said yes—if he had a favor. So when I came to the cotillion it took four young men to carry my favors—and afterward I had them—the favors—pinned all over my bedroom."

I asked Edwin how he became such an authority on food when his mother really didn't seem to care much. "It's because Mother has always had wonderful cooks. I have none, so I had to learn to cook."

"He began it as a small boy in France," Mrs. Post explained. "His father and I went off on trips and left the children with their French nurse."

Edwin and I talked for a bit about some of his special cookery tricks. "Don't cook shrimp as most cookbooks advise," he told me. "Instead, take off their shells first, then boil the shells in wine and make a sauce of the liquid and cream. Or fry them in butter, turning them round and round, for three minutes only, adding the shell liquid to make a sauce. I guarantee you'll never again do a barbaric thing like boiling shrimp in their shells."

There was a pause and then Edwin added, "But if I'm cooking for Mother, she'd rather have milk and chocolate pudding than anything else in the world."

I had the feeling he liked cooking for his mother. He seemed to be a devoted son. Not all sons of famous parents are. I was always wondering what went on in their minds—in Winston Churchill's daughter Sarah's, for instance. They were a handsome, happy young couple, Sarah Churchill and her husband, Antony Beauchamp, that day they were my guests. But I couldn't get Sarah to talk about her distinguished father, Sir Winston Churchill. There was some awful inhibition locked away inside her, possibly along with the seeds of rebellion and tragedy which were to make such sad headlines. But at this, their first radio interview together, those two were gay and he at least was talkative.

The talented photographer, whose suicide shocked the world a decade later, explained that his name was pronounced Beacham—Beauchamp like Cholmondeley.

I was writing a magazine article at the moment about how to make people talk, and I said I hoped I would not have to put in Sarah Churchill as one I couldn't get to do it. Antony Beauchamp interposed.

"She never *stops* talking. I don't read books at all any more because I get them all from Sarah. A home evening with Sarah is a lot of her pacing up and down the room while I sit smoking a cigarette and listening. She starts with politics—that lasts only about thirty seconds, thank heaven—then on to the theater, to books."

Here Sarah interrupted. "I'm really very much interested in politics, but I try to keep the home happy by not discussing them too much."

She added apropos of nothing that she was just as fond of politics as of avocado pears. She and Antony giggled, in the classic, endearing fashion of newlyweds, and then Antony told admiringly of Sarah's poise when a fire broke out in a summer theater in Norwich, Connecticut ("pronounced Norrich—see, you Americans do it, too, and how about Arkansas City and Arkansaw"). On the occasion of the theater fire, Antony went on, Sarah had stepped in front of the footlights and calmed the audience with an impromptu joke.

"Ladies and gentlemen—we hope the only way we are going to burn you up this evening is by our performances."

I said, wistfully, that I still longed to get Sarah to talk about her family.

Sarah sympathized. "I'm always much more sorry for anybody who interviews me than I am for myself. It's the journalistic strain in me. Having a father and brother who are journalists, I know it's harder to pose the questions than to answer them."

I asked Sarah whether it was true that C. B. Cochran, the producer, had asked her at an audition, "Does your father know you're here?" Sarah said yes, and that Mr. Cochran had also advised her to stop using made-up names because people would recognize her anyhow.

"They used to say, 'What's the matter—do you think it's a disadvantage to be the daughter of the most important man in England?' and I could only say that it couldn't be a disadvantage to be the daughter of my father.'"

Antony told how Sarah, then his favorite sitter for photographic portraits, had started out as a problem. "I could never get her at the right angle or the right moment—she wanted to talk too much. Finally, because she was always in action, I tried what in England is called electronic blotting—a flash bulb put inside a studio lamp so you can take a picture in a fraction of a second. The first one I got had Sarah throwing back her head, talking, with an expression that was really her own. That was the picture on the cover of *Life* magazine."

A little before we were to go off the air Sarah announced that she'd never enjoyed a broadcast so much (of course Antony and I had been doing nearly all the talking). "You do seem to have an influence on people," she declared. "I feel I should be doing this every day."

And then she got a loquacious spurt that made me believe that perhaps Antony had been right when he said she talked a lot.

"I wanted to be a doctor, but I started too late," she confessed. "So I thought I ought to do something different and went into stock in England. It just grew. It seems funny for someone as shy as I am to go on the stage, but the minute I pass through a stage door I'm over being timid or scared; and it doesn't matter what country I'm in, if I'm on the stage I'm talking my own language."

She urged Antony to tell about taking the daughter-in-law of the Nizam of Hyderabad (richest man in the world) to see a performance by Mae West. The princess, an exquisitely beautiful young woman, asked to meet the actress. When Tony took her backstage the inimitable Mae said, "Now, honey, I want to teach you a little lesson in sex appeal—how to get your man."

"And then," Tony went on, "she got this beautiful girl to repeat after her, 'Come up and see me sometime,' and it was the most devastating thing I ever heard."

It really was two o'clock closing time now, and I hadn't succeeded in getting Sarah Churchill to talk about her father. Sarah said, "Maybe someday I will do it."

They sailed soon afterward for England, and I never saw either one of them again. It's sad to lose people when a contact has been so stimulating and pleasant.

Many of my interviewees, though, still send me Christmas cards—at least Irene Castle does. One summer when I was broadcasting from Marjorie Evans' home in Larchmont, New York, a letter came from Irene Castle in Chicago telling me how the programs brought back memories to her of long ago when she used to drive in a carriage to her grandfather's house in Larchmont and go swimming in Horseshoe Bay.

Of course I immediately invited her to be a guest any time she was in New York. She agreed with a proviso that I give her special cause—anti-vivisection—a fair hearing. She explained on the air, "I was born stage-struck, and I've loved animals ever since I can remember. My aunt was a doctor and used to bring home every stray she saw—and at one time my father had seventy-five dogs. If a dog bit my sister or me we never dared complain to Father because he'd always say, 'What did *you* do to the dog?' "

So we talked about vivisection and then I asked her about the days when she caused a sensation, if not a scandal, by bobbing her hair. Ministers inveighed against the shorn female head, the hairpin industry was ruined, and an inventive manufacturer had to dream up the bobby pin.

That wasn't all. When Irene Castle danced across the American scene her slim, boyish figure sent millions of American women on diets. She and her husband, creators of the Castle Walk, billed themselves as Mr. and Mrs. Vernon Castle, first husband-and-wife team in the entertainment world to admit they were married and proud of it.

"It had a sentimental touch that people seemed to like," she said. She met Vernon Castle not far from where we were broadcasting—at the New Rochelle Yacht Club.

"New Rochelle was a center for theater people. Remember George M. Cohan's *Forty-Five Minutes from Broadway?* Vernon was visiting some theatrical friends on that Sunday and was invited to my home for dinner. He was homesick for England, and Mother was a cosmopolitan and great traveler. He fell in love with her first and later with me. So when his Broadway show, *The Hen-Pecks*, reopened in the fall he found two lines in it for me. Later when a French producer wanted *The Hen-Pecks*, Vernon said I must go along and *I* said, 'Why don't we tell the producer that a dance has been added, a dance by the Castles?' That's how we got to Paris."

They hadn't much money, but they took along an old family serv-ant who said he didn't want a salary, only a chance to travel. Even so, Paris was a grim experience. Their show had been rewritten. It was unfunny, vulgar, and so they quit, walking back to their attic rooms with thirty francs to their names. The old family retainer kept bringing home baskets of food. The Castles were alarmed, and one day they followed him to see whether he'd been stealing in their be-half. Not at all. He'd organized a crap game with the French elevator operators.

Finally, an agent found the Castles and offered to put them in the Café Paris, run by Papa Louis. "Fifty francs a night was what we got and the agent was collecting a hundred," recalled Irene indignantly. "When Papa Louis discovered that he fired the agent and gave us the hundred.

"Overnight we were a success. People used to invite us to their tables and offer us tips. Vernon, with British dignity, wanted to refuse, but not me with my Yankee thrift. I told him it was rude not to accept a gift. After Café Paris we never had any more struggle."

When Vernon Castle, young, handsome, idolized, was killed in an airplane crash in Texas in 1918, the whole country wept, and for a time it seemed the end of the world to Irene.

But they had made their impact. They had introduced the Castle Walk, changing the ballroom habits of continents. They had invented the one-step and the Hesitation Waltz. And all over America, due to Irene Castle's influence, women were wearing bobbed hair and shed-ding hiplines.

Two other guests that summer at Larchmont were the exiled King Peter and Queen Alexandra of Yugoslavia. At the time the two were living in a small apartment in New York with their small son, Alex-ander. Queen Alexandra was doing all the cooking.

"I don't like anybody around. It's much more amusing to do it all myself, even if it means burned fingers now and then," she explained.

The king commented, "She's a very good cook."

"At least he eats what I make," she told me. "I stand over him until he does. He cooks sometimes, too, but he uses up every pot and pan in the kitchen."

"But I clean up," he protested.

"Yes, but you put everything back in the wrong place."

"Well, I often do the greasy pots. You make me!"

"Just like any husband and wife," gratified listeners wrote.

They had never abdicated and both young people were sure they would some day reign again. "We'll be better at it, too, because we've learned to be ordinary people and live an ordinary life," declared King Peter hopefully. "We learned a lot that our forefathers didn't know, and we can put our experience into practice in our country. We can adapt a lot of American ways of living and thinking too."

Peter's cherished dream was that with the help of American engineers Yugoslavian boys might be taught how to develop the natural resources of the country so that Yugoslavia might be a miniature United States of America—the United States of Yugoslavia.

Said King Peter: "I was eleven and at school in England when the headmaster came to my bedroom at six in the morning to tell me I had to leave school. He and the headmistress were crying, but they didn't tell me why. As I came out the door there were two bobbies in helmets and I thought, 'They're going to arrest me. What have I done?' In the car they told me that my father had been assassinated and I would now be king. War came two weeks later. My people were unprepared, so they had to give up after twelve days."

The government was taken first to Greece, then to Egypt, next to England, and in 1942 Peter came to the United States. "I feel if we could have a free election I'd be in as king, not to mix in politics but to safeguard the liberties of my people," he declared. "Kings may have been dictators in the past, but now we realize that we have more duties than rights."

"I have lived most of my life in exile," sighed Alexandra. "My father died three months before I was born."

Her boy was born at Claridge's in London. "When a royal child is born," explained Alexandra, "the prime minister has to be there and various representatives of the government. We had Titoites as well as a delegation of royalists."

"Even had two doctors, one from each side," added Peter. "I was rushing around madly with one delegation in the bathroom, the other in the lobby outside. It wouldn't do to have them meet!"

After the birth, which took place in her mother's apartment because it was larger, they took the baby back into her apartment on one mattress and the queen on another.

"It was a bumpy trip and the courtiers had been eating garlic," Alexandra commented.

The person I addressed irreverently as Spiderlegs Kalty covered many a queen and king, too, in his time. I called the dignified dean of radio correspondents and master ad libber, H. V. Kaltenborn, Spiderlegs Kalty the first time I interviewed him because I had learned that his friends back in his native Merrill, Wisconsin, did. Mr. Kaltenborn presented me with a bunch of violets and bowed from the waist like a courtier.

"Both the United States and I came of age as the twentieth century opened," he told me. "My war record began with the Spanish American War, and going to war was my first time away from Merrill. I went in at twenty and came out at twenty-one, a top sergeant and a self-styled war correspondent for the Merrill *Advocate*. I had to stuff myself on bananas and milk to make top sergeant, for I was the lightest, thinnest, youngest man in my company. It wasn't much of a war, but I enjoyed it.

"When it was over I decided to travel a bit, but I had no money. Most of my fellow soldiers didn't care what railroad they used to get home and agreed to travel on the Louisville & Nashville as a favor to me. The competition in those days was keen, and the Louisville & Nashville gave me a free pass in return for my advice to Company F. In these days of easy travel it is hard to realize that a rail trip to the South was almost like going to a foreign country. From New Orleans I rode up the Mississippi for twenty-two dollars, and it was a marvelous experience, bringing back the post-Civil War days that Mark Twain wrote about. I almost signed up on a boat to work my way round the world, but I was homesick and so I went back to Merrill.

"The travel bug had bitten me, though, and I was determined to see the world. I worked for a while on the Merrill *Advocate* and later for a lumber camp in northern Wisconsin. I used to read aloud to my fellow lumberjacks. The head of the firm scolded, 'You read too much. You'll never amount to anything.' When I met him many years later, he said, 'You were always such a great reader I knew you were sure to amount to something.'

"Through the *Advocate* I got a pass—papers exchanged advertisements for passes in those days—and came to New York. I had very little money, but I found I could sleep for ten cents a night in the

Mills Hotel on Bleecker Street and for a penny I could buy a newspaper, a small dab of ice cream known as a penny lick, two or three bananas, or a piece of watermelon. Although New York was exciting I wanted to get to Europe. I read in the *Sun* an account of somebody who had worked his way on a cattle boat. Soon I was signed up as nursemaid to five hundred steers on a freighter bound for Liverpool."

He was down to his last twenty francs in Paris when he got a job selling stereoscopes. He spoke no French, but his employer wrote out a little sales talk in French which he pasted in his order book.

"I never made a fortune during the fifteen months I sold stereoscopes, but I certainly learned French and it all helped me when, after my return to America, I tackled New York determined to become a big-city journalist. I wanted to work on a newspaper. Nothing else would do. There were no jobs on the Manhattan papers, but the sight of workers hurrying home at night across Brooklyn Bridge inspired me to write a paraphrase of Southey's poem "The Cataract of Lodore" which I took to the Brooklyn *Daily Eagle*. The editor paid me five dollars for the poem and best of all gave me a job at eight dollars a week."

Before he left the *Eagle* to go to Harvard for a year as a special student, he had done almost everything on the paper, including dramatic criticism, and he was earning twenty-five dollars a week. After his graduation from Harvard the *Eagle* rehired him at forty a week and assigned him to an editorial desk with quick prospects for advancement. Later he was Washington correspondent and, in World War I, war editor for the *Eagle*. In 1921 he took part in an experiment that was to influence his life. He spoke over the radio from Newark, New Jersey, and was heard by a chamber-of-commerce group gathered in Brooklyn for a demonstration of the new invention.

"The next year I began a series of radio talks on current events," he recalled. "These were the first spoken editorials ever heard by a radio audience. Hardly a week went by in which there was not some threat to have me put off the air for my frank expression of opinion."

This training is what fitted Mr. Kaltenborn to become the greatest ad libber of all time. In 1938, during the twenty days and nights of the Czechoslovakian crisis, he made a hundred and two broadcasts, ranging from two minutes to two hours in length. Portable radio sets had just been developed and people listened everywhere. Kaltenborn's name became a household word.

"News bulletins were handed to me as I talked," he said. "Speeches of foreign leaders had to be analyzed and sometimes translated while they were being delivered. I had to keep a constant eye on the control room for signs telling me when I was on or off the air. Sometimes when I had just launched into an analysis of a foreign leader's speech I was given a signal to wind up my talk in exactly one minute. On other occasions I was told to comment on a new development for exactly three minutes before the network switched to a foreign capital. Then suddenly they would discover that connections with Europe could not be made and the engineer would signal me to continue my comments and expand until further notice.

"During routine broadcasting the networks kept a staff of musicians or at least a pianist standing by, ready to fill any odd seconds or minutes that might develop due to technical failure or the nonappearance of a performer. During this crisis period CBS dispensed with musicians and free moments were filled with Kaltenborn.

"I had little sleep during those days and not much in the way of substantial food. I napped occasionally on an army cot in one of the offices, and my wife brought up from the drugstore below an occasional container of coffee and a sandwich, or from home a container of my favorite soup."

I couldn't resist asking Mr. Kaltenborn to tell one more story that had nothing to do with broadcasting but was a sort of ad-libbing. He had been captured by Chinese bandits in 1927 in Canton. They contemplated shooting him.

"They picked me up as a communist; they thought I looked like a communist. They arrested me and at that time were making short shrift of communists. The president of Canton Christian College tried to explain that I was an American newspaper reporter, but they didn't believe him. He begged them not to shoot me until he had spoken to their commander.

"They looked glowering and glum and that was rather uncomfortable, so I thought I'd try to cheer them up. I had some oranges in my pocket and started to juggle them. The Chinese have a great sense of humor, and, seeing what looked like a dignified chap juggling these oranges, they roared with delight. When I saw my show was going so well I started to balance a straw on my nose. I learned juggling as a boy and spent hours practicing and got so I could balance three chairs on my chin!"

## 19.  TRIUMPHANT MOMENT

A special light always glowed in the eyes of guests when they came to telling of triumph after long agonies of disappointment, hope deferred, and failure. I enjoyed that moment in an interview more than any other.

Phil Stong had the look of the mischievous small boy he must have been in his farm days in Iowa when he told me of thirteen novels refused before his best-seller *State Fair* was accepted.

I can remember any number of novelists whose first success dazed almost more than it dazzled them. Betty Smith, Kathleen Winsor, and Rosemary Taylor had two things in common—unexpected fame as best-selling authors and a little black dress apiece.

The little black dress was the uniform of the newly arrived literary celebrity in the forties. If the writer didn't know about it somebody in her publishing firm took over and led the way to an expensive couturier's for the outfitting that prepared for those inevitable cocktail parties, encounters with book sellers, and interviews with press and radio.

The day she arrived to launch *A Tree Grows in Brooklyn*, Betty Smith was not wearing the little black dress. Thin, dark-haired, olive-skinned, Betty was quite right in believing black did nothing for her. So a dress for which she had reluctantly paid several hundred dollars had been permanently exiled to her darkest closet. Betty was still a little dazed by fame.

"One day you're just Betty Smith," she marveled, "and the next you're The-Tree-Grows-in-Brooklyn Betty Smith, and you hear the oddest things being said about yourself. Just today two women in my hotel lobby were talking about me. One told her friend that I live entirely on meat and black coffee and the other said, 'Yes, she takes

walks at midnight and her hobby is chopping wood.' So I walked right
up to them and announced, 'Everything you've said about Betty Smith
is completely untrue.'

" 'Oh, do *you* know Betty Smith? What is she *really* like?' I answered
unhesitatingly, 'She's very noble and she gives to the poor.' Then I
walked away. All this made me very nervous. In the subway I felt
everybody was staring at me. Then I realized they weren't. Really, *I*
was staring at them to see whether *they* were staring at me."

As a child Betty's ambition had been not to write but to read all the
books in the world.

"I started in the Greenpoint branch library in Brooklyn. I read
through the A's and thought I was nearly through the B's when I
happened to spot a whole section of Browns. And then I learned that
Greenpoint was only one of eleven branch libraries, all with A-to-Z
authors I hadn't read. So I settled for copying my favorite book, *When
Knighthood Was in Flower*, by hand in penny notebooks. When I
finished I thought, 'Well, that proves that it's at least physically possible for me to write a book.' "

Rosemary Taylor didn't protest anything about her good black dress
except the price which, however, was not the wild extravagance she had
feared. She wore it happily to press conferences and parties, along
with a giddy pink hat and the inevitable orchids.

Rosemary, too, was getting the full publicity treatment because her
book, *Chicken Every Sunday*, soared up the best-seller list, was bought
by Hollywood, optioned for a Broadway play, and condensed by
*Reader's Digest*.

"Can you imagine?" she said to me, still unbelieving. "I wrote it for
my mother's birthday present, not even for publication!"

The story is about her family in Tucson, Arizona, especially about
her mother.

"Mother has a talent for taking in boarders," Rosemary explained.
"At seventy-eight, she still has eleven roomers. It began by her moving
out of her own room into the dining room because she wanted an
extra room ready to rent in case somebody nice came along.

"My father, a traveling salesman, got home from a trip to find a
strange man sitting on our front porch. He was 'somebody nice' who'd
come along, and Mother couldn't resist renting him her own room.
It isn't so much the money as her craving to 'do' for somebody. One

of her boarders was on a raw-vegetable diet and Mother worried about his not getting his money's worth, so she fed double portions to his wife!"

Somebody suggested that Mother's birthday gift should be published, so Rosemary sent it to several magazines. No luck. Then on a trip to Canada she read it to some officers' wives. One knew a publisher and that's how this particular best seller got into print.

Rosemary finally thus reconciled her torturing ambition to write deathless prose!

"After all, the carpenter who builds a hen house has his place as well as the man who constructs a cathedral. To me, as I write my pedestrian prose, this is very comforting."

The new author who got the most glamorous treatment of all was Kathleen Winsor of *Forever Amber* fame. Kathleen was young and beautiful, and the experts dressed her in long, mystery-provoking veils and slinky dresses with heavy eye shadow and exotic foundation make-up.

It was a shock to find this spectacular-looking woman almost tongue-tied with fright. She said afterward that if I hadn't known her book so well she couldn't have gone on. But I found, midway in the broadcast, that Kathleen had a phenomenal memory for an incredible array of dates and statistics from her research for the turbulent plague and disaster-ridden period of Amber's career. It was quite true that she had begun her investigations to help her husband with a college thesis! Which adds one more strange item to my list of how books get written.

From their own lives came material for the books written by two delightful sisters from the West Coast, Betty MacDonald of *The Egg and I* fame, and Mary Bard, who is married to a doctor and wrote a very funny first opus called *The Doctor Wears Three Faces*.

Betty confided that New York frightened her so much that the minute she got there she wanted to turn right around and go back to Washington. She also gave it as her opinion that chickens are the dumbest, most unlovable creatures that live.

"I suppose it's ungrateful to say that," she admitted, "when they have done so well by me. But they got in their innings on me long before I got in mine by writing a book about them."

Mary and Betty's father was a mining engineer, and to keep the family together the mother had moved her brood all over the country.

"We had to adjust ourselves at a moment's notice to new schools, new playmates, new climates," Mary said, and added reflectively, "but nothing prepared us for being a success in New York; not even being a doctor's wife, and that's really saying something.

"The real reason I'm in town is that my husband is attending a medical meeting. No wife of a doctor ever travels unless it's to a city where there's a medical meeting."

"Are doctors so different?" I asked innocently.

Mary just looked at me and then quoted from her book: "A doctor is a man who is licensed to practice medicine. A husband is a man who is licensed to come home every night on the five-ten, eat dinner, play with the children, read *Time*, and work in the garden. Combine the two and what do you get? A husband who is licensed to come home every night on the five-ten, eat dinner, play with the children, read *Time*, work in the garden, and also practice medicine? No. You get a draught in the the hall, a slammed door, an empty chair at dinner, and a voice on the telephone."

It disturbed me if any of the triumphant ones were not savoring to the full the sweets of their victory, and I often lectured them a little. Mary Martin, Texas small-town girl who made good, was one who never had to be urged by me or anybody else to enjoy her new acclaim. She had gone through so much discouragement that she was keenly aware of every bit of good fortune.

There's a threadbare yarn about Mary that she tells me is true. Billy Rose was masterminding a show in Fort Worth, Texas, when little Mary applied for a chorus job. After auditioning her Billy Rose earnestly advised her to give up any idea of a stage career and go back to the little dancing school she ran in her home town of Weatherford.

"And don't try to sing," Billy added kindly.

Later the persistent girl got the nickname of Audition Mary because she auditioned as many as ten times a week.

"I'd go to Hollywood to take courses and to audition in the summer, and then I'd go back to my dancing school. One summer my father said I could stay, and so I did for two years.

"People said I'd never get anywhere with a plain name like Mary Martin. They wanted to spell it Merry and Mary Martini and all kinds of ways, but I think you and I have done well with our plain vanilla names—Mary Margaret, Mary Martin."

On her first trip to New York, Mary heard they were auditioning girls for a part in *Leave It to Me* and decided to try for it.

"Vinton Freedley asked whether I'd ever been on the stage. I had to say no, but I added, 'I can do anything.' When I got to the theater they were in rehearsal and Billy Gaxton inquired whether I'd ever been on the stage before. I had to say no again and Billy admonished, 'All you have to do is talk very loud.' I said the first line as loud as I could—and got the part.

"I didn't dare tell my family, because I had to do a kind of strip tease and I knew they'd object. But when they learned about it from my singing teacher it turned out they didn't know what a strip tease was so it was all right."

In *Leave It to Me*, Cole Porter had written a song which Mary was to sing. Porter coached her in how to put it over. But even he couldn't have suspected how she *would* put it over until opening night when little Audition Mary from Texas stopped the show with "My Heart Belongs to Daddy."

The day after *South Pacific* opened to triumph of a magnitude seldom seen on Broadway, I greeted Mary Martin with: "You know who I'd rather be than anyone else in the world today? *You*—the girl they used to call Audition Mary in Hollywood!"

Mary laughed, that infectious, Texas laugh of hers that neither years nor success ever change. She kissed me and Ezio Pinza, who was beaming too.

"It's wonderful," she said, starry-eyed.

For once the overworked and usually exaggerated word wonderful seemed inadequate. The critics themselves did better. Superlatives rolled off their typewriters. The lines at the box office stretched for blocks. Record companies were begging for commitments, offers were pouring in on Mary and Ezio though it was obvious they would be thoroughly occupied for years.

"Mary, Dick Rodgers told me you refused the part at first," I teased.

"Well, I did," she admitted sheepishly. "I said I wouldn't dream of singing in the same show with Ezio Pinza—that I couldn't ever match my small voice to his."

That objection was settled by Oscar Hammerstein and Dick Rodgers' promising she wouldn't sing once with Mr. Pinza. And they kept their word.

For Ezio Pinza, opera star, it was a brand-new career, starting when he was fifty-odd years old and had already won fame in opera.

When I got Moss Hart's autobiography, *Act One,* I read it backward because I wanted to find out whether he'd put in the wonderful story about what happened when he got his first big Broadway hit—*Once in a Lifetime.* I always thought he might have been teasing me with a fantastic made-up tale. But sure enough, there it was just as he had told it on the program. I wondered, as I had when he first told it, whether I'd ever have had the nerve to do it.

On the morning after that show opened Mr. Hart tucked the rave notices under his arm and took a cab to the far reaches of Brooklyn where his family lived. He woke everybody up and said, "Come on. We are moving to New York. We are walking out of here with just the clothes on our backs and nothing else. We'll go to a hotel until we can find an apartment. There's nothing to pack. We're just walking out the door."

In less than an hour he'd bundled the astonished and somewhat dubious Hart family into a taxicab. He drew five hundred dollars from the theater box office to pay immediate bills, and the Harts never did go back to Brooklyn.

The moment of triumph is often preceded by years of preparation, doubts, fears, even agony. Alec Templeton's whole life has been a victory. He overcame sightlessness by ignoring it, never talking about it, not letting others talk about it.

Alec is one of a small group I used to introduce on the air as one of my favorite men in the world. "I have lived music all my life," he told me. "My earliest memories are all musical. An old neighbor of mine in Cardiff, Wales, told me just a year ago how I used to play on her son's bicycle bell. I remembered it too—it was in F sharp, a key I like."

When Alec was only two years old he climbed on a piano stool and did an imitation of an organ grinder who'd just gone by. At four he wrote a nocturne in B major, a difficult key with five sharps. Born with absolute pitch, he remembered as a child the first time he heard Rachmaninoff's "Prelude in C-Sharp Minor" played by a famous band in a park in Wales.

"Next day I asked my teacher to play the prelude. She began and I said, 'Oh you're playing it in a different key,' and she was because the band had transposed it."

Alec's own idea of a real triumph was when he went back to Cardiff for the jubilee anniversary of his music teacher and gave a recital in honor of the woman who'd helped him see his world in terms of music.

Was he born with a burning ambition to act? I asked Basil Rathbone.

"Not at all," said Basil. "I simply got bored working in an insurance office in England and quit. Since I had a cousin in a Shakespearean repertory company I went to him. He happened to be a famous artist —Frank Benson. He asked me whether I had any readings I could do for an audition.

"I said, 'Yes, that would be very easy.' When you're eighteen you talk that way. And I did a scene using three different voices—Shylock, Salerio, and Bassanio. Only at eighteen would one dare to do that, unless he were Emlyn Williams. When I finished, Frank Benson said, 'Actors are like young horses. I look at them as I look at a two-year-old colt. Now you seem to have some of the qualities of a winner so I'll give you a chance.' And that, Mary Margaret, is how it all started."

Anne Nichol's triumph with *Abie's Irish Rose* was so mixed up with tribulation at first that if she hadn't been a very valiant woman, it wouldn't have been a triumph at all.

She got the plot from a true story told by guests at her dinner table about an Irish girl who married a Jewish boy. The dramatic possibilities of the situation kept going round and round in her mind until she had to write the play. After opening night on Broadway, critic Heywood Broun said *Abie* wouldn't last two nights. Critic Percy Hammond denounced it as mawkish sentimentality.

"About half the reviews were kinder," Anne Nichols told me, "but we had hit the first hot spell of the season when people stay away from the theater in droves. I managed to keep the show going all that summer of 1922. And some good surprises came along, such as David Belasco coming to see *Abie* several times, loving it, talking about it.

"The actors took less salary, we sold tickets cut-rate. But by November, I'd paid back the actors' salaries with interest."

*Abie's Irish Rose* ran for 2327 performances—nearly seven years! As a result of it—and Anne Nichols is proud of this—Hitler included her and *Abie* in *Mein Kampf*.

Marc Connelly's triumph included that of another person. It all started when Marc was given a book by Rollin Kirby, a cartoonist friend.

"He thought it had a philosophy I'd enjoy," Marc explained. "It was called *Ol' Man Adam an' His Chillun* and was by a man I'd never heard of—Roark Bradford. When I read it I was so excited that I rushed down to New Orleans to find the author."

That's how the classic *Green Pastures* was born.

Marc Connelly peered owlishly at me over the microphone and recalled with relish the events that went into the making of that great drama.

"We roamed all over the countryside so that I could hear the talk of the people. Then when I began writing I remembered that Robert Burns used to test his poetry on people in village inns in Scotland. So I went back and tested my dialogue on the country people around St. Francisville and above Baton Rouge. I thought if it got the approval of the originals of my characters—people who for the most part couldn't read or write but could recognize the imagery and the simple speech—then I was on the right track. Sometimes I was on the wrong track and had to make changes until I got it."

Marc Connelly visited me again in 1951, when a revival of *The Green Pastures* had opened.

"The problem was finding someone to play De Lawd. Then William Marshall came to see me."

Mr. Marshall, sitting next to Mr. Connelly at the microphone, told how at the time he was so discouraged he was almost ready to give up trying to get anywhere in the theater.

Marc Connelly took up the story: "There he was, six feet five—but too young, I thought—and then as he read I told myself that God, after all, is ageless. When the little girl in the play asks what God looks like she's told he's like the Reverend. So God, I decided, could be anybody who had about him a mildness, a serenity, an inner beauty, and a look of dignity and nobility. William Marshall had it all."

Result: a second triumph for *Green Pastures*.

Sometimes triumph is an accident. Cab Calloway was rehearsing an arrangement with a band one afternoon. There was a break where the music stopped and he was supposed to sing the words. But he forgot them and filled in with "'skeep-ippa-dee-peep-ip and a heigh-dee-ho' and everybody laughed, so I thought maybe I'd hit on something. We didn't have a theme song so I decided to concoct one around this 'heigh-dee-ho' with the orchestra answering."

The rest is jazz history.

Igor Gorin sang a lovely haunting melody for me and then talked about it.

"We were living in a cellar in Paris. It was wartime and Mother wouldn't let us children go out. But she went and always came back with food for us. Then she'd sing for us this old, old Ukranian song. It says that sometimes in life it is stormy but always the storm goes away and sunshine follows."

The Gorins had plenty of storm before the sun shone. Igor was six when with his mother, sister, and brother he fled Russia. They were hungry and the sound of guns was never far off, but they had the song.

"After the war in Vienna, when I auditioned for a scholarship, 'Stormy Breezes' was my lucky song."

That audition led him eventually to America and a dream came true.

"It was my ambition to become part of this great, living democracy. I speak it, I sing it, and I live it as much as I know how. My prayers of gratitude are said best through music."

A pretty teen-ager walked up to Tallulah Bankhead at a cocktail party somewhere in the South. "I'd like to act. How do I go about it?" she demanded.

Tallulah, unsurprised, told her to write to Eva Le Gallienne, then go to New York. The girl was Uta Hagen. When I heard the story she was married to José Ferrer and they were starring together on Broadway in *Vickie*.

"Miracle of miracles, Eva Le Gallienne answered," marveled Uta. "She said if or when I came to New York she'd see me. I took my week's spring vacation, came on, and Miss Le Gallienne auditioned me. That was in April. In June when I was signing up for summer school a letter came from Miss Le Gallienne. She was producing *Hamlet* and would I be interested in playing Ophelia?

"I cried and cried, and then I began to pack. Ophelia was wonderful, and I never went back to college. I was very broke for five months and finally I called designer Lee Simonson, who knew my father. I didn't want to trade on my family, but I only had nine dollars left. I told Mr. Simonson I wanted to meet the Lunts.

"'You, too,' he groaned. Half an hour later he called back: 'Well, you can meet them tonight!'"

Here Uta's story was briskly interrupted by José Ferrer. "She won't tell it right," he deplored, "so I will. The point is that when she met the Lunts that night, they agreed to audition her in five or six weeks. Uta said, 'Oh no, I couldn't afford to stay in New York that long.' And so they fitted her in a few nights later. They told her they didn't want her to do comedy, nothing serious, no tragedy, no poetry, no Shakespeare, especially no *Sea Gull*, which is the play they were casting.

"Her appointment was for eleven. She went home and read through every play she could find and at last she thought, 'Well, it's *The Sea Gull* they're doing and it's *The Sea Gull* I want to be in, so whether they want me to or not, I'm going to read it.'

"She got to the appointment at eleven and waited until two, when the matinee audience began to arrive. Then she realized they'd meant eleven at night. It was raining and she wandered about the city, ending up soaking wet and bedraggled.

"At 11 P.M. six girls were auditioned. When they came to Uta she was cold and nervous, but she kicked off her shoes, ran on the stage and right into the *Sea Gull* scene they'd told her not to do. Then she ran off stage, put her shoes and coat on, and was ready to leave when someone said Lynn Fontanne and Alfred Lunt wished her to wait. They rehearsed until two that morning, and Uta went on in the part that night. Now isn't that an exciting story?"

I asked Uta whether she'd have told it that way.

"No," she answered meekly.

Once when I was doing a newspaper column I wrote an open letter to Dinah Shore (open letters are helpful when you must find a new column theme every day in the week—I also wrote one to the Collector of Internal Revenue!). The letter to Dinah thanked her for being such a delightfully modest, nice person, and I meant every word.

Dinah Shore was really Frances Rose Shore—"only everybody called me Fannie and I hated it. The kids used to say, 'Fannie sat on a tack—Fannie *Rose*. The crowd roared and Fannie rose. Did Fannie Rose? Shore!' Well, I took about as much of that as I could and when

I got to New York, I made up my mind nobody would ever know Fannie Rose Shore. There was a song I used to use as a theme song, 'Dinah,' so I took that name.

"I used to sing, dance, recite, or play the piano every time Mother could rope the members of her bridge club or ladies' aid society into listening, but I didn't really sing professionally until one evening when I was fourteen and in my sister's borrowed dress went to this night club. I was going to get ten dollars. I made an entrance, and there sitting grimly at a front table were my mother and father—they took me home after the first eight bars! I didn't get the ten dollars, either.

"The summer before I was graduated from Vanderbilt University, I had been to a Panhellenic meeting in New Hampshire and stopped off to do an audition at CBS which came to nothing. But I sang on WNEW and they were kind enough to take me, so I sang there for two weeks. Daddy said if I would come home and finish school I could go back to New York the following summer. So I went home and then off to New York when school ended. They told me at the radio station that I had a new style, but I didn't know what they meant. I sang the only way I knew how. And I was fired off my first commercial because I didn't sing loud enough or fast enough. Then I came back and NBC put on 'Chamber Music Society of Lower Basin Street,' which kidded the classics and jazz. I sang on that, my first really big break. After that came the Eddie Cantor show, which was the finest thing that could happen to any singer—being with Eddie. I'm amazed all the time. I can't believe it yet. You don't feel any different; just grateful and can't believe it's you."

The day Elaine Malbin was on the air with me for the first time, she was almost heartbreakingly frank about herself.

"I was ugly and fat and poor as a little girl, and that's part of the reason I'm a singer; it makes up for everything. When they discovered I had a voice I seized on it; it was a hope that I would have something in my life.

"Yes, it's lonely developing a talent like this. But if I go to parties I find I do not have the pleasure I get from studying and singing. Young men don't understand my feeling about my work—they're not interested."

We took Elaine while she was still in high school to Newark, New

York, to sing at the Jackson & Perkins rose festival. A deluge of mail was her first big public recognition.

"I have a burning desire to be good—to be a great artist," she said. Well, little Elaine has grown into a beautiful, glamorous star, and I feel a glow of pride every time I hear her.

Anita Loos wrote her first motion-picture scenario when she was twelve. She'd been watching pictures ever since she was six. She copied an address from a can of film and mailed the script to David Wark Griffith. He bought it and produced it with Mary Pickford and Lionel Barrymore as the stars!

"When I finally met Mr. Griffith he took me to lunch at a drugstore and asked me to tell him something about myself. I must have been a brat at twelve because I said I lived in San Diego, California, which was a very dull place, so I spent my time in the library there. He asked what I'd been reading, and I told him Kant's *Critique of Pure Reason*. He said, 'Give me a résumé of it,' and I did. Then he said please to discuss something easier—and I talked about the ethics of Spinoza! But do you know, I converted him to that; he remained a great Spinoza admirer as long as he lived."

By the time she was fifteen this little prodigy had sold ninety stories. And notwithstanding Kant and Spinoza, her *Gentlemen Prefer Blondes* was translated into thirteen languages, including Chinese.

John and Margaret Farrar were picked by destiny to be a success story. John is one of our great editors and publishers; Margaret is the creator of the crossword puzzle epidemic. They're both successes but it's their marriage I believe to have been foreordained.

"When I was a sophomore at Smith College," says Margaret, "I had to compose a song for a final examination. I thought I wanted to be a musician at the time. Anyhow, I needed a lyric to set my melody to, and I borrowed one from our school magazine. It had been reprinted from the Yale literary journal and was duly credited as to source, but not as to author. I turned in my masterpiece and got an A.

"One night, after I'd been graduated and was going to work for John O'Hara Cosgrave on the old New York *World*, I went to dinner at the Cosgrave home. There I met a young man named John Farrar and found that it was his poem I'd set to music two years before!"

Margaret's fame as a creator of crossword puzzles was not due to John Farrar, however, but to Franklin P. Adams, whose "Conning

Tower," signed F.P.A., was must reading for millions. F.P.A. was a fan of young Margaret's, and when he saw that she was taking the newspaper's dull puzzles and making them bright, accurate, and original he boosted the feature until it was as popular as his own column.

It's a cliché about poets starving in attics, but for Joseph Auslander it was a cliché which came uncomfortably true.

"I gave up my teaching job," he explained, "because it took so much of me that there was nothing left for poetry. I moved to a cheap room and lived on ten cents a day—two doughnuts and a scuttle of java twice a day and all the free sugar I could get away with. I had one friend in those days—Socrates. Socrates was a mouse and he went everywhere in my pocket.

"I had a poem in one of those little poetry magazines, and a poem by somebody named Audrey Wurdemann faced mine. I read hers and was terribly excited. 'I've got to meet that girl,' I thought. I called a friend on the magazine and asked about her. He chuckled and said: 'She just called me about you.' Then he told me she was only fourteen, and I couldn't believe it. I still can't imagine how she could write such a wise poem at that age.

"Then she telephoned to invite me to dinner, but I wouldn't go. I was afraid I'd eat too much."

The turning point came when a former pupil of Joseph Auslander's, now the famous Ogden Nash, tracked him down to his cold-water flat and said, "I want you to write a book about poetry."

Joe Auslander with Frank E. Hill wrote *The Winged Horse*. It was a best seller. He could go to Audrey's house to dinner now. And that's how the two poets met and fell in love and were married.

What I called on the air "The Burning of the Clothes" is gloriously triumphant.

Since the day in 1952 when Henry Viscardi told it, he has gone on to organize Abilities, Inc., the Long Island concern run entirely by the handicapped, with the Viscardi motto: "I do not choose to be a common man. It is my right to be uncommon if I can."

You have to know about Hank—that he was born with stumps for legs so that he stood about three feet from the floor. But of items like courage, stick-to-itiveness, and enterprise he had at least triple equipment. And eventually he had an operation that made it possible for him to have legs that made him normal height.

Through the years I watched him win over to his cause everybody he ever tackled: Mrs. Franklin D. Roosevelt, Bernard Baruch, Dr. Howard A. Rusk, and people much harder to move—hard-boiled, self-absorbed businessmen.

"I did not tell the family when I was coming home after the operation," he said. "The whole business, especially the experimental fitting of artificial legs, was risky. I did not want them to build up hope and then be disappointed. But when at last I could walk—when I knew I could get away with it—I simply walked in the front door.

"They were at dinner at the kitchen table, and as I came in I called out: 'It's myself.' When I came into the kitchen they couldn't say much, for feeling. My mother cried a little. I tried to ease the tension —told them how I'd had to borrow some trousers from the leg-maker, and then everyone talked at once.

"I walked over to the mantel and saw the clock on it. I'd never seen the top of the mantel before. And when I stood next to my mother, she only came up to my shoulder. Then the girls began talking about teaching me to dance and how I could drive the car. It was as if my life had just begun.

"It doesn't seem like a big thing, but it was thrilling to march up to a telephone and put in a coin; to walk along a street and see the tops of automobiles. And being able to hang on to a strap in the subway was fascinating! Always before I'd played a game in the subway, dividing people into the starers and the nonstarers. I found myself still doing it, but there was no need. I was like everybody else.

"The burning of the clothes was the greatest bonfire ever lit. It kind of smelled up the neighborhood for a while, but those old clothes of mine that had encased my three-foot body represented a life that had ended, and the whole family decided we'd burn them as a sort of celebration of victory. Such a victory was it that people would come to the house and say, 'Where's your cousin who used to be around here—that little fellow who looked a lot like you?' The shoemaker asked me that one day when I walked in, a tall young man, to call for my sister's shoes. I told him truthfully, 'That little boy is dead.'"

## 20. VSP (VERY SPECIAL PEOPLE)

*"I don't lose my temper and rage, but I get kind of cold and then the children say, 'Maw's mad!' "   Eleanor Roosevelt*

Interviewers have often asked me to name the guests who stand out in my mind. I immediately want to include them all, which is obviously not possible when there are years of them. So perhaps it would help to narrow down the list if I defined the outstanding radio guest. First that person has something important to say; then he (or just as often she) is frank, gracious, and giving, has a good vocabulary, is quick on the uptake, talkative but not loquacious, and tells a story well.

Mrs. Franklin Delano Roosevelt is my nomination for first place on this roster. And after her, Pearl Buck, Fannie Hurst, and Carl Van Doren. Fannie once said, "The important thing is to be the caring kind of person."

I agree, and these VSPs of mine are the caring kind. Honorable mention on this highly personal list goes to John Mason Brown and Hendrik Willem Van Loon—John for his especially felicitous way with words and his graceful ability always to leave me feeling smarter and more charming than I ever could be; Hendrik because he invariably flattered me by seeming to get brand-new thoughts and ideas as we talked before the microphone.

I have plenty of reason to know about Mrs. Roosevelt's concern for other human beings. It has been evident in every contact I've had with her. The first time I spoke to her a magazine had asked me to write an article about how famous men were helped by their wives. Mrs. Roosevelt was one of the suggested wives. Franklin Delano Roosevelt was then governor of New York. Two days after I got the assignment

I was walking along the street in New York City, thinking about the article, when suddenly I saw Mrs. Roosevelt advancing toward me. It seemed a heaven-sent chance, so when we came abreast I said, "Excuse me, Mrs. Roosevelt, I'm Mary Margaret McBride and *Country Gentleman* has asked me to interview you for a piece on how wives help their husbands."

Mrs. Roosevelt smiled, thought a minute, then answered, "Well, I really think you should see Franklin about that. You'd better come up to Albany. Can you make it next Friday?"

So I went to Albany and spent the night at the governor's mansion. Mrs. Roosevelt met me at the train and put me next to the governor at dinner. He spoke warmly of the great help she had been to him since his illness, which he mentioned frankly and without embarrassment. He said she could go places he couldn't and that he depended upon her eyes and ears as much as his own. I thought it was a pleasant, even merry household and enjoyed myself.

The next time I needed an interview with Mrs. Roosevelt she was the wife of the President of the United States and guest of honor at a luncheon presided over by Mrs. William Dick Sporborg. I asked Mrs. Sporborg how I was to get time with Mrs. Roosevelt, who was rushing in just in time for lunch and afterward speeding away to another appointment.

Mrs. Sporborg said, "Well, if you can come to the head table without making too much fuss about it, I'll see that you get to talk to Mrs. Roosevelt."

To avoid fuss, as Mrs. Sporborg requested, I crawled underneath the table and emerged standing at Mrs. Sporborg's side. She got up unobtrusively and I slid into her seat. Down the table I could hear somebody worrying about time. Mrs. Roosevelt heard, too, and she looked round calmly to say, "It's all right. I'm watching the clock." So we talked and everybody waited.

It was then that I told her a little story I'd heard in my own Middle West. A new congressman had been elected and his friends and neighbors were giving a party for his wife. She confessed she was nervous about going to Washington where she didn't know anybody and she was sure she'd miss her sewing circle. "Oh now, Susie," comforted her sister, "don't you worry about being lonesome. Mrs. Roosevelt will be there and she'll see that you meet people and have a real good time."

The Queen of Greece must have felt the same way. She had confided to Mrs. Roosevelt, visiting her country, that there were certain things she especially wanted to see in New York. When Mrs. Roosevelt got in touch with her here it turned out that she hadn't yet found any of the places she had named. The former first lady therefore took over for a day as guide. In the course of the expedition they passed a city firehouse. The queen looked curiously through the big open doors at the brass fire poles.

"Do you think they'd mind if I went in?" she asked. Mrs. Roosevelt assured her the firemen would be delighted. She introduced the queen all round, and the royal guest asked so many questions and seemed so interested that Mrs. Roosevelt suggested to the firemen that they demonstrate how they answer an alarm. Almost instantly a bell rang and men began sliding down the brass poles from the second floor; after them their mascot cat slid down. The queen was enchanted. I'll wager it is her favorite story about the United States!

When Bess Furman told Mrs. Roosevelt about the difficult time I was having in Florida during the citrus contract that blessed woman promptly telegraphed me an invitation to spend the night at the White House on my way back to New York. Florida newspapers featured the telegram, and my lot was considerably bettered because of it.

Mrs. Roosevelt's amused description of the number and size of the closets at Buckingham Palace compared to the amount of her wardrobe when she stayed there just after the war convinces me that she would sympathize with the way I felt when my own wardrobe humiliated me at her house.

After dinner the night I spent at the White House she sent her guests with an usher on a tour of the upstairs rooms. Finally we came to the Lincoln room. The usher threw open the door with a flourish, all the time talking eloquently about the great Abe. A maid had evidently unpacked for me, and over on the antique dresser was my old hairbrush with a tuft of bristles missing and my comb with three teeth out. Flung across what had been Mrs. Taft's favorite rocking chair was my best blue dressing gown, spotted and torn in one place after the Florida siege. Hastily the usher shut the door, murmuring apologetically, "I didn't know it was occupied." (I could have sunk through the floor.)

Another time, after a big change in my life, I was feeling low and talking pessimistically to anybody who would listen. Mrs. Roosevelt invited me to lunch. We had it alone in her apartment, and after we finished eating she said, "Now tell me about your circumstances." I did and she asked thoughtfully, "Would you like to do a program with me?" I was too overcome to do more than stammer, "Of course."

"I thought perhaps we could do a once-a-week conversation," she explained, "just about everything important that's going on. Women need to think about what's happening. Maybe we can help."

She ended by suggesting that I telephone her agent. He had us make a tape. Midway he stopped us. "Look here, Mary Margaret," he accused. "You're interviewing Mrs. Roosevelt. This is supposed to be a conversation—not an interview."

Mrs. Roosevelt broke in. "It's my fault. I'm afraid I'm talking too much. Never mind, I'll fix it."

Of course it wasn't her fault. I was so used to interviewing her, so certain that her opinions were more important than mine that naturally I *was* interviewing her. But we started over again and produced a conversation about what was happening in the world at the moment —the Russians were in it, and the cold war, labor relations, politics. We skipped nothing, not even a cookbook of mine which had come out a short time before.

Mrs. Roosevelt admitted that her chief cooking knowledge was confined to scrambling eggs, which she used to do in the White House on Sunday evenings for supper. I asked her how she did them, and she said, "Oh, I just make them." But a little probing revealed that she uses cream.

Mrs. Roosevelt works to make money to give away, but the best things she gives are time, energy, and understanding. One day when she was broadcasting with me, we had lunch together and got talking about what else she was going to do that day. She said a young woman who wanted to get into television was coming to make a recording with her. She'd had a letter from the girl, and something in the way she wrote made Mrs. Roosevelt feel she ought to have a chance. She rearranged her entire day so as to devote several hours to advising and making contacts for this complete stranger.

But it's hard to do anything for her. If you ask her to lunch she counters with, "You come here. I want you to see my new house."

When she did a broadcast with me, I usually went to the street with her afterward to find a taxicab. But she always saw one first and before I could say good-by was skittering across the street and into the vehicle.

That makes all the funnier the story she told me about our mutual friend, John Golden, the producer. When she got back to New York after her husband's death, Mr. Golden and another friend of hers came to see her one day, very solemn and portentous. She waited, a bit anxiously, to hear what they had on their minds, and Mr. Golden told her they had constituted themselves a committee of two to look after her and advise her. They intimated that she didn't have much business sense and might get into a lot of trouble. Mrs. Roosevelt after a moment of startled silence laughed and let them know emphatically that she was capable of looking after herself and intended to do it.

One of the times I was to have her on the program I said I'd call for her. She was living then on Washington Square; it was after she'd left the White House. Something had delayed her so we were late leaving. Then when we got a taxicab, the traffic was bad, and pretty soon I found myself sitting on the edge of my seat. Mrs. Roosevelt said, "Do you think it would help if we got out and ran? I'm willing." And she meant it too.

I once lost a sponsor because of this wonderful woman. I went to a big party in Washington where she, then first lady, was guest of honor. Her cousin, Alice Longworth, had a seat at a table near me, and when Mrs. Roosevelt came into the room everybody rose spontaneously and applauded except Mrs. Longworth, who sat a few minutes too long and kept on laughing and talking. When I got back to New York, I mildly deplored this on the air, and the sponsor, a Republican, took my remarks as an affront to his party and went off my program summarily.

One day I expected Mrs. Roosevelt when she didn't come. The Girl Scouts had asked me to have Eleanor Roosevelt on to make a plea for funds for their organization. I said, "Of course, any time." The day came and I'd prepared a number of questions about recent columns, her page in *McCall's* magazine, and her travels. But no Mrs. Roosevelt. We went on the air without her. Suddenly I saw Mrs.

Theodore Roosevelt patiently sitting in the front row. A great light broke. She was Eleanor Roosevelt too.

Mrs. Theodore told the story later in an interview with Mike Wallace and said I was furious. I wasn't and I hope she didn't really believe I was. I was just flabbergasted because I had not prepared for *her*. True, I'd interviewed her several times before, but for the moment everything I knew about her went out of my head. I am an ad libber, but I have to know what I'm going to ad-lib about!

She was a wonderful sport and laughingly assured me that she was used to belonging to the Oyster Bay branch—the out-of-season Roosevelts.

Last summer Kathleen McLaughlin of the New York *Times* asked Emma Bugbee of the *Herald Tribune* and me to dinner with Mrs. Roosevelt. The evening is one of my treasured memories. Emma and Kathleen covered Mrs. Roosevelt for many years in the White House and out. Their relationship with her is easy and friendly. We ranged conversationally from queens to recipes. Kathleen served a wonderful orange dessert. We all took down the way to make it.

Mrs. Roosevelt was at her warmest. She told about Queen Wilhelmina of Holland, who was visiting her at Hyde Park, coming out one sunny day with a pillow tucked under one arm and a book under the other. A lady in waiting immediately sprang to take the pillow and book. Queen Wilhelmina shook her head decidedly. "No, no, I'm going off by myself," she insisted. "I'm going to sit under a tree and read."

Even a queen feels like relaxing at Val Kill Cottage.

When Emperor Haile Selassie of Ethiopia went to the cottage for luncheon the protocol authority informed the hostess that His Imperial Highness must have twenty minutes alone to rest before luncheon. But first he was eager to see himself on television in a taped interview.

Mrs. Roosevelt established her guest before the television set and went off to other duties.

"He still seemed happily absorbed when I peeped in at him a half hour later," she related. "Luncheon was to be in about twenty minutes, so I debated about breaking in on him to warn him that if he intended to rest for twenty minutes, he must be about it. I finally told him, and he smiled up at me beatifically.

" 'I just wanted to take off my shoes,' he explained. 'I have them off so I don't need time to rest.' "

Mrs. Roosevelt involuntarily glanced down, and there he was in his stocking feet, wiggling his toes.

I think Mrs. Roosevelt's favorite among royalty was Queen Mary. She admired Queen Mary's spirit, which was quite like her own.

She told about one time when she was supposed to leave Buckingham Palace early in the morning and Queen Mary said to her son, King George, "Of course you're going to see Mrs. Roosevelt off."

"Oh no, please," Mrs. Roosevelt pleaded, "don't. It's much too early for anyone to be up."

"I shall get up," asserted the queen mother, looking severely at her son. "And I shall expect to see you too." Sure enough, in the chill gray dawn of the next morning not only Queen Mary but the obedient King George saw the guest off.

Kathleen, who had recently stayed overnight at my barn in the Catskills, told about the view. Mrs. Roosevelt said, "I don't see why I can't see your house!"

I told her it was my dream to have her there and she said, "Send me a choice of dates." I did and she chose a Thursday in July. She brought me some jars of jelly which she presented with the comment, "My housekeeper sent these, but she didn't want to because she thinks you are an authority on food. I talked her out of that, though."

Of course that day—it's always true when you want to show off anything; a child, a garden, or a view—the mountains were completely shrouded in mist, but she looked at everything else.

"I want to see all of your house," she said, so I gave her the complete tour. Luckily I had cleaned carefully everywhere that showed, but in the kitchen there's a utility closet for mops and brooms and that very morning I had thrown some dust rags on the floor, thinking, "She won't look in here." Which hasty judgment only proved I'd never before accompanied Mrs. Roosevelt on an inspection trip. She said, "I want to see everything," opened the door, and there the rags were, all tumbled untidily together.

In the long entrance hall she tried a closet door and found it locked. "But it's locked," she protested. "What do you have in there?"

Confused, I muttered, "Moths."

"Moths!" she exclaimed in horror. "You oughtn't to have moths!"

She was all for opening the closet then and there and beginning a foray on the insects, so I had to explain that I had already begun to fight them and that what I had tried to lock in was really the smell of moth balls.

I could always count on her on the air to say exactly what she thought. I remarked that Khrushchev of Russia seemed rather childish. He wanted what he wanted when he wanted it, and he lost his temper when he didn't get it.

She corrected me: "Don't think of him as a child. He knows exactly what he's doing every minute. Don't think of him as a drunkard either!"

All these earlier pictures with Khrushchev smiling jovially as if he'd had a few too many didn't fool her, who had talked to the Russian leader for hours. She added sagely, "I doubt if he'd ever have too many drinks when anything important engaged him. He's a very canny man."

The picture on television of Mrs. Roosevelt entertaining Mr. Khrushchev and his wife at Hyde Park and, because of their many appointments which kept them from staying to lunch, sending them off with a bag of rolls made me smile. It reminded me of a story she told me of a woman who wanted to talk to her about a pet cause.

Characteristically, Mrs. Roosevelt said, "Come to lunch," and the woman warned, "I'll have to bring seven other women with me." Mrs. Roosevelt said, "All right," and had luncheon prepared for eight women, but when the party came there were four extras.

The hostess was a little surprised, and I guess her expression showed it.

Mrs. X of the cause explained airily: "Oh, don't worry. I told the extra four to bring their own buns."

The extra four did, too, and contentedly ate their own buns. Mrs. Roosevelt supplied the coffee. She commented to me rather dubiously, "I suppose it was all right. Mrs. X said so, anyhow."

She takes joking and unpleasant comment with the same calmness she accords to praise. Perhaps she's a little more calm under attack— real or jocular—because she's likely to be embarrassed by effusiveness. A newspaper friend of mine told me about walking through the White House with Mrs. Roosevelt and coming upon one of the women employees lightheartedly taking the first lady off for the benefit of her fellows.

The subject of the satire stood still until the girl had finished, then stepped into view and applauded. She said to the girl, "You must do that for my party on Friday."

The culprit, scarlet with embarrassment, tried to apologize but Mrs. Roosevelt insisted, "No apology is necessary. Just come to the party!" (The girl came but was too ill at ease to do the sketch.)

Mrs. Roosevelt has had plenty of critics (though they have decreased almost to the vanishing point recently), but she usually beats them to the punch. She told me, and laughed heartily, about one young man writing a college paper on columnists who said a reader would have to have several years of college to comprehend the columns of Walter Lippmann but only needed a fifth-grade education to understand Mrs. Roosevelt.

Sometimes I wish she were not so important. It would be nice to feel free to telephone her whenever I want to, to ask her for regular weekends as I do other friends whom I enjoy. But I am always afraid I'll be presuming, because after all, informal though she seems, she *is* the world's first lady.

She's appeared on every radio and television program I've ever asked her to be on. I've done recordings from her Val Kill Cottage at Hyde Park. I've lunched and dined with her, but I'm sure she doesn't know how I really feel about her, how I long to be able to talk to her not as an interviewer, but as a friend.

I used to have a recurring dream about her. We were hurrying across fields and I was trying, not very successfully, to keep up with her. I guess that dream is symbolical.

A friend told me about a conversation with one of the Roosevelt grandsons. He was talking about a rather distinguished man who had, as the boy put it, sucked up to Nanna—even called her by her first name a few times but, said the grandson, he soon stopped that!

"Why did he, do you suppose?" I asked my friend, who opined that, though Mrs. Roosevelt didn't say much, the atmosphere grew chilly.

I doubt that, though, because she's always courteous. But sometimes when I go away from her, I have the impression that I've made a fool of myself. And what can you do? Maybe write: "Dear Mrs. Roosevelt, I know I said something very stupid the other day and I wish I hadn't because the way I feel about you, I want to appear to you in the very best light." But there's the danger that I didn't seem more foolish than usual and that even if I did, she'd forgotten by now because she has so many people and plans always on her mind.

So I never wrote the letter until now—and I'm glad I've done it at last.

Mrs. Roosevelt helped give me social consciousness, and in all the too brief years I knew him Carl Van Doren was my balance wheel. When the radio witch hunt was on and my conscience was troubled because I felt I was taking the cowardly way, he didn't agree and was so logical about his belief that sometimes after listening to him, I gained a few hours of peace within myself.

He felt it was important for me to stay on the air—and if I didn't lie or bear false witness he thought the small compromise of tailoring my guest list for expediency was not too important.

Once, introducing him, I applied to Carl a phrase that he had used about Washington and Franklin: "too honest to feel suspicion, too great to feel envy."

Carl commented thoughtfully: "I doubt if you are ever suspicious unless you're a little crooked yourself, or envious if you have any real confidence in yourself."

I cherish particularly two notes of the many he sent me, these like lots of others written at one forty-five, just after I'd gone off the air. This day I had said with some bitterness that I was sick of being accused of too much sweetness and light.

Carl wrote: "Mary Margaret darling, But you must not object to the charge of sweetness and light in you. Think what sweetness is: the balanced state of health between the green and the unripe on one side and the over-ripe and rotten on the other. Sweetness is another word for strength and harmony. Sweetness unachieved is immaturity; sweetness past is decay. So stick where you are, sweetness. And as to light, what on earth else is so searching and even cruel? Didn't you ever turn a bright light into a dark corner and see the noisome bats scuttle into hiding? You have let so many lights fall into corners of prejudice and unkindness that I think of you as a healing agent on the air. And remember again: no light, no life. I'm sending you the Portable Swift, with strict urgings that you read what Swift has to say about sweetness and light. Love—Carl."

After I did a broadcast at the Kentucky Derby he wrote: "Dearest Mary Margaret, You were wonderful in Louisville today. Sometime I must tell you about my passion for that enchanting town. But today I almost wriggled off the couch where I was lolling to listen while you talked about fillies in the Derby. Haven't I told you about Colonel Matt Winn's saying there was a romantic aspect to that? If so few have won, it is—he said—because fillies will not run away from horses in the spring! You could have said that as safely as what you said about the Craig hussy [one of my ancestors] who had a baby by her captain! Love—Carl."

In a slightly different way all her own, novelist Fannie Hurst helps keep me on an even keel. Fannie is one of the most interesting and complicated people I've ever met, and I tell her things I never tell anybody else.

Long before I was on the air I met Fannie at a dinner where we were both to be speakers. Later when she was sitting across the microphone from me, I reminded her of that night (I doubt if she remembered it as vividly as I).

"You'd evidently just decided to go out and make speeches if it killed you, because you said to me: 'I've been living in an ivory tower—this is a dreary conclusion but true—and now I've made the decision to come out of it here I am with icy cold hands and this expensive dinner going to waste.'" (Seven-fifty it cost—big for those days.)

I wasn't eating either. We both got up finally and made two dreadful speeches. Today Fannie talks privately or publicly better than anybody I know. Under special conditions I like to talk, but I have to feel that my audience knows and loves me—that they are, in short, listeners!

Fannie doesn't need a special audience. I suppose that's because she has more to say, and of course besides being amusing she is wise and compassionate. Capricious, too, frequently changing her mind in mid-air.

As with all my VSPs the most wonderful thing about Fannie is her passionate caring for miserable people deprived of rights; for the sick, the sad. Not that any more than Mrs. Roosevelt she permits you to waste time feeling sorry for yourself. When I try to cry on her shoulder she lets me know very quickly she has no time for puny self-pitiers. But should you have a real crisis, she's there.

When I am sentimental about Fannie I always think of the time Stella Karn was in the hospital and Ohio had a day for Fannie Hurst. The last thing at the airport Fannie telephoned Stella and right in the middle of the celebration remembered to send her a telegram.

And one time when she started on a trip to Maine with her secretary, the brilliant writer Zora Neale Hurston, they ended up in Niagara Falls because Fannie discovered Zora had never been there. Zora told me that story of course, not Fannie.

Long before she won the Nobel prize Pearl Buck's books about her mother (*The Exile*) and her father (*Fighting Angel*) were on my shelf of special favorites kept within easy reach in my bedroom, along with *Green Mansions, Alice in Wonderland*, and all of Dickens.

So when Pearl Buck finally consented to come on my program, I was excited. At first she was a difficult guest—reserved and suspicious, I thought, of both me and the microphone. Because her books had revealed her to me, I persevered and over the years we became friends.

The last time I interviewed her she stunned me and made news in Broadway columns by announcing that she was a rock-'n'-roll enthusiast.

"I've been listening to a lot of the music the youngsters like," she said with her usual calm deliberation. "I always want to know why anything new catches on."

Author of best sellers under a male nom de plume, John Sedgwick, as well as her own, what I respect most about Pearl Buck is her courage. She has often come on the air with me and talked about her own retarded child so that parents of other retarded children should understand and know how to deal with such a tragic problem.

Another time her theme was to arrange adoption for orphans of American soldier-fathers and Chinese, Indian, Polynesian, or Japanese mothers.

Pearl and her husband, Richard Walsh, kept taking these children into their own Pennsylvania home until there was no longer any room. Then they bought another farmhouse and engaged a Quaker couple to try to give these wartime orphans a decent start in life.

She once said to me: "I'm a product of the crossing of several breeds. I had a French grandmother, a Dutch grandfather, and on my father's side they were all Germans who came here in 1760. So I understand these children."

"Hate and bigotry are becoming rather unfashionable," she told me in June 1952. "Americans are beginning to think about their prejudices, beginning to do some self-examining.

"If we can just stave off the accident of war month by month, we stand a good chance to enter into a wonderful and prosperous era."

## 21. STAR DASH

Years ago, when I worked on the Cleveland *Press*, I used to be sent to get what the editor called star-dash material on some special event like a parade or a big meeting. This meant that I would pick up bits of color from the crowd, a few sentences expressing opinions, a little anecdote, in no particular sequence, to be run and separated one from the other by stars and dashes.

* — * — * — * — * — * —

Leon Rothier of the Metropolitan Opera, telling about a visit to Enrico Caruso: "I was told it was customary for newcomers to pay a visit to Caruso so I went to his hotel. A nice man, his valet, said, 'He will be pleased to see you.' Just as I was handing the valet my coat and cane and was about to give him my hat Caruso came into the hall. To free my hand to shake hands, I threw my hat through an open door. It was the bedroom of Caruso, and my hat fell on the bed. I saw Caruso get white. He jumped on my hat and said, 'Never do that again.' I did not know what to think of the great tenor.

"When I came back to the Metropolitan, I told the story and somebody said, 'You did *that!* That is the worst luck in the world!' For more than a month Caruso said nothing more than hello to me—never even shook hands. Then one day he patted me on the shoulder and I understood I was forgiven."

* — * — * — * — * — * —

Julia Field, zoo director, pretty blonde, weight a hundred and ten pounds: "I liked and was fascinated by wild animals all my life. I learned by watching experienced trainers, and the longer I watched, the more I understood the animals. I began to see mistakes the men made and thought I could do better. One day I went in with seven lions—just walked in and felt perfectly at home. They were trained animals and I knew what they could do, although they hadn't been working for a few months. It isn't a matter of just liking them, or having no fear. You could have no fear and be killed very quickly. The secret is to know the animals so well you can predict what they're going to do and to have enough skill to bluff them into thinking you're far stronger than they."

\* — \* — \* — \* — \* — \* —

I never got the great Albert Einstein on the air, but I did have the privilege of meeting him in his plain little office in Princeton, New Jersey, when I was doing a broadcast about Princeton Graduate School. His hair was long and white and mussed, his smile crinkled his whole face. My hosts sprang me on him and him on me, and we were both shy. I stammered a request that he give me some statement to take back to my radio audience.

He hesitated but kept smiling. At last he shook his head. "No, I couldn't give you a statement so suddenly," he told me. "With the tensions in the world today, we must think before we make any statement at all. But I will tell you one wrong thing we do in this country—we try to segregate scholarship; and it is wrong for only the young people to study."

\* — \* — \* — \* — \* — \* —

Years of admiration and headlines and applause never cured prima donna Lily Pons of what she called "nervocity." The tiny singer told me that eating was impossible for her on a day when she was to sing.

"I am seasick that day. The best thing for me is to do something with my hands. Ironing—that is very good for my nervocity. Right up to the time I begin, it is seasickness, fear. Confidence comes only when I feel my public—and the feeling is right."

\* — \* — \* — \* — \* — \* —

Playwright Robert Sherwood, arriving a few minutes late for the broadcast, explains: "I was held up by a matter of prejudice and opinion. I've been called up for jury duty and I was being questioned as to suitability to serve on the jury of a trial involving a candy manufacturer. The question was: 'Are you in any way or to any degree prejudiced against chocolate marshmallows?'"

\* — \* — \* — \* — \* — \* —

Barnaby Conrad, who writes about bull fighting, arguing with me about his favorite sport. "The bull if he had a chance either to go to the stockyard or fight a glorious battle for twenty minutes in the ring—the bull would always choose the fight. It's the only pain or actual conflict he's ever met in his four years of perfect existence. I know that had I lived as ideal a life as a bull leads for four years and then had twenty minutes of struggle before the end, I'd like that."

* — * — * — * — * — * —

Sidney Baldwin of the Peoria, Illinois, *Star,* in town on a visit: "I miss the old days in New York of double-decker buses on Fifth Avenue and the florists' windows. Instead of being full of chrysanthemums and roses and the old flowers, they now feature lots of new-fangled flowers and foliage they bring in by airplane from all over and the flowers we know and love are pushed way back. And no more stoops on the houses—they've cut them all down. I miss, too, the special table in the corner of the old Waldorf-Astoria. And the Astor stable tearoom with the horses' names still over the stalls."

* — * — * — * — * — * —

Author Louis Bromfield, who came back from France in 1939, took up four or five abandoned farms in Ohio, and set about building up the soil and trying for quality yields in terms of nutrition, told me: "It's ridiculous to say just anybody can be a farmer! What we had for many years were earth scratchers and men who hated their land and their animals. They never belonged on the farm and are in the towns now. The new farmer is knowledgeable and interested—and we're turning broken-down farms in the South into good productive institutions. It's exciting and encouraging."

* — * — * — * — * — * —

I have a lot of the preacher's zeal, only just at the critical moment I get uncertain. Irwin Edman, who used often to leave his philosophy classes at Columbia University to delight my listeners and me with ideas and speculations, advised me to stay unconvinced.

"It's the convinced who are dangerous," he declared. "They may become the intolerant, the fanatic, the dictators. They have closed minds, for they don't want to find out about other people's ideas. They don't want their own precious convictions disturbed."

* — * — * — * — * — * —

Former ambassador and world traveler Hugh Gibson: "The llama is a very funny animal and absolutely stupid except for one thing. He will carry up to a hundred pounds, and if you put on one pound more he'll go on a sit-down strike and you can build a fire under him and he won't budge. The only thing that will finally make him move is if you pick up a handful of little pebbles and flick them at his nose, his one tender spot. He'll get more and more irritated and finally stumble to his feet but only after you've taken off the surplus load. This is passive resistance!"

* — * — * — * — * — * —

Actress Helen Hayes, who came one day when I was feeling low about my own common sense: "I was so relieved when you said you didn't know how to organize your life. What do you do with a case of black despair? I've tried talking it over, but I just find new things to worry about."

* — * — * — * — * — * —

Alan Villiers, who writes about the sea, was born in a gale in North Melbourne; and for a long time at sea, gales played a part in his life.

"Any kid born in Australia kept one eye over the horizon looking at the ships, all right—and my uncles would take me to the docks to see the ships; they were a link with the rest of the world. Way back in those days you felt a bit cut off there in Australia. There was a nice man I met on the docks named Christian Christianson. I brought him home, and I liked him so much I just took his name for a while. The family didn't want me to go to sea so they got some old boy to try to discourage me, and instead of discouraging me, he almost got my father to go too. He'd been to sea forty years and he could talk, that fellow. We all went to sea after that. My father used to say: 'Never forget that your time on earth is a gift from God which you ought to use with his other gifts to enrich all living if you can.'"

* — * — * — * — * — * —

Anthropologist Margaret Mead: "If we live long enough [the human race], we'll come out all right. We need patience, belief, and trust. It's despair and desperation that drive people into quick temporary solutions that don't get us anywhere.

"Parents are scared because we have emphasized the harsher and more damaging things that can happen to children. We know how very important early childhood is and how much we should give children of security and love. It isn't true that you will do irreparable harm if you leave a child for one night, but the early memory that creates a feeling of safety and love is terribly important.

"A child who has had love and security and then sees flogging and shooting and people dying can still come back and have a normal life —with their kittens and their dogs and the whole circle of loving people around them."

\* — \* — \* — \* — \* — \* —

James Farley, political leader: "You can't keep a democracy going without participation. Colleges should give time to the science of government. Too many people refuse to take a part in public affairs, yet complain about those who do. When women started in public affairs the men didn't want them. In America people always find a way of meeting every crisis. When the solution comes the hard way we're the better for it."

\* — \* — \* — \* — \* — \* —

Dr. Marynia F. Farnham, psychiatrist and writer: "I have never met in my office the woman who is glad she's a woman, the one who honestly enjoys homemaking and wants more than anything else in the world to raise a family of healthy, normal youngsters. This is because that woman has never needed help. She's adjusted to what she's doing, having chosen to do the very thing she's best fitted for by training, background, and natural biological and psychological endowments. She's an adult woman."

\* — \* — \* — \* — \* — \* —

Henry Morton Robinson, author of *The Cardinal*: "I can't get away from my worries—they couldn't be torn out of me. They're in my blood. Anxiety is part of the writer's burden. He's never free of it. During the writing of a book I'm in a highly nauseated state all the time, driven by some compulsion that's very painful to bear and impossible to throw off; so I may say that in the last thirty years I've never been free, even during dreams, of worry and anxiety about the outcome of my work. The very process of writing is not an external thing. It comes from the deepest part of one's life. It's an enormous pressure and comes out that way. And in letting it come out you release the anxiety that generates it.

"When I go into my studio in the morning, having prepared by a very simple process of clearing everything else out of my life, I am in the condition of a radio tube—a receptor tube that picks up waves from heaven knows where, and my job is to be in good condition to set them down . . . and I have to trust those waves. I've often compared it to a man driving an automobile through a thick fog. It is not necessary that you see the end. It is only necessary that you see as far ahead as the immediate light will throw its beam—one step at a time. And you must trust the unconscious absolutely.

"I was under such pressure that if ordinary writing things weren't available, if I didn't have pen and ink, I would have scratched this story, *The Cardinal*, on rocks, on the bark of trees; I would have scratched it on the parchment of my own skin!"

\* — \* — \* — \* — \* — \* —

Bela Kornitzer, who did a book about American fathers and sons, explains why: "I was so startled at the way prominent Americans were always being written about in connection with their mothers, while in Europe when you think about a great man you think about his father. The European father is a sort of dictator. He is a disciplinarian; he runs the family. He is a symbol of power and strength. The relationship between an American father and his children is rather amiable and chummy, and he's sort of a pal to his boys."

\* — \* — \* — \* — \* — \* —

R. E. Gould, Maine storekeeper, remembered the stick of striped candy a man gave him when he was seven. "It was the first I ever had and the most beautiful thing I ever saw, and I decided then and there I'd have a store when I was grown up and give sticks of candy to little boys . . . The oddest customer I ever had? The man who wanted poor butter—two pounds of it. He had his stepson visiting him!"

\* — \* — \* — \* — \* — \* —

Irma Rombauer, whose cookbook sold millions: "Someday I'm going to write a novel, and I plan to let my heroine go wrong. That's because I've always had to make my recipes go right."

\* — \* — \* — \* — \* — \* —

R. G. Waldeck, born into a liberal and cultured German family, said she did not believe there was anything in a people themselves which gave them a talent for democracy. "Isn't it rather education, environment? I, myself, came from a completely liberal house, but my father thought it very bad for me to read the newspapers. He thought I should read Goethe and the good books. Because in Germany the so-called liberals were educated for art and belles-lettres, but not for politics."

* — * — * — * — * — * —

Lewis E. Lawes, famous warden of Sing Sing, did not believe that brutalizing men in prison achieved any useful purpose. Part of his formula for handling prisoners was contained in these words: "People must be kept busy. Idleness, especially three or four years of it in prison, is no good. Men come out a complete mess. I think, too, that juvenile delinquency is tied up with the fact that children are not given enough to do."

* — * — * — * — * — * —

Dr. Samuel Shoemaker, New York minister: "We can't win freedom with bullets and industry. We have to fight the wrong kind of beliefs— materialism, communism, godlessness—which is why leadership in the church is so terribly important. Religion might hold the balance of power. Man needs to be changed. He's like an animal, and an angel. We have to get the animal out of him and the angel into him."

* — * — * — * — * — * —

Eve Curie, writer and daughter of scientist Marie Curie: "There are people who feel in their bodies the misery of others—and have a sense of guilt because all didn't have their opportunities."

* — * — * — * — * — * —

I asked dancer-choreographer Agnes de Mille whether she'd consider retiring. Her answer: "I heard a man say once that he'd stayed married through sheer inertia, and some of us stay on our jobs for the same reason. Yes, I think I'd like to retire."

* — * — * — * — * — * —

The lovely ballet star, Vera Zorina, laughed when I asked whether she'd always wanted to dance.

"I'm told that I clicked my heels together as my diapers were being changed. I've had mothers come backstage and ask me to discourage their daughters from studying ballet. I always refuse. If the dancing is in them it will come out."

\* — \* — \* — \* — \* — \* —

Prima donna Mary Garden, whom I did not meet until some years after she retired as one of opera's great stars and went to live in her little house in Aberdeen, Scotland, had a brisk answer when I asked if she regretted giving up marriage for a career:

"Too busy. I didn't have time. I chose a career and I'm very glad. A husband would be a bore. I never met a man who wouldn't be, never. I like a man—his friendship and his company—but I couldn't bear one trailing after me.

"I never liked dolls or toys, only music and drama, and as a child I wrote to all the great stars, asking for their autographs. I never got one, and I was heartbroken. When I got to be an opera singer I gave autographs to everybody."

\* — \* — \* — \* — \* — \* —

Singer Jessica Dragonette: "My world was a singing world and a world to dream in, and I made my dreams come true. When you have no more dreams, no more world flourishes for you. The secret is *faith*. The whole world is singing. Your song is your speaking on the air, Mary Margaret."

\* — \* — \* — \* — \* — \* —

Playwright Channing Pollock, who said he was never unhappy for as much as a whole hour in his entire life: "I can't understand how an intelligent person can be unhappy," he insisted. "I'm happy because I work seven days a week, seventeen hours a day. A man is happy as long as he's in love with something or somebody. I'm going to die with my boots on. I've got them beside my bed."

\* — \* — \* — \* — \* — \* —

Author Catherine Marshall, widow of the Reverend Peter Marshall, who was Chaplain in the United States Senate: "Peter firmly believed that God could tell him what he ought to do in any given situation because he had had so many examples of that in his own life. And that was in a sense the backbone of his message to other people: that God does have a plan for each person's life and that if we found that plan we'd be happier, more successful, have peace of mind, have all the things we really long for.

"It was the basis on which we formed our marriage too. We actually prayed about whether or not we should get married. There was no question about our being in love, but we had to be sure that there was God's blessing on it and that our lives fused together would be of greater benefit than our lives apart. We both became convinced that God had placed that love in our hearts and that God's very much in favor of romance—and the romances that God plants are much much nicer than any other kind."

* — * — * — * — * — * —

Food miracle-worker Herman Smith, talking about Christmas back home in Michigan: "We always went to the barn to fetch the special sheaf of wheat my father saved for the birds. It was tied with gay ribbon and hung with bits of suet and soft bread. We hoisted it on a pole in our kitchen garden. For Christmas breakfast we had eggs fried in rosemary butter and apple pancakes with our own buckwheat honey.

"Then on watch night, New Year's Eve, it was the custom to jump from a chair into the new year, wearing your best clothes and with money in your pocket. On New Year's Day we children went calling, carrying sprigs of laurel or evergreen. At our farmhouse the children callers left their sprigs in a wicker basket on a marble-topped table in the hall and were then given a new penny and a heart-shaped cookie with the year numerals on it in pink icing.

"Lady callers on New Year's were given thimble-size glasses of strawberry and cowslip wine. The men were fortified with glasses of whisky, hot water, lemon peel, and spices."

* — * — * — * — * — * —

Erle Stanley Gardner, king of mystery-story writers, when I asked him if he enjoyed doing the Perry Mason stories, answered: "If I didn't enjoy them I wouldn't do them. I believe in doing work you're enthusiastic about instead of getting work to do and then trying to generate the enthusiasm for it. When I named Perry Mason, I wanted something that meant strength and ruggedness. I thought of Mason be-

cause it had something to do with stone and Perry went nicely with
it."

\* — \* — \* — \* — \* — \* —

Said author Cid Ricketts Sumner: "The worst tragedy would be to
have to say of life at your last gasp, 'Oh, was *that* all there was to it!'
Each period of life has to be lived not only fully but used as a preparation for the next period. Every young person should look ahead and
find something to be interested in doing when he is old and alone.
I have my writing, and that keeps me from being an interfering
mother-in-law and grandmother. But if I didn't write I would hang
paper, make dresses or model them, or maybe I'd go back to medical
school and finish my course."

Cid Ricketts Sumner's rugged eight-point credo for life is this.
"*Legs:* It's the legs that go back on you. Use your legs. Don't let them
jellify or ossify. Keep going. Walk, ride, go up and down stairs fast.
Never mind if it kills you. *Things:* Don't be a slave to them. Your
heirs and assigns will probably throw out most of that junk you
cherish. Better do it yourself. *Memories:* Throw them out too. Go live
in a new place. Here is a new life, a different one. Never think back
or regret. Go ahead. *Friends:* Don't give up the old ones, but make one
good new one every year—one real friend, not just an acquaintance.
*Work:* If you don't know how to do anything, learn. Never stop learning. My mother took up the violin at seventy-nine. *Perspective:* Now
is the time to get a good look at life and try to see what it's all about.
If you're ever going to have any sense it will be now. This is quite
exciting, figuring out things and taking a long look. *Time:* It is precious
now as never before. Use it. Do quickly the things you've always
wanted to do 'sometime.' *Risks:* Take them. It's the young who should
be cautious. They have so much to lose. Live dangerously."

\* — \* — \* — \* — \* — \* —

Father of the blues, W. C. Handy, on the day before his birthday
and mine, November 16, telling about how he wrote "St. Louis Blues":
"That song seemed to spring right out of nowhere. In just one evening
at the piano I wrote it. Only it didn't *really* spring from nowhere. It
sprang out of all that misery years before when I slept in vacant lots
or on the cobblestones of the Mississippi levee. I had to keep my feet
moving because the police could pick up a sleeping man for vagrancy

and they had a test—if your eyes were closed and your feet still, they could arrest you; you were a bum. But if you kept your feet swinging you got away with it. The boys in the poolroom used to tell me that the minute I heard those official steps my feet began swinging. I envied one man with a glass eye because he'd pull his hat over his good eye and there would be the glass one wide awake when the cops came."

\* — \* — \* — \* — \* — \* —

General MacArthur's biographers, Frank Kelley and Cornelius Ryan, are telling about the time MacArthur was turned down at West Point because of physical difficulties: "His mother would have none of it. For a full year she put her son through a regimen of exercises. He applied again and West Point admitted him. He led his class."

\* — \* — \* — \* — \* — \* —

Colonel Bernt Balchen, explorer and pioneer polar flier, who offered to fly me over the North Pole himself way back in the winter of 1950, talking about how he got to be an American citizen: "I'd been trying to hurry things up, for my time in this country was nearly over. Then one day a man handed me a sealed envelope containing an order for my deportation. Depressed, I was sitting in my hotel room when the telephone rang. Congressman Fiorello La Guardia said: 'I've just introduced a special bill in Congress to make you a United States citizen.'"

\* — \* — \* — \* — \* — \* —

Dr. Norman Vincent Peale, best-selling author of books that have helped millions and famous pastor of Marble Collegiate Church, about his childhood: "The kids called me skinny, and that bothered me no end. I didn't want to be skinny and I was a preacher's son, too, and they sort of take it out on you for that. They gave me the feeling all the time that I was some special type of person that had to be different. I worked my head off to get over that thin business—ate thousands of chocolate sundaes and pies and cakes, but it did no good. I stayed thin until I got to be about thirty years of age, when I burst at the seams. I got very fat and then had to go to work to take off forty pounds, so I've always had problems with my avoirdupois. That was part of my inferiority complex."

\* — \* — \* — \* — \* — \* —

*Life* photographer Margaret Bourke-White describing her audience with Joseph Stalin: "When I came into the room I was looking up because I'd seen all those enormous statues of him and thought he'd be as tall as a mountain. But I had to look down, because Stalin was an inch shorter than I. His mustache had a kind of chewed-up, straw-like look. He was gray and tired and his cheeks were pock-marked. Most pictures you see are retouched and the pock marks removed. I was nervous but I kept saying to myself, 'Now talk to Joe as you would to anybody else. Just tell him to sit down and look natural.'

"Once I had to crawl on hands and knees to get from one low camera angle to another, and Stalin burst out laughing when I did it. But when he stopped laughing, his face became granite again—as if a veil had fallen over it.

"I went back to my hotel and worked all night developing the prints. They were shelling all night, and I was afraid something would happen and I'd lose my film."

* — * — * — * — * — * —

Jesse Stuart, Kentucky poet, telling what it was like when he came home to the hills: " 'Chickens come home to roost,' my mother told me. I did too, and that country never looked as good to me as then. The dogwood blossoms were a little whiter, the redbud a little pinker, the water in the streams a little bluer. It was then I began writing poems as I never had before. I was away from college, away from towns, back to the life I knew. I was home—and the poems came to me. I wrote forty-two in a half day and never revised them."

* — * — * — * — * — * —

Christopher Isherwood, author: "Yes, I really wanted to get sent down from Cambridge, and I did too. It was a terrible thing to do, but I've never regretted it. What I did was write answers to an important examination in verse and limericks—any rubbish that came into my head—because I had this problem of getting myself expelled at all costs. To one solemn question I wrote: 'I really can't answer this question because I am so bothered by this room; there's something hanging from the ceiling that distracts me, and that portrait of Prince Albert on the wall!' After this book was written I got word that I was forgiven and would be received back."

* — * — * — * — * — * —

John Mason Brown, author, lecturer, and critic, after traveling for some days with candidates for the presidency—Eisenhower and Stevenson: "It's been a wonderful experience, not only from the point of view of a political lesson but in seeing an America that I have never seen before. As a lecturer I have traveled all over the country, but an America that is exercising the privilege of choice is different. When you see these people—pouring out in front of silos, at whistle stops and Civil War monuments—that have probably listened to more campaign oratory than any figures in the world; and when you see, as once I saw with General Eisenhower late at night—we were going toward Aurora in a motorcade past a little farmhouse—a family on the road lighting a bonfire and holding up the children in the dark to see what was a symbol of choice as the general drove by—well, it is a terrifically exciting, eye-opening and mind-stretching experience."

\* — \* — \* — \* — \* — \* —

Playwright Robert E. Sherwood (he came often to the program) talking about a typographical error that wasn't. "Lots of people wrote in because of what they thought was a typographical error in one of my books. I was writing about Harry Hopkins and General Marshall when they were in Scotland waiting for a plane in a tiny village. They were on a secret mission and nobody in the Scottish village knew who they were or why they were there. Harry went to a telephone booth in the little inn where they were staying and said to the operator, 'Get me the President of the United States in the White House in Washington, D.C.' Instead she notified the local police that there was a maniac loose.

"Hopkins, getting no result on the Washington call, requested: 'Get me Winston Churchill at 10 Downing Street in London.' Then the telephone operator was sure he was crazy. The police were moving in, and I commented in the book: '*unfortunately* General Marshall and Harry Hopkins were not arrested!' My critics thought it was a typographical error—that I meant to say fortunately, but I didn't. I meant unfortunately because if they *had* been arrested it would have made a much better story for me to write!"

\* — \* — \* — \* — \* — \* —

Will Durant, historian and author, told me the first gossip columnist was probably Pietro Aratino, who used to threaten kings, emperors, popes with items which would turn their hair white, unless they sent him gifts.

"They were all afraid of him—Francis I, Charles V, even Clement VII all took care of him very nicely."

Talking seriously, Dr. Durant declared that civilization doesn't die, it migrates. "The Renaissance isn't dead. It ended as a period in Italy, but much of it is alive today. I could use up five lifetimes studying it and still be an amateur on the subject. We Americans spend too much time learning what went on in the past twenty-four hours and not enough finding out what happened in the past six thousand years. The result is, no matter how well informed we are about current events, we haven't the background of knowledge with which to understand them. We are choked with news and starved of history."

\* — \* — \* — \* — \* — \* —

Madeleine Carroll, about what the war had done for her: "As an actress you are very remote and away from people. You are built up by publicity departments to be some strange creature, to be looked at from afar. You lose contact with humanity, which is a sad thing and a bad thing for anybody. During the war I learned, like many people, the basic truth—that we're all part of one another; that we can't live without each other. The GI was as useful to me as I was to him. If I helped him, he helped me even more."

\* — \* — \* — \* — \* — \* —

Faye Emerson, actress, writer, television star, and one of my favorite people in all the world: "I know the feeling of the little girl who was crying, and when her distressed mother asked her why, wailed: 'I'm just so afraid I'll grow up not to say what I mean, like you and Aunt Kate!'"

\* — \* — \* — \* — \* — \* —

Emily Kimbrough, popular lecturer and writer, another of my favorites, telling about lecturing and especially about an English professor who came to her hotel room to borrow a copy of *The Atlantic Monthly*: "With no warning, standing there in the middle of my room, he launched into a speech which I can only describe as highly personal. He was short and plump—and not young. But his voice had depths of emotion that jarred both of us. He was magnificent in his pauses and his long dependent clauses. I couldn't think of a single answer except, 'No, thank you,' and I said that in a sort of awful falsetto so that I could clear my throat and say it again. I turned my back and stared out the window, hoping he would go away. To my intense relief I heard him walk across the room, then a door slammed.

"Immediately there was a great thrashing in my clothes closet. Before he came I'd hung some underwear in there to dry, and as he emerged, head down, from the closet—which he had mistaken for the exit door—I saw dangling down his back three of my precious nylon stockings and my best brassiere."

*—*—*—*—*—*—

The one time I diet is when I have to speak in public. That's because I'm too scared to swallow. One night in Kansas City when I had to make a speech I found myself sitting beside ex-President Harry Truman.

"Eat a little," he urged, "it'll do you good." He added comfortingly, "Everybody feels like that."

"Not you?" I asked in astonishment, remembering how calm he always seemed.

The former president nodded, and suddenly I felt so much better that I choked down a little chicken.

"How long do you think anybody should talk?" I asked, and hung on his answer, which came quickly: "From twenty to forty minutes, and nearer twenty than forty."

*—*—*—*—*—*—

Columnist Hedda Hopper, about her mother visiting Hollywood: "Mother was quite deaf. When I introduced her to Hedy Lamarr she looked at her and said, 'You're a very pretty girl; you should be in the movies.' And I said, 'Mother, this is Hedy Lamarr.' And she said, 'Well, she could change her name. You did.'

"One night we went to Ciro's with Edgar Bergen and Ken Murray. Mother ordered milk so I did, too, and the waiters almost dropped dead. Of course she hadn't caught our hosts' names, but next morning she said, 'Darling, I suppose they were celebrated people we were with last night,' and when I told her she looked blank so I said, 'You know, Charlie McCarthy.' She said, 'Was it now? Why, he doesn't look a bit like he sounds!' You see, she'd heard Charlie McCarthy on the radio, but Edgar Bergen never entered her consciousness. She said, 'Ken Murray looked so sad for a funnyman.' I told her, 'Mother, all funnymen look sad.'"

\* — \* — \* — \* — \* — \* —

Prima donna Lotte Lehmann: "My fondest memory, and earliest, is of a lovely spring day. I was in the park and saw my mother approaching at the end of a long path. I remember being filled with the beauty of the day and thinking as I ran to Mother, 'This is spring. This is beautiful.' And that has been in my life always. In spring, especially, this picture comes back to me—running into the arms of my mother at the end of that path."

\* — \* — \* — \* — \* — \* —

Joe Laurie, Jr., talking about Dr. Cook, the explorer. "Vaudevillians didn't believe in him. Why? He was supposed to have been to the North Pole, and yet when he went to Hammerstein's to appear in vaudeville he told the stage manager his dressing room at the theater was too cold!"

\* — \* — \* — \* — \* — \* —

Al Capp, creator of Li'l Abner: "I'm a simple guy, actually, not complicated at all as the stories have me. Many interviewers come to me with a preconceived idea, and as soon as I sense that and feel they'll be comfortable if I affirm their ideas, I do. I'm just genial to them. I want to turn out exactly the kind of guy they hope I am. I don't want them to have to work too hard on their stories.

"They like me to have been poor, but when I was a boy we ate occasionally so I guess we were just moderately poor. My mother was a tremendous woman, and one of the reasons I look at you so fascinatedly is that you have her coloring—your hair is like hers, her eyes were bright and dark brown like yours. She was a remarkable woman, enormously practical, so that she rejected everyone else's practicality as concerned me, her oldest son and the hope of her family, when I decided I wanted to be an artist.

"That was a blow to all my relatives, who felt no artist could ever make a living. However, my mother insisted I go to art school, and it was because of her and a series of miracles she performed that I went as far as I did. She followed my strip very carefully; I really don't think she read it. She was the kind of person who wanted something gripping, and here I was drawing all these strange creatures. I don't think she understood it, probably thought it was a little silly, but she realized that other people understood the drawings and she was grateful for that.

"Occasionally she had a criticism. Once she looked at a Sunday page of mine and said, 'Alfred, don't you think you used too many words in this one? Why didn't you save a few for next Sunday?' Another time she said, 'Now, Alf, you're doing well. Why don't you get these people some clothes?'

"My wife has a curious attitude toward my strip. Whenever it gets lusty or violent she lectures. She's afraid that the neighbors at Southampton might not think well of our family if the head of it can draw such mayhem and violence in a comic strip."

\* — \* — \* — \* — \* — \* —

Will Rogers, Jr., and his wife Collier, telling of the unloading from the *Exodus* at Cyprus: "Collier was one of 144 newspaper correspondents, and all were astonished at the British display of military might when the *Exodus* tried to unload the refugees. At the dock they saw three thousand British soldiers fully armed, piles of tear-gas cannisters, gun carriers, lorries full of ammunition, piles of fire hose rigged up; a cordon was thrown around the docks with hundreds and hundreds of soldiers standing elbow to elbow with truncheons and guns ready.

"Then when we got permission, after much censorship, to get to the dockside to see the boat brought alongside, there coming down the gangplank was what all this British military might was geared to club —men, women, and children but mostly women, children, and old people. They were very tired. They'd been two months in the slimy hold of these cargo ships. They hadn't been on deck for two months because there was no room—little children with tear-stained faces, men holding infants in arms, and then the lines of unconscious. Seventy people came off on stretchers, some bound down with raincoats, so we couldn't see the conditions of their skulls. Some streamed blood; children streamed blood from their knees and wrists. There was hatred on their faces, and grief and pain. The British were clubbing them on the gangplank as they came down, nudging them with truncheons."

\* — \* — \* — \* — \* — \* —

Dancer Pearl Primus, back from Africa: "I carried no beads, no gifts but the gift of my heart. When I smiled they knew it meant 'I love you.' I danced with them too; there is no audience, everybody is part of the dance. I learned their dances by letting them embrace me so I could feel the movements of their muscles. Each person is given one note to hum or chant which will fit into the whole pattern of the group.

"Truth is truth whether through the dance or through singing or from a person bringing the spoken message, and in these times, when the world is so upset, if I can bring the truth of these people, with their beauty, to Americans, I am happy."

\* — \* — \* — \* — \* — \* —

From an interview with attorney Arthur Garfield Hays, champion of underdogs: "Everybody's being pushed around one way or another, and the only protection you have in life is to live in a democracy where at least the government has no legal right to push you around. It's bad enough that society can do it. 'The human being,' Clarence Darrow once said, when defending some poor person he thought was being pushed around unjustly, 'is made up of stuff that you'd pay ninety cents for in a drugstore.' Once when we were defending some Negroes charged with murder and he was expressing his usual philosophy that it didn't make any difference whether they were sent to jail for life or not, Clarence Darrow said: 'After all, in life there's a certain line of habit—anything above that line gives you pleasure, anything below that line makes you depressed.' He said it doesn't make any difference where that line is—if these people go to jail for life and their habits are formed that way, they get the same reactions from things that are pleasurable and things that are annoying. So I asked: 'Clarence, if you feel that way why do you sear your life out defending these folks?' And he said: 'Well, you know, I've often wondered about that. I just feel I'd be uncomfortable if I didn't!' "

\* — \* — \* — \* — \* — \* —

Author Roger Butterfield, who had just compiled *The American Past:* "President Grant was fond of driving fast horses. One day on a Washington street a policeman stopped him and realized it was the President. Then he tried to apologize, but Grant insisted on surrendering the vehicle and asked that he be arrested just like any other citizen who drove a fast horse. The policeman refused to arrest him but confiscated his horse and wagon. Grant walked home from the police station!

"President Wilson wrote his message to Congress calling for the war on Germany on a portable typewriter, picking it out with one finger [although Billy Rose elsewhere in this book says President Wilson was good at shorthand]. He couldn't sleep afterward and sat on the veranda of the White House with a glass of milk late that night in April 1917."

* — * — * — * — * — * —

I said to John Gunther, famous author of the "Inside" books: "My favorite book of yours is *Death Be Not Proud,* the memoir of your son Johnny, who died at seventeen of a brain tumor. Your other work will live as history, John, but Johnny's book—— Well, do you remember his three wishes? His first was for happiness, his second for an extra week's vacation, but his third was to do some good in the world. And I wouldn't be surprised if Johnny wouldn't do more good for the world through his book than all the other things you've ever written."

John: "That book about Johnny was really his book. I was very little more than just a medium transferring things he had said and done to paper. Nine tenths of it is his own conversation, so it was really written by him."

* — * — * — * — * — * —

Cleveland Amory, social historian: "The first gigolos came into being at Long Branch, New Jersey, where ladies hired them to help them when they were in the water and couldn't swim . . . A house with a hundred rooms in the mountains was considered a cottage by Mrs. Stuyvesant Fish and her set. One son telegraphed his mother to say he was bringing ninety-six boys from Yale home for the weekend. She telegraphed back: 'Many guests already here. Have only room for fifty.'

"When an important guest once came to Newport, Mrs. Fish said: 'Oh, I'd quite forgotten I'd asked you.' Once she coughed on leaving the house and her husband said, 'Can I get you something for your throat, my dear?' She answered, 'Yes, you can—that diamond and pearl necklace I saw at Tiffany's yesterday.'"

* — * — * — * — * — * —

Benjamin A. Javits, brother of Senator Jacob Javits, who had a plan for peace: "My idea is to build the world as we did the United States; to take the same ingredients we discovered here as being so marvelous for constructing a new civilization. The elements we now have in this country will do the job—faith, affection, know-how, skill, manpower, and money. How do people live in countries where the standard of living is low? They live on hope. We've got to give hope to the world, and with that goes a sense of security. If we win the cold war we've tied to us the peoples who have been uncertain where to go, what to do."

\* — \* — \* — \* — \* — \* —

Lloyd C. Douglas told us how he happened to write his best seller *The Robe*. "I had a letter from a saleswoman in a department store in Ohio, and she asked if I'd ever heard what happened to Jesus' robe after the soldiers cast lots for it. I answered that I hadn't but I'd try to find out. I sent the woman every chapter of the book that answered her question and kept up with her for a long time after that."

Douglas' father was a country preacher. "We got eighteen gallons of apple butter at a donation party one time, and my mother mournfully demanded, 'What'll I do with it all?' My father said, 'We'll paint the barn with it!'

"My father would rather I'd swear than make a mistake in grammar. He said, 'You can cure a boy of saying *damn* but not *have went!*'"

\* — \* — \* — \* — \* — \* —

Historian Carl Van Doren: "Just as the states in our early days needed something that would do away with their quarreling, sovereignties, jealousies, and ignorance about each other, so I feel very strongly that the countries of the world are in a somewhat similar predicament and that the United Nations is a great rehearsal in the United States for a *real* United Nations."

In his middle-western childhood, Carl read all the books he could get at. "We read greedily and uncritically. The whole Van Doren family grew up in the village of Hope, Illinois, not many miles from the farm my grandfather had carved out with five yoke of oxen from the prairie sod. None of us knew or cared about literary chronology. Books for us were like stars, all looking the same from a distance, only some shining brighter than others. Books were to us the experiences we couldn't have in our small town. But when we did come to travel, later on, we knew a surprising number of things. Books had enlarged our village."

* — * — * — * — * — * —

Years ago I began having Willy Ley, rocket and space expert, more as a joke than because I believed his weird predictions. I asked him then:

"What would it be like to go to the moon?" His answer: "You'd go of course by rocket. You'd have to imagine a future spaceship shaped somewhat like the Viking Rockets—large cylindrical things with tailfins at the end taking off vertically. They accelerate, starting off if possible at the top of a mountain and if possible near the equator, because there the earth turns fastest on its axis and you can utilize this speed which you get from the earth's turning—Mother Earth's last gift to her probing child, this speed of turning. It's quite high; it amounts to about twelve hundred feet per second. Well, you're in this ship, probably flat on your back on something that might be called a mattress, only it's a highly scientific variety with all the shock-absorbing devices which engineers can think up. You weigh about four times as much as you do normally, at least you feel that in the first seven or eight minutes, depending on a number of factors too complicated to mention here. After this period of acceleration is over, you are moving with a velocity of about seven miles per second and then an instrument shuts the fuel flow off automatically and all of a sudden you are weightless—you don't weigh an ounce—everything then moves in the same direction and is no longer subject to gravitation or strain.

"The remainder of the trip to the moon from the earth would be just coasting—ninety-six hours of it to be precise—four days. In these four days you would not experience any gravity at all—you would feel very light. You might feel hungry because your stomach is perfectly empty, but you would still have no desire to eat anything."

* — * — * — * — * — * —

I told John K. Hutchens, daily book reviewer of the New York *Herald Tribune*, about my unrealized ambition in the twenties to be a great writer. He said: "The twenties were full of people who tried to write, and fortunately a lot of them did. It was an era that started with the end of the war and ended with the big crash. The freedom and individualism came to a disastrous stop. In the thirties writers began following more or less political and sociological lines in their writing—they tended to conform.

"If you lived through the twenties it's almost impossible not to feel a particular affection for them. As Edmund Wilson has said: 'There was a lot of waste and nonsense, but the best that was done was awfully good and a great influence on later writers.'

"The good things about the little magazines of that day was that they gave a chance to everybody who wanted to be a writer to appear in print. A great number got their start that way—Hemingway and Sherwood Anderson among them. Even if they only lasted an issue or two those magazines were marvelous for the thrill they gave new writers to see their work set down.

"You can get homesick for the twenties looking back at newspapers of those times, too—F.P.A.'s 'Conning Tower,' in which contributions from Edna St. Vincent Millay and Dorothy Parker were printed. Then there was Christopher Morley's 'Bowling Green,' Don Marquis' 'Sun Dial,' and all those wonderful Chicago columnists who criticized, commented, and published readers' letters.

"The satire in the twenties was a reaction to the extreme materialism and disillusion that followed World War I. Strange things happened to that satire. Sinclair Lewis was satirizing the small-town businessman in *Babbitt*, and yet you came to feel Lewis liked *Babbitt* very much—at least I got that feeling when I reread *Babbitt*."

\* — \* — \* — \* — \* — \* —

Franc and Jean Shor, writers who have traveled everywhere and found a Shangri-la—a place where nobody's poor, they have no taxes, no army—Hunza. Jean said: "In Hunza they work all day but they are happy and there is no crime. . . .

"I saw Casino just after it was bombed, and I hope never again will I see such utter destruction. I feel they should have put a wall around it and left it just as it was. It would have been impressive in future years to see what the results of war can be."

\* — \* — \* — \* — \* — \* —

Novelist Zora Neale Hurston, talking about her childhood feeling about the moon: "I run and the moon follows me. I thought I was special and I was shocked when I found other people making the same claim on the moon."

Zora, on a rather different subject: "In 1936, in Haiti, I photographed a living, moving woman whom death and burial records showed to have been dead since 1907."

\* — \* — \* — \* — \* — \* —

Gracie Fields on success: "I taught myself to sing by playing the records of Caruso, Galli-Curci, and others . . . My rules for life? Just be honest—don't look at things through too rose-colored glasses. Work hard—you can't just sit back. Be fair—you can't grab from somebody and succeed."

\* — \* — \* — \* — \* — \* —

Maurice Evans had flown from Hollywood and forfeited big money to do a revival of Shakespeare's *Richard II* at the City Center, where everybody works at minimum salary. I asked if anybody ever ad-libbed Shakespeare.

Maurice said yes: "Remember the famous speech—'This blessed plot, this earth, this realm, this England . . . is now leased out . . . like to a tenement or a pelting farm . . .' Well, one well-known actor got to that line and the word 'tenement' went completely out of his head. But he never faltered: 'Is now leased out like to a phonograph,' he said. The word phonograph has the same number of syllables as tenement and nobody in the audience noticed.

"Another time I was in a production of *Antony and Cleopatra* at the Old Vic. We'd been rehearsing our next play, *Julius Caesar*, all day long and we were tired. Came the scene where a character finds Cleopatra, her crown awry, dead. This performer, entering, went at once into a long scene from *Julius Caesar*. Cleopatra startled, opened one eye in surprise. But he went right through with the speech he had started. The other actors let him finish, then continued with *Antony and Cleopatra*. If the audience knew, it made no demonstration."

\* — \* — \* — \* — \* — \* —

My own observation: Little Jeannie Helmericks, who spent her beginning years with her explorer parents, Bud and Constance Helmericks, in the Far North, pines for such delicacies as agutuk, Eskimo ice cream made of warm bear's grease poured over whole cranberries and frozen. "And of course *all* children love raw frozen fish eyes," said her father casually (the Helmericks were frequent guests), adding that you never have to coax a child to eat what's good for it in the polar lands. "A finicky child is such a nuisance," he finished.

\* — \* — \* — \* — \* — \* —

Fulton Oursler, whom I had known first as a rather sophisticated, hard-boiled editor, telling about his search for a better life: "I had that kind of contented agnosticism; I thought I was just fine—I didn't know I was bitter or discouraged. Live today because tomorrow you die. Oh yes, you would be honest up to a point where it hurt, but then you'd start telling yourself you had to be realistic because you had your family to think about and principle became something less and less important and expediency became not always the wisest thing but the smart thing. Yet I found all those years that nothing really satisfied me.

"I looked forward to a wonderful time, and when I got there it wasn't as wonderful as I expected. There was always a letdown, and I was always hoping that the next time it would be a perfect experience. Life was a disappointment. That sums it up. And it became increasingly tasteless.

"It was a fortunate thing for me that some unhappy things happened to me. We have to hit bottom before we can start for the top if we are stubborn and learn hard. As I began to change I didn't say I believe in God or that I want to believe in God, but at least I got as far as to say I want to want to believe in God. That is all a man needs. If he has an impulse to seek the truth and to look for infinity and to ask if this is a mad, schemeless world or does it have law and order and justice and wisdom and mercy in it; if he applies himself to that as a willing partaker and is willing to contribute to it he very soon finds the answer. And once having found the answer, life is not tasteless any more and experiences are greater than one's expectations and one looks on life with completely new senses and the experience of living becomes an experience of being close to a Divine Father whose relationship to one is an intensification and a glorification of a relationship with an earthly father who is kind and loving."

\* — \* — \* — \* — \* — \* —

Ruth Chatterton, actress and writer, on how she got started acting: "I was introduced to the manager of a stock company in Washington when I was twelve. I had put my hair up and pretended to be sixteen. I got the job and a rise in salary after the first week—from five to ten dollars—and was on my way. Henry Miller's son saw me and wired his father: 'This is the girl you want for your daughter in *The Rainbow*'—and they hired me by telephone. Later I was down on my luck and had made five tests in Hollywood. Then Joe Sternberg was showing the one he had made and Emil Jannings waddled down the aisle, kissed the screen, and rumbled: 'Ziss is za voman I vill!' And that's how I got started in the movies."

* — * — * — * — * — * —

Actor Charles Laughton discussing accents: "I learned in England to talk American for a play by listening all night to a recording of President Wilson but decided not to take the job because America would think I was faking. I turned down the family hotel business to go into the theater. My mother—my word, she's a sparky old dame—taught me staunchness, steadfastness, and determination to build my own life. She's a real old terror and I adore her."

* — * — * — * — * — * —

Quentin Reynolds: "In my life I think I've only met three brave men—men who seem to have been born without fear. *One*, Father Callahan—his absence of fear was founded completely on faith. *Two*, Jimmy Doolittle, who carries religion in his heart. He is without fear because he calculates every risk to a mathematical certainty, without emotion. *Three*, Sidney Bernstein, a civilian in England, partner of Alfred Hitchcock, so intent on his own work that he was too busy to bother with bombings in London."

* — * — * — * — * — * —

James Michener of *South Pacific*, in 1951, talking about the Polynesian fault-finder who cried out: " 'Why hasn't the governor supplied social services for our Polynesian Islands?' And the governor replied: 'We have not provided old-age pensions because in Polynesia old people are cared for; we haven't put orphanages there because no child is without a home; we have no mental hospitals because Polynesian life doesn't produce nervous breakdowns; and we don't need unemployment insurance because no islander would see his brother starve.'

"It's all true and it sounds like paradise. But anyone living in any society has to weigh the good against the bad and pray to heaven the good outweighs the bad. I certainly wouldn't change my life in New York for any tropical island right now, because, balancing it out, they do live in an enormous backwater and we live where the future history of the world is being written. Since life is pretty short, I think I'll go along with the people who are writing history. When I am older and worn out I might like living on a Pacific Island very much, but I think a good many people who believe they would like to right now have to make the basic decision about what's good in their life and what's bad in that other.

"Polynesians are a dying race, a race absorbed by other peoples. They dance to other people's music, and they're caught up in a conflict of wanting to hold on to their old way of life which they like very much and also wanting the new way which they also like."

* — * — * — * — * — * —

Janet Flanner, *The New Yorker* columnist in France: "The English don't educate princes very well to be kings, but they are nervous about women so they carefully educate a princess to be a queen."

* — * — * — * — * — * —

Lillian Smith, author of *Strange Fruit*, speaking in November 1945 about discrimination: "A human being cannot be shunned, discriminated against, looked down upon without great injury to his personality. A life full of social shame, social shunning, breeds feelings of shame, despair, hate, frustration that even the strongest, the heathiest personality, the most stable nerves cannot long endure. Sometimes I wonder how long Negroes can maintain their self-control, their equanimity, their forbearance, their sanity. The quick sure road to disaster is hate, despair, and loss of faith."

* — * — * — * — * — * —

John Crosby, radio and television columnist: "I think I'm quite a gentle critic, and I hope I don't fall into the pitfall of unfairness just for effect. I have drawers full of notes on programs neither bad nor good enough to be commented on. I cannot think of anything I've ever written that I would want to take back."

\* — \* — \* — \* — \* — \* —

Nobel prize winner Sigrid Undset, during World War II: "The American elm is one of the most graceful trees I've ever seen anywhere, and streets lined with elms are too beautiful for words . . . In my country, Norway, we have long winters, short summers, very little arable land, and very rocky, stormy shores; but we have built a good life with kind people and standards of decency. We've been exiles during the war and we've been given much to do—the young people and the old at home who were born to face the tortures of their oppressors. What I want more than anything in the world is for my country to be free and swept clean from the forces of evil."

\* — \* — \* — \* — \* — \* —

Edward R. Hewitt, seventy-eight-year-old grandson of Peter Cooper, talking about the horseless carriages: "Mrs. Hamilton Fish, who lived on Gramercy Park, bought a fine-looking electric open car. We saw it delivered at her house. A demonstrator showed her how to run it. The lever which turned on the power was at the driver's side. All you had to do was to push the lever forward to go forward and back to go backward, and keep it upright in order to stand still. This was simplicity itself; but the makers did not know Mrs. Fish.

"She started out alone toward Third Avenue. Just as she had got going, a big man crossed in front of the car. She tried to slow down, but pushed the lever forward, making the car speed forward. The car hit the man and knocked him down. Mrs. Fish then tried to stop the car; but she moved the lever too far back, so the car backed slowly and ran over the man again. This got her rattled. Again she moved the lever too far forward, and ran over him once more. This time the man sprang up and yelled: ''Fore God, ma'am, you sure are goin' to run over me!' He disappeared around the corner at high speed, and was never seen again. Mrs. Fish left the car right there, and this was the only ride she ever had in it."

\* — \* — \* — \* — \* — \* —

Meredith Willson, telling about sounds he remembers from his Iowa childhood: "The old flatiron you put between your knees and

cracked black walnuts and hickory nuts on with the old family hammer. And Mama scraping the burnt toast when you came down in
the morning in your long winter underwear."

\* — \* — \* — \* — \* — \* —

Mari Sandoz wrote a thrilling biography about her pioneer father,
*Old Jules,* who had, said one critic, "a spirit as fierce and tenacious
as the American eagle." She gave me cold shivers when she told me:
"My father had warned these two men to keep off his place, but the
much traveled road, the only road in the valley, ran through our yard.
So the two men came riding and my father saw them. Shaking with
anger, he limped to the house, grabbed his rifle, and pushed his head
out of the door as they stopped at the gate.

" 'Hello,' they called. But there was no greeting in Old Jules. 'I
told you to keep off my place!' he yelled. 'This is a public road,' they
told him.

"My father jerked his rifle to his shoulder. 'I told you to keep off.
Now you git it!' But as his finger jerked on the trigger I struck the
barrel upward. There was a report, an echo, and the sound of horses
running hard.

"Jules ejected the steaming cartridge from the chamber, drove another into place. Then he whirled upon me. For a long moment the
two frozen eyes looked down the blued barrel an inch from my chest. I
stood frozen in fear. Suddenly he dropped the rifle across his arm,
pushed his cap back, and limped out of the house, across the yard,
and up the yellow slope out of sight."

\* — \* — \* — \* — \* — \* —

Spinster Nell Snead, of the Kansas City *Star,* with a wonderful
sense of humor and proportion, said to me half jokingly one day (but
I agree with her wholeheartedly): "Every woman ought to be allowed
one baby and no questions asked."

**Part III**  *HOME*

## 22.  TRAGEDY

When I came back from Norway in the summer of 1953, I found Stella Karn sick. Unbeknownst to me, she had been ailing when I went away and that was why she had asked Cynthia Lowry to go with me. In February 1954 she had an operation.

It was cancer, the doctor told me, and, while the operation was successful, he was not sure about the future. I pleaded with him not to let her know, at least not right away. But on his very first visit after she was conscious, she got it out of him and also learned that I had tried to keep it from her. She gave me such a dressing down as I had seldom had from her.

She said, "I want the truth. I have to know what's the matter and I have to face it. You must never lie to me again or let anyone else—promise!" So I promised and nobody ever did lie to her again. Through all her nearly four years of suffering she knew everything the doctors knew about her case.

It was she who decided we must give up the program. I'd thought of it but hadn't dared to suggest it for fear of hurting her pride. She didn't admit even then that she was too sick to go on. Rather she said I needed a rest after twenty years of broadcasting, that she was sick of fighting with an executive at ABC who annoyed her. I agreed and suggested that our twentieth anniversary in May would be the perfect time to close the program. So it was decided that after May 15 we would no longer be on the air.

Most of our other beginnings and endings had sent Stella into a mad revel of publicity and preparation. This time she let others plan. Our dear Gene Leone persuaded me that it must be a party with food, and he brought magnificent squabs, lobsters, shrimp, ham, great salads, fruit, and cheese with a staff of waiters from Leone's to see that everybody was superbly fed. Other friends wanted to come, too, and so I let them. But instead of choosing the biggest possible place, we had our farewell in my apartment facing the park from which I had been broadcasting during the years at ABC.

The guests waited upstairs until each was called down to broadcast. Everybody was crying. There were gifts and poems and compliments, but it was not gay. President Kintner of ABC came to say he was sorry we were leaving. My radio family and special friends were all there: Stella, Mrs. Deichler, Janice, Nikki, Hattie, Tex and Jinx, Ben Gross, Jane Redfield, Fannie Hurst, John and Margaret Kieran, Alec Templeton (he read a poem), Patricia Collinge, John Golden (he sang a song dedicated to me), John Farrar, and Myra Washington. Wes Gallagher of the Associated Press (I was doing a column for him) was there, and on hand to represent my two oldest sponsors were Fred W. Meyer and Morris Scheck. Imra Mirante, who had interviewed me when she was a schoolgirl, talked about that interview. My godson, Calvin Lee, of whom I am so proud, made a sweet little speech. Finally, Dr. Norman Vincent Peale said a prayer. There is a candid-camera picture of the last few moments. I am sobbing with my head bowed on the broadcasting table. The clock behind says one minute to two.

We dried our tears eventually and ate Gene's wonderful food. But we were still not gay. We knew it was the end of something we'd greatly cared about.

John Farrar arranged a party for me that week to which the publishers came. They gave me a citation because they said I had helped sell a lot of books in the twenty years. They all paid me compliments, and John Hutchens wrote a beautiful quarter of a page about my interviews. In a way it was like going to my own funeral.

After the party I went up to Stella's farm in the Catskills and tried to relax, but I couldn't. I had trouble sleeping and if I did finally drop off, I would jerk awake moaning from a recurring nightmare. It was always one o'clock in the dream and I could hear Vincent's voice announcing me—but although I did my best to speak, nothing came out of my paralyzed lips and I could not get on the air. My dear Dr. Anthony Tocco, who serves so well an area of fifty miles or more up here in the Catskills, finally got me calm again, but it was weeks before

I could turn on the radio or television. I couldn't bear to hear or see others doing what I wanted so much to be doing too.

At least I was busy enough, for I was writing five columns a week for the Associated Press that were being run in two hundred newspapers, and later Stella and Ted Cott fixed it up for me to tape a five-minute commentary (mostly about books) for the NBC network. It wasn't the same though. It could never be the same again, and I knew it. For Stella was dying.

Hardly anybody except those closest to her knew the truth. For a long time she had had a herniated esophagus, and when anybody asked how she was she made a dramatic and funny story of her ruptured esophagus. She didn't want pity.

The time I hurt her most, I think, was when I said to her one day (she was being stubborn), "Stella, you're just using your sickness to get your own way." An hour later she telephoned me. In a sober, rather sad voice she asked, "Do you really think I'm using my sickness to get my own way? Because I don't want to do that."

As a matter of fact, she never behaved like a sick woman. In the hospital the night she died she demanded that I give her medicine out of her own purse. That wasn't allowed in the hospital, and I tried to protest. By this time every breath for her was a major effort, but she gasped in her poor little wisp of a voice, "Yes," and I had to give her what she wanted.

During the long terrible months before her death she was taking radiation in massive doses. She'd get up at six o'clock, and by seven she'd be in the hospital. She went alone, and after the treatment was over she'd go to the office and stay until Janice could persuade her to pack up the mail and start for her hotel. They often went by bus because traffic was heavy and taxicabs were not found easily. One night on a bus an elderly woman got up and gave Stella her seat. Later Stella, with a crooked little smile, said to Janice, "I must really look sick when a gray-haired old lady gets up to let me sit down."

She insisted upon delivering herself boxes of candy that Christmas for the nurses who had helped with her treatments at the hospital. She slowly went up the stairs past the carefully sealed and guarded rooms where radiation therapy was given, saw each nurse in person, and handed out the candy—asked one about her children, another about her dog, then collapsed against a window ledge. Later one of the nurses telephoned the office and left a message. "Tell Miss Karn she's earned her vacation and we wish her a blessed Christmas. She's the bravest woman we ever knew!"

I didn't believe she was dying. Perhaps I would not believe that anybody so vital and enthusiastic about life could die. But some instinct made me close up the farm and come into town the first of January to be with her as much as she would let me. Usually I'd telephone her several times a day and come over to the Waldorf about five o'clock in the afternoon to stay until midnight. She'd lie on the bed, and I would sit in a chair close by.

Florence and Al Herman had given her a little portable television, and she liked to have it on. Sometimes we'd hardly talk at all, but it was a wonderful companionship we had then. I hardly went anywhere else those months and was miserable when I did leave her. One night someone invited me to *My Fair Lady*. Stella insisted that I go. I thought it was a wonderful show but sat with tears under my eyelids all evening because Stella couldn't see it too.

We never quarreled now, and each day I saw she was weaker. It was an effort for her even to walk to the bathroom. She ate hardly at all. Finally just before I took her to the hospital she was drinking through a straw a little Coca-Cola with milk in it. She wouldn't let us call an ambulance, though she couldn't walk. We got her downstairs in a wheel chair. She was wearing her favorite Chinese housecoat, and as usual she organized the expedition.

Janice and I packed just what she told us to—nightgown, robe, bed jacket, perfume, checkbook, notebook, pencils. She took her radio and her portable television set plus a stack of stock-market current reports and a load of magazines. As we passed through the Waldorf her favorite house detective, a huge man with a wide, red face, told her she looked fine. Stella grinned up at him and said, "I'll bet you never thought you'd see me in one of these things."

Her friends hurried to the hospital—the Hermans, the Haders, the Robisons, Myrta Ross, Poppy Cannon. Poppy brought an African doctor who had just come to New York for observation and study. She thought he would interest Stella, and he did. Every word was an agonizing drain on her ebbing strength, but she talked to the young man about his plans and before Poppy took him away asked him to come to see her at her office and was full of ideas for some letters she wanted to give him.

She told me that she thought she would be able to go to the farm in May, and I talked cheerily of what we would do. I really felt optimistic, for I believed she would be better soon. Thirty-six hours later she was dead.

The housekeeper at the Waldorf told me that the staff went into mourning when they heard the news. Stella was a tough woman and some of them had suffered from her toughness when things didn't suit her, but her generosity and gallantry under suffering had won all their hearts. Almost every group of employees sent flowers.

When it came to the service I never hesitated. It seemed to me that Stella was telling me what to do. I engaged not the largest room at the funeral parlor but a medium-sized one, because Stella believed in standing room only. "No vacant seats, baby," she always admonished. When friends telephoned I told them about the service and said to each, "I'd like you to come if you'd like to, but I don't want anybody there who doesn't actually want to be. Don't come because you think you should."

They all came. All kinds of people. Old friends of hers I'd never met, some who'd been estranged from both of us for a while—celebrities, maids and telephone girls from the hotel, even her doctors. For an hour we talked about Stella. I tried to express in words what a friend she had been to me. Jane Pickens told about how Stella put the Pickens Sisters into show business, Fannie Hurst how amusing she'd always found Stella in her long friendship with her. Ben Gross told about the time Stella had come to his office and asked him to give me another chance. Eddie Dowling read a psalm, Dr. Emory Ross said a prayer; we laughed and we cried. There were banks of flowers—and people were standing in the aisles. I knew Stella would have liked it.

After Stella died everybody tried to help me. Beautiful Poppy Cannon, the best possible traveling companion because of her amiability, insisted that I go with her on a gourmet tour of Europe—Scotland, Ireland, England, Holland, France. When we came back I found that my friends in the radio and television business were outdoing one another in efforts on my behalf—Henry Jaffe, Ted Cott, Lester and Julie Lewis, who became my agents, and especially that wonderful pair, Tex and Jinx McCrary. I cannot possibly live long enough to repay the debt I owe those two. With anxious and unselfish affection they made elaborate plans for my future and ended by installing me as a permanent Friday fixture on their television show.

Every now and then I would get into a despondent mood and decide, because I felt neither of them would ever ask me to go, that I ought to leave the show. Tex would listen patiently to my muddled misgivings and then, with that way he has of lifting his head and looking directly into the eyes of the person to whom he is talking, he would say with affectionate firmness, "I'll tell you when to leave!"

Of course he never did, and I continued on the show until they gave it up, sometimes taking over for them on days when they had to be away. It was exactly the kind of job I needed, for it gave me an association with two people I loved and something to look forward to every week. Yet I had no burdensome responsibility to sponsor or network.

Later Joe Rosenfield invited me to appear for three hours every Sunday night on his "Happiness Exchange." He, Dolly (his wife), and Julie (Dolly's sister), hospitable southerners all, were not only sympathetic, but fed me banquets of country ham, collard greens, and corn bread.

I had a very pleasant once-a-week experience with kindly Sam Levenson and his television program on CBS, and others—Mike Wallace, Jack Paar, Dave Garroway, Barry Gray, Josie McCarthy, Nan Garcia, Joan Taylor, Professor Warren Bower—have been kind enough to ask me to appear now and then. I enjoy these diversions, but more and more lately I have been glad to come back to my barn.

It's a frightening world out yonder, lipsticks that poison the wearer, women my age raped and beaten in the streets and public parks, deliberate plans going on everywhere to destroy the earth and eventually, I suppose, all the other heavenly bodies. I don't expect to escape entirely, but at least here in my barn is a reasonable facsimile of peace and contentment.

The barn is where I live in the Catskills. And I'm still a little surprised about it. That's because I never was a logical candidate for barn remodeling. I have, in fact, poked a bit of fun at those who turn old coffee grinders into lamps, cranberry scoops into ivy holders, and cobblers' benches into coffee tables. It would never have occurred to me under ordinary circumstances to convert a two-hundred-year-old barn into a house.

And the only reason I ever contemplated becoming a houseowner at all was first to be able to get away from Stella's too generous inviting of guests when I was spending the weekend with her, and second, to have permanently for my own what I believe to be the most beautiful view in the world. While I enjoy cooking, sweeping, and even dusting, I have never yearned for the responsibility of radiators that make funny noises, plaster that cracks, or faucets that drip. For the past thirty-five years I have been quite happy to turn such problems over to superintendents of various Manhattan apartment houses I have occupied. Indeed, I have often been vocal about the voluntary bondage of home-owning friends.

I could afford to be superior since I had no compelling reason to become a property owner. My broadcasting and writing kept me, most of the time, in the city. I had no children to bring up amid fresh air and bird song. I'm a dedicated nature lover, but when I fell in love with a view it was luckily the magnificent one to be seen from Stella's porch. And I was always welcome there, sometimes as renter, sometimes as guest.

Stella, not really believing me at first, said certainly, she'd let me have an acre or so of her hillside. And there the matter stood until a spring weekend when I was frantically busy and Stella's house was full of more than usually active guests, including indulgent parents with a spoiled child who had one screaming tantrum after another. Out in Stella's front yard, waving relieved farewells to the departing guests, I announced firmly that I was going to build my house—right away.

Of course I was totally unprepared for what lay ahead. Like every other literate person, I've been frequently exposed to magazine literature on the popular subject of building and remodeling. I'd read and laughed at Mr. Blandings. But at such times housebuilding was not even a hazy, happy daydream.

As this story proceeds it probably will seem strange that I was so willing to turn the building project over to others and to play only the role of an off-stage moaning noise. But it did not—it does not—seem at all illogical to me. In the first place, I own a highly specialized imagination. I can visualize a story from a few words and usually get one written or told in some form or other. But I have a blind spot when it comes to visualizing how an empty lot will look when there's a house on it. When I get a room redecorated I find great difficulty in seeing the windows with the draperies up, the green chair slip-covered in pink, the parquet carpeted.

So I turned the whole project over to the logical person: my manager, who certainly could visualize a house on a vacant lot and who also adored tackling big jobs from scratch, organizing, negotiating, haggling, and planning. Moreover, she had already gone through several construction and remodeling jobs. And she certainly knew, or I thought she knew, exactly what I had in mind, including the modest amount I had decided to spend. Besides, as only she and I were aware at the time, she desperately needed something to occupy her thoughts.

Anybody who has ever built a house knows what is coming now. I can't make any sense of blueprints, but if one were drawn of my building adventures I am certain it would be a complete and comprehensive plan on how *not* to acquire a home.

Stella, having instantly accepted her commission to major-domo the construction of my dream house, was on the telephone within minutes, looking for a builder. The first dozen or so she reached were too busy even to consider other work for months. And I, of course, couldn't wait, now that my mind was made up.

Eventually we had a great stroke of luck: a builder who had done some work for Stella in the past had been on a year-long sabbatical and was beginning to think about getting back to work—provided the job was something that interested him.

The following weekend Mr. Smith drove up. He was a tall, good-looking man with an impressive head of white hair. The three of us sat around the dining-room table as I outlined what I wanted. Mr. Smith nodded and was sympathetic and understanding. I pointed to the spot on the hillside above the apple orchard where I wanted the house. Then Stella and Mr. Smith went out to look the situation over.

They disappeared almost instantly from the site I had proposed and were gone about three hours. When I saw them again they were so excited they were incoherent. What had happened was, according to the preliminary version, that they had both decided what I really wanted was to remodel the unused two-hundred-year-old barn fifty yards or so down the road from Stella's farmhouse.

"Chestnut beams," Mr. Smith breathed reverently. "The size of them. Do you know what that means?" I didn't, but he assured me that remodeling the old barn so that every last one of those huge and magnificent beams was displayed to full advantage would make the most glorious, wonderful, and interesting country home ever seen. I would even have natural split levels built into the hillside.

Stella, in the throes of old-beam love too, was dreaming more ecstatically than even Mr. Smith. The bewitched pair, it turned out, had decided that rather than spoil the barnlike appearance of the place they would just leave the two fore and aft barn doors and arrange for me to drive my nonexistent automobile right into the middle of the building. Then the west side of the barn, beside the road, would supply a complete, if small, apartment on the second floor ("for the caretaker," explained Stella grandly) and below that would be a glass front area ("A conservatory," tossed off my manager. "You can grow orange trees in it.").

As for my living quarters, there would also be two floors. The ground floor would be a beamed kitchen, with a huge fireplace, modern cooking and laundry equipment, pine paneling, a picture window on the view, and an open porch leading to lawn and garden. Over it would be the huge living room with all those beams showing as well as the peaked roof in its pristine woody beauty, a fireplace, paneling, book-cases everywhere, picture window, and then a screened porch in the treetops overlooking the grandeur of mountains and lakes.

I listened with a feeling of mounting apprehension. Somehow this was not exactly what I had in mind. And it sounded wildly expensive. I timidly mentioned cost, but Stella told me soothingly, as if speaking to a very young child, that it wouldn't cost much more, maybe not as much as my little dream house. For, she said, the barn is there, the beams are there. With the foundation patched a bit, new roofing over the old, new siding over the old, a chimney and two fireplaces, plumb-ing—there you are!

My whole idea, I protested to indifferent ears, was to have every-thing on one floor. I reminded them that I don't like to climb stairs.

"We'll build ramps," said Stella.

"I wasn't planning on having caretakers," I objected feebly.

"You might, sometime," maintained Stella briskly. "And besides you could rent it as an apartment if you wanted to. What you'd get would probably carry the whole place."

"You'll be so happy in it," said Mr. Smith. "It will be beautiful!"

"We'll have redwood siding," dreamed Stella.

"Redwood in the Catskills?" I demurred. "Isn't that more native to California?"

"Pine, then," said Mr. Smith.

"Redwood," said Stella decisively. "I'll have a carload shipped from the Coast."

Right then, of course, I could have put my foot down. I didn't because it seemed that the barn was the best solution. Stella was pant-ing to get the project started. She looked and seemed to feel better than she had for months.

For the next few days she and Mr. Smith spent the daylight hours at the barn. When they did return to the house for a bite to eat or a cup of coffee they talked a language strange to me.

"I think we should have two septic tanks," I heard Stella say, "so the caretaker's apartment can be completely separate. And finger drains for the garbage-disposal unit in the sink. And the panelboard in the furnace room should be oversize for the heavy equipment."

"I don't really think it's necessary to have the furnace room paneled," I muttered.

"That's for the electricity," said Stella, patiently, as to an idiot.

"Well," she announced upon my arrival from the city one Friday evening, "you can plan on Thanksgiving dinner in your new house. The workmen are starting on the foundations Monday."

A surveyor came up to measure off my new acreage, a lawyer drew some papers, and on Monday a flock of cars drew up around the barn. Trucks arrived to dump sand, gravel, cement mixers outside the yard. It seemed every time I looked at the road another truck was being unloaded. Strange men streamed in and out, occasionally knocking on Stella's kitchen door with bills for me.

Screeching, grinding, grating sounds issued from the barn—all, I supposed, involved in patching up the foundation. One day I walked over to the busy site and found the lower level of the barn resting on jacks while workmen pulled away great bluestone slabs and replaced them with concrete blocks.

"I thought the foundations were all right," I said worriedly to a workman there.

"Just want to make them more solid," he said soothingly. "It's so we can lay the concrete for the kitchen floor and the porch."

I fled. And the next time I forced myself to go over, there was a bastion of concrete, thick enough surely to hold up the Empire State Building, running down the south side of the barn.

"Had to do it," said the workman. "One of those beams was pretty weak at the base. But it's like Gibraltar now."

Occasionally Stella and Mr. Smith threw me a crumb of encouraging information. They had decided, they said, the bowed and peaked effect on the west side of the barn (built originally to make bale-raising easier) was charming and should be retained even if it meant more expensive handling of the redwood siding. Stella looked over samples, checked bills for hours, and in her spare time thought up expensive additions for my barn.

"You really ought to have murals," she suggested one evening. "The rising sun over one barn door, the setting sun over the other. And we can have them floodlighted."

From time to time money was mentioned, but not very often in my presence. A few times I received hints that the barn might cost just a little bit more than the modest sum I had mentioned as my limit. I knew in a way, though I didn't quite understand, that Mr. Smith was operating on something called a "cost-plus basis." They both told me I was getting nothing but the best, from the brass piping inside to the copper gutters outside.

At this stage I was testy with apprehensive friends, homeowners all, who expertized about my house-to-be. One was interested mainly in leaks and drainage and kept muttering about footing tiles and the importance of plenty of flashing around the chimney. He was the one, I think, who prowled the ground making sample routes for carrying off water.

Another was concerned entirely with electric wiring and kept throwing out suggestions about having every wire accessible in case of trouble.

A gardening friend was perhaps the most maddening. She returned from the building site with dire news: workmen had ruthlessly chopped through the main roots of a big sugar maple which was needed to shade the porch, bulldozers had dumped five feet of soil around the mountain ash out front and it was dying (look at the leaves dropping!). Most irritating of all, she informed me disapprovingly that I should have insisted on having all the topsoil scraped into one pile before the digging started.

"But it's too late now," she said. "You'll have to buy topsoil."

There wasn't an optimist among them. Everybody seemed to have positive and disagreeable ideas about what was going to be wrong with my house. "You'll see," they Job-comforted.

I realize now that the day I really began to fear the worst was the one when I strolled over to the barn to demand one of my rare progress reports. Everyone stopped work and proudly showed me about. Some of the men were chiseling away and treating the beams. Masons were laying bluestone slabs on the downstairs fireplace. The concrete automobile runway in the center of the barn was dry enough to walk on. I nodded agreeably as they displayed accomplishments and pointed out where this or that would ultimately be. I walked upstairs (by the ramp from the runway) to the living room, where Stella gestured widely to outline the panorama windows on the south.

"And where," I inquired innocently, "will the bedrooms be?"

"Bedrooms!" repeated a helpful friend.

"Bedrooms!" echoed Stella.

Then they looked at each other blankly. It was soon obvious that we all had been so steamed up about the living room and kitchen that the little matter of sleeping quarters, plus bathrooms, had been quite overlooked. Two days later the bulldozers came back and pretty soon workmen were laying concrete block foundations to a large addition beside the living-room end of the barn.

"It's just as well," concluded Stella. "It was too small anyway. And you need a storeroom underneath for firewood and garden tools."

But of course the real reason I had to have the addition was that to install even the most modest of sleeping quarters would have concealed some of their precious beams. The second floor of the addition, they informed me, would be just the right size to provide me with a master bedroom and adjoining bath, a room and bath for a housekeeper, plus two guest rooms, each with private bath—tiled.

"This is getting a little larger than I'd planned," I told them. "Isn't it also getting pretty expensive?" For the first time they failed to reassure me. In fact, I thought they looked dashed. And gradually the estimated cost of my dream house went up, up, up. Also at this point someone started mentioning something he called "resale value." This did not help much, since I was intending to live in the house, not sell it for profit.

It was a pay-as-you-go project, too, and I was writing checks at a rate to give me finger cramps. About every week, it seemed, I'd have to arrange to replenish my checking account.

I got a little bored with explaining to local residents and visitors alike that the roadside roof was *supposed* to bow in and come to a peak.

The old barn had already cost more than three times what I had planned to spend. Of course the living room was beautiful. It opened onto the view and had a wonderful screened-in porch. The barn was a lovely place to visit, but you couldn't live in it yet. By spending several thousand dollars more, we made everything all right. The outlets in the proposed downstairs kitchen were inadequate for what we wanted, so we turned the housekeeper's room into a kitchen. Then the downstairs room became what is probably the largest guest room in the United States. Of course this also involved moving a door, adding more window space, and ripping out existing plumbing.

So now I live in the barn the year round and love every moment, every creature, every season. Each time of the year has its special charm. June is filled with brilliant blue and gold days, the lake shimmers, the rolling hills beyond are colored a tender young green by millions of new shoots on the conifers. It seems always to be a vintage lilac year, for the old bushes (one is much more than a hundred years old) are invariably bent from the weight of lavender blooms. The little weigela, growing lushly from the one scrawny root left after some careless helper ran over the shrub with his tractor, is in full pink flower in the shadow of the big straight Norwegian maple.

Here and there in the meadow, their feathery heads bobbing over the grass, are columbines, deep purple and pink. The pink and red rambler roses are in bloom and the peony buds are swelling with promise. The irises that Berta planted so lovingly are opening in droves. The meadows are full of tiny woods strawberries. Later there will be blackberries and dewberries.

Golden October days with the mountains clothed defiantly in scarlet and orange turn me into a shameless putter-offer, and I find myself making any kind of excuse to get outdoors. Often I take a ride over the winding Catskill mountain and valley trails at the peak of the fall color. Birch, beech, and poplars with their yellow foliage light sections of the road like floodlights.

Some of the red maples, outer leaves flaming crimson against a background of clean hard green, look from a distance like Christmas trees hung with red balls, while bunched stands of wild cherry trees can almost be mistaken for spring's forsythia, they are so deeply and gaily yellow. Here and there clumps of oak and sumac, shading from the oak's bronze to the hunter's-cap red of sumac, make dramatic contrast against the frosted green of the pines and the emerald depths of hemlock and spruces. So richly colored are they that it is impossible to feel unfriendly toward even poison ivy or the too ubiquitous Virginia creeper. Wine-colored poison ivy festoons the gray trunks of ancient gnarled apple trees, long abandoned to the windfall-hunting deer. And a mailbox on a stump is furled with the scarlet of Virginia creeper.

But star billing in the annual show must go this year, as every year, to the infinite variety of the sugar maples. Before you have more than caught your breath after coming upon a tree entirely dressed in purest orange, you lose it again over one of palest green under yellow, like chartreuse. So if I sound a little giddy it's only the harmless hang-over of my annual scenery binge—a good soul-cleansing intoxication which overcomes me in October every year.

Summer and fall, when I'm up early enough, and every evening just before dusk, I spend a quiet time with a family of white-tailed deer who have become my good friends. Most often as I watch, the shy, graceful mother and her gamboling fawn come gaily out of the woods at the top of the hill. Less frequently the antlered father joins them in the old apple orchard beyond the meadow where they nose around under the trees to see if there have been any windfalls since their last visit.

The tawny mother frequently stops eating to gaze anxiously at me. A slammed door, a whistle, or an automobile on the road many yards away makes her start and turn her head. The baby switches its perky white tail and pays me little heed because, I like fatuously to imagine, it knows I won't do it any harm. The buck is too lordly to acknowledge my existence, but now and then a quiver of awareness runs through his body and I know every nerve is attuned to sense possible danger.

As the nights grow more chill and the leaves turn, my pleasure in these charming creatures is marred by the dread that their time may be running out. November is open season for deer hunting and though these acres will be plastered with posters, hunters don't always heed and I'm afraid my family of deer may have grown too trusting. What worries me most is that I may have helped to make them so. And there is little I can do now to save them from the brave men in red caps who find deer killing exciting and somehow justify the slaying of wild creatures by calling it "sport."

It's peaceful at all seasons here, but in winter the quiet is like something felt. For hours there is no sound at all except the whisper of snow and the surging of the wind. Even the postman's smooth-running car sounds noisy in the hush. The sun is bright, but the wind carries a sharp biting cold. Bundled to the eyebrows, I go out bravely to walk but come hurrying back, nose tingling, eyes watering, ready for endless cups of hot tea.

Over beyond the pond, silent now because the frogs have dug in for a winter's sleep, the shiny green leaves of laurel, nature's thermometer, curl farther and farther under as the temperature drops lower and lower. The sparrows, nuthatches, and chickadees are around, but the only time they have much to say is when they hop to the terrace for handouts of sunflower seeds or swing on the coffee-can feeding station that my neighbors, Victor and Angela Bitterman, have put up for me. Poison ivy, by the way, comes into its own as a useful plant in winter. The birds, not at all allergic, love the gray berries.

The leaves of maples, birches, oaks, and elms have dropped onto the floor of the woods and crackle and whisper as an occasional rabbit or deer whisks along some private path. There's a thick film of ice on the pond and the steady splash of the overflow that widens into a brook is interrupted by the plink of ice.

On a day of bleak cold the earth seems dead, yet within it is life dormant, waiting. Without cold, many flowers would never be so beautiful. Mother Nature knows best. The ever-changing view from the stone terrace continues to enchant; the lake with its strand of white sand moving into water which sometimes looks forbiddingly gray and choppy, sometimes emerald green and sometimes deeply blue; the mountains, pink at sunset, with the deep greens of the conifers massed low over the lake and laced above with white snow which usually falls early here. I like my view in all moods—somber, brilliantly sunlit, and most especially in the cold silver sparkle of the moon.

My oldest friends up here in the mountains are Connie and Ethel Heiselman. If it weren't for them I doubt if I'd be living today in a reconverted barn. When Connie was mayor of Kingston he sent identical and very flattering invitations to Mary Margaret McBride and Martha Deane to visit Kingston in May and help crown the apple blossom queen. We thought it a great joke that he had invited both of me and assured each of us that she was the very best woman broadcaster, so I gravely wrote two separate letters to say we'd come.

Connie, who likes a laugh even when it's on himself, was amused when I told him what he had done, and we became great friends. We crowned the apple blossom queen without apple blossoms—they hadn't yet bloomed—and spent the weekend with Connie looking at lovely old Kingston and the beautiful mountains. We were thrilled with all of it. So much so that Stella, who had been wanting to buy a farm, immediately decided that here was the perfect location. And later she found the farm.

Next to the Heiselmans, I have known Pat and Claire Kearney (he's a well-known writer) the longest of anybody in West Shokan. Claire and her sister Anne run Watson Hollow Inn, a wonderful place to take guests for delicious meals planned by Anne and served at tables beautifully decorated by Claire. Another friendly neighbor who feeds me exquisite food from time to time is Judie, whose excellent restaurant is in Kingston.

The Kearneys and all my neighbors are the kind I can call on in time of trouble. The Bittermans—Angela, who weaves beautiful fabrics, and Victor, who worries that I don't eat the right foods—watch over me affectionately, and Angela and I have started a garden club. We hope to make West Shokan the most beautiful village in America. (What I need most of course is a handyman for my own house and grounds who could weed and mow and plow, fix faucets, furnaces, and washing machines.)

The Hesleys, from whom this land I love was bought by Stella, are good friends too. Lottie planted many of the shrubs and trees I now treasure. Katherine has a green thumb and is a wonderful help with my African violets. Irving gets called in when I have a real scare, like the well failing to pump. The Eckers, Harry and Ruth, deliver my mail every day and taxi my guests and me back and forth. I have a warm conviction that they, too, would be refuges in time of trouble, as would the Larges, the Tracys on the hill, the Heidenstroms nearby, the De-Sannas, Elwyn Davis, Ollie Bergher.

The only complaint I have against the Johansens next door is that they go to Florida in winter. I don't understand how they can bear to miss the beauty of a Catskill winter. It is typical of her that one day after a drenching rain that followed a long dry spell I looked out to see kind Stephanie Johansen busily weeding my pansy bed. When I tried to thank her she said, "Well, you have to do it when the ground's moist, and I thought you might not get to it."

Then there are Belle Woods, a darling little wren of a woman who makes the pants and smocks that I wear up here; Art Scofield, who keeps me carpentered and painted; John Daly, the politest man in the mountains; Mrs. Bergmann and Bob Donovan, who are kind enough to help me out in crises; the Kelders; the Lanes; the Scheicks; the postmistress, Mabel Weidner, with a wry and delightful sense of humor; Jean and Bob Johansen; Thor and Irene Krogh, who ably edit our local weekly; Edna and Lester Davis and Joe Winkler, who run the general store where I buy my supplies and upon whom I call for everything from baiting a mousetrap to advice on roasting veal. Carl, the Davises' son, a fine pianist, is going to help teach me to play the organ, a project already started by the gifted Dorothy Narel, who writes a column for the Kingston *Freeman*, sings, and plays the piano.

Not too far away is my adopted daughter, Mary Cay Di Donna, with her nice husband and two darling children, and in Kingston are my good friends Sam and Hannah Scudder.

This is dreadful! I am doing exactly what I used to scold guests for during a broadcast when they tried to put in the names of all their friends and relatives. It's because I want my neighbors to know I value them that I'm trying to get them all in.

Alan Devoe, who observed nature and wrote about it, once told me that most naturalists live to a great old age. He believed that watching plants and animals made for longevity. I hope so for I'd like to live a long time on my hill with my neighbors, my friends who come for weekends, my brother Milton and his wife, Sally, who vacation with me, my organ, my garden, and my reading. For years I've been saving Joyce and Proust. I wonder how I'll like them. I've enjoyed my life and don't regret any of it. But I can see that, taken altogether, it is faintly, sometimes even blatantly, ridiculous.

But perhaps I am not unique. From my present pleasant haven I look at other lives, those of pontifical prelates who seem to feel that they and God share all secrets, snobbish intellectuals with their pretensions; windy politicians perpetually promising. And I find them all rather ridiculous.

I do have to acknowledge that life has defeated me in one particular. I wanted to be a great writer, and now I never shall be. The trouble was, I suppose, that I wanted to be a writer but I didn't especially want to write, and, anyway, I had nothing of consequence to say. So I was far better off as a day-to-day talker than as a would-be creative writer breaking my heart trying to reach the stars. I touched a good many lives in the years, and I hope I alleviated some loneliness and awakened a few to the horrors of cruelty and injustice. If so, I am reasonably content.